MASS CALENDAR

Date

The Value of a Missal

"Hand Missals which are drawn up according to the requirements of the modern liturgical renewal and which contain not only the Ordinary of the Mass but a version of all the liturgical texts approved by the competent authority are still necessary for the more perfect understanding of the total mystery of salvation celebrated during the liturgical year, for drawing meditation and fervor from the inexhaustible riches of the liturgical texts, and for facilitating actual participation.

"This demands not only that the Word of God be proclaimed within the gathered community and attentively listened to by it, but also that the holy people respond to the Word of God which they have received and celebrate the Sacred (Mysteries) by singing or reciting the parts of the Ordinary and Proper [of the Mass], hymns and Psalms.

"[Missals are] especially necessary for . . . those who participate in daily Mass, or who desire to live and pray every day in the spirit of the liturgy; those who because of sickness or inconvenience or other similar reasons cannot assemble with their own liturgical community, so that they may be joined to their prayer more truly and intimately; children who are to be initiated progressively into the mystery of the liturgy."

Postconciliar Commission for the Implementation
of the Constitution on the Sacred Liturgy.

This Missal belongs to

....

Cycle A

For 2010-2011

New *Saint Joseph*

SUNDAY MISSAL

PRAYERBOOK AND HYMNAL

This new Missal has been especially designed to help you participate at Mass . . . in the fullest and most active way possible.

How easy it is to use this Missal

- Refer to the Calendar inside the front cover for the page of the Sunday Mass (the "Proper").

- This arrow (↓) means continue to read. This arrow (→) indicates a reference back to the Order of Mass ("Ordinary") or to another part of the "Proper."

- Boldface type always indicates the people's parts that are to be recited aloud.

*The People of God together with Christ worship
the heavenly Father*

New . . . St. Joseph

SUNDAY MISSAL

PRAYERBOOK AND HYMNAL

For 2010-2011

THE COMPLETE MASSES FOR SUNDAYS, HOLYDAYS, and the EASTER TRIDUUM

With the People's Parts of Holy Mass
Printed in Boldface Type
and Arranged for Parish Participation

WITH THE "NEW AMERICAN BIBLE" TEXT
FROM THE REVISED SUNDAY LECTIONARY,
SHORT HELPFUL NOTES AND EXPLANATIONS,
AND A TREASURY OF POPULAR PRAYERS

Dedicated to St. Joseph
Patron of the Universal Church

CATHOLIC BOOK PUBLISHING CORP.
New Jersey

NIHIL OBSTAT: Sr. M. Kathleen Flanagan, S.C., Ph.D.
        Censor Librorum

IMPRIMATUR: ✠ Arthur J. Serratelli, S.S.L., S.T.D., D.D.
        Bishop of Paterson

The St. Joseph Missals have been diligently prepared with the invaluable assistance of a special Board of Editors, including specialists in Liturgy and Sacred Scripture, Catechetics, Sacred Music and Art.

In this new Sunday Missal Edition the musical notations for responsorial antiphons are by Rev. John Selner, S.S.

The Scriptural Readings and Responsorial Psalms are taken from the *Lectionary for Mass, Vol. 1* © 1998, 1997, 1970 by Confraternity of Christian Doctrine, Washington, D.C. All rights reserved.

The poetic English translations of the sequences of the Roman Missal are taken from *The Roman Missal* approved by the National Conference of Catholic Bishops of the United States © 1964 by the National Catholic Welfare Conference, Inc. All rights reserved.

English translation of the Roman Missal, Rites for Holy Week, original texts of The Alternative Opening Prayers, Invitatories, and the Penitential Rites; The Rite of Marriage; The Rite of Penance; The Rite of Christian Initiation of Adults; titles, responsorial psalms and alleluia verses of the Lectionary for Mass, Copyright © 1969, 1970, 1973, 1974, 1981, 1985, 1997, International Committee on English in the Liturgy, Inc. All rights reserved.

All other texts and illustrations © Copyright by Catholic Book Publishing Corp., N.J.

(T-2011)

ISBN 978-0-89942-647-1

© 2010 by *Catholic Book Publishing Corp.*, N.J.
Printed in the U.S.A.

PREFACE

IN the words of the Second Vatican Council in the *Constitution on the Liturgy*, the *Mass* "is an action of Christ the priest and of his body which is the Church; it is a sacred action surpassing all others; no other action of the Church can equal its efficacy by the same title and to the same degree" (art. 7). Hence the Mass is a sacred sign, something visible which brings the invisible reality of Christ to us in the worship of the Father.

The Mass was first instituted as a meal at the Last Supper and became a living memorial of Christ's sacrifice on the cross:

"At the Last Supper, on the night when he was betrayed, our Savior instituted the Eucharistic sacrifice of his body and blood. He did this in order to perpetuate the sacrifice of the Cross throughout the centuries until he should come again, and so to entrust to his beloved spouse, the Church, a memorial of his death and resurrection: a sacrament of love, a sign of unity, a bond of charity, a Paschal banquet in which Christ is eaten, the mind is filled with grace, and a pledge of future glory is given to us.

"The Church, therefore, earnestly desires that Christ's faithful, when present at this mystery of faith, should not be there as strangers or silent spectators; on the contrary, through a good understanding of the rites and prayers they should take part in the sacred action conscious of what they are doing, with devotion and full collaboration. They should be instructed by God's word and be nourished at the table of the Lord's body; they should give thanks to God; by offering the immaculate Victim, not only through the hands of the priests but also with him, they should learn also to offer themselves; through Christ the Mediator, they should be drawn day by day into ever more perfect union with God and with each other, so that . . . God may be all in all" (art. 47-48).

Accordingly, this new Sunday Missal has been edited, in conformity with the latest findings of modern liturgists, especially to enable the people to attain the most active participation.

To insure that "each . . . lay person who has an office to perform [will] do all of, but only, those parts which pertain to his office" (art. 28), a simple method of instant identification of the various parts of the Mass, has been designed, using different type faces:

(1) **boldface type** — clearly identifies all people's parts for each Mass.

(2) lightface type—indicates the priest's or lector's parts.

In order to enable the faithful to prepare for each Mass AT HOME and so participate more actively AT MASS, the editors have added short helpful explanations of the new scripture readings, geared to the spiritual needs of daily life. A large selection of hymns for congregational singing has been included as well as a treasury of private prayers.

We trust that all these special features will help Catholics who use this new St. Joseph Missal to be led— in keeping with the desire of the Church—"to that full, conscious, and active participation in liturgical celebrations which is demanded by the very nature of the liturgy. Such participation by the Christian people as a chosen race, a royal priesthood, a holy nation, a redeemed people (1 Pt 2, 9; cf. 2, 4-5), is their right and duty by reason of their baptism" (art. 14).

PLAN OF THE MASS

INTRODUCTORY RITES
1. Entrance Antiphon **(Proper)**
2. Greeting
3. Blessing and Sprinkling Water
4. Penitential Rite
5. Kyrie
6. Gloria
7. Opening Prayer **(Proper)**

LITURGY OF THE WORD
8. First Reading **(Proper)**
9. Responsorial Psalm **(Proper)**
10. Second Reading **(Proper)**
11. Alleluia **(Proper)**
12. Gospel **(Proper)**
13. Homily
14. Profession of Faith **(Creed)**
15. General Intercessions

(Preparation of the Gifts)
16. Offertory Song
17. Preparation of the Bread
18. Preparation of the Wine
19. Invitation to Prayer
20. Prayer over the Gifts **(Proper)**

(Eucharistic Prayer)
LITURGY OF THE EUCHARIST
21. Introductory Dialogue
22. Preface
23. Sanctus
    Eucharistic Prayer
    1, 2, 3, 4
    Children 1, 2, 3
    Reconciliation 1, 2

(Communion Rite)
24. Lord's Prayer
25. Sign of Peace
26. Breaking of the Bread
27. Prayers Before Communion
28. Reception of Communion
29. Communion Antiphon **(Proper)**
30. Silence After Communion
31. Prayer After Communion **(Proper)**

CONCLUDING RITE
32. Greeting
33. Blessing
34. Dismissal

THE ORDER OF MASS

Options are indicated by A, B, C, D in the margin.

INTRODUCTORY RITES

Acts of prayer and penitence prepare us to meet Christ as he comes in Word and Sacrament. We gather as a worshiping community to celebrate our unity with him and with one another in faith.

1 ENTRANCE ANTIPHON `STAND`

If it is not sung, it is recited by all or some of the people.

Joined together as Christ's people, we open the celebration by raising our voices in praise of God who is present among us. This song should deepen our unity as it introduces the Mass we celebrate today.

→ `Turn to Today's Mass`

2 GREETING (3 forms)

When the priest comes to the altar, he makes the customary reverence with the ministers and kisses the altar. Then, with the ministers, he goes to his seat. After the entrance song, all make the sign of the cross:

Priest: In the name of the Father, ✚ and of the Son, and of the Holy Spirit.

PEOPLE: **Amen.**

The priest welcomes us in the name of the Lord. We show our union with God, our neighbor, and the priest by a united response to his greeting.

A

Priest: The grace of our Lord Jesus Christ and the love of God and the fellowship of the Holy Spirit be with you all.

PEOPLE: And also with you.

B ——————OR——————

Priest: The grace and peace of God our Father and the Lord Jesus Christ be with you.

PEOPLE: Blessed be God, the Father of our Lord Jesus Christ.

or:

And also with you.

C ——————OR——————

Priest: The Lord be with you.

PEOPLE: And also with you.

[Bishop: Peace be with you.

People: **And also with you.**]

3 RITE OF BLESSING and SPRINKLING HOLY WATER

The rite of blessing and sprinkling holy water may be celebrated in all churches and chapels at all Sunday Masses celebrated on Sunday or Saturday evening. See pp. 72-74.

4 PENITENTIAL RITE (3 forms)

(Omitted when the rite of blessing and sprinkling holy water has taken place or some part of the liturgy of the hours has preceded.)

Before we hear God's word, we acknowledge our sins humbly, ask for mercy, and accept his pardon.

Invitation to repent:

After the introduction to the day's Mass, the priest invites the people to recall their sins and to repent of them in silence:

A As we prepare to celebrate the mystery of Christ's love,
　　let us acknowledge our failures
　　and ask the Lord for pardon and strength.

B Coming together as God's family,
　　with confidence let us ask the Father's forgiveness,
　　for he is full of gentleness and compassion.

C My brothers and sisters,
　　to prepare ourselves to celebrate the sacred mysteries,
　　let us call to mind our sins.

Then, after a brief silence, one of the following forms is used.

A

Priest and **PEOPLE:**
　　　I confess to almighty God,
　　　and to you, my brothers and sisters,
　　　that I have sinned through my own fault

They strike their breast:
　　　in my thoughts and in my words,
　　　in what I have done,

and in what I have failed to do;
and I ask blessed Mary, ever virgin,
all the angels and saints,
and you, my brothers and sisters,
to pray for me to the Lord our God.

B ————————OR————————

Priest: Lord, we have sinned against you:
Lord, have mercy.

PEOPLE: **Lord, have mercy.**

Priest: Lord, show us your mercy and love.

PEOPLE: **And grant us your salvation.**

C ————————OR————————

Priest or other minister:

You were sent to heal the contrite:
Lord, have mercy.

PEOPLE: **Lord have mercy.**

Priest or other minister:

You came to call sinners:
Christ, have mercy.

PEOPLE: **Christ, have mercy.**

Priest or other minister:

You plead for us at the right hand of the
Father:
Lord, have mercy.

PEOPLE: **Lord, have mercy.**

(Other invocations may be used as on pp. 75-77.)

Absolution:

At the end of any of the forms of the penitential rite:

Priest: May almighty God have mercy on us,
          forgive us our sins,
          and bring us to everlasting life.

PEOPLE: **Amen.**

5 KYRIE

Unless included in the penitential rite, the Kyrie is sung or said by all, with alternating parts for the choir or cantor and for the people:

℣. Lord have mercy.

℟. **Lord, have mercy.**

℣. Christ, have mercy.

℟. **Christ, have mercy.**

℣. Lord, have mercy.

℟. **Lord, have mercy.**

6 GLORIA

As the Church assembled in the Spirit we praise and pray to the Father and the Lamb.

When the Gloria is sung or said, the priest or the cantors or everyone together may begin it:

**Glory to God in the highest,
    and peace to his people on earth.**

**Lord God, heavenly King,
almighty God and Father,
    we worship you, we give you thanks,
    we praise you for your glory.**

Lord Jesus Christ, only Son of the Father,
Lord God, Lamb of God,
you take away the sin of the world:
  have mercy on us;
you are seated at the right hand of the Father:
  receive our prayer.

For you alone are the Holy One,
you alone are the Lord,
you alone are the Most High,
  Jesus Christ,
  with the Holy Spirit,
  in the glory of God the Father. Amen.

7 OPENING PRAYER

The priest invites us to pray silently for a moment and then, in our name, expresses the theme of the day's celebration and petitions God the Father through the mediation of Christ in the Holy Spirit.

Priest: Let us pray.

→ **Turn to Today's Mass**

Priest and people pray silently for a while. Then the priest says the opening prayer and concludes:

Priest: For ever and ever.
PEOPLE: Amen.

LITURGY OF THE WORD

The proclamation of God's Word is always centered on Christ, present through his Word. Old Testament writings prepare for him; New Testament books speak of him directly. All of scripture calls us to believe once more and to follow. After the reading we reflect on God's words and respond to them.

As in Today's Mass　　　　SIT

8　FIRST READING

At the end of the reading: Reader: The word of the Lord.

PEOPLE: Thanks be to God.

9　RESPONSORIAL PSALM

The people repeat the response sung by the cantor the first time and then after each verse.

10　SECOND READING

At the end of the reading: Reader: The word of the Lord.

PEOPLE: Thanks be to God.

11　ALLELUIA (Gospel Acclamation)　　STAND

Jesus will speak to us in the Gospel. We rise now out of respect and prepare for his message with the alleluia.

The people repeat the alleluia after cantor's alleluia and then after the verse. During Lent one of the following invocations is used as a response instead of the alleluia:

(a)　Glory and praise to you, Lord Jesus Christ!
(b)　Glory to you, Lord Jesus Christ, Wisdom of God the Father!
(c)　Glory to you, Word of God, Lord Jesus Christ!
(d)　Glory to you, Lord Jesus Christ, Son of the Living God!

(e) **Praise and honor to you, Lord Jesus Christ!**
(f) **Praise to you, Lord Jesus Christ, King of endless glory!**
(g) **Marvelous and great are your works, O Lord!**
(h) **Salvation, glory, and power to the Lord Jesus Christ!**

12 GOSPEL

Before proclaiming the Gospel, the deacon asks the priest:
Father, give me your blessing. *The priest says:*

The Lord be in your heart and on your lips
that you may worthily proclaim his gospel.
In the name of the Father, and of the Son, ✠ and of
the Holy Spirit. *The deacon answers:* Amen.

If there is no deacon, the priest says inaudibly:

Almighty God, cleanse my heart and my lips that I
may worthily proclaim your gospel.

Deacon (or Priest):
     The Lord be with you.

PEOPLE: And also with you.

Deacon (or Priest):

✠ A reading from the holy Gospel according to N.

PEOPLE: Glory to you, Lord.

At the end:

Deacon (or priest):
     The Gospel of the Lord.

PEOPLE: Praise to you, Lord Jesus Christ.

Then the deacon (or priest) kisses the book, saying inaudibly: May the words of the Gospel wipe away our sins.

13 HOMILY   `SIT`

God's word is spoken again in the homily. The Holy Spirit speaking through the lips of the preacher explains and applies today's biblical readings to the needs of this particular congregation. He calls us to respond to Christ through the life we lead.

14 PROFESSION OF FAITH (CREED) `STAND`

As a people we express our acceptance of God's message in the scriptures and homily. We summarize our faith by proclaiming a creed handed down from the early Church.

All say the profession of faith on Sundays.

THE NICENE CREED

We believe in one God,
    the Father, the Almighty,
    maker of heaven and earth,
    of all that is seen and unseen.
We believe in one Lord, Jesus Christ,
    the only Son of God,
    eternally begotten of the Father,
    God from God, Light from Light,
    true God from true God,
    begotten, not made, one in Being with the Father.
    Through him all things were made.
For us men and for our salvation
      he came down from heaven:
by the power of the Holy Spirit
    he was born of the Virgin Mary,   } *bow*
    and became man.
For our sake he was crucified under Pontius Pilate;
    he suffered, died, and was buried.
    On the third day he rose again
      in fulfillment of the Scriptures;
    he ascended into heaven
      and is seated at the right hand of the Father.
He will come again in glory to judge the living
      and the dead,
    and his kingdom will have no end.
We believe in the Holy Spirit, the Lord, the giver of
      life,
    who proceeds from the Father and the Son.
    With the Father and the Son he is worshiped and
      glorified.
    He has spoken through the Prophets.

We believe in one holy catholic and apostolic Church.
We acknowledge one baptism for the forgiveness of
    sins.
We look for the resurrection of the dead,
    and the life of the world to come. Amen.

OR ——————— APOSTLES' CREED ———————

In celebrations of Masses with children, the Apostles' Creed
may be said after the homily.

I believe in God, the Father almighty,
    creator of heaven and earth.

I believe in Jesus Christ, his only Son, our Lord.
    He was conceived by the power of the Holy Spirit
        and born of the Virgin Mary.
    He suffered under Pontius Pilate,
        was crucified, died, and was buried.
    He descended to the dead.
    On the third day he rose again.
    He ascended into heaven,
        and is seated at the right hand of the Father.
    He will come again to judge the living and the dead.

I believe in the Holy Spirit,
    the holy catholic Church,
    the communion of saints,
    the forgiveness of sins,
    the resurrection of the body,
    and the life everlasting. Amen.

15 GENERAL INTERCESSIONS   (Prayer of the Faithful)

As a priestly people we unite with one another to pray for today's
needs in the Church and the world.

After the priest gives the introduction the deacon or other
minister sings or says the invocations.

PEOPLE: Lord, hear our prayer.
(or other response, according to local custom)
At the end the priest says the concluding prayer:

PEOPLE: Amen.

LITURGY OF THE EUCHARIST

Made ready by reflection on God's Word, we enter now into the eucharistic sacrifice itself, the Supper of the Lord. We celebrate the memorial which the Lord instituted at his Last Supper. We are God's new people, the redeemed brothers and sisters of Christ, gathered by him around his table. We are here to bless God and to receive the gift of Jesus' body and blood so that our faith and life may be transformed.

PREPARATION OF THE GIFTS

16 OFFERTORY SONG   `SIT`

The bread and wine for the Eucharist, with our gifts for the Church and the poor, are gathered and brought to the altar. We prepare our hearts by song or in silence as the Lord's table is being set.

While the people's gifts are brought forward to the priest and are placed on the altar, the offertory song is sung.

17 PREPARATION OF THE BREAD

Before placing the bread on the altar, the priest says inaudibly:

Blessed are you, Lord, God of all creation.
Through your goodness we have this bread to offer,
which earth has given and human hands have made.
It will become for us the bread of life.

If there is no singing, the priest may say this prayer aloud, and the people may respond:

PEOPLE: **Blessed be God for ever.**

18 PREPARATION OF THE WINE

When he pours wine and a little water into the chalice, the deacon (or the priest) says inaudibly:

20

By the mystery of this water and wine
may we come to share in the divinity of Christ,
who humbled himself to share in our humanity.

Before placing the chalice on the altar, he says:

Blessed are you, Lord, God of all creation.
Through your goodness we have this wine to offer,
fruit of the vine and work of human hands.
It will become our spiritual drink.

*If there is no singing, the priest may say this prayer
aloud, and the people may respond:*

PEOPLE: Blessed be God for ever.

The priest says inaudibly:

Lord God, we ask you to receive us
and be pleased with the sacrifice we offer you
with humble and contrite hearts.

Then he washes his hands, saying:

Lord, wash away my iniquity;
cleanse me from my sin.

19 INVITATION TO PRAYER   `STAND`

Priest: Pray, brethren, that our sacrifice may be accept-
          able to God, the almighty Father.

PEOPLE:

**May the Lord accept the sacrifice at your hands
for the praise and glory of his name,
for our good, and the good of all his Church.**

20 PRAYER OVER THE GIFTS

*The priest, speaking in our name, asks the Father to bless
and accept these gifts.*

➡ `Turn to Today's Mass`

At the end, **PEOPLE: Amen.**

EUCHARISTIC PRAYER

We begin the eucharistic service of praise and thanksgiving, the center of the entire celebration, the central prayer of worship. We lift our hearts to God, and offer praise and thanks as the priest addresses this prayer to the Father through Jesus Christ. Together we join Christ in his sacrifice, celebrating his memorial in the holy meal and acknowledging with him the wonderful works of God in our lives.

21 INTRODUCTORY DIALOGUE

Priest: The Lord be with you.
PEOPLE: And also with you.
Priest: Lift up your hearts.
PEOPLE: We lift them up to the Lord.
Priest: Let us give thanks to the Lord our God.
PEOPLE: It is right to give him thanks and praise.

22 PREFACE

As indicated in the individual Masses of this Missal, the priest may say one of the following Prefaces (listed in numerical order).

23   ACCLAMATION

Priest and **PEOPLE:**

Holy, holy, holy Lord, God of power and might, heaven and earth are full of your glory.

> **Hosanna in the highest.**

Blessed is he who comes in the name of the Lord.

> **Hosanna in the highest.**   `KNEEL`

Then the priest continues with one of the following Eucharistic Prayers.

EUCHARISTIC PRAYER...................Choice of nine

EUCHARISTIC PRAYER No. 1

The Roman Canon

(This Eucharistic Prayer is especially suitable for Sundays and Masses with proper "Communicantes" and "Hanc igitur.")

[The words within brackets may be omitted.]

[Praise to the Father]

We come to you, Father,
with praise and thanksgiving,
through Jesus Christ your Son.
Through him we ask you to accept and bless
these gifts we offer you in sacrifice.

[Intercessions: For the Church]

We offer them for your holy catholic Church,
watch over it, Lord, and guide it;
grant it peace and unity throughout the world.
We offer them for N. our Pope,
for N. our bishop,
and for all who hold and teach the catholic faith
that comes to us from the apostles.
Remember, Lord, your people,
especially those for whom we now pray, N. and N.

Remember all of us gathered here before you.
You know how firmly we believe in you
and dedicate ourselves to you.
We offer you this sacrifice of praise
for ourselves and those who are dear to us.
We pray to you, our living and true God,
for our well-being and redemption.

In union with the whole Church*
we honor Mary,
the ever-virgin mother of Jesus Christ our Lord and
     God.
We honor Joseph, her husband,
the apostles and martyrs
Peter and Paul, Andrew,
[James, John, Thomas,
James, Philip,
Bartholomew, Matthew, Simon and Jude;
we honor Linus, Cletus, Clement, Sixtus,
Cornelius, Cyprian, Lawrence, Chrysogonus,
John and Paul, Cosmas and Damian]
and all the saints.
May their merits and prayers
gain us your constant help and protection.
[Through Christ our Lord. Amen.]

Father, accept this offering*
from your whole family.
Grant us your peace in this life,
save us from final damnation,
and count us among those you have chosen.
[Through Christ our Lord. Amen.]

Bless and approve our offering;
make it acceptable to you,
an offering in spirit and in truth.
Let it become for us
the body and blood of Jesus Christ,
your only Son, our Lord.
[Through Christ our Lord. Amen.]

*See p. 90 for special Communicantes and Hanc Igitur.

1

[The Lord's Supper]

The day before he suffered
he took bread in his sacred hands
and looking up to heaven,
to you, his almighty Father,
he gave you thanks and praise.
He broke the bread,
gave it to his disciples, and said:

Take this, all of you, and eat it:
this is my body which will be given up for you.

When supper was ended,
he took the cup.
Again he gave you thanks and praise,
gave the cup to his disciples, and said:

Take this, all of you, and drink from it:
this is the cup of my blood,
the blood of the new and everlasting covenant.
It will be shed for you and for all
so that sins may be forgiven.
Do this in memory of me.

[Memorial Acclamation]

Priest: Let us proclaim the mystery of faith.

PEOPLE:

A Christ has died,
  Christ is risen,
  Christ will come again.

B Dying you destroyed our death,
  rising you restored our life.
  Lord Jesus, come in glory.

1

C When we eat this bread and drink this cup,
   we proclaim your death, Lord Jesus,
   until you come in glory.

D Lord, by your cross and resurrection
   you have set us free.
   You are the Savior of the world.

[The Memorial Prayer]

Father, we celebrate the memory of Christ, your
   Son.
We, your people and your ministers,
recall his passion,
his resurrection from the dead,
and his ascension into glory;
and from the many gifts you have given us
we offer to you, God of glory and majesty,
this holy and perfect sacrifice:
the bread of life
and the cup of eternal salvation.
Look with favor on these offerings
and accept them as once you accepted
the gifts of your servant Abel,
the sacrifice of Abraham, our father in faith,
and the bread and wine offered by your priest
   Melchisedech.
Almighty God,
we pray that your angel may take this sacrifice
to your altar in heaven.
Then, as we receive from this altar
the sacred body and blood of your Son,
let us be filled with every grace and blessing.
[Through Christ our Lord. Amen.]

1 *[For the Dead]*

Remember, Lord, those who have died
and have gone before us marked with the sign of
　　faith,
especially those for whom we now pray, N. and N.
May these, and all who sleep in Christ,
find in your presence
light, happiness, and peace.
[Through Christ our Lord. Amen.]

For ourselves, too, we ask
some share in the fellowship of your apostles and
　　martyrs,
with John the Baptist, Stephen, Matthias, Barnabas,
[Ignatius, Alexander, Marcellinus, Peter, Felicity, Perpetua,
Agatha, Lucy, Agnes, Cecilia, Anastasia]
and all the saints.
Though we are sinners,
we trust in your mercy and love.
Do not consider what we truly deserve,
but grant us your forgiveness.
Through Christ our Lord.

Through him you give us all these gifts.
You fill them with life and goodness,
you bless them and make them holy.

[Concluding Doxology]

Through him,
with him,
in him,
in the unity of the Holy Spirit,
all glory and honor is yours,
almighty Father, for ever and ever.

All reply: **Amen.** *Continue with the Mass, as on p. 66.*

(This Eucharistic Prayer is particularly suitable on Weekdays or for special circumstances)

STAND

℣. The Lord be with you.
℟. **And also with you.**
℣. Lift up your hearts.
℟. **We lift them up to the Lord.**
℣. Let us give thanks to the Lord our God.
℟. **It is right to give him thanks and praise.**

PREFACE   *[Praise to the Lord]*

Father, it is our duty and our salvation,
always and everywhere
to give you thanks
through your beloved Son, Jesus Christ.

He is the Word through whom you made the universe,
the Savior you sent to redeem us.

By the power of the Holy Spirit
he took flesh and was born of the Virgin Mary.

For our sake he opened his arms on the cross;
he put an end to death
and revealed the resurrection.

In this he fulfilled your will
and won for you a holy people.

And so we join the angels and the saints
in proclaiming your glory
as we sing (say):

2 SANCTUS

[First Acclamation of the People]

**Holy, holy, holy Lord, God of power and might,
heaven and earth are full of your glory.**
    Hosanna in the highest.
Blessed is he who comes in the name of the Lord.
    Hosanna in the highest.

KNEEL

[Invocation of the Holy Spirit]

Lord, you are holy indeed,
the fountain of all holiness.

Let your Spirit come upon these gifts to make
    them holy,
so that they may become for us
the body and blood of our Lord, Jesus Christ.

[The Lord's Supper]

Before he was given up to death,
a death he freely accepted,
he took bread and gave you thanks.
He broke the bread,
gave it to his disciples, and said:

Take this, all of you, and eat it:
this is my body which will be given up for you.

When supper was ended, he took the cup.
Again he gave you thanks and praise,
gave the cup to his disciples, and said:

Take this, all of you, and drink from it:
this is the cup of my blood,
the blood of the new and everlasting covenant.
It will be shed for you and for all
so that sins may be forgiven.
Do this in memory of me.

[Memorial Acclamation] **2**

Priest: Let us proclaim the mystery of faith.

PEOPLE:

A **Christ has died,
Christ is risen,
Christ will come again.**

B **Dying you destroyed our death,
rising you restored our life.
Lord Jesus, come in glory.**

C **When we eat this bread and drink this cup,
we proclaim your death, Lord Jesus,
until you come in glory.**

D **Lord, by your cross and resurrection
you have set us free.
You are the Savior of the world.**

[The Memorial Prayer]

In memory of his death and resurrection,
we offer you, Father, this life-giving bread,
this saving cup.
We thank you for counting us worthy
to stand in your presence and serve you.

[Invocation of the Holy Spirit]

May all of us who share in the body and blood of
     Christ
be brought together in unity by the Holy Spirit.

2 *[Intercessions: For the Church]*

Lord, remember your Church throughout the
    world;
make us grow in love,
together with N. our Pope,
N. our bishop, and all the clergy. *

[For the Dead]

Remember our brothers and sisters
who have gone to their rest
in the hope of rising again;
bring them and all the departed
into the light of your presence.

[In Communion with the Saints]

Have mercy on us all;
make us worthy to share eternal life
with Mary, the virgin Mother of God,
with the apostles, and with all the saints
who have done your will throughout the ages.
May we praise you in union with them,
and give you glory
through your Son, Jesus Christ.

[Concluding Doxology]

Through him,
with him,
in him,
in the unity of the Holy Spirit,
all glory and honor is yours,
almighty Father,
for ever and ever.

All reply: **Amen.** *Continue with the Mass, as on p. 66.*

---

* *In Masses for the Dead the following may be added:*

Remember N, whom you have called from this life.
In baptism he (she) died with Christ:
may he (she) also share his resurrection.

(This Eucharistic Prayer may be used with any Preface and preferably on Sundays and feast days)

KNEEL

[Praise to the Father]

Father, you are holy indeed,
and all creation rightly gives you praise.
All life, all holiness comes from you
through your Son, Jesus Christ our Lord,
by the working of the Holy Spirit.

From age to age you gather a people to yourself,
so that from east to west
a perfect offering may be made
to the glory of your name.

[Invocation of the Holy Spirit]

And so, Father, we bring you these gifts.
We ask you to make them holy by the power of
     your Spirit,
that they may become the body and blood
of your Son, our Lord Jesus Christ,
at whose command we celebrate this eucharist.

[The Lord's Supper]

On the night he was betrayed,
he took bread and gave you thanks and praise.
He broke the bread, gave it to his disciples, and
     said:

Take this, all of you, and eat it:
this is my body which will be given up for you.

3 When supper was ended, he took the cup.
Again he gave you thanks and praise,
gave the cup to his disciples, and said:

Take this, all of you, and drink from it:
this is the cup of my blood,
the blood of the new and everlasting covenant.
It will be shed for you and for all
so that sins may be forgiven.
Do this in memory of me.

[Memorial Acclamation]

Priest: Let us proclaim the mystery of faith.

PEOPLE:

A Christ has died,
Christ is risen,
Christ will come again.

B Dying you destroyed our death,
rising you restored our life.
Lord Jesus, come in glory.

C When we eat this bread and drink this cup,
we proclaim your death, Lord Jesus,
until you come in glory.

D Lord, by your cross and resurrection
you have set us free.
You are the Savior of the world.

[The Memorial Prayer]

Father, calling to mind the death your Son
endured for our salvation,
his glorious resurrection and ascension into heaven,
and ready to greet him when he comes again,
we offer you in thanksgiving this holy and living
sacrifice.

3

Look with favor on your Church's offering
and see the Victim whose death has reconciled us
   to yourself.

[Invocation of the Holy Spirit]

Grant that we, who are nourished by his body
   and blood,
may be filled with his Holy Spirit,
and become one body, one spirit in Christ.

[Intercessions: In Communion with the Saints]

May he make us an everlasting gift to you
and enable us to share in the inheritance of your
   saints,
with Mary, the virgin Mother of God;
with the apostles, the martyrs,
(Saint *N.*) and all your saints,
on whose constant intercession we rely for help.

[For the Church]

Lord, may this sacrifice,
which has made our peace with you,
advance the peace and salvation of all the world.
Strengthen in faith and love your pilgrim Church
   on earth;
your servant, Pope *N.*, our bishop *N.*,
and all the bishops,
with the clergy and the entire people your Son
   has gained for you.
Father, hear the prayers of the family you have
   gathered here before you.
In mercy and love unite all your children
wherever they may be.*

[For the Dead]

Welcome into your kingdom our departed
   brothers and sisters,

*See p. 36 for special prayer for Masses for the Dead.

3 and all who have left this world in your friendship.
We hope to enjoy for ever the vision of your glory,
through Christ our Lord, from whom all good
    things come.

[Concluding Doxology]

Through him,
with him,
in him,
in the unity of the Holy Spirit,
all glory and honor is yours,
almighty Father,
for ever and ever.

All reply: **Amen.**

Continue with the Mass, as on p. 66.

*In the Masses for the Dead the following is said:

Remember N.
In baptism he (she) died with Christ:
may he (she) also share his resurrection,
when Christ will raise our mortal bodies
and make them like his own in glory.
Welcome into your kingdom our departed brothers
    and sisters,
and all who have left this world in your friendship.
There we hope to share in your glory
when every tear will be wiped away.
On that day we shall see you, our God, as you are.
We shall become like you
and praise you for ever through Christ our Lord,
from whom all good things come.
Through him, etc., as above.

℣. The Lord be with you.   STAND

℟. **And also with you.**

℣. Lift up your hearts.

℟. **We lift them up to the Lord.**

℣. Let us give thanks to the Lord our God.

℟. **It is right to give him thanks and praise.**

PREFACE

Father in heaven,
it is right that we should give you thanks and glory:
you are the one God, living and true.
Through all eternity you live in unapproachable
    light.
Source of life and goodness, you have created all
    things,
to fill your creatures with every blessing
and lead all men to the joyful vision of your light.
Countless hosts of angels stand before you to do
    your will;
they look upon your splendor
and praise you, night and day.
United with them,
and in the name of every creature under heaven,
we too praise your glory as we sing (say):

SANCTUS   *[First Acclamation of the People]*

**Holy, holy, holy Lord, God of power and might,
heaven and earth are full of your glory.**
   Hosanna in the highest.
Blessed is he who comes in the name of the Lord.
   Hosanna in the highest.

4 *[Praise to the Father]* **KNEEL**

Father, we acknowledge your greatness:
all your actions show your wisdom and love.
You formed man in your own likeness
and set him over the whole world
to serve you, his creator,
and to rule over all creatures.
Even when he disobeyed you and lost your
   friendship
you did not abandon him to the power of death,
but helped all men to seek and find you.
Again and again you offered a covenant to man,
and through the prophets taught him to hope for
   salvation.
Father, you so loved the world
that in the fullness of time you sent your only Son
   to be our Savior.
He was conceived through the power of the Holy
   Spirit,
and born of the Virgin Mary,
a man like us in all things but sin.
To the poor he proclaimed the good news of salvation,
to prisoners, freedom,
and to those in sorrow, joy.
In fulfillment of your will
he gave himself up to death;
but by rising from the dead,
he destroyed death and restored life.
And that we might live no longer for ourselves
   but for him,
he sent the Holy Spirit from you, Father,
as his first gift to those who believe,

to complete his work on earth
and bring us the fullness of grace.

[Invocation of the Holy Spirit]

Father, may this Holy Spirit sanctify these offer-
    ings.
Let them become the body ✛ and blood of Jesus
    Christ our Lord
as we celebrate the great mystery
which he left us as an everlasting covenant.

[The Lord's Supper]

He always loved those who were his own in the
    world.
When the time came for him to be glorified by
    you, his heavenly Father,
he showed the depth of his love.
While they were at supper,
he took bread, said the blessing, broke the bread,
and gave it to his disciples, saying:

Take this, all of you, and eat it:
this is my body which will be given up for you.

In the same way, he took the cup, filled with
    wine.
He gave you thanks, and giving the cup to his dis-
    ciples, said:

Take this, all of you, and drink from it:
this is the cup of my blood,
the blood of the new and everlasting covenant.
It will be shed for you and for all
so that sins may be forgiven.
Do this in memory of me.

[Memorial Acclamation]

Priest: Let us proclaim the mystery of faith.

4 PEOPLE:

A Christ has died,
Christ is risen,
Christ will come again.

B Dying you destroyed our death,
rising you restored our life.
Lord Jesus, come in glory.

C When we eat this bread and drink this cup,
we proclaim your death, Lord Jesus,
until you come in glory.

D Lord, by your cross and resurrection
you have set us free.
You are the Savior of the world.

[The Memorial Prayer]

Father, we now celebrate this memorial of our
redemption.

We recall Christ's death, his descent among the
dead,

his resurrection, and his ascension to your right
hand;

and, looking forward to his coming in glory, we
offer you his body and blood,

the acceptable sacrifice

which brings salvation to the whole world.

Lord, look upon this sacrifice which you have
given to your Church;

and by your Holy Spirit, gather all who share this
one bread and one cup

into the one body of Christ, a living sacrifice of
praise.

4

[Intercessions: For the Church]

Lord, remember those for whom we offer this
    sacrifice,
especially N., our Pope,
N., our bishop, and bishops and clergy every-
    where.
Remember those who take part in this offering,
those here present and all your people,
and all who seek you with a sincere heart.

[For the Dead]

Remember those who have died in the peace of
    Christ
and all the dead whose faith is known to you alone.

[In Communion with the Saints]

Father, in your mercy grant also to us, your chil-
    dren,
to enter into our heavenly inheritance
in the company of the Virgin Mary, the Mother of
    God,
and your apostles and saints.
Then, in your kingdom, freed from the corruption
    of sin and death,
we shall sing your glory with every creature
    through Christ our Lord,
through whom you give us everything that is good.

[Concluding Doxology]

Through him,
with him,
in him,
in the unity of the Holy Spirit,
all glory and honor is yours,
almighty Father,
for ever and ever.

All reply: **Amen.** *Continue with the Mass, as on p. 66.*

EUCHARISTIC PRAYER FOR MASSES WITH CHILDREN I

STAND

℣. The Lord be with you.
℟. **And also with you.**
℣. Lift up your hearts.
℟. **We lift them up to the Lord.**
℣. Let us give thanks to the Lord our God.
℟. **It is right to give him thanks and praise.**

God our Father,
you have brought us here together
so that we can give you thanks and praise
for all the wonderful things you have done.

We thank you for all that is beautiful in the world
and for the happiness you have given us.
We praise you for daylight
and for your word which lights up our minds.
We praise you for the earth,
and all the people who live on it,
and for our life which comes from you.

We know that you are good.
You love us and do great things for us.
[So we all sing (say) together:

**Holy, holy, holy Lord, God of power and might,
heaven and earth are full of your glory.**
      Hosanna in the highest.]

Father,
you are always thinking about your people;
you never forget us.

You sent us your Son Jesus,
who gave his life for us
and who came to save us.
He cured sick people;
he cared for those who were poor
and wept with those who were sad.
He forgave sinners
and taught us to forgive each other.
He loved everyone
and showed us how to be kind.
He took children in his arms and blessed them.
[So we are glad to sing (say):

**Blessed is he who comes in the name of the
Lord. Hosanna in the highest.]**

God our Father,
all over the world your people praise you.
So now we pray with the whole Church:
with N., our pope and N., our bishop.
In heaven the blessed Virgin Mary,
the apostles and all the saints
always sing your praise.
Now we join with them and with the angels
to adore you as we sing (say):

PEOPLE:

**Holy, holy, holy Lord, God of power and might,
heaven and earth are full of your glory.**
     Hosanna in the highest.
Blessed is he who comes in the name of the Lord.
     Hosanna in the highest.

C1 God our Father,
you are most holy
and we want to show you that we are grateful.

We bring you bread and wine
and ask you to send your Holy Spirit to make these gifts
the body ✠ and blood of Jesus your Son.
Then we can offer to you
what you have given to us.

On the night before he died,
Jesus was having supper with his apostles.
He took bread from the table.
He gave you thanks and praise.
Then he broke the bread, gave it to his friends, and said:

Take this, all of you, and eat it:
this is my body which will be given up for you.

When supper was ended,
Jesus took the cup that was filled with wine.
He thanked you, gave it to his friends, and said:

Take this, all of you, and drink from it:
this is the cup of my blood,
the blood of the new and everlasting covenant.
It will be shed for you and for all
so that sins may be forgiven.
Then he said to them:
do this in memory of me.

We do now what Jesus told us to do.
We remember his death and his resurrection

and we offer you, Father, the bread that gives us
    life,
and the cup that saves us.
Jesus brings us to you;
welcome us as you welcome him.

Priest: Let us proclaim the mystery of faith.

PEOPLE:

A   **Christ has died,**
     Christ is risen,
     Christ will come again.

B   **Dying you destroyed our death,**
     rising you restored our life.
     Lord Jesus, come in glory.

C   **When we eat this bread and drink this cup,**
     we proclaim your death, Lord Jesus,
     until you come in glory.

D   **Lord, by your cross and resurrection**
     you have set us free.
     You are the Savior of the world.

Father,
because you love us,
you invite us to come to your table.
Fill us with the joy of the Holy Spirit
as we receive the body and blood of your Son.

Lord,
you never forget any of your children.
We ask you to take care of those we love,
especially of *N.* and *N.*;
and we pray for those who have died.

C 1 Remember everyone who is suffering from pain or
           sorrow.
Remember Christians everywhere
and all other people in the world.

We are filled with wonder and praise
when we see what you do for us
through Jesus your Son,
and so we sing:

Through him,
with him,
in him,
in the unity of the Holy Spirit,
all glory and honor is yours,
almighty Father,
for ever and ever.

The people respond: **Amen.**

Continue with the Mass, as on p. 66.

EUCHARISTIC PRAYER FOR MASSES WITH CHILDREN II

℣. The Lord be with you.

℟. **And also with you.**

℣. Lift up your hearts.

℟. **We lift them up to the Lord.**

℣. Let us give thanks to the Lord our God.

℟. **It is right to give him thanks and praise.**

God our loving Father,
we are glad to give you thanks and praise
because you love us.
With Jesus we sing your praise:

All say:

Glory to God in the highest.

> *or:*

Hosanna in the highest.

Because you love us,
you gave us this great and beautiful world.
With Jesus we sing your praise:

All say:

Glory to God in the highest.

> *or:*

Hosanna in the highest.

Because you love us,
you sent Jesus your Son
to bring us to you
and to gather us around him
as the children of one family.
With Jesus we sing your praise:

47

C
2

All say:

Glory to God in the highest.

or:

Hosanna in the highest.

For such great love
we thank you with the angels and saints
as they praise you and sing (say):

All say:

**Holy, holy, holy Lord, God of power and might,
heaven and earth are full of your glory.**
    Hosanna in the highest.
Blessed is he who comes in the name of the Lord.
    Hosanna in the highest.

Blessed be Jesus, whom you sent
to be the friend of children and of the poor.

He came to show us
how we can love you, Father,
by loving one another.
He came to take away sin,
which keeps us from being friends,
and hate, which makes us all unhappy.

He promised to send the Holy Spirit,
to be with us always
so that we can live as your children.

All say:

Blessed is he who comes in the name of the Lord.
    Hosanna in the highest.

God our Father,
we now ask you
to send your Holy Spirit
to change these gifts of bread and wine
into the body ✠ and blood
of Jesus Christ, our Lord.

The night before he died,
Jesus your Son showed us how much you love us.
When he was at supper with his disciples,
he took bread,
and gave you thanks and praise.
Then he broke the bread,
gave it to his friends, and said:

Take this, all of you, and eat it:
This is my body which will be given up for you.

All say:
Jesus has given his life for us.

When supper was ended,
Jesus took the cup that was filled with wine.
He thanked you, gave it to his friends, and said:

Take this, all of you, and drink from it:
this is the cup of my blood,
the blood of the new and everlasting covenant.
It will be shed for you and for all
so that sins may be forgiven.

All say:
Jesus has given his life for us.

Then he said to them:
do this in memory of me.

C 2 And so, loving Father,
we remember that Jesus died and rose again
to save the world.
He put himself into our hands
to be the sacrifice we offer you.

All say:
We praise you, we bless you, we thank you.

Lord our God,
listen to our prayer.
Send the Holy Spirit
to all of us who share in this meal.
May this Spirit bring us closer together
in the family of the Church,
with N., our pope,
N., our bishop,
all other bishops,
and all who serve your people.

All say:
We praise you, we bless you, we thank you.

Remember, Father, our families and friends (. . .),
    and all those we do not love as we should.
Remember those who have died (. . .).
Bring them home to you
to be with you for ever.

All say:
We praise you, we bless you, we thank you.

Gather us all together into your kingdom.
There we shall be happy for ever

C 2

with the Virgin Mary, Mother of God and our
    mother.
There all the friends
of Jesus the Lord
 will sing a song of joy.

All say:

We praise you, we bless you, we thank you.

Through him,
with him,
in him,
in the unity of the Holy Spirit,
all glory and honor is yours,
almighty Father,
for ever and ever.

The people respond: **Amen.**

Continue with the Mass, as on p. 66.

EUCHARISTIC PRAYER FOR MASSES WITH CHILDREN III

STAND

℣. The Lord be with you.
℟. **And also with you.**
℣. Lift up your hearts.
℟. **We lift them up to the Lord.**
℣. Let us give thanks to the Lord our God.
℟. **It is right to give him thanks and praise.**

Outside Easter season:

We thank you,
God our Father.
You made us to live for you and for each other.
We can see and speak to one another,
and become friends,
and share our joys and sorrows.

During Easter Season:

We thank you,
God our Father.
You are the living God;
you have called us to share in your life,
and to be happy with you for ever.
You raised up Jesus, your Son,
the first among us to rise from the dead,
and gave him new life.
You have promised to give us new life also,
a life that will never end,
a life with no more anxiety and suffering.

**C
3**

And so, Father, we gladly thank you
with every one who believes in you;
with the saints and the angels,
we rejoice and praise you, saying:

**Holy, holy, holy Lord, God of power and might,
heaven and earth are full of your glory.**
Hosanna in the highest.
Blessed is he who comes in the name of the Lord.
Hosanna in the highest.

Yes, Lord, you are holy;   **KNEEL**
you are kind to us and to all.
For this we thank you.
We thank you above all for your Son, Jesus Christ.

Outside Easter season:

You sent him into this world
because people had turned away from you
and no longer loved each other.
He opened our eyes and our hearts
to understand that we are brothers and sisters
and that you are Father of us all.

During Easter season:

He brought us the good news
of life to be lived with you for ever in heaven.
He showed us the way to that life,
the way of love.
He himself has gone that way before us.

He now brings us together to one table
and asks us to do what he did.

C 3

Father,
we ask you to bless these gifts of bread and wine
and make them holy.
Change them for us into the body ✛ and blood of
   Jesus Christ, your Son.

On the night before he died for us,
he had supper for the last time with his disciples.
He took bread
and gave you thanks.
He broke the bread
and gave it to his friends, saying:

Take this, all of you, and eat it:
this is my body which will be given up for you.

In the same way he took a cup of wine.
He gave you thanks
and handed the cup to his disciples, saying:

Take this, all of you, and drink from it:
this is the cup of my blood,
the blood of the new and everlasting covenant.
It will be shed for you and for all
so that sins may be forgiven.
Then he said to them:
do this in memory of me.

God our Father,
we remember with joy
all that Jesus did to save us.
In this holy sacrifice,
which he gave as a gift to his Church,
we remember his death and resurrection.

**C
3**

Father in heaven,
accept us together with your beloved Son.
He willingly died for us,
but you raised him to life again.
We thank you and say:

All say:

Glory to God in the highest.

(Or some other suitable acclamation of praise.)

Jesus now lives with you in glory,
but he is also here on earth, among us.
We thank you and say:

All say:

Glory to God in the highest.

(Or some other suitable acclamation of praise.)

One day he will come in glory
and in his kingdom
there will be no more suffering,
no more tears, no more sadness.
We thank you and say:

All say:

Glory to God in the highest.

(Or some other suitable acclamation of praise.)

Father in heaven,
you have called us
to receive the body and blood of Christ at this table
and to be filled with the joy of the Holy Spirit.

C 3

Through this sacred meal
give us strength to please you more and more.

Lord, our God,
remember N., our pope,
N., our bishop, and all other bishops.

Outside Easter season:

Help all who follow Jesus
to work for peace
and to bring happiness to others.

During Easter season:

Fill all Christians with the gladness of Easter.
Help us to bring this joy
to all who are sorrowful.

Bring us all at last
together with Mary, the Mother of God,
and all the saints,
to live with you
and to be one with Christ in heaven.

Through him,
with him,
in him,
in the unity of the Holy Spirit,
all glory and honor is yours,
almighty Father,
for ever and ever.

The people respond: **Amen.**

Continue with the Mass, as on p. 66.

EUCHARISTIC PRAYER FOR MASSES OF RECONCILIATION I

STAND

℣. The Lord be with you.
℟. **And also with you.**
℣. Lift up your hearts.
℟. **We lift them up to the Lord.**
℣. Let us give thanks to the Lord our God.
℟. **It is right to give him thanks and praise.**

Father, all-powerful and ever-living God,
we do well always and everywhere to give you
        thanks and praise.
You never cease to call us
to a new and more abundant life.

God of love and mercy,
you are always ready to forgive;
we are sinners,
and you invite us
to trust in your mercy.

Time and time again
we broke your covenant,
but you did not abandon us.
Instead, through your Son, Jesus our Lord,
you bound yourself even more closely to the
        human family
by a bond that can never be broken.

Now is the time
for your people to turn back to you
and to be renewed in Christ your Son,
a time of grace and reconciliation.

R 1 You invite us
to serve the family of mankind
by opening our hearts
to the fullness of your Holy Spirit.

In wonder and gratitude,
we join our voices with the choirs of heaven
to proclaim the power of your love
and to sing of our salvation in Christ:

All say:

**Holy, holy, holy Lord, God of power and might,
heaven and earth are full of your glory.**
Hosanna in the highest.
Blessed is he who comes in the name of the Lord.
Hosanna in the highest.

`KNEEL`

Father,
from the beginning of time
you have always done what is good for man
so that we may be holy as you are holy.

Look with kindness on your people
gathered here before you:
send forth the power of your Spirit
so that these gifts may become for us
the body ✠ and blood of your beloved Son, Jesus
the Christ,
in whom we have become your sons and daughters.

When we were lost
and could not find the way to you,
you loved us more than ever:
Jesus, your Son, innocent and without sin,
gave himself into our hands
and was nailed to a cross.
Yet before he stretched out his arms between
    heaven and earth
in the everlasting sign of your covenant,
he desired to celebrate the Paschal feast
in the company of his disciples.

While they were at supper,
he took bread and gave you thanks and praise.
He broke the bread, gave it to his disciples, and
    said:

Take this, all of you, and eat it:
this is my body which will be given up for you.

At the end of the meal,
knowing that he was to reconcile all things in
    himself
by the blood of his cross,
he took the cup, filled with wine.
Again he gave you thanks,
handed the cup to his friends, and said:

Take this, all of you, and drink from it:
this is the cup of my blood,
the blood of the new and everlasting covenant.
It will be shed for you and for all
so that sins may be forgiven.
Do this in memory of me.

R 1

Priest: Let us proclaim the mystery of faith.

PEOPLE:

A Christ has died,
Christ is risen,
Christ will come again.

B Dying you destroyed our death,
rising you restored our life.
Lord Jesus, come in glory.

C When we eat this bread and drink this cup,
we proclaim your death, Lord Jesus,
until you come in glory.

D Lord, by your cross and resurrection
you have set us free.
You are the Savior of the world.

We do this in memory of Jesus Christ,
our Passover and our lasting peace.
We celebrate his death and resurrection
and look for the coming of that day
when he will return to give us the fullness of joy.
Therefore we offer you, God ever faithful and
true,
the sacrifice which restores man to your friendship.

Father,
look with love
on those you have called
to share in the one sacrifice of Christ.
By the power of your Holy Spirit
make them one body,
healed of all division.

Keep us all
in communion of mind and heart
with N., our pope, and N., our bishop.
Help us to work together
for the coming of your kingdom,
until at last we stand in your presence
to share the life of the saints,
in the company of the Virgin Mary and the
      apostles,
and of our departed brothers and sisters
whom we commend to your mercy.

Then, freed from every shadow of death,
we shall take our place in the new creation
and give you thanks
with Christ, our risen Lord.

Through him,
with him,
in him,
in the unity of the Holy Spirit,
all glory and honor is yours,
almighty Father,
for ever and ever.

The people respond: **Amen.**

Continue with the Mass, as on p. 66.

STAND

℣. The Lord be with you.
℟. **And also with you.**
℣. Lift up your hearts.
℟. **We lift them up to the Lord.**
℣. Let us give thanks to the Lord our God.
℟. **It is right to give him thanks and praise.**

Father, all-powerful and ever-living God,
we praise and thank you through Jesus Christ
  our Lord
for your presence and action in the world.

In the midst of conflict and division,
we know it is you
who turn our minds to thoughts of peace.
Your Spirit changes our hearts:
enemies begin to speak to one another,
those who were estranged join hands in friendship,
and nations seek the way of peace together.

Your Spirit is at work
when understanding puts an end to strife,
when hatred is quenched by mercy,
and vengeance gives way to forgiveness.

For this we should never cease
to thank and praise you.
We join with all the choirs of heaven
as they sing for ever to your glory:

R 2

All say:

**Holy, holy, holy Lord, God of power and might,
heaven and earth are full of your glory.**
   Hosanna in the highest.
Blessed is he who comes in the name of the Lord.
   Hosanna in the highest.

God of power and might,   **KNEEL**
we praise you through your Son, Jesus Christ,
who comes in your name.
He is the Word that brings salvation.
He is the hand you stretch out to sinners.
He is the way that leads to your peace.

God our Father,
we had wandered far from you,
but through your Son you have brought us back.
You gave him up to death
so that we might turn again to you
and find our way to one another.

Therefore we celebrate the reconciliation
Christ has gained for us.

We ask you to sanctify these gifts
by the power of your Spirit,
as we now fulfill your Son's ✝ command.

While he was at supper
on the night before he died for us,
he took bread in his hands,
and gave you thanks and praise.
He broke the bread,
gave it to his disciples, and said:

Take this, all of you, and eat it:
this is my body which will be given up for you.

R 2 At the end of the meal he took the cup.
Again he praised you for your goodness,
gave the cup to his disciples, and said:

Take this, all of you, and drink from it:
this is the cup of my blood,
the blood of the new and everlasting covenant.
It will be shed for you and for all
so that sins may be forgiven.
Do this in memory of me.

Priest: Let us proclaim the mystery of faith.

PEOPLE:

A   **Christ has died,**
    Christ is risen,
    Christ will come again.

B   **Dying you destroyed our death,**
    rising you restored our life.
    Lord Jesus, come in glory.

C   **When we eat this bread and drink this cup,**
    we proclaim your death, Lord Jesus,
    until you come in glory.

D   **Lord, by your cross and resurrection**
    you have set us free.
    You are the Savior of the world.

Lord our God,
your Son has entrusted to us
this pledge of his love.
We celebrate the memory of his death and resurrection
and bring you the gift you have given us,
the sacrifice of reconciliation.

R 2

Therefore, we ask you, Father,
to accept us, together with your Son.

Fill us with his Spirit
through our sharing in this meal.
May he take away all that divides us.

May this Spirit keep us always in communion
with N., our pope, N., our bishop,
with all the bishops and all your people.
Father, make your Church throughout the world
a sign of unity and an instrument of your peace.

You have gathered us here
around the table of your Son,
in fellowship with the Virgin Mary, Mother of God,
    and all the saints.

In that new world where the fullness of your peace
    will be revealed,
gather people of every race, language, and way of
    life
to share in the one eternal banquet
with Jesus Christ the Lord.

Through him,
with him,
in him,
in the unity of the Holy Spirit,
all glory and honor is yours,
almighty Father,
for ever and ever.

The people respond: **Amen.**

COMMUNION RITE

To prepare for the paschal meal, to welcome the Lord, we pray for forgiveness and exchange a sign of peace. Before eating Christ's body and drinking his blood, we must be one with him and with all our brothers and sisters in the Church.

24 LORD'S PRAYER

Priest:　　　　　　　　　　　　　　**STAND**

A Let us pray with confidence to the Father
in the words our Savior gave us:

B Jesus taught us to call God our Father,
and so we have the courage to say:

C Let us ask our Father to forgive our sins
and to bring us to forgive those who sin against
us.

D Let us pray for the coming of the kingdom
as Jesus taught us.

Priest and **PEOPLE**:

**Our Father, who art in heaven,
hallowed be thy name;
thy kingdom come;
thy will be done on earth as it is in heaven.
Give us this day our daily bread;
and forgive us our trespasses
as we forgive those who trespass against us;
and lead us not into temptation,
but deliver us from evil.**

Priest:　Deliver us, Lord, from every evil,
and grant us peace in our day.

In your mercy keep us free from sin
and protect us from all anxiety
as we wait in joyful hope
for the coming of our Savior, Jesus Christ.

PEOPLE: **For the kingdom, the power, and the glory
are yours, now and for ever.**

25 SIGN OF PEACE

The Church is a community of Christians joined by the Spirit in
love. It needs to express, deepen, and restore its peaceful unity
before eating the one Body of the Lord and drinking from the
one cup of salvation. We do this by a sign of peace.

The priest says the prayer for peace:

Lord Jesus Christ, you said to your apostles:
I leave you peace, my peace I give you.
Look not on our sins, but on the faith of your
     Church,
and grant us the peace and unity of your kingdom
where you live for ever and ever.

PEOPLE: **Amen.**

Priest: The peace of the Lord be with you always.

PEOPLE: **And also with you.**

Deacon (or priest):
  Let us offer each other the sign of peace.

*The people exchange a sign of peace and love, according
to local custom.*

26 BREAKING OF THE BREAD

Christians are gathered for the"breaking of the bread," another
name for the Mass. In communion, though many we are made
one body in the one bread, which is Christ.

Then the following is sung or said:

PEOPLE:

> **Lamb of God, you take away the sins of the world:**
>> **have mercy on us.**
> **Lamb of God, you take away the sins of the world:**
>> **have mercy on us.**
> **Lamb of God, you take away the sins of the world:**
>> **grant us peace.**

The hymn may be repeated until the breaking of the bread is finished, but the last phrase is always: "Grant us peace."

Meanwhile the priest breaks the host over the paten and places a small piece in the chalice, saying inaudibly:

May this mingling of the body and blood of our
    Lord Jesus Christ
bring eternal life to us who receive it.

KNEEL

27 PRAYERS BEFORE COMMUNION

We pray in silence and then voice words of humility and hope
as our final preparation before meeting Christ in the eucharist.

Before communion, the priest says inaudibly one of the following prayers:

Lord Jesus Christ, Son of the living God, by the will
of the Father and the work of the Holy Spirit your
death brought life to the world. By your holy body
and blood free me from all my sins and from every
evil. Keep me faithful to your teaching, and never
let me be parted from you.

OR

Lord Jesus Christ, with faith in your love and
mercy I eat your body and drink your blood. Let it
not bring me condemnation, but health in mind
and body.

28 RECEPTION OF COMMUNION*

*The priest genuflects. Holding the host elevated slightly
over the paten, the priest says:*

Priest: This is the Lamb of God
who takes away the sins of the world.
Happy are those who are called to his supper.

Priest and **PEOPLE** (once only):
**Lord, I am not worthy to receive you,
but only say the word and I shall be healed.**

Before receiving communion, the priest says inaudibly:

May the body of Christ bring me to everlasting life.
May the blood of Christ bring me to everlasting life.

He then gives communion to the people.

Priest: The body of Christ. Communicant: **Amen.**
Priest: The blood of Christ. Communicant: **Amen.**

29 COMMUNION SONG or ANTIPHON

*The Communion Psalm or other appropriate Song or
Hymn is sung while Communion is given to the faithful. If
there is no singing, the Communion Antiphon is said:*

➡ **Turn to Today's Mass**

*The vessels are cleansed by the priest or deacon or
acolyte. Meanwhile he says inaudibly:*

Lord, may I receive these gifts in purity of heart.
May they bring me healing and strength, now and
for ever.

*See Guidelines on pp. 662-663.

30 PERIOD OF SILENCE or Song of Praise

After communion there may be a period of silence, or a song of praise may be sung.

31 PRAYER AFTER COMMUNION STAND

The priest prays in our name that we may live the life of faith since we have been strengthened by Christ himself. Our *Amen* makes his prayer our own.

Priest: **Let us pray.**

Priest and people may pray silently for a while. Then the priest says the prayer after communion.

→ **Turn to Today's Mass**

At the end, **PEOPLE: Amen.**

CONCLUDING RITE

We have heard God's Word and eaten the body of Christ. Now it is time for us to leave, to do good works, to praise and bless the Lord in our daily lives.

32 GREETING STAND

After any brief announcements (sit), the blessing and dismissal follow:

Priest: **The Lord be with you.**

PEOPLE: And also with you.

33 BLESSING

A Simple form

Priest: **May almighty God bless you,
the Father, and the Son, ✠ and the Holy Spirit.**

PEOPLE: Amen.

On certain days or occasions another more solemn form of blessing or prayer over the people may be used as the rubrics direct.

B Solemn blessing

Texts of all the solemn blessings are given on pp. 92-99.

Deacon: **Bow your heads and pray for God's blessing.**

The priest always concludes the solemn blessings by adding:

**May almighty God bless you,
the Father, and the Son, ✠ and the Holy Spirit.**

PEOPLE: Amen.

C Prayer over the people

Texts of all prayers over the people are given on pp. 99-103.

After the prayer over the people, the priest always adds:

**May almighty God bless you,
the Father, and the Son, ✠ and the Holy Spirit.**

PEOPLE: Amen.

34 DISMISSAL
Deacon (or priest):

A Go in the peace of Christ.

B The Mass is ended, go in peace.

C Go in peace to love and serve the Lord.

PEOPLE: Thanks be to God.

If any liturgical service follows immediately, the rite of dismissal is omitted.

RITE OF BLESSING AND
SPRINKLING HOLY WATER

*When this rite is celebrated it takes the place of the peni-
tential rite at the beginning of Mass. The Kyrie is also
omitted.*

*After greeting the people the priest remains standing at
his chair. A vessel containing the water to be blessed is
placed before him. Facing the people, he invites them to
pray, using these or similar words:*

Dear friends,
this water will be used
to remind us of our baptism.
Let us ask God to bless it,
and to keep us faithful
to the Spirit he has given us.

After a brief silence, he joins his hands and continues:

A.

God our Father,
your gift of water
brings life and freshness to the earth;
it washes away our sins
and brings us eternal life.

We ask you now
to bless ✠ this water,
and to give us your protection on this day
which you have made your own.
Renew the living spring of your life within us
and protect us in spirit and body,
that we may be free from sin
and come into your presence
to receive your gift of salvation.
We ask this through Christ our Lord. ℟. **Amen.**

B. Or:

Lord God almighty,
creator of all life,
of body and soul,
we ask you to bless ✤ this water:
as we use it in faith
forgive our sins
and save us from all illness
and the power of evil.

Lord,
in your mercy
give us living water,
always springing up as a fountain of salvation:
free us, body and soul, from every danger,
and admit us to your presence
in purity of heart.
Grant this through Christ our Lord. ℞. **Amen.**

C. Or (during the Easter season):

Lord God almighty,
hear the prayers of your people:
we celebrate our creation and redemption.
Hear our prayers and bless ✤ this water
which gives fruitfulness to the fields,
and refreshment and cleansing to man.
You chose water to show your goodness
when you led your people to freedom
through the Red Sea
and satisfied their thirst in the desert
with water from the rock.
Water was the symbol used by the prophets
to foretell your new covenant with man.
You made the water of baptism holy
by Christ's baptism in the Jordan:
by it you give us a new birth
and renew us in holiness.
May this water remind us of our baptism,
and let us share the joy

of all who have been baptized at Easter.
We ask this through Christ our Lord. ℟. **Amen.**

*Where it is customary, salt may be mixed with the holy water.
The priest blesses the salt, saying:*

Almighty God,
we ask you to bless ✠ this salt
as once you blessed the salt scattered over the water
by the prophet Elisha.
Wherever this salt and water are sprinkled,
drive away the power of evil,
and protect us always
by the presence of your Holy Spirit.
Grant this through Christ our Lord. ℟. **Amen.**

Then he pours the salt into the water in silence.

*Taking the sprinkler, the priest sprinkles himself and his
ministers, then the rest of the clergy and people. He may
move through the church for the sprinkling of the people.
Meanwhile, an antiphon or another appropriate song is
sung.*

*When he returns to his place and the song is finished, the
priest faces the people and, with joined hands, says:*

May almighty God cleanse us of our sins,
and through the eucharist we celebrate
make us worthy to sit at his table
in his heavenly kingdom.

The people answer: **Amen.**

When it is prescribed, the Gloria is then sung or said.

PENITENTIAL RITE

ALTERNATIVE FORMS FOR C (p. 13)

ii

Priest or other minister:
Lord Jesus, you came to gather the nations
into the peace of God's kingdom:
Lord, have mercy.

People: **Lord, have mercy.**

Priest or other minister:
You come in word and sacrament to strengthen us in
holiness:
Christ, have mercy.

People: **Christ, have mercy.**

Priest or other minister:
You will come in glory with salvation for your people:
Lord, have mercy.

People: **Lord, have mercy.** (➔ p. 14)

iii

Priest or other minister:
Lord Jesus, you are mighty God and Prince of peace:
Lord, have mercy.

People: **Lord, have mercy.**

Priest or other minister:
Lord Jesus, you are Son of God and Son of Mary:
Christ, have mercy.

People: **Christ, have mercy.**

Priest or other minister:
Lord Jesus, you are Word made flesh and splendor of the
Father:
Lord, have mercy.

People: **Lord, have mercy.** (➔ p. 14)

iv

Priest or other minister:
Lord Jesus, you came to reconcile us
to one another and to the Father:
Lord, have mercy.

People: **Lord, have mercy.**

Priest or other minister:
Lord Jesus, you heal the wounds of sin and division:
Christ, have mercy.

People: **Christ, have mercy.**

Priest or other minister:
Lord Jesus, you intercede for us with your Father:
Lord, have mercy.

People: **Lord, have mercy.**   (➜ p. 14)

v

Priest or other minister:
You raise the dead to life in the Spirit:
Lord, have mercy.

People: **Lord, have mercy.**

Priest or other minister:
You bring pardon and peace to the sinner:
Christ, have mercy.

People: **Christ, have mercy.**

Priest or other minister:
You bring light to those in darkness:
Lord, have mercy.

People: **Lord, have mercy.**   (➜ p. 14)

vi

Priest or other minister:
Lord Jesus, you raise us to new life:
Lord, have mercy.

People: **Lord, have mercy.**

Priest or other minister:
Lord Jesus, you forgive us our sins:

Christ, have mercy.
People: **Christ, have mercy.**
Priest or other minister:
Lord Jesus, you feed us with your body and blood:
Lord, have mercy.
People: **Lord, have mercy.** (➜ p. 14)

vii

Priest or other minister:
Lord Jesus, you have shown us the way to the Father:
Lord, have mercy.
People: **Lord, have mercy.**
Priest or other minister:
Lord Jesus, you have given us the consolation of the truth:
Christ, have mercy.
People: **Christ, have mercy.**
Priest or other minister:
Lord Jesus, you are the Good Shepherd,
leading us into everlasting life:
Lord, have mercy.
People: **Lord, have mercy.** (➜ p. 14)

viii

Priest or other minister:
Lord Jesus, you healed the sick:
Lord, have mercy.
People: **Lord, have mercy.**
Priest or other minister:
Lord Jesus, you forgave sinners:
Christ, have mercy.
People: **Christ, have mercy.**
Priest or other minister:
Lord Jesus, you give us yourself to heal us and bring us
    strength:
Lord, have mercy.
People: **Lord, have mercy.** (➜ p. 14)

PREFACES

ADVENT I (P 1)

The Two Comings of Christ
(From the First Sunday of Advent to December 16)

Father, all-powerful and ever-living God,
we do well always and everywhere to give you thanks
through Jesus Christ our Lord.

When he humbled himself to come among us as a man,
he fulfilled the plan you formed long ago
and opened for us the way to salvation.

Now we watch for the day,
hoping that the salvation promised us will be ours
when Christ our Lord will come again in his glory.

And so, with all the choirs of angels in heaven
we proclaim your glory
and join in their unending hymn of praise: ➜ No. 23, p. 23

ADVENT II (P 2)

Waiting for the Two Comings of Christ
(From December 17 to December 24)

Father, all-powerful and ever-living God,
we do well always and everywhere to give you thanks
through Jesus Christ our Lord.

His future coming was proclaimed by all the prophets.
The virgin mother bore him in her womb
with love beyond all telling.
John the Baptist was his herald
and made him known when at last he came.

In his love he has filled us with joy
as we prepare to celebrate his birth,
so that when he comes he may find us watching in prayer,
our hearts filled with wonder and praise.

And so, with all the choirs of angels in heaven
we proclaim your glory
and join in their unending hymn of praise: → No. 23, p. 23

CHRISTMAS I (P 3)

Christ the Light

(From Christmas to Saturday before Epiphany)

Father, all-powerful and ever-living God,
we do well always and everywhere to give you thanks
through Jesus Christ our Lord.

In the wonder of the incarnation
your eternal Word has brought to the eyes of faith
a new and radiant vision of your glory.
In him we see our God made visible
and so are caught up in love of the God we cannot see.

And so, with all the choirs of angels in heaven
we proclaim you glory
and join in the unending hymn of praise: → No. 23, p. 23

CHRISTMAS II (P 4)

Christ Restores Unity to All Creation

(From Christmas to Saturday before Epiphany)

Father, all-powerful and ever-living God,
we do well always and everywhere to give you thanks
through Jesus Christ our Lord.

Today you fill our hearts with joy
as we recognize in Christ the revelation of your love.
No eye can see his glory as our God,
yet now he is seen as one like us.

Christ is your Son before all ages,
yet now he is born in time.
He has come to lift up all things to himself,
to restore unity to creation,
and to lead mankind from exile into your heavenly kingdom.

With all the angels of heaven
we sing our joyful hymn of praise: → No. 23, p. 23

CHRISTMAS III (P 5)

*Divine and Human Exchange in the
Incarnation of the Word*
(From Christmas to Saturday before Epiphany)

Father, all-powerful and ever-living God,
we do well always and everywhere to give you thanks
through Jesus Christ our Lord.

Today in him a new light has dawned upon the world:
God has become one with man,
and man has become one again with God.

Your eternal Word has taken upon himself our human
       weakness,
giving our mortal nature immortal value.
So marvelous is this oneness between God and man
that in Christ man restores to man the gift of everlasting life.

In our joy we sing to your glory
with all the choirs of angels: ➔ No. 23, p. 23

LENT I (P 8)

The Spiritual Meaning of Lent

Father, all-powerful and ever-living God,
we do well always and everywhere to give you thanks
through Jesus Christ our Lord.

Each year you give us this joyful season
when we prepare to celebrate the paschal mystery
with mind and heart renewed.
You give us a spirit of loving reverence for you, our Father,
and of willing service to our neighbor.

As we recall the great events that gave us new life in Christ,
you bring the image of your Son to perfection within us.
Now, with angels and archangels,
and the whole company of heaven,
we sing the unending hymn of your praise: ➔ No. 23, p. 23

LENT II (P 9)

The Spirit of Penance

Father, all-powerful and ever-living God,
we do well always and everywhere to give you thanks.

This great season of grace is your gift to your family
to renew us in spirit.
You give us strength to purify our hearts,
to control our desires,
and so to serve you in freedom.
You teach us how to live in this passing world
with our heart set on the world that will never end.

Now, with all the saints and angels,
we praise you for ever: ➤ No. 23, p. 23

EASTER I (P 21)
The Paschal Mystery

(Easter Vigil, Easter Sunday and during the octave and season)

Father, all-powerful and ever-living God,
we do well always and everywhere to give you thanks
through Jesus Christ our Lord.

We praise you with greater joy than ever
on this Easter night (day) (in this Easter season),
when Christ became our paschal sacrifice.

He is the true Lamb who took away the sins of the world.
By dying he destroyed our death;
by rising he restored our life.

And so, with all the choirs of angels in heaven
we proclaim your glory
and join in their unending hymn of praise: ➤ No. 23, p. 23

EASTER II (P 22)
New Life in Christ

Father, all-powerful and ever-living God,
we do well always and everywhere to give you thanks
through Jesus Christ our Lord.

We praise you with greater joy than ever in this Easter season,
when Christ became our paschal sacrifice.

He has made us children of the light,
rising to new and everlasting life.
He has opened the gates of heaven
to receive his faithful people.

His death is our ransom from death;
his resurrection is our rising to life.

The joy of the resurrection renews the whole world,
while the choirs of heaven sing for ever to your glory:

→ No. 23, p. 23

EASTER III (P 23)

Christ Lives and Intercedes for Us For Ever

Father, all-powerful and ever-living God,
we do well always and everywhere to give you thanks
through Jesus Christ our Lord.

We praise you with greater joy than ever in this Easter season,
when Christ became our paschal sacrifice.

He is still our priest,
our advocate who always pleads our cause.
Christ is the victim who dies no more,
the Lamb, once slain, who lives for ever.

The joy of the resurrection renews the whole world,
while the choirs of heaven sing for ever to your glory:

→ No. 23, p. 23

EASTER IV (P 24)

*The Restoration of the Universe through the
Paschal Mystery*

Father, all-powerful and ever-living God,
we do well always and everywhere to give you thanks
through Jesus Christ our Lord.

We praise you with greater joy than ever in this Easter season,
when Christ became our paschal sacrifice.

In him a new age has dawned,
the long reign of sin is ended,
a broken world has been renewed,
and man is once again made whole.

The joy of the resurrection renews the whole world,
while the choirs of heaven sing for ever to your glory:

→ No. 23, p. 23

EASTER V (P 25)
Christ Is Priest and Victim

Father, all-powerful and ever-living God,
we do well always and everywhere to give you thanks
through Jesus Christ our Lord.

We praise you with greater joy than ever in this Easter season,
when Christ became our paschal sacrifice.

As he offered his body on the cross,
his perfect sacrifice fulfilled all others.
As he gave himself into your hands for our salvation,
he showed himself to be the priest, the altar, and the lamb
of sacrifice.

The joy of the resurrection renews the whole world,
while the choirs of heaven sing for ever to your glory:

➙ No. 23, p. 23

ASCENSION I (P 26)
The Mystery of the Ascension
(Ascension to the Saturday before Pentecost inclusive)

Father, all-powerful and ever-living God,
we do well always and everywhere to give you thanks.

[Today] the Lord Jesus, the king of glory,
the conqueror of sin and death,
ascended to heaven while the angels sang his praises.

Christ, the mediator between God and man,
judge of the world and Lord of all,
has passed beyond our sight,
not to abandon us but to be our hope.
Christ is the beginning, the head of the Church;
where he has gone, we hope to follow.

The joy of the resurrection and ascension renews the whole
world,
while the choirs of heaven sing for ever to your glory:

➙ No. 23, p. 23

ASCENSION II (P 27)

The Mystery of the Ascension
(Ascension to the Saturday before Pentecost inclusive)

Father, all-powerful and ever-living God,
we do well always and everywhere to give you thanks
through Jesus Christ our Lord.

In his risen body he plainly showed himself to his disciples
and was taken up to heaven in their sight
to claim for us a share in his divine life.

And so, with all the choirs of angels in heaven
we proclaim your glory
and join in their unending hymn of praise: ➔ No. 23, p. 23

SUNDAYS IN ORDINARY TIME I (P 29)

The Paschal Mystery and the People of God

Father, all-powerful and ever-living God,
we do well always and everywhere to give you thanks
through Jesus Christ our Lord.

Through his cross and resurrection
he freed us from sin and death
and called us to the glory that has made us
a chosen race, a royal priesthood,
a holy nation, a people set apart.

Everywhere we proclaim your mighty works
for you have called us out of darkness
into your own wonderful light.

And so, with all the choirs of angels in heaven
we proclaim your glory
and join in their unending hymn of praise: ➔ No. 23, p. 23

SUNDAYS IN ORDINARY TIME II (P 30)

The Mystery of Salvation

Father, all-powerful and ever-living God,
we do well always and everywhere to give you thanks
through Jesus Christ our Lord.

Out of love for sinful man,
he humbled himself to be born of the Virgin.

By suffering on the cross
he freed us from unending death,
and by rising from the dead
he gave us eternal life.

And so, with all the choirs of angels in heaven
we proclaim your glory
and join in their unending hymn of praise: → No. 23, p. 23

SUNDAYS IN ORDINARY TIME III (P 31)

The Salvation of Man by Man

Father, all-powerful and ever-living God,
we do well always and everywhere to give you thanks.

We see your infinite power
in your loving plan of salvation.
You came to our rescue by your power as God,
but you wanted us to be saved by one like us.
Man refused your friendship,
but man himself was to restore it
through Jesus Christ our Lord.

Through him the angels of heaven offer their prayer of adoration
as they rejoice in your presence for ever
May our voices be one with theirs
in their triumphant hymn of praise: → No. 23, p. 23

SUNDAYS IN ORDINARY TIME IV (P 32)

The History of Salvation

Father, all-powerful and ever-living God,
we do well always and everywhere to give you thanks
through Jesus Christ our Lord.

By his birth we are reborn.
In his suffering we are freed from sin.
By his rising from the dead we rise to everlasting life.
In his return to you in glory
we enter into your heavenly kingdom.

And so, we join the angels and the saints
as they sing their unending hymn of praise: → No. 23, p. 23

SUNDAYS IN ORDINARY TIME V (P 33)

Creation

Father, all-powerful and ever-living God,
we do well always and everywhere to give you thanks.

All things are of your making,
all times and seasons obey your laws,
but you chose to create man in your own image,
setting him over the whole world in all its wonder.
You made man the steward of creation,
to praise you day by day for the marvels of your wisdom
   and power,
through Jesus Christ our Lord.
We praise you, Lord with all the angels in their song of
   joy: → No. 23, p. 23

SUNDAYS IN ORDINARY TIME VI (P 34)

The Pledge of an Eternal Easter

Father, all-powerful and ever-living God,
we do well always and everywhere to give you thanks.

In you we live and move and have our being.
Each day you show us a Father's love;
your Holy Spirit, dwelling within us,
gives us on earth the hope of unending joy.

Your gift of the Spirit,
who raised Jesus from the dead,
is the foretaste and promise
of the paschal feast of heaven.

With thankful praise,
in company with the angels,
we glorify the wonders of your power: → No. 23, p. 23

SUNDAYS IN ORDINARY TIME VII (P 35)

Salvation through the Obedience of Christ

Father, all-powerful and ever-living God,
we do well always and everywhere to give you thanks.

So great was your love
that you gave us your Son as our redeemer.
You sent him as one like ourselves,

though free from sin,
that you might see and love in us
what you see and love in Christ.
Your gifts of grace, lost by disobedience,
are now restored by the obedience of your Son.

We praise you, Lord, with all the angels and saints
in their song of joy: ➤ No. 23, p. 23

SUNDAYS IN ORDINARY TIME VIII (P 36)
The Church United in the Mystery of the Trinity

Father, all-powerful and ever-living God,
we do well always and everywhere to give you thanks.

When your children sinned
and wandered far from your friendship,
you reunited them with yourself
through the blood of your Son
and the power of the Holy Spirit.

You gather them into your Church,
to be one as you, Father, are one
with your Son and the Holy Spirit.
You call them to be your people,
to praise your wisdom in all your works.
You make them the body of Christ
and the dwelling-place of the Holy Spirit.

In our joy we sing to your glory
with all the choirs of angels: ➤ No. 23, p. 23

HOLY EUCHARIST I (P 47)
The Sacrifice and Sacrament of Christ

Father, all-powerful and ever-living God,
we do well always and everywhere to give you thanks
through Jesus Christ our Lord.

He is the true and eternal priest
who established this unending sacrifice.
He offered himself as a victim for our deliverance
and taught us to make this offering in his memory.
As we eat his body which he gave for us,

we grow in strength.
As we drink his blood which he poured out for us,
we are washed clean.

Now, with angels and archangels,
and the whole company of heaven,
we sing the unending hymn of your praise: ➔ No. 23, p. 23

HOLY EUCHARIST II (P 48)
The Effects of the Holy Eucharist

Father, all-powerful and ever-living God,
we do well always and everywhere to give you thanks
through Jesus Christ our Lord.

At the last supper,
as he sat at table with his apostles,
he offered himself to you as the spotless lamb,
the acceptable gift that gives you perfect praise.
Christ has given us this memorial of his passion
to bring us its saving power until the end of time.

In this great sacrament you feed your people
and strengthen them in holiness,
so that the family of mankind
may come to walk in the light of one faith,
in one communion of love.
We come then to this wonderful sacrament
to be fed at your table
and grow into the likeness of the risen Christ.

Earth unites with heaven
to sing the new song of creation
as we adore and praise you for ever: ➔ No. 23, p. 23

CHRISTIAN DEATH I (P 77)
The Hope of Rising in Christ

Father, all-powerful and ever-living God,
we do well always and everywhere to give you thanks
through Jesus Christ our Lord.

In him, who rose from the dead,
our hope of resurrection dawned.
The sadness of death gives way
to the bright promise of immortality.

Lord, for your faithful people life is changed, not ended.
When the body of our earthly dwelling lies in death
we gain an everlasting dwelling place in heaven.

And so, with all the choirs of angels in heaven
we proclaim your glory
and join in their unending hymn of praise: → No. 23, p. 23

CHRISTIAN DEATH II (P 78)

Christ's Death, Our Life

Father, all-powerful and ever-living God,
we do well always and everywhere to give you thanks
through Jesus Christ our Lord.

He chose to die
that he might free all men from dying.
He gave his life
that we might live to you alone for ever.

In our joy we sing to your glory
with all the choirs of angels: → No. 23, p. 23

CHRISTIAN DEATH III (P 79)

Christ, Salvation and Life

Father, all-powerful and ever-living God,
we do well always and everywhere to give you thanks
through Jesus Christ our Lord.

In him the world is saved,
man is reborn,
and the dead rise again to life.

Through Christ the angels of heaven
offer their prayer of adoration
as they rejoice in your presence for ever.
May our voices be one with theirs
in their triumphant hymn of praise: → No. 23, p. 23

CHRISTIAN DEATH IV (P 80)

From Earthly Life to Heaven's Glory

Father, all-powerful and ever-living God,
we do well always and everywhere to give you thanks.

By your power you bring us to birth.
By your providence you rule our lives.

By your command you free us at last from sin
as we return to the dust from which we came.
Through the saving death of your Son
we rise at your word to the glory of the resurrection.

Now we join the angels and the saints
as they sing their unending hymn of praise: → No. 23, p. 23

CHRISTIAN DEATH V (P 81)
Our Resurrection through Christ's Victory

Father, all-powerful and ever-living God,
we do well always and everywhere to give you thanks
through Jesus Christ our Lord.

Death is the just reward for our sins,
yet, when at last we die,
your loving kindness calls us back to life
in company with Christ,
whose victory is our redemption.

Our hearts are joyful,
for we have seen your salvation,
and now with the angels and saints
we praise you for ever: → No. 23, p. 23

PROPER COMMUNICANTES
AND HANC IGITUR

FOR EUCHARISTIC PRAYER I

Communicantes for Christmas

In union with the whole Church
we celebrate that day (night)
when Mary without loss of her virginity
gave the world its savior.
We honor Mary,
the ever-virgin mother of Jesus Christ, our Lord and God,
    etc., p. 25.

Communicantes for the Epiphany

In union with the whole Church
we celebrate that day

when your only Son,
sharing your eternal glory,
showed himself in a human body.
We honor Mary, etc., p. 25.

Communicantes for Easter

In union with the whole Church
we celebrate that day (night)
when Jesus Christ, our Lord,
rose from the dead in his human body.
We honor Mary, etc., p. 25.

Hanc Igitur for Easter

Father, accept this offering
from your whole family
and from those born into the new life
of water and the Holy Spirit,
with all their sins forgiven.
Grant us your peace in this life,
save us from final damnation,
and count us among those you have chosen.
[Through Christ our Lord. Amen.]

→ *Canon, p. 25: Bless, etc.*

Communicantes for the Ascension

In union with the whole Church
we celebrate that day
when your Son, our Lord,
took his place with you
and raised our frail human nature to glory.
We honor Mary, etc., p. 25.

Communicantes for Pentecost

In union with the whole Church
we celebrate the day of Pentecost
when the Holy Spirit appeared to the apostles
in the form of countless tongues.
We honor Mary, etc., p, 25.

SOLEMN BLESSINGS

The following blessings may be used, at the discretion of the priest, at the end of Mass, or after the liturgy of the word, the office, and the celebration of the sacraments.

The deacon gives the invitation, or in his absence the priest himself may also give it: Bow your heads and pray for God's blessing. *Another form of invitation may be used. Then the priest extends his hands over the people while he says or sings the blessings. All respond:* Amen.

I. Celebrations during the Proper of Seasons

1. ADVENT

You believe that the Son of God once came to us;
you look for him to come again.
May his coming bring you the light of his holiness
and free you with his blessing. ℟. **Amen.**

May God make you steadfast in faith,
joyful in hope, and untiring in love
all the days of your life. ℟. **Amen.**

You rejoice that our Redeemer came to live with us as man.
When he comes again in glory,
may he reward you with endless life. ℟. **Amen.**

May almighty God bless you,
the Father, and the Son, ✠ and the Holy Spirit. ℟. **Amen.**

2. CHRISTMAS

When he came to us as man,
the Son of God scattered the darkness of this world,
and filled this holy night (day) with his glory.
May the God of infinite goodness
scatter the darkness of sin
and brighten your hearts with holiness. ℟. **Amen.**

God sent his angels to shepherds
to herald the great joy of our Savior's birth.
May he fill you with joy
and make you heralds of his gospel. ℟. **Amen.**

When the Word became man,
earth was joined to heaven.

May he give you his peace and good will,
and fellowship with all the heavenly host. R̸. **Amen.**

May almighty God bless you,
the Father, and the Son, ✠ and the Holy Spirit. R̸. **Amen.**

3. BEGINNING OF THE NEW YEAR

Every good gift comes from the Father of light.
May he grant you his grace and every blessing,
and keep you safe throughout the coming year. R̸. **Amen.**

May he grant you unwavering faith,
constant hope, and love that endures to the end. R̸. **Amen.**

May he order your days and work in his peace,
hear your every prayer,
and lead you to everlasting life and joy. R̸. **Amen.**

May almighty God bless you,
the Father, and the Son, ✠ and the Holy Spirit. R̸. **Amen.**

4. EPIPHANY

God has called you out of darkness
into his wonderful light.
May you experience his kindness and blessings,
and be strong in faith, in hope, and in love. R̸. **Amen.**

Because you are followers of Christ,
who appeared on this day as a light shining in darkness,
may he make you a light to all your sisters and brothers.
R̸. **Amen.**

The wise men followed the star,
and found Christ who is light from light.
May you too find the Lord
when your pilgrimage is ended. R̸. **Amen.**

May almighty God bless you,
the Father, and the Son, ✠ and the Holy Spirit. R̸. **Amen.**

5. PASSION OF THE LORD

The Father of mercies has given us an example of unselfish
love
in the sufferings of his only Son.

Through your service of God and neighbor
may you receive his countless blessings. ℟. **Amen.**

You believe that by his dying
Christ destroyed death for ever.
May he give you everlasting life. ℟. **Amen.**

He humbled himself for our sakes.
May you follow his example
and share in his resurrection. ℟. **Amen.**

May almighty God bless you,
the Father, and the Son, ✠ and the Holy Spirit. ℟. **Amen.**

6. EASTER VIGIL AND EASTER SUNDAY

May almighty God bless you on this solemn feast of Easter,
and may he protect you against all sin. ℟. **Amen.**

Through the resurrection of his Son
God has granted us healing.
May he fulfill his promises,
and bless you with eternal life. ℟. **Amen.**

You have mourned for Christ's sufferings;
now you celebrate the joy of his resurrection.
May you come with joy to the feast which lasts for ever.
℟. **Amen.**

May almighty God bless you,
the Father, and the Son, ✠ and the Holy Spirit. ℟. **Amen.**

7. EASTER SEASON

Through the resurrection of his Son
God has redeemed you and made you his children.
May he bless you with joy. ℟. **Amen.**

The Redeemer has given you lasting freedom.
May you inherit his everlasting life. ℟. **Amen.**

By faith you rose with him in baptism.
May your lives be holy,
so that you will be united with him for ever. ℟. **Amen.**

May almighty God bless you,
the Father, and the Son, ✠ and the Holy Spirit. ℟. **Amen.**

8. ASCENSION

May almighty God bless you on this day
when his only Son ascended into heaven
to prepare a place for you. ℟. **Amen.**

After his resurrection, Christ was seen by his disciples.
When he appears as judge
may you be pleasing for ever in his sight. ℟. **Amen.**

You believe that Jesus has taken his seat in majesty
at the right hand of the Father.
May you have the joy of experiencing
that he is also with you to the end of time,
according to his promise. ℟. **Amen.**

May almighty God bless you,
the Father, and the Son, ✠ and the Holy Spirit. ℟. **Amen.**

9. HOLY SPIRIT

(This day) the Father of light
has enlightened the minds of the disciples
by the outpouring of the Holy Spirit.
May he bless you
and give you the gifts of the Spirit for ever. ℟. **Amen.**

May that fire which hovered over the disciples
as tongues of flame
burn out all evil from your hearts
and made them glow with pure light. ℟. **Amen.**

God inspired speech in different tongues
to proclaim one faith.
May he strengthen your faith
and fulfill your hope of seeing him face to face. ℟. **Amen.**

May almighty God bless you,
the Father, and the Son, ✠ and the Holy Spirit. ℟. **Amen.**

10. ORDINARY TIME I
Blessing of Aaron (Num 6:24-26)

May the Lord bless you and keep you. ℟. **Amen.**

May his face shine upon you,
and be gracious to you. ℟. **Amen.**

May he look upon you with kindness,
and give you his peace. ℟. **Amen.**

May almighty God bless you,
the Father, and the Son, ✛ and the Holy Spirit. ℟. **Amen.**

11. ORDINARY TIME II *(Phil 4:7)*

May the peace of God
which is beyond all understanding
keep your hearts and minds
in the knowledge and love of God
and of his Son, our Lord Jesus Christ. ℟. **Amen.**

May almighty God bless you,
the Father, and the Son, ✛ and the Holy Spirit. ℟. **Amen.**

12. ORDINARY TIME III

May almighty God bless you in his mercy,
and make you always aware of his saving wisdom. ℟. **Amen.**

May he strengthen your faith with proofs of his love,
so that you will persevere in good works. ℟. **Amen.**

May he direct your steps to himself,
and show you how to walk in charity and peace. ℟. **Amen.**

May almighty God bless you,
the Father, and the Son, ✛ and the Holy Spirit. ℟. **Amen.**

13. ORDINARY TIME IV

May the God of all consolation
bless you in every way
and grant you peace all the days of your life. ℟. **Amen.**

May he free you from all anxiety
and strengthen your hearts in his love. ℟. **Amen.**

May he enrich you with his gifts of faith, hope, and love,
so that what you do in this life
will bring you to the happiness of everlasting life. ℟. **Amen.**

May almighty God bless you,
the Father, and the Son, ✛ and the Holy Spirit. ℟. **Amen.**

14. ORDINARY TIME V

May almighty God keep you from all harm
and bless you with every good gift. ℟. **Amen.**

May he set his Word in your heart
and fill you with lasting joy. ℟. **Amen.**

May you walk in his ways,
always knowing what is right and good,
until you enter your heavenly inheritance. ℟. **Amen.**

May almighty God bless you,
the Father, and the Son, ✠ and the Holy Spirit. ℟. **Amen.**

II. Celebrations of Saints

15. BLESSED VIRGIN MARY

Born of the Blessed Virgin Mary,
the Son of God redeemed mankind.
May he enrich you with his blessings. ℟. **Amen.**

You received the author of life through Mary.
May you always rejoice in her loving care. ℟. **Amen.**

You have come to rejoice at Mary's feast.
May you be filled with the joys of the Spirit
and the gifts of your eternal home. ℟. **Amen.**

May almighty God bless you,
the Father, and the Son, ✠ and the Holy Spirit. ℟. **Amen.**

16. PETER AND PAUL

The Lord has set you firm within his Church,
which he built upon the rock of Peter's faith.
May he bless you with a faith that never falters. ℟. **Amen.**

The Lord has given you knowledge of the faith
through the labors and preaching of St. Paul.
May his example inspire you to lead others to Christ
by the manner of your life. ℟. **Amen.**

May the keys of Peter, and the words of Paul,
their undying witness and their prayers,
lead you to the joy of that eternal home
which Peter gained by his cross, and Paul by the sword.
℟. **Amen.**

May almighty God bless you,
the Father, and the Son, ✠ and the Holy Spirit. ℟. **Amen.**

17. APOSTLES

May God who founded his Church upon the apostles
bless you through the prayers of St. N. (and St. N.). ℟. **Amen.**

May God inspire you to follow the example of the apostles,
and give witness to the truth before all men. ℟. **Amen.**

The teaching of the apostles has strengthened your faith.
May their prayers lead you
to your true and eternal home. ℟. **Amen.**

May almighty God bless you,
the Father, and the Son, ✚ and the Holy Spirit. ℟. **Amen.**

18. ALL SAINTS

God is the glory and joy of all his saints,
whose memory we celebrate today.
May his blessing be with you always. ℟. **Amen.**

May the prayers of the saints deliver you from present evil.
May their example of holy living
turn your thoughts to service of God and neighbor. ℟. **Amen.**

God's holy Church rejoices that her saints
have reached their heavenly goal,
and are in lasting peace.
May you come to share all the joys of our Father's house.
℟. **Amen.**

May almighty God bless you,
the Father, and the Son, ✚ and the Holy Spirit. ℟. **Amen.**

III. Other Blessings

19. DEDICATION OF A CHURCH

The Lord of earth and heaven
has assembled you before him this day
to dedicate this house of prayer
(to recall the dedication of this church).
May he fill you with the blessings of heaven. ℟. **Amen.**

God the Father wills that all his children
scattered throughout the world
become one family in his Son.

May he make you his temple,
the dwelling-place of his Holy Spirit. ℞. **Amen.**

May God free you from every bond of sin,
dwell within you and give you joy.
May you live with him for ever
in the company of all his saints. ℞. **Amen.**

May almighty God bless you,
the Father, and the Son, ✤ and the Holy Spirit. ℞. **Amen.**

20. THE DEAD

In his great love,
the God of all consolation gave man the gift of life.
May he bless you with faith
in the resurrection of his Son,
and with the hope of rising to new life. ℞. **Amen.**

To us who are alive
may he grant forgiveness,
and to all who have died
a place of light and peace. ℞. **Amen.**

As you believe that Jesus rose from the dead,
so may you live with him for ever in joy. ℞. **Amen.**

May almighty God bless you,
the Father, and the Son, ✤ and the Holy Spirit. ℞. **Amen.**

PRAYERS OVER THE PEOPLE

*The following prayers may be used, at the discretion of
the priest, at the end of the Mass, or after the liturgy of
the word, the office, and the celebration of the sacraments.*

*The deacon gives the invitation, or in his absence the
priest himself may also give it:* Bow your heads and pray
for God's blessing. *Another form of invitation may be
used. Then the priest extends his hands over the people
while he says or sings the prayer. All respond:* Amen.

After the prayer, the priest always adds:

May Almighty God bless you,
the Father, and the Son, ✤ and the Holy Spirit. ℞. **Amen.**

1. Lord,
   have mercy on your people.
   Grant us in this life the good things
   that lead to the everlasting life you prepare for us.
   We ask this through Christ our Lord.

2. Lord,
   grant your people your protection and grace.
   Give them health of mind and body,
   perfect love for one another,
   and make them always faithful to you.
   Grant this through Christ our Lord.

3. Lord,
   may all Christian people both know and cherish
   the heavenly gifts they have received.
   We ask this in the name of Jesus the Lord.

4. Lord,
   bless your people and make them holy
   so that, avoiding evil,
   they may find in you the fulfillment of their longing.
   We ask this through Christ our Lord.

5. Lord,
   bless and strengthen your people.
   May they remain faithful to you
   and always rejoice in your mercy.
   We ask this in the name of Jesus the Lord.

6. Lord,
   you care for your people even when they stray.
   Grant us a complete change of heart,
   so that we may follow you with greater fidelity.
   Grant this through Christ our Lord.

7. Lord,
   send your light upon your family.
   May they continue to enjoy your favor
   and devote themselves to doing good.
   We ask this through Christ our Lord.

8. Lord,
   we rejoice that you are our creator and ruler.

As we call upon your generosity,
renew and keep us in your love.
Grant this through Christ our Lord.

9. Lord,
we pray for your people who believe in you.
May they enjoy the gift of your love,
share it with others
and spread it everywhere.
We ask this in the name of Jesus the Lord.

10. Lord,
bless your people who hope for your mercy.
Grant that they may receive
the things they ask for at your prompting.
Grant this through Christ our Lord.

11. Lord,
bless us with your heavenly gifts,
and in your mercy make us ready to do your will.
We ask this through Christ our Lord.

12. Lord,
protect your people always,
that they may be free from every evil
and serve you with all their hearts.
We ask this through Christ our Lord.

13. Lord,
help your people to seek you with all their hearts
and to deserve what you promise.
Grant this through Christ our Lord.

14. Father,
help your people to rejoice in the mystery of redemption
and to win its reward.
We ask this in the name of Jesus the Lord.

15. Lord,
have pity on your people;
help them each day to avoid what displeases you
and grant that they may serve you with joy.
We ask this through Christ our Lord.

16. Lord,
   care for your people and purify them.
   Console them in this life
   and bring them to the life to come.
   We ask this in the name of Jesus the Lord.

17. Father,
   look with love upon your people,
   the love which our Lord Jesus Christ showed us
   when he delivered himself to evil men
   and suffered the agony of the cross,
   for he is Lord for ever.

18. Lord,
   grant that your faithful people
   may continually desire to relive the mystery of the
      eucharist
   and so be reborn to lead a new life.
   We ask this through Christ our Lord.

19. Lord God,
   in your great mercy,
   enrich your people with your grace
   and strengthen them by your blessing
   so that they may praise you always.
   Grant this through Christ our Lord.

20. May God bless you with every good gift from on high.
   May he keep you pure and holy in his sight at all times.
   May he bestow the riches of his grace upon you,
   bring you the good news of salvation,
   and always fill you with love for all men.
   We ask this through Christ our Lord.

21. Lord,
   make us pure in mind and body,
   that we will avoid all evil pleasures
   and always delight in you.
   We ask this in the name of Jesus the Lord.

22. Lord,
   bless your people and fill them with zeal.
   Strengthen them by your love to do your will.
   We ask this through Christ our Lord.

23. Lord,
    come, live in your people
    and strengthen them by your grace.
    Help them to remain close to you in prayer
    and give them a true love for one another.
    Grant this through Christ our Lord.

24. Father,
    look kindly on your children who put their trust in you;
    bless them and keep them from all harm,
    strengthen them against the attacks of the devil.
    May they never offend you
    but seek to love you in all they do.
    We ask this through Christ our Lord.

FEASTS OF SAINTS

25. God our Father,
    may all Christian people rejoice in the glory of your
      saints.
    Give us fellowship with them
    and unending joy in your kingdom.
    We ask this in the name of Jesus the Lord.

26. Lord,
    you have given us many friends in heaven.
    Through their prayers we are confident
    that you will watch over us always
    and fill our hearts with your love.
    Grant this through Christ our Lord.

"*Holy Mother Church is conscious that she must celebrate the saving work of her divine Spouse by devoutly recalling it on certain days throughout the course of the year. Every week, on the day which she has called the Lord's day, she keeps the memory of the Lord's resurrection, which she also celebrates once in the year, together with his blessed passion, in the most solemn festival of Easter.*

"*Within the cycle of a year, moreover, she unfolds the whole mystery of Christ, from the incarnation and birth until the ascension, the day of Pentecost, and the expectation of blessed hope and of the coming of the Lord.*

"*Recalling thus the mysteries of redemption, the Church opens to the faithful the riches of her Lord's powers and merits, so that these are in some way made present for all time, and the faithful are enabled to lay hold upon them and become filled with saving grace*" (Vatican II: Constitution on the Sacred Liturgy, no. 102).

OUR CHURCH'S YEAR OF PRAYER

Advent
> We prepare for the coming of Jesus,
> who is here and yet to come

Christmas Season
> We celebrate the gift of our Father's love:
> Jesus is our brother and our Lord

Ordinary Time
> With Jesus
> we enter into the work of his body, the Church

Lent
> In our daily life and prayer
> we die with Christ to sin,
> and live with him for God

Easter triduum
> We celebrate Jesus' dying and rising
> and our sharing with him through baptism

Easter season
> Sharing in the new life of Christ
> we are filled with his Spirit

Ordinary time
> Guided by the Spirit of Jesus
> we build the kingdom of God by our lives

"In those days before the flood, they were eating and drinking. . . ."

YEAR A

NOVEMBER 28, 2010

1st SUNDAY OF ADVENT

ENTRANCE ANT. Ps 25:1-3 [Hope]

To you, my God, I lift my soul, I trust in you; let me never come to shame. Do not let my enemies laugh at me. No one who waits for you is ever put to shame.

➔ No. 2, p. 10 (Omit Gloria)

OPENING PRAYER [Welcome for Christ]

Let us pray

   [that we may take Christ's coming seriously]

All-powerful God,

increase our strength of will for doing good

that Christ may find an eager welcome at his coming

and call us to his side in the kingdom of heaven,

where he lives and reigns with you and the Holy Spirit,

one God, for ever and ever. ℟. **Amen.** ↓

ALTERNATIVE OPENING PRAYER   [Longing for Christ]

Let us pray
  [in Advent time
  with longing and waiting
  for the coming of the Lord]
Father in heaven,
our hearts desire the warmth of your love
and our minds are searching for the light of your
    Word.
Increase our longing for Christ our Savior
and give us the strength to grow in love,
that the dawn of his coming
may find us rejoicing in his presence
and welcoming the light of his truth.
We ask this in the name of Jesus the Lord.
℞. **Amen.** ↓

FIRST READING Is 2:1-5   [The Messianic Time]

    In a vision the prophet sees the promise of salvation being
    fulfilled. The Word of the Lord is personified; he shall
    judge. Let us walk in the light of the Lord.

  A reading from the Book of the Prophet Isaiah

T HIS is what Isaiah, son of Amoz,
  saw concerning Judah and Jerusalem.
    In days to come,
the mountain of the LORD's house
    shall be established as the highest mountain
    and raised above the hills.
All nations shall stream toward it;
    many peoples shall come and say:
"Come, let us climb the LORD's mountain,
    to the house of the God of Jacob,
that he may instruct us in his ways,
    and we may walk in his paths."
For from Zion shall go forth instruction,
    and the word of the LORD from Jerusalem.

He shall judge between the nations,
　　and impose terms on many peoples.
They shall beat their swords into plowshares
　　and their spears into pruning hooks;
one nation shall not raise the sword against another,
　　nor shall they train for war again.
O house of Jacob, come,
　　let us walk in the light of the LORD!
The word of the Lord. ℟. **Thanks be to God.** ↓

RESPONSORIAL PSALM Ps 122 [Joy in the Lord's House]

℟. Let　us　go　re - joic - ing

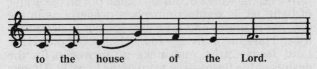

to　the　house　of　the　Lord.

I rejoiced because they said to me,
　　"We will go up to the house of the LORD."
And now we have set foot
　　within your gates, O Jerusalem.—℟.

Jerusalem, built as a city
　　with compact unity.
To it the tribes go up,
　　the tribes of the LORD.—℟.

According to the decree for Israel,
　　to give thanks to the name of the LORD.
In it are set up judgment seats,
　　seats for the house of David.—℟.

Pray for the peace of Jerusalem!
　　May those who love you prosper!
May peace be within your walls,
　　prosperity in your buildings.—℟.

Because of my relatives and friends
    I will say, "Peace be within you!"
Because of the house of the LORD, our God,
    I will pray for your good.

℞. **Let us go rejoicing to the house of the Lord.** ↓

SECOND READING Rom 13:11-14   [Put On the Lord]
    **The apostle urges us to come out of the darkness of sin
    into the protective light—Jesus is the light.**

A reading from the Letter of Saint Paul to the Romans

BROTHERS and sisters: You know the time; it is
the hour now for you to awake from sleep. For our
salvation is nearer now than when we first believed;
the night is advanced, the day is at hand. Let us then
throw off the works of darkness and put on the armor
of light; let us conduct ourselves properly as in the
day, not in orgies and drunkenness, not in promiscu-
ity and lust, not in rivalry and jealousy. But put on the
Lord Jesus Christ, and make no provision for the
desires of the flesh.—The word of the Lord. ℞. **Thanks
be to God.** ↓

ALLELUIA (Ps 85:8)   [Love and Salvation]
℞. **Alleluia, alleluia.**
Show us, Lord, your love;
and grant us your salvation.
℞. **Alleluia, alleluia.** ↓

GOSPEL Mt 24:37-44   [Stay Awake!]
    **We must always be prepared for the coming of Christ, for
    no one knows the day or hour. Even though we are pre-
    pared, his coming will be unexpected; we must not be
    caught off guard.**

℣. The Lord be with you. ℞. **And also with you.**
✝ A reading from the holy Gospel according to
Matthew. ℞. **Glory to you, Lord.**

JESUS said to his disciples: "As it was in the days of Noah, so it will be at the coming of the Son of Man. In those days before the flood, they were eating and drinking, marrying and giving in marriage, up to the day that Noah entered the ark. They did not know until the flood came and carried them all away. So will it be also at the coming of the Son of Man. Two men will be out in the field; one will be taken, and one will be left. Two women will be grinding at the mill; one will be taken and one will be left. Therefore stay awake! For you do not know on which day your Lord will come. Be sure of this: if the master of the house had known the hour of the night when the thief was coming, he would have stayed awake and not let his house be broken into. So too, you also must be prepared, for at an hour you do not expect, the Son of Man will come."—The Gospel of the Lord. ℟. **Praise to you, Lord Jesus Christ.**   ➜ No. 14, p. 18

PRAYER OVER THE GIFTS   [Promise of Eternal Life]

Father,
from all you give us
we present this bread and wine.
As we serve you now,
accept our offering
and sustain us with your promise of eternal life.
Grant this through Christ our Lord.
℟. **Amen.**   ➜ No. 21, p. 22 (Pref. P 1)

COMMUNION ANT. Ps 85:13   [A New World]

The Lord will shower his gifts, and our land will yield its fruit. ↓

PRAYER AFTER COMMUNION   [Love for Heaven]

Father,
may our communion
teach us to love heaven.

May its promise and hope
guide our way on earth.
We ask this through Christ our Lord.
℟. **Amen.**   ➜ No. 32, p. 70

Optional Solemn Blessings, p. 92, and Prayers Over the People, p. 99

"Repent, for the kingdom of heaven is at hand."

DECEMBER 5

2nd SUNDAY OF ADVENT

ENTRANCE ANT. See Is 30:19, 30   [Lord of Salvation]

**People of Zion, the Lord will come to save all nations,
and your hearts will exult to hear his majestic voice.**
                    ➜ No. 2, p. 10 (Omit Gloria)

OPENING PRAYER   [Receiving Christ]

Let us pray
  [that nothing may hinder us
  from receiving Christ with joy]
God of power and mercy,
open our hearts in welcome.
Remove the things that hinder us from receiving Christ
  with joy,

so that we may share his wisdom
and become one with him
when he comes in glory,
for he lives and reigns with you and the Holy Spirit,
one God, for ever and ever. ℞. **Amen.** ↓

ALTERNATIVE OPENING PRAYER   [Christ's Wisdom]

Let us pray
   [in Advent time
   for the coming Savior to teach us wisdom]
Father in heaven,
the day draws near when the glory of your Son
will make radiant the night of the waiting world.
May the lure of greed not impede us from the joy
which moves the hearts of those who seek him.
May the darkness not blind us
to the vision of wisdom
which fills the minds of those who find him.
We ask this in the name of Jesus the Lord.
℞. **Amen.** ↓

FIRST READING Is 11:1-10   [Messiah of Peace]

   **Jesse, the father of David, is the ancestor of the Messiah.
   All nations will turn to him.**

   A reading from the Book of the Prophet Isaiah

O N that day a shoot shall sprout from the stump
      of Jesse,
   and from his roots a bud shall blossom.
The spirit of the Lord shall rest upon him:
   a spirit of wisdom and of understanding,
a spirit of counsel and of strength,
   a spirit of knowledge and of fear of the LORD,
   and his delight shall be the fear of the LORD.
Not by appearance shall he judge,
   nor by hearsay shall he decide,

but he shall judge the poor with justice,
　　and decide aright for the land's afflicted.
He shall strike the ruthless with the rod of his mouth,
　　and with the breath of his lips he shall slay the
　　　wicked.
Justice shall be the band around his waist,
　　and faithfulness a belt upon his hips.
Then the wolf shall be a guest of the lamb,
　　and the leopard shall lie down with the kid;
the calf and the young lion shall browse together,
　　with a little child to guide them.
The cow and the bear shall be neighbors,
　　together their young shall rest;
　　the lion shall eat hay like the ox.
The baby shall play by the cobra's den,
　　and the child lay his hand on the adder's lair.
There shall be no harm or ruin on all my holy
　　　mountain;
　　for the earth shall be filled with knowledge of the
　　　LORD,
　　as water covers the sea.
On that day, the root of Jesse,
　　set up as a signal for the nations,
the Gentiles shall seek out,
　　for his dwelling shall be glorious.
The word of the Lord. ℟. **Thanks be to God.** ↓

RESPONSORIAL PSALM Ps 72　　　　[Justice and Peace]

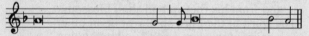

℟. Justice shall flourish in his time, and fullness of peace for ev - er.

O God, with your judgment endow the king,
　　and with your justice, the king's son;
he shall govern your people with justice
　　and your afflicted ones with judgment.—℟.

Justice shall flower in his days,
   and profound peace, till the moon be no more.
May he rule from sea to sea,
   and from the River to the ends of the earth.

℟. **Justice shall flourish in his time,**
   and fullness of peace for ever.

For he shall rescue the poor man when he cries out,
   and the afflicted when he has no one to help him.
He shall have pity for the lowly and the poor;
   the lives of the poor he shall save.

℟. **Justice shall flourish in his time,**
   and fullness of peace for ever.

May his name be blessed forever;
   as long as the sun his name shall remain.
In him shall all the tribes of the earth be blessed;
   all the nations shall proclaim his happiness.

℟. **Justice shall flourish in his time,**
   and fullness of peace for ever. ↓

SECOND READING Rom 15:4-9   [Instruction from Scripture]
   Remember that the Scriptures are written for our instruc-
   tion. In Christ the promise of Scripture is fulfilled.

A reading from the Letter of Saint Paul to the Romans

BROTHERS and sisters: Whatever was written previously was written for our instruction, that by
endurance and by the encouragement of the
Scriptures we might have hope. May the God of
endurance and encouragement grant you to think in
harmony with one another, in keeping with Christ
Jesus, that with one accord you may with one voice
glorify the God and Father of our Lord Jesus Christ.

   Welcome one another, then, as Christ welcomed
you, for the glory of God. For I say that Christ became

a minister of the circumcised to show God's truthfulness, to confirm the promises to the patriarchs, but so that the Gentiles might glorify God for his mercy. As it is written:

Therefore, I will praise you among the Gentiles
and sing praises to your name.

The word of the Lord. ℞. **Thanks be to God.** ↓

ALLELUIA Lk 3:4, 6　　　　　　　[Prepare the Way]

℞. **Alleluia, alleluia.**
Prepare the way of the Lord, make straight his paths:
all flesh shall see the salvation of God.
℞. **Alleluia, alleluia.** ↓

GOSPEL Mt 3:1-12　　　　　　　[Prepare for the Lord]

John the Baptist calls the people to prepare for the Messiah. He urges a change in life-style and calls for repentance.

℣. The Lord be with you. ℞. **And also with you.**
✛ A reading from the holy Gospel according to Matthew. ℞. **Glory to you, Lord.**

JOHN the Baptist appeared, preaching in the desert of Judea and saying, "Repent, for the kingdom of heaven is at hand!" It was of him that the prophet Isaiah had spoken when he said:

A voice of one crying out in the desert,
Prepare the way of the Lord,
make straight his paths.

John wore clothing made of camel's hair and had a leather belt around his waist. His food was locusts and wild honey. At that time Jerusalem, all Judea, and the whole region around the Jordan were going out to him and were being baptized by him in the Jordan River as they acknowledged their sins.

When he saw many of the Pharisees and Sadducees coming to his baptism, he said to them, "You brood of vipers! Who warned you to flee from the coming wrath? Produce good fruit as evidence of your repentance. And do not presume to say to yourselves, 'We have Abraham as our father.' For I tell you, God can raise up children to Abraham from these stones. Even now the ax lies at the root of the trees. Therefore every tree that does not bear good fruit will be cut down and thrown into the fire. I am baptizing you with water, for repentance, but the one who is coming after me is mightier than I. I am not worthy to carry his sandals. He will baptize you with the Holy Spirit and fire. His winnowing fan is in his hand. He will clear his threshing floor and gather his wheat into his barn, but the chaff he will burn with unquenchable fire."—The Gospel of the Lord. ℟. **Praise to you, Lord Jesus Christ.**   → No. 14, p. 18

PRAYER OVER THE GIFTS   [Our Offering]

Lord,
we are nothing without you.
As you sustain us with your mercy,
receive our prayers and offerings.
We ask this through Christ our Lord.
℟. **Amen.**   → No. 21, p. 22 (Pref. P 1)

COMMUNION ANT. Bar 5:5; 4:36   [Coming Joy]

Rise up, Jerusalem, stand on the heights, and see the joy that is coming to you from God. ↓

PRAYER AFTER COMMUNION   [Wise Judgment]

Father,
you give us food from heaven.
By our sharing in this mystery,
teach us to judge wisely the things of earth

and to love the things of heaven.
Grant this through Christ our Lord.
℟. **Amen.** → No. 32, p. 70

Optional Solemn Blessings, p. 92, and Prayers Over the People, p. 99

"Hail, full of grace! The Lord is with you."

DECEMBER 8

IMMACULATE CONCEPTION

ENTRANCE ANT. Is 61:10 [Mary's Joy in the Lord]

I exult for joy in the Lord, my soul rejoices in my God; for he has clothed me in the garment of salvation and robed me in the cloak of justice, like a bride adorned with her jewels. → No. 2, p. 10

OPENING PRAYER [Living in God's Presence]

Let us pray
    [that through the prayers of the sinless Virgin Mary,
    God will free us from our sins]
Father,
you prepared the Virgin Mary
to be the worthy mother of your Son.
You let her share beforehand
in the salvation Christ would bring by his death,

and kept her sinless from the first moment of her conception.
Help us by her prayers
to live in your presence without sin.
We ask this through our Lord Jesus Christ, your Son,
who lives and reigns with you and the Holy Spirit,
one God, for ever and ever. ℟. **Amen.** ↓

ALTERNATIVE OPENING PRAYER   [Mary's Faith and Love]
Let us pray
   [on this feast of Mary
   who experienced the perfection
   of God's saving power]
Father,
the image of the Virgin is found in the Church.
Mary had a faith that your Spirit prepared
and a love that never knew sin,
for you kept her sinless from the first moment of her
   conception.
Trace in our actions the lines of her love,
in our hearts her readiness of faith.
Prepare once again a world for your Son
who lives and reigns with you and the Holy Spirit,
one God, for ever and ever. ℟. **Amen.** ↓

FIRST READING Gn 3:9-15, 20   [Promise of the Redeemer]
Adam and Eve, male and female, humankind has dis-
obeyed God. Sin is the source of all trouble. In his mercy
God promises redemption.

A reading from the Book of Genesis

AFTER the man, Adam, had eaten of the tree, the
   LORD God called to the man and asked him, "Where
are you?" He answered, "I heard you in the garden; but I
was afraid, because I was naked, so I hid myself." Then
he asked, "Who told you that you were naked? You have
eaten, then, from the tree of which I had forbidden you

to eat!" The man replied, "The woman whom you put here with me—she gave me fruit from the tree, and so I ate it." The LORD God then asked the woman, "Why did you do such a thing?" The woman answered, "The serpent tricked me into it, so I ate it."

Then the LORD God said to the serpent:

"Because you have done this, you shall be banned
     from all the animals
     and from all the wild creatures;
on your belly shall you crawl,
     and dirt shall you eat
     all the days of your life.
I will put enmity between you and the woman,
     and between your offspring and hers;
he will strike at your head,
     while you strike at his heel."

The man called his wife Eve, because she became the mother of all the living.—The word of the Lord. ℟. **Thanks be to God.** ↓

RESPONSORIAL PSALM Ps 98   [God's Salvation]

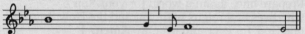

℟. **Sing to the Lord a new song, for he has done marvelous deeds.**

Sing to the LORD a new song,
     for he has done wondrous deeds;
his right hand has won victory for him,
     his holy arm.—℟.

The LORD has made his salvation known:
     in the sight of the nations he has revealed his justice.
He has remembered his kindness and his faithfulness
     toward the house of Israel.—℟.

All the ends of the earth have seen
     the salvation by our God.

Sing joyfully to the L<small>ORD</small>, all you lands;
   break into song; sing praise.—R̸. ↓

SECOND READING Eph 1:3-6, 11-12   [God's Saving Plan]

Glory and praise to God the Father who sent us Christ the Redeemer—our Savior and Lord.

A reading from the Letter of Saint Paul to
the Ephesians

BROTHERS and sisters: Blessed be the God and Father of our Lord Jesus Christ, who has blessed us in Christ with every spiritual blessing in the heavens, as he chose us in him, before the foundation of the world, to be holy and without blemish before him. In love he destined us for adoption to himself through Jesus Christ, in accord with the favor of his will, for the praise of the glory of his grace that he granted us in the beloved.

In him we were chosen, destined in accord with the purpose of the One who accomplishes all things according to the intention of his will, so that we might exist for the praise of his glory, we who first hoped in Christ. —The word of the Lord. R̸. **Thanks be to God.** ↓

ALLELUIA Cf. Lk 1:28

R̸. **Alleluia, alleluia.**
Hail, Mary, full of grace, the Lord is with you;
blessed are you among women.
R̸. **Alleluia, alleluia.** ↓

GOSPEL Lk 1:26-38   [Mary's Great Holiness]

Mary, the virgin of Nazareth, is chosen by God to be the mother of his Son. Because of this she is highly favored— full of grace. In true humility she accepts the will of God.

V̸. The Lord be with you. R̸. **And also with you.**
✛ A reading from the holy Gospel according to Luke. R̸. **Glory to you, Lord.**

THE angel Gabriel was sent from God to a town of Galilee called Nazareth, to a virgin betrothed to a man named Joseph, of the house of David, and the virgin's name was Mary. And coming to her, he said, "Hail full of grace! The Lord is with you." But she was greatly troubled at what was said and pondered what sort of greeting this might be. Then the angel said to her, "Do not be afraid, Mary, for you have found favor with God. Behold, you will conceive in your womb and bear a son, and you shall name him Jesus. He will be great and will be called Son of the Most High, and the Lord God will give him the throne of David his father, and he will rule over the house of Jacob forever, and of his kingdom there will be no end." But Mary said to the angel, "How can this be, since I have no relations with a man?" And the angel said to her in reply, "The Holy Spirit will come upon you, and the power of the Most High will overshadow you. Therefore the child to be born will be called holy, the Son of God. And behold, Elizabeth, your relative, has also conceived a son in her old age, and this is the sixth month for her who was called barren; for nothing will be impossible for God." Mary said: "Behold, I am the handmaid of the Lord. May it be done to me according to your word." Then the angel departed from her.—The Gospel of the Lord. ℟. **Praise to you, Lord Jesus Christ.**

➜ No. 14, p. 18

PRAYER OVER THE GIFTS   [Helped by Mary's Prayers]

Lord,
accept this sacrifice
on the feast of the sinless Virgin Mary.
You kept her free from sin
from the first moment of her life.
Help us by her prayers,
and free us from our sins.
We ask this in the name of Jesus the Lord. ℟. **Amen.** ↓

PREFACE (P 58)   [Mary Our Advocate]

℣. The Lord be with you. ℟. **And also with you.**
℣. Lift up your hearts. ℟. **We lift them up to the Lord.**
℣. Let us give thanks to the Lord our God. ℟. **It is right to give him thanks and praise.**

Father, all-powerful and ever-living God,
we do well always and everywhere to give you thanks.
You allowed no stain of Adam's sin
to touch the Virgin Mary.
Full of grace, she was to be a worthy mother of your
    Son,
your sign of favor to the Church at its beginning,
and the promise of its perfection as the bride of Christ,
    radiant in beauty.
Purest of virgins, she was to bring forth your Son,
the innocent lamb who takes away our sins.
You chose her from all women to be our advocate with
    you
and our pattern of holiness.
In our joy we sing to your glory
with all the choirs of angels: → No. 23, p. 23

COMMUNION ANT.   [All Honor to Mary]

All honor to you, Mary! From you arose the sun of justice, Christ our God. ↓

PRAYER AFTER COMMUNION   [Free from Sin]

Lord our God,
in your love, you chose the Virgin Mary
and kept her free from sin.
May this sacrament of your love
free us from our sins.
Grant this through Christ our Lord.
℟. **Amen.**   → No. 32, p. 70

Optional Solemn Blessings, p. 92, and Prayers Over the People, p. 99

"[John] heard in prison of the works of the Christ [and] sent his disciples to Jesus."

DECEMBER 12

3rd SUNDAY OF ADVENT

ENTRANCE ANT. Phil 4:4, 5   [Mounting Joy]

Rejoice in the Lord always; again I say, rejoice! The Lord is near.   ➜ No. 2, p. 10 (Omit Gloria)

OPENING PRAYER   [Joy of Salvation]

Let us pray
   [that God will fill us with joy
   at the coming of Christ]
Lord God,
may we, your people,
who look forward to the birthday of Christ
experience the joy of salvation
and celebrate that feast with love and thanksgiving.
We ask this through our Lord Jesus Christ, your Son,
who lives and reigns with you and the Holy Spirit,
one God, for ever and ever. ℟. **Amen.** ↓

ALTERNATIVE OPENING PRAYER   [Joy and Hope]

Let us pray
    [this Advent
    for joy and hope in the coming Lord]
Father of our Lord Jesus Christ,
ever faithful to your promises
and ever close to your Church:
the earth rejoices in hope of the Savior's coming
and looks forward with longing
to his return at the end of time.
Prepare our hearts and remove the sadness
that hinders us from feeling the joy and hope
which his presence will bestow,
for he is Lord for ever and ever. ℟. **Amen.** ↓

FIRST READING Is 35:1-6, 10   [Here Is Your God]

This vision of the Messiah describes his work—not only in restoring health and well-being to the infirm, but also in bringing the mercy and forgiveness of salvation.

A reading from the Book of the Prophet Isaiah

THE desert and the parched land will exult;
    the steppe will rejoice and bloom.
They will bloom with abundant flowers,
    and rejoice with joyful song.
The glory of Lebanon will be given to them,
    the splendor of Carmel and Sharon;
they will see the glory of the LORD,
    the splendor of our God.
Strengthen the hands that are feeble,
    make firm the knees that are weak,
say to those whose hearts are frightened:
    Be strong, fear not!
Here is your God,
    he comes with vindication;
with divine recompense
    he comes to save you.

Then will the eyes of the blind be opened,
　　the ears of the deaf be cleared;
then will the lame leap like a stag,
　　then the tongue of the dumb will sing.

Those whom the Lord has ransomed will return
　　and enter Zion singing,
　　crowned with everlasting joy;
they will meet with joy and gladness,
　　sorrow and mourning will flee.
The word of the Lord. ℟. **Thanks be to God.** ↓

RESPONSORIAL PSALM Ps 146   [The Lord Our Savior]

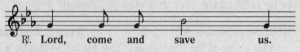

℟. Lord, come and save us.

℟. Or: **Alleluia.**

The Lord God keeps faith forever,
　　secures justice for the oppressed,
　　gives food to the hungry.
The Lord sets captives free.—℟.

The Lord gives sight to the blind;
　　the Lord raises up those that were bowed down.
The Lord loves the just;
　　the Lord protects strangers.—℟.

The fatherless and the widow he sustains,
　　but the way of the wicked he thwarts.
The Lord shall reign forever;
　　your God, O Zion, through all generations.

℟. **Lord, come and save us.** ↓

℟. Or: **Alleluia.** ↓

SECOND READING Jas 5:7-10 [The Lord's Coming Is at Hand]

Look to the example of prophets and learn patience under severe hardships.

A reading from the Letter of Saint James

BE patient, brothers and sisters, until the coming of the Lord. See how the farmer waits for the precious fruit of the earth, being patient with it until it receives the early and the late rains. You too must be patient. Make your hearts firm, because the coming of the Lord is at hand. Do not complain, brothers and sisters, about one another, that you may not be judged. Behold, the Judge is standing before the gates. Take as an example of hardship and patience, brothers and sisters, the prophets who spoke in the name of the Lord.—The word of the Lord. ℟. **Thanks be to God.** ↓

ALLELUIA Is 61:1 (cited in Lk 4:18)   [Witness to the Poor]

℟. **Alleluia, alleluia.**
The Spirit of the Lord is upon me,
because he has anointed me
to bring glad tidings to the poor.
℟. **Alleluia, alleluia.** ↓

GOSPEL Mt 11:2-11   [Effects of the Lord's Coming]

Jesus applies the words of Isaiah to himself. He proclaims the good news of salvation, freedom, and joy.

℣. The Lord be with you. ℟. **And also with you.**
✝ A reading from the holy Gospel according to Matthew. ℟. **Glory to you, Lord.**

WHEN John the Baptist heard in prison of the works of the Christ, he sent his disciples to Jesus with this question, "Are you the one who is to come, or should we look for another?" Jesus said to them in reply, "Go and tell John what you hear and see: the blind regain their sight, the lame walk, lepers are cleansed, the deaf hear, the dead are raised, and the poor have the good news proclaimed to them. And blessed is the one who takes no offense at me."

As they were going off, Jesus began to speak to the crowds about John, "What did you go out to the desert to see? A reed swayed by the wind? Then what did you go out to see? Someone dressed in fine clothing? Those who wear fine clothing are in royal palaces. Then why did you go out? To see a prophet? Yes, I tell you, and more than a prophet. This is the one about whom it is written:

Behold, I am sending my messenger ahead of you;
he will prepare your way before you.

Amen, I say to you, among those born of women there has been none greater than John the Baptist; yet the least in the kingdom of heaven is greater than he."
—The Gospel of the Lord. ℟. **Praise to you, Lord Jesus Christ.**   ➔ No. 14, p. 18

PRAYER OVER THE GIFTS   [Continual Sacrifice]
Lord,
may the gift we offer in faith and love
be a continual sacrifice in your honor
and truly become our eucharist and our salvation.
Grant this through Christ our Lord.
℟. **Amen.**   ➔ No. 21, p. 22 (Pref. P 1 or 2)

COMMUNION ANT. See Is 35:4   [Trust in God]
Say to the anxious: be strong and fear not, our God will come to save us. ↓

PRAYER AFTER COMMUNION   [Preparation for Christ]
God of mercy,
may this eucharist bring us your divine help,
free us from our sins,
and prepare us for the birthday of our Savior,
who is Lord for ever and ever.
℟. **Amen.**   ➔ No. 32, p. 70

Optional Solemn Blessings, p. 92, and Prayers Over the People, p. 99

"Joseph . . . took his wife [Mary] into his home."

DECEMBER 19

4th SUNDAY OF ADVENT

ENTRANCE ANT. Is 45:8   **[The Advent Plea]**
Let the clouds rain down the Just One, and the earth bring forth a Savior.   ➜ No. 2, p. 10 (Omit Gloria)

OPENING PRAYER   **[From Suffering to Glory]**
Let us pray
   [as Advent draws to a close,
    that Christ will truly come into our hearts]
Lord,
fill our hearts with your love,
and as you revealed to us by an angel
the coming of your Son as man,
so lead us through his suffering and death
to the glory of his resurrection,
for he lives and reigns with you and the Holy Spirit,
one God, for ever and ever. ℟. **Amen.** ↓

ALTERNATIVE OPENING PRAYER   **[Operative Faith]**
Let us pray
   [as Advent draws to a close

for the faith that opens our lives
  to the Spirit of God]
Father, all-powerful God,
your eternal Word took flesh on our earth
when the Virgin Mary placed her life
at the service of your plan.
Lift our minds in watchful hope
to hear the voice which announces his glory
and open our minds to receive the Spirit
who prepares us for his coming.
We ask this through Christ our Lord.
℞. **Amen.** ↓

FIRST READING Is 7:10-14   **[The Virgin with Child]**

The words of the prophet spoken to the king are applied to the birth of the Savior.

A reading from the Book of the Prophet Isaiah

THE LORD spoke to Ahaz, saying: Ask for a sign from the LORD, your God; let it be deep as the netherworld, or high as the sky! But Ahaz answered, "I will not ask! I will not tempt the LORD!" Then Isaiah said: Listen, O house of David! Is it not enough for you to weary people, must you also weary my God? Therefore the Lord himself will give you this sign: the virgin shall conceive, and bear a son, and shall name him Immanuel.—The word of the Lord. ℞. **Thanks be to God.** ↓

RESPONSORIAL PSALM Ps 24   **[The King of Glory]**

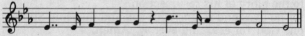

℞.   **Let the Lord en-ter;   he is king of glo-ry.**

The LORD's are the earth and its fullness;
  the world and those who dwell in it.
For he founded it upon the seas
  and established it upon the rivers.

℟. **Let the Lord enter; he is king of glory.**

Who can ascend the mountain of the LORD?
   or who may stand in his holy place?
He whose hands are sinless, whose heart is clean,
   who desires not what is vain.

℟. **Let the Lord enter; he is king of glory.**

He shall receive a blessing from the LORD,
   a reward from God his savior.
Such is the race that seeks for him,
   that seeks the face of the God of Jacob.

℟. **Let the Lord enter; he is king of glory.** ↓

SECOND READING Rom 1:1-7   [Jesus the Savior]
   **The Messiah is a descendant of David according to the
   flesh and the Son of God according to the Spirit. His salvation is for all humankind.**

A reading from the Letter of Saint Paul to the Romans

PAUL, a slave of Christ Jesus, called to be an apostle and set apart for the gospel of God, which he
promised previously through his prophets in the holy
Scriptures, the gospel about his Son, descended from
David according to the flesh, but established as Son of
God in power according to the Spirit of holiness
through resurrection from the dead, Jesus Christ our
Lord. Through him we have received the grace of apos-
tleship, to bring about the obedience of faith, for the
sake of his name, among all the Gentiles, among
whom are you also, who are called to belong to Jesus
Christ; to all the beloved of God in Rome, called to be
holy. Grace to you and peace from God our Father and
the Lord Jesus Christ.—The word of the Lord. ℟.
Thanks be to God. ↓

ALLELUIA Mt 1:23 [Emmanuel]

℟. **Alleluia, alleluia.**
The virgin shall conceive, and bear a son,
and they shall name him Emmanuel.
℟. **Alleluia, alleluia.** ↓

GOSPEL Mt 1:18-24 [God-with-Us]
Emmanuel means God is with us. He is conceived by the Holy Spirit and born of the Virgin Mary.

℣. The Lord be with you. ℟. **And also with you.**
✠ A reading from the holy Gospel according to Matthew. ℟. **Glory to you, Lord.**

THIS is how the birth of Jesus Christ came about. When his mother Mary was betrothed to Joseph, but before they lived together, she was found with child through the Holy Spirit. Joseph her husband, since he was a righteous man, yet unwilling to expose her to shame, decided to divorce her quietly. Such was his intention when, behold, the angel of the Lord appeared to him in a dream and said, "Joseph, son of David, do not be afraid to take Mary your wife into your home. For it is through the Holy Spirit that this child has been conceived in her. She will bear a son and you are to name him Jesus, because he will save his people from their sins." All this took place to fulfill what the Lord had said through the prophet:
  Behold, the virgin shall conceive and bear a son,
    and they shall name him Emmanuel,
which means "God is with us." When Joseph awoke, he did as the angel of the Lord had commanded him and took his wife into his home.
—The Gospel of the Lord. ℟. **Praise to you, Lord Jesus Christ.** → No. 14, p. 18

PRAYER OVER THE GIFTS   [Power of the Spirit]

Lord,
may the power of the Spirit,
which sanctified Mary the mother of your Son,
make holy the gifts we place upon this altar.
Grant this through Christ our Lord.
℞. **Amen.**   → No. 21, p. 22 (Pref. P 2)

COMMUNION ANT. Is 7:14   [The Virgin-Mother]

**The Virgin is with child and shall bear a son, and she
will call him Emmanuel.** ↓

PRAYER AFTER COMMUNION   [Growth in Holiness]

Lord,
in this sacrament
we receive the promise of salvation;
as Christmas draws near
make us grow in faith and love
to celebrate the coming of Christ our Savior,
who is Lord for ever and ever.
℞. **Amen.**   → No. 32, p. 70

Optional Solemn Blessings, p. 92, and Prayers Over the People, p. 99

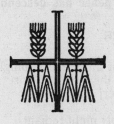

The Word is made flesh.

DECEMBER 25

CHRISTMAS

MASS AT MIDNIGHT

ENTRANCE ANT. Ps 2:7   [Son of God]

The Lord said to me: You are my Son; this day have I begotten you.

OR   [True Peace]

Let us all rejoice in the Lord, for our Savior is born to the world. True peace has descended from heaven.
→ No. 2, p. 10

OPENING PRAYER   [Eternal Joy]

Let us pray
  [in the peace of Christmas midnight
  that our joy in the birth of Christ
  will last for ever]
Father,
you make this holy night radiant
with the splendor of Jesus Christ our light.
We welcome him as Lord, the true light of the world.

Bring us to eternal joy in the kingdom of heaven,
where he lives and reigns with you and the Holy Spirit,
one God, for ever and ever. R. **Amen.** ↓

ALTERNATIVE OPENING PRAYER   [Joy, and Hope]

Let us pray
  [with joy and hope
  as we await the dawning of the Father's Word]
Lord our God,
with the birth of your Son
your glory breaks on the world.
Through the night hours of the darkened earth
we your people watch for the coming of your promised
  Son.
As we wait, give us a foretaste of the joy that you will
  grant us
when the fullness of his glory has filled the earth,
who lives and reigns with you for ever and ever.
R. **Amen.** ↓

FIRST READING Is 9:1-6   [The Messiah's Kingdom]

**The spell of darkness, the shame of sin is broken—the
Prince of light is born to us.**

A reading from the Book of the Prophet Isaiah

THE people who walked in darkness
  have seen a great light;
upon those who dwelt in the land of gloom
  a light has shone.
You have brought them abundant joy
  and great rejoicing,
as they rejoice before you as at the harvest,
  as people make merry when dividing spoils.
For the yoke that burdened them,
  the pole on their shoulder,

and the rod of their taskmaster
  you have smashed, as on the day of Midian.
For every boot that tramped in battle,
  every cloak rolled in blood,
  will be burned as fuel for flames.
For a child is born to us, a son is given us;
  upon his shoulder dominion rests.
They name him Wonder-Counselor, God-Hero,
  Father-Forever, Prince of Peace.
His dominion is vast
  and forever peaceful,
from David's throne, and over his kingdom,
  which he confirms and sustains
by judgment and justice,
  both now and forever.
The zeal of the Lord of hosts will do this!
The word of the Lord. ℟. **Thanks be to God.** ↓

RESPONSORIAL PSALM Ps 96   [Bless the Lord]

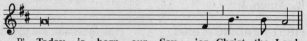

℟. Today is born our Sav - ior, Christ the Lord.

Sing to the Lord a new song;
  sing to the Lord, all you lands.
Sing to the Lord; bless his name.

℟. **Today is born our Savior, Christ the Lord.**

Announce his salvation, day after day.
  Tell his glory among the nations;
  among all peoples, his wondrous deeds.

℟. **Today is born our Savior, Christ the Lord.**

Let the heavens be glad and the earth rejoice;
  let the sea and what fills it resound;
  let the plains be joyful and all that is in them!
Then shall all the trees of the forest exult.—℟.

They shall exult before the LORD, for he comes;
   for he comes to rule the earth.
He shall rule the world with justice
   and the peoples with his constancy.

℟. **Today is born our Savior, Christ the Lord.** ↓

SECOND READING Ti 2:11-14   [Salvation for All]
   **We look to the second coming of Christ in glory. Through
   his cross we are freed from the darkness of sin.**

   A reading from the Letter of Saint Paul to Titus

BELOVED: The grace of God has appeared, saving
all and training us to reject godless ways and
worldly desires and to live temperately, justly, and
devoutly in this age, as we await the blessed hope, the
appearance of the glory of our great God and savior
Jesus Christ, who gave himself for us to deliver us
from all lawlessness and to cleanse for himself a people as his own, eager to do what is good.—The word of
the Lord. ℟. **Thanks be to God.** ↓

ALLELUIA Lk 2:10-11   [Great Joy]

℟. **Alleluia, alleluia.**
I proclaim to you good news of great joy:
today a Savior is born for us,
Christ the Lord.
℟. **Alleluia, alleluia.** ↓

GOSPEL Lk 2:1-14   [Birth of Christ]
   **Rejoice in the good news—our Savior is born, and he is
   revealed to us by the witness of shepherds.**

℣. The Lord be with you. ℟. **And also with you.**
✠ A reading from the holy Gospel according to Luke.
℟. **Glory to you, Lord.**

IN those days a decree went out from Caesar
Augustus that the whole world should be enrolled.
This was the first enrollment, when Quirinius was gov-

ernor of Syria. So all went to be enrolled, each to his own town. And Joseph too went up from Galilee from the town of Nazareth to Judea, to the city of David that is called Bethlehem, because he was of the house and family of David, to be enrolled with Mary, his betrothed, who was with child. While they were there, the time came for her to have her child, and she gave birth to her firstborn son. She wrapped him in swaddling clothes and laid him in a manger, because there was no room for them in the inn.

Now there were shepherds in that region living in the fields and keeping the night watch over their flock. The angel of the Lord appeared to them and the glory of the Lord shone around them, and they were struck with great fear. The angel said to them, "Do not be afraid; for behold, I proclaim to you good news of great joy that will be for all the people. For today in the city of David a savior has been born for you who is Christ and Lord. And this will be a sign for you: you will find an infant wrapped in swaddling clothes and lying in a manger." And suddenly there was a multitude of the heavenly host with the angel, praising God and saying:

"Glory to God in the highest
    and on earth peace to those on whom his favor
    rests."

The Gospel of the Lord. ℞. **Praise to you, Lord Jesus Christ.**   ➜ No. 14, p. 18

In the profession of faith, all genuflect at the words, and became man.

PRAYER OVER THE GIFTS   [Become Like Christ]

Lord,
accept our gifts on this joyful feast of our salvation.
By our communion with God made man
may we become more like him

who joins our lives to yours,
for he is Lord for ever and ever.
℟. **Amen.**   → No. 21, p. 22 (Pref. P 3-5)

*When Eucharistic Prayer I is used, the special Christmas
form of* In union with the whole Church *is said.*

COMMUNION ANT. Jn 1:14   [Glory of Christ]
The Word of God became man; we have seen his glory. ↓

PRAYER AFTER COMMUNION   [Following Christ]
God our Father,
we rejoice in the birth of our Savior.
May we share his life completely
by living as he has taught.
We ask this in the name of Jesus the Lord.
℟. Amen.   → No. 32, p. 70

Optional Solemn Blessings, p. 92, and Prayers Over the People, p. 99

———

MASS AT DAWN

ENTRANCE ANT. See Is 9:2, 6; Lk 1:33   [Prince of Peace]
**A light will shine on us this day, the Lord is born for
us: he shall be called Wonderful God, Prince of peace,
Father of the world to come; and his kingship will
never end.**   → No. 2, p. 10

OPENING PRAYER   [Light of Faith]
Let us pray
   [that the love of Christ
   will be a light to the world]
Father,
we are filled with the new light
by the coming of your Word among us.
May the light of faith

shine in our words and actions.
Grant this through our Lord Jesus Christ, your Son,
who lives and reigns with you and the Holy Spirit,
one God, for ever and ever. ℟. **Amen.** ↓

ALTERNATIVE OPENING PRAYER   [Christ's Peace]

Let us pray
   [for the peace
   that comes from the Prince of Peace]
Almighty God and Father of light,
a child is born for us and a son is given to us.
Your eternal Word leaped down from heaven
in the silent watches of the night,
and now your Church is filled with wonder
at the nearness of her God.
Open our hearts to receive his life
and increase our vision with the rising of dawn,
that our lives may be filled with his glory and his
   peace,
who lives and reigns for ever and ever. ℟. **Amen.** ↓

FIRST READING Is 62:11-12   [The Savior's Birth]

Our Savior comes. He makes us a holy people and redeems us.

A reading from the Book of the Prophet Isaiah

SEE, the LORD proclaims
to the ends of the earth:
say to daughter Zion,
   your savior comes!
Here is his reward with him,
   his recompense before him.
They shall be called the holy people,
   the redeemed of the LORD,
and you shall be called "Frequented,"
   a city that is not forsaken.
The word of the Lord. ℟. **Thanks be to God.** ↓

RESPONSORIAL PSALM Ps 97   [Be Glad in the Lord]

℟.   **A light will shine on us this day: the Lord is born for us.**

The LORD is king; let the earth rejoice;
  let the many isles be glad.
The heavens proclaim his justice,
  and all peoples see his glory.

℟. **A light will shine on us this day:
  the Lord is born for us.**

Light dawns for the just;
  and gladness, for the upright of heart.
Be glad in the LORD, you just,
  and give thanks to his holy name.

℟. **A light will shine on us this day:
  the Lord is born for us.** ↓

SECOND READING Ti 3:4-7   [Saved by God's Mercy]

**By God's mercy we are saved from sin. Jesus became man
that we might through him receive the Spirit.**

A reading from the Letter of Saint Paul to Titus

B ELOVED: When the kindness and generous love
of God our savior appeared, not because of any
righteous deeds we had done but because of his mercy,
he saved us through the bath of rebirth and renewal by
the Holy Spirit, whom he richly poured out on us
through Jesus Christ our savior, so that we might be
justified by his grace and become heirs in hope of eternal life.—The word of the Lord. ℟. **Thanks be to
God.** ↓

ALLELUIA Lk 2:14   [Glory to God]

℟. **Alleluia, alleluia.**
Glory to God in the highest,

and on earth peace to those
on whom his favor rests.
℟. **Alleluia, alleluia.** ↓

GOSPEL Lk 2:15-20   [Jesus, the God-Man]
   The wonder of salvation is revealed to the shepherds and
   to us. The love of God is manifest because he is with us.

℣. The Lord be with you. ℟. **And also with you.**
✛ A reading from the holy Gospel according to Luke.
℟. **Glory to you, Lord.**

W HEN the angels went away from them to heaven,
   the shepherds said to one another, "Let us go,
then, to Bethlehem to see this thing that has taken
place, which the Lord has made known to us." So they
went in haste and found Mary and Joseph, and the
infant lying in the manger. When they saw this, they
made known the message that had been told them
about this child. All who heard it were amazed by what
had been told them by the shepherds. And Mary kept
all these things, reflecting on them in her heart. Then
the shepherds returned, glorifying and praising God
for all they had heard and seen, just as it had been told
to them. —The Gospel of the Lord. ℟. **Praise to you,
Lord Jesus Christ.**   → No. 14, p. 18

In the profession of faith, all genuflect at the words, and
became man.

PRAYER OVER THE GIFTS   [Gift of Divine Life]
Father,
may we follow the example of your Son
who became man and lived among us.
May we receive the gift of divine life
through these offerings here on earth.
We ask this in the name of Jesus the Lord.
℟. **Amen.**   → No. 21, p. 22 (Pref. P 3-5)

When Eucharistic Prayer I is used, the special Christmas form of In union *with the whole Church is said.*

COMMUNION ANT. See Zec 9:9   [The Holy One]
Daughter of Zion, exult; shout aloud, daughter of Jerusalem! Your King is coming, the Holy One, the Savior of the world. ↓

PRAYER AFTER COMMUNION   [Riches Revealed in Christ]
Lord,
with faith and joy
we celebrate the birthday of your Son.
Increase our understanding and our love
of the riches you have revealed in him,
who is Lord for ever and ever.
℟. **Amen.**   → No. 32, p. 70

Optional Solemn Blessings, p. 92, and Prayers Over the People, p. 99

————————

MASS DURING THE DAY

ENTRANCE ANT. Is 9:6   [The Gift of God's Son]
A child is born for us, a son given to us; dominion is laid on his shoulder, and he shall be called Wonderful-Counselor.   → No. 2, p. 10

OPENING PRAYER   [Share in Christ's Glory]
Let us pray
   [for the glory promised by the birth of Christ]
Lord God,
we praise you for creating man,
and still more for restoring him in Christ.
Your Son shared our weakness:
may we share his glory,
for he lives and reigns with you and the Holy Spirit,
one God, for ever and ever. ℟. **Amen.** ↓

ALTERNATIVE OPENING PRAYER   [People of Light]

Let us pray
  [in the joy of Christmas
  because the Son of God lives among us]
God of love, Father of all,
the darkness that covered the earth
has given way to the bright dawn of your Word made
  flesh.
Make us a people of this light.
Make us faithful to your Word,
that we may bring your life to the waiting world.
Grant this through Christ our Lord. ℟. **Amen.** ↓

FIRST READING Is 52:7-10   [Your God Is King]

**The good news, the Gospel—the Lord comforts his people
by announcing our salvation.**

A reading from the Book of the Prophet Isaiah

HOW beautiful upon the mountains
  are the feet of him who brings glad tidings,
announcing peace, bearing good news,
    announcing salvation, and saying to Zion,
    "Your God is King!"
Hark! Your sentinels raise a cry,
    together they shout for joy,
for they see directly, before their eyes,
    the LORD restoring Zion.
Break out together in song,
    O ruins of Jerusalem!
For the LORD comforts his people,
    he redeems Jerusalem.
The LORD has bared his holy arm
    in the sight of all the nations;
all the ends of the earth will behold
    the salvation of our God.
The word of the Lord. ℟. **Thanks be to God.** ↓

RESPONSORIAL PSALM Ps 98   [Sing a New Song]

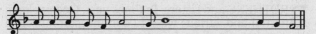

℟. All the ends of the earth have seen the saving   power of God.

Sing to the LORD a new song,
  for he has done wondrous deeds;
his right hand has won victory for him,
  his holy arm.

℟. **All the ends of the earth have seen the saving power of God.**

The LORD has made his salvation known:
  in the sight of the nations he has revealed his justice.
He has remembered his kindness and his faithfulness
  toward the house of Israel.

℟. **All the ends of the earth have seen the saving power of God.**

All the ends of the earth have seen
  the salvation by our God.
Sing joyfully to the LORD, all you lands;
  break into song; sing praise.

℟. **All the ends of the earth have seen the saving power of God.**

Sing praise to the LORD with the harp,
  with the harp and melodious song.
With trumpets and the sound of the horn
  sing joyfully before the King, the LORD.

℟. **All the ends of the earth have seen the saving power of God.** ↓

SECOND READING Heb 1:1-6   [God Speaks through Jesus]

> Now God speaks to us more clearly than ever before. His Son is with us—God is with us; we are his people.

A reading from the Letter to the Hebrews

BROTHERS and sisters: In times past, God spoke in partial and various ways to our ancestors through the prophets; in these last days, he has spoken to us through the Son, whom he made heir of all things and through whom he created the universe,
who is the refulgence of his glory,
    the very imprint of his being,
and who sustains all things by his mighty word.
When he had accomplished purification from sins,
he took his seat at the right hand of the Majesty on
        high,
as far superior to the angels
as the name he has inherited is more excellent than
        theirs.
For to which of the angels did God ever say:
You are my son; this day I have begotten you?
Or again:
I will be a father to him, and he shall be a son to me?
And again, when he leads the firstborn into the world, he says:
Let all the angels of God worship him.
The word of the Lord. ℟. **Thanks be to God.** ↓

ALLELUIA   [Adore the Lord]

℟. **Alleluia, alleluia.**
A holy day has dawned upon us.
Come, you nations, and adore the Lord.
Today a great light has come upon the earth.
℟. **Alleluia, alleluia.** ↓

GOSPEL Jn 1:1-18 or 1:1-5, 9-14   [The True Light]
The Word of God is the living Word. The Word became flesh and lives in our midst.

[If the "Shorter Form" is used, the indented text in brackets is omitted.]

℣. The Lord be with you. ℟. **And also with you.**
✠ A reading from the holy Gospel according to John.
℟. **Glory to you, Lord.**

IN the beginning was the Word,
and the Word was with God,
  and the Word was God.
He was in the beginning with God.
All things came to be through him,
  and without him nothing came to be.
What came to be through him was life,
  and this life was the light of the human race;
the light shines in the darkness,
  and the darkness has not overcome it.

> [A man named John was sent from God. He
> came for testimony, to testify to the light, so
> that all might believe through him. He was not
> the light, but came to testify to the light.]

The true light, which enlightens everyone, was coming into the world.
He was in the world,
  and the world came to be through him,
  . but the world did not know him.
He came to what was his own,
  but his own people did not accept him.

But to those who did accept him he gave power to become children of God, to those who believe in his name, who were born not by natural generation nor by human choice nor by a man's decision but of God.

And the Word became flesh
  and made his dwelling among us,
  and we saw his glory,
  the glory as of the Father's only Son,
  full of grace and truth.

> [John testified to him and cried out, saying,
> "This was he of whom I said, 'The one who is
> coming after me ranks ahead of me because

he existed before me.' " From his fullness we have all received, grace in place of grace, because while the law was given through Moses, grace and truth came through Jesus Christ. No one has ever seen God. The only Son, God, who is at the Father's side, has revealed him.]

The Gospel of the Lord. ℟. **Praise to you, Lord Jesus Christ.**   ➙ No. 14, p. 18

In the profession of faith, all genuflect at the words, and became man.

PRAYER OVER THE GIFTS   [Peace and Praise]

Almighty God,
the saving work of Christ
made our peace with you.
May our offering today
renew that peace within us
and give you perfect praise.
We ask this in the name of Jesus the Lord.
℟. Amen.   ➙ No. 21, p. 22 (Pref. P 3-5)

When Eucharistic Prayer I is used, the special Christmas form of In union with the whole Church *is said.*

COMMUNION ANT. Ps 98:3   [God's Power]

All the ends of the earth have seen the saving power of God. ↓

PRAYER AFTER COMMUNION   [Children of God]

Father,
the child born today is the Savior of the world.
He made us your children.
May he welcome us into your kingdom
where he lives and reigns with you for ever and ever.
℟. **Amen.**   ➙ No. 32, p. 70

Optional Solemn Blessings, p. 92, and Prayers Over the People, p. 99

"Rise, take the child and his mother, [and] flee . . . ."

DECEMBER 26

HOLY FAMILY

ENTRANCE ANT. Lk 2:16   [Jesus, Mary, and Joseph]
The shepherds hastened to Bethlehem, where they found Mary and Joseph, and the baby lying in a manger. ➙ No. 2, p. 10

OPENING PRAYER   [Peace in Families]

Let us pray
   [for peace in our families]
Father,
help us to live as the holy family,
united in respect and love.
Bring us to the joy and peace of your eternal home.
Grant this . . . for ever and ever.
℟. **Amen.** ↓

ALTERNATIVE OPENING PRAYER   [Value of Family Life]

Let us pray
   [as the family of God,
   who share in his life]
Father in heaven, creator of all,
you ordered the earth to bring forth life

149

and crowned its goodness by creating the family of man.
In history's moment when all was ready,
you sent your Son to dwell in time,
obedient to the laws of life in our world.
Teach us the sanctity of human love,
show us the value of family life,
and help us to live in peace with all men
that we may share in your life for ever.
We ask this through Christ our Lord. ℟. **Amen.** ↓

FIRST READING Sir 3:2-7, 12-14   [Duties toward Parents]

**Fidelity to Yahweh implies many particular virtues, and
among them Sirach gives precedence to duties toward parents. He promises atonement for sin to those who honor
their parents.**

A reading from the Book of Sirach

GOD sets a father in honor over his children;
a mother's authority he confirms over her sons.
Whoever honors his father atones for sins,
    and preserves himself from them.
When he prays, he is heard;
    he stores up riches who reveres his mother.
Whoever honors his father is gladdened by children,
    and when he prays, is heard.
Whoever reveres his father will live a long life;
    he obeys his father who brings comfort to his
    mother.

My son, take care of your father when he is old;
    grieve him not as long as he lives.
Even if his mind fail, be considerate of him;
    revile him not all the days of his life;
kindness to a father will not be forgotten,
    firmly planted against the debt of your sins
    —a house raised in justice to you.
The word of the Lord. ℟. **Thanks be to God.** ↓

RESPONSORIAL PSALM Ps 128   [Happiness in Families]

℟. Bles-sed are those who fear the Lord and walk in his ways.

Blessed is everyone who fears the LORD,
  who walks in his ways!
For you shall eat the fruit of your handiwork;
  blessed shall you be, and favored.—℟.

Your wife shall be like a fruitful vine
  in the recesses of your home;
your children like olive plants
  around your table.—℟.

Behold, thus is the man blessed
  who fears the LORD.
The LORD bless you from Zion:
  may you see the prosperity of Jerusalem
  all the days of your life.—℟. ↓

SECOND READING Col 3:12-21   [Plan for Family Life]
  Paul describes the life a Christian embraces through baptism.

[If the "Shorter Form" is used, the indented text in brackets is omitted.]

  A reading from the Letter of Saint Paul to the Colossians

BROTHERS and sisters: Put on, as God's chosen ones, holy and beloved, heartfelt compassion, kindness, humility, gentleness, and patience, bearing with one another and forgiving one another, if one has a grievance against another; as the Lord has forgiven you, so must you also do. And over all these put on love, that is, the bond of perfection. And let the peace of Christ control your hearts, the peace into which you were also called in one body. And be thankful. Let the word of Christ dwell in you richly, as in all wisdom you teach and admonish one another, singing psalms, hymns, and spiritual songs with gratitude in your hearts to God. And whatever you do, in word or in deed, do everything in the name of the Lord Jesus, giving thanks to God the Father through him.

[Wives, be subordinate to your husbands, as is proper in the Lord. Husbands, love your wives, and avoid any bitterness toward them. Children, obey your parents in everything, for this is pleasing to the Lord. Fathers, do not provoke your children, so they may not become discouraged.]

The word of the Lord. ℟. **Thanks be to God.** ↓

ALLELUIA Col 3:15a, 16a [Peace of Christ]

℟. **Alleluia, alleluia.**
Let the peace of Christ control your hearts;
let the word of Christ dwell in you richly.
℟. **Alleluia, alleluia.** ↓

GOSPEL Mt 2:13-15, 19-23 [Escape into Egypt]

In Christ all the prophecies are fulfilled. He is the Messiah, the dominant one—the Son of God. In all things he carries out the will of his Father.

℣. The Lord be with you. ℟. **And also with you.**
✛ A reading from the holy Gospel according to Matthew. ℟. **Glory to you, Lord.**

WHEN the magi had departed, behold, the angel of the Lord appeared to Joseph in a dream and said, "Rise, take the child and his mother, flee to Egypt, and stay there until I tell you. Herod is going to search for the child to destroy him." Joseph rose and took the child and his mother by night and departed for Egypt. He stayed there until the death of Herod, that what the Lord had said through the prophet might be fulfilled, *Out of Egypt I called my son.*

When Herod had died, behold, the angel of the Lord appeared in a dream to Joseph in Egypt and said,

"Rise, take the child and his mother and go to the land of Israel, for those who sought the child's life are dead." He rose, took the child and his mother, and went to the land of Israel. But when he heard that Archelaus was ruling over Judea in place of his father Herod, he was afraid to go back there. And because he had been warned in a dream, he departed for the region of Galilee. He went and dwelt in a town called Nazareth, so that what had been spoken through the prophets might be fulfilled, *He shall be called a Nazorean.*—The Gospel of the Lord. ℟. **Praise to you, Lord Jesus Christ.** →No. 14, p. 18

PRAYER OVER THE GIFTS [Unite Our Families]

Lord,
accept this sacrifice
and through the prayers of Mary, the virgin Mother of
   God,
and of her husband, Joseph,
unite our families in peace and love.
We ask this in the name of Jesus the Lord.
℟. **Amen.** → No. 21, p. 22 (Pref. P 3-5)

When Eucharistic Prayer I is used, the special Christmas form of In union with the whole Church *is said.*

COMMUNION ANT. Bar 3:38 [God with Us]

Our God has appeared on earth, and lived among men. ↓

PRAYER AFTER COMMUNION [Strength for Families]

Eternal Father,
we want to live as Jesus, Mary, and Joseph,
in peace with you and one another.
May this communion strengthen us
to face the troubles of life.
Grant this through Christ our Lord.
℟. **Amen.** → No. 32, p. 70

Optional Solemn Blessings, p. 92, and Prayers Over the People, p. 99

"He was named Jesus. . . ."

JANUARY 1, 2011

SOLEMNITY OF MARY, MOTHER OF GOD

ENTRANCE ANT. See Is 9:2, 6; Lk 1:33   [Wonderful God]

A light will shine on us this day, the Lord is born for us: he shall be called Wonderful God, Prince of peace, Father of the world to come; and his kingship will never end.

OR Sedulius   [Hail, Holy Mother]

Hail, holy Mother! The child to whom you gave birth is the King of heaven and earth for ever.   → No. 2, p. 10

OPENING PRAYER   [Mary's Prayers]

Let us pray
  [that Mary, the mother of the Lord,
  will help us by her prayers]
God our Father,
may we always profit by the prayers
of the Virgin Mother Mary,
for you bring us life and salvation
through Jesus Christ her Son
who lives and reigns with you and the Holy Spirit,
one God, for ever and ever. ℟. **Amen.** ↓

ALTERNATIVE OPENING PRAYER   [Gift of a Mother's Love]

Let us pray
  [in the name of Jesus,
  born of a virgin and Son of God]
Father,
source of light in every age,
the virgin conceived and bore your Son
who is called Wonderful God, Prince of Peace.
May her prayer, the gift of a mother's love,
be your people's joy through all ages.
May her response, born of a humble heart,
draw your Spirit to rest on your people.
Grant this through Christ our Lord. ℞. **Amen.** ↓

FIRST READING Nm 6:22-27   [The Aaronic Blessing]

Aaron and the Israelites are to pray that God will answer their prayers with blessings.

A reading from the Book of Numbers

THE Lord said to Moses: "Speak to Aaron and his
  sons and tell them: This is how you shall bless the
Israelites. Say to them:
The LORD bless you and keep you!

The LORD let his face shine upon you, and be gracious
    to you!
The LORD look upon you kindly and give you peace!

So shall they invoke my name upon the Israelites and
I will bless them."—The word of the Lord. ℞. **Thanks
be to God.** ↓

RESPONSORIAL PSALM Ps 67   [God Bless Us]

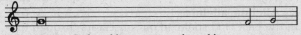

  ℞. May God bless us in his mer - cy.
May God have pity on us and bless us;
    may he let his face shine upon us.

So may your way be known upon earth;
   among all nations, your salvation.

℟. **May God bless us in his mercy.**

May the nations be glad and exult
   because you rule the peoples in equity;
   the nations on the earth you guide.

℟. **May God bless us in his mercy.**

May the peoples praise you, O God;
   may all the peoples praise you!
May God bless us,
   and may all the ends of the earth fear him!

℟. **May God bless us in his mercy.** ↓

SECOND READING Gal 4:4-7   [Heirs by God's Design]
   God sent Jesus, his Son, born of Mary, to deliver all from
   the bondage of sin and slavery of the law. By God's choice
   we are heirs of heaven.

A reading from the Letter of Saint Paul to the Galatians

B ROTHERS and sisters: When the fullness of time
   had come, God sent his Son, born of a woman,
born under the law, to ransom those under the law, so
that we might receive adoption as sons. As proof that
you are sons, God sent the Spirit of his Son into our
hearts, crying out, "Abba, Father!" So you are no longer
a slave but a son, and if a son then also an heir,
through God.—The word of the Lord. ℟. **Thanks be to
God.** ↓

ALLELUIA Heb 1:1-2   [God Speaks]
℟. **Alleluia, alleluia.**
In the past God spoke to our ancestors through the
   prophets;
in these last days, he has spoken to us through the Son.
℟. **Alleluia, alleluia.** ↓

GOSPEL Lk 2:16-21   [The Name of Jesus]

When the shepherds came to Bethlehem, they began to understand the message of the angels. Mary prayed about this great event. Jesus received his name according to the Jewish ritual of circumcision.

℣. The Lord be with you. ℟. **And also with you.**

✠ A reading from the holy Gospel according to Luke.

℟. **Glory to you, Lord.**

THE shepherds went in haste to Bethlehem and found Mary and Joseph, and the infant lying in the manger. When they saw this, they made known the message that had been told them about this child. All who heard it were amazed by what had been told them by the shepherds. And Mary kept all these things, reflecting on them in her heart. Then the shepherds returned, glorifying and praising God for all they had heard and seen, just as it had been told to them.

When eight days were completed for his circumcision, he was named Jesus, the name given him by the angel before he was conceived in the womb.—The Gospel of the Lord. ℟. **Praise to you, Lord Jesus Christ.**   → No. 14, p. 18

PRAYER OVER THE GIFTS   [Salvation Fulfilled]

God our Father,
we celebrate at this season
the beginning of our salvation.
On this feast of Mary, the Mother of God,
we ask that our salvation
will be brought to its fulfillment.
We ask this through Christ our Lord. ℟. **Amen.** ↓

PREFACE (P 56)   [Mary, Virgin and Mother]

℣. The Lord be with you. ℟. **And also with you.**

℣. Lift up your hearts. ℟. **We lift them up to the Lord.**

℣. Let us give thanks to the Lord our God. ℟. **It is right to give him thanks and praise.**

Father, all-powerful and ever-living God,
we do well always and everywhere to give you thanks
(as we celebrate . . . of the Blessed Virgin Mary).
Through the power of the Holy Spirit,
she became the virgin mother of your only Son,
our Lord Jesus Christ,
who is for ever the light of the world.
Through him the choirs of angels
and all the powers of heaven
praise and worship your glory.
May our voices blend with theirs
as we join in their unending hymn: → No. 23, p. 23

*When Eucharistic Prayer I is used, the special Christmas
form of* In union with the whole Church *is said.*

COMMUNION ANT. Heb 13:8   **[Jesus Forever]**
**Jesus Christ is the same yesterday, today, and for
ever.** ↓

PRAYER AFTER COMMUNION   **[Mother of the Church]**
Father,
as we proclaim the Virgin Mary
to be the mother of Christ and the mother of the
   Church,
may our communion with her Son
bring us to salvation.
We ask this through Christ our Lord.
℟. **Amen.**   → No. 32, p. 70

Optional Solemn Blessings, p. 92, and Prayers Over the People, p. 99

"They prostrated themselves and did him homage."

JANUARY 2

EPIPHANY OF THE LORD

ENTRANCE ANT. See Mal 3:1; 1 Chr 29:12 **[Lord and Ruler]**

The Lord and ruler is coming; kingship is his, and government and power.   → No. 2, p. 10

OPENING PRAYER   **[Light of Faith]**

Let us pray
   [that we will be guided by the light of faith]
Father,
you revealed your Son to the nations
by the guidance of a star.
Lead us to your glory in heaven
by the light of faith.
We ask this through our Lord Jesus Christ, your Son,
who lives and reigns with you and the Holy Spirit,
one God, for ever and ever. ℟. **Amen.** ↓

ALTERNATIVE OPENING PRAYER   **[God's Love Is Near]**

Let us pray
   [grateful for the glory revealed today
     through God made man]
Father of light, unchanging God,
today you reveal to men of faith

159

the resplendent fact of the Word made flesh.
Your light is strong,
your love is near;
draw us beyond the limits which this world imposes,
to the life where your Spirit makes all life complete.
We ask this through Christ our Lord. ℟. **Amen.** ↓

FIRST READING Is 60:1-6   **[Glory of God's Church]**

Jerusalem is favored by the Lord. Kings and peoples will come before you. The riches of the earth will be placed at the gates of Jerusalem.

A reading from the Book of the Prophet Isaiah

RISE up in splendor, Jerusalem! Your light has come,
    the glory of the Lord shines upon you.
See, darkness covers the earth,
    and thick clouds cover the peoples;
but upon you the LORD shines,
    and over you appears his glory.
Nations shall walk by your light,
    and kings by your shining radiance.
Raise your eyes and look about;
    they all gather and come to you:
your sons come from afar,
    and your daughters in the arms of their nurses.

Then you shall be radiant at what you see,
    your heart shall throb and overflow,
for the riches of the sea shall be emptied out before you,
    the wealth of nations shall be brought to you.
Caravans of camels shall fill you,
    dromedaries from Midian and Ephah;
all from Sheba shall come
    bearing gold and frankincense,
    and proclaiming the praises of the LORD.
The word of the Lord. ℟. **Thanks be to God.** ↓

RESPONSORIAL PSALM Ps 72   [The Messiah-King]

℟. Lord, every nation on earth will adore you.

O God, with your judgment endow the king,
    and with your justice, the king's son;
he shall govern your people with justice
    and your afflicted ones with judgment.

℟. **Lord, every nation on earth will adore you.**

Justice shall flower in his days,
    and profound peace, till the moon be no more.
May he rule from sea to sea,
    and from the River to the ends of the earth.

℟. **Lord, every nation on earth will adore you.**

The kings of Tarshish and the Isles shall offer gifts;
    the kings of Arabia and Seba shall bring tribute.
All kings shall pay him homage,
    all nations shall serve him.

℟. **Lord, every nation on earth will adore you.**

For he shall rescue the poor man when he cries out,
    and the afflicted when he has no one to help him.
He shall have pity for the lowly and the poor;
    the lives of the poor he shall save.

℟. **Lord, every nation on earth will adore you.** ↓

SECOND READING Eph 3:2-3a, 5-6   [Good News for All]

    Paul admits that God has revealed the divine plan of salvation to him. Not only the Jews, but also the whole Gentile world, will share in the Good News.

A reading from the Letter of Saint Paul to the Ephesians

BROTHERS and sisters: You have heard of the stewardship of God's grace that was given to me for your benefit, namely, that the mystery was made known to me by revelation. It was not made known to people in other generations as it has now been revealed to his holy apostles and prophets by the Spirit: that the Gentiles are coheirs, members of the same body, and copartners in the promise in Christ Jesus through the gospel.—The word of the Lord. ℟. **Thanks be to God.** ↓

ALLELUIA Mt 2:2   [Leading Star]

℟. **Alleluia, alleluia.**
We saw his star at its rising
and have come to do him homage.
℟. **Alleluia, alleluia.** ↓

GOSPEL Mt 2:1-12   [Magi with Gifts]

King Herod, being jealous of his earthly crown, was threatened by the coming of another king. The magi from the east followed the star to Bethlehem from which a ruler was to come.

℣. The Lord be with you. ℟. **And also with you.**
✢   A reading from the holy Gospel according to Matthew. ℟. **Glory to you, Lord.**

WHEN Jesus was born in Bethlehem of Judea, in the days of King Herod, behold, magi from the east arrived in Jerusalem, saying, "Where is the newborn king of the Jews? We saw his star at its rising and have come to do him homage." When King Herod heard this, he was greatly troubled, and all Jerusalem with him. Assembling all the chief priests and the scribes of the people, he inquired of them where the Christ was to be born. They said to him, "In Bethlehem of Judea, for thus it has been written through the prophet:

And you, Bethlehem, land of Judah,
    are by no means least among the rulers of Judah;
since from you shall come a ruler,
    who is to shepherd my people Israel."
Then Herod called the magi secretly and ascertained from them the time of the star's appearance. He sent

them to Bethlehem and said, "Go and search diligently
for the child. When you have found him, bring me
word, that I too may go and do him homage." After
their audience with the king they set out. And behold,
the star that they had seen at its rising preceded them,
until it came and stopped over the place where the
child was. They were overjoyed at seeing the star, and
on entering the house they saw the child with Mary his
mother. They prostrated themselves and did him homage. Then they opened their treasures and offered him
gifts of gold, frankincense, and myrrh. And having
been warned in a dream not to return to Herod, they
departed for their country by another way.—The
Gospel of the Lord. ℟. **Praise to you, Lord Jesus
Christ.**
→ No. 14, p. 18

PRAYER OVER THE GIFTS   [Offering of Jesus]

Lord,
accept the offerings of your Church,
not gold, frankincense and myrrh,
but the sacrifice and food they symbolize:
Jesus Christ, who is Lord for ever and ever.
℟. **Amen.** ↓

PREFACE (P 6)   [Jesus Revealed to All]

℣. The Lord be with you. ℟. **And also with you.**
℣. Lift up your hearts. ℟. **We lift them up to the Lord.**
℣. Let us give thanks to the Lord our God. ℟. **It is right
to give him thanks and praise.**

Father, all-powerful and ever-living God,
we do well always and everywhere to give you thanks.
Today you revealed in Christ your eternal plan of sal-
    vation
and showed him as the light of all peoples.
Now that his glory has shone among us
you have renewed humanity in his immortal image.

Now, with angels and archangels,
and the whole company of heaven,
we sing the unending hymn of your praise:

→ No. 23, p. 23

*When Eucharistic Prayer I is used, the special Epiphany
form of* In union with the whole Church *is said.*

COMMUNION ANT. See Mt 2:2   [Adore the Lord]

**We have seen his star in the east, and have come with
gifts to adore the Lord. ↓**

PRAYER AFTER COMMUNION   [Christ in the Eucharist]

Father,
guide us with your light.
Help us to recognize Christ in this eucharist
and welcome him with love,
for he is Lord for ever and ever.
℟. **Amen.**   → No. 32, p. 70

Optional Solemn Blessings, p. 92, and Prayers Over the People, p. 99

"This is my beloved Son, with whom I am well pleased."

JANUARY 9

BAPTISM OF THE LORD

ENTRANCE ANT. See Mt 3:16-17   **[Beloved Son]**

When the Lord had been baptized, the heavens opened, and the Spirit came down like a dove to rest on him. Then the voice of the Father thundered: This is my beloved Son, with him I am well pleased.

→ No. 2, p. 10

OPENING PRAYER   **[Faithful to Our Baptism]**

Let us pray
   [that we will be faithful to our baptism]
Almighty, eternal God,
when the Spirit descended upon Jesus
at his baptism in the Jordan,
you revealed him as your own beloved Son.
Keep us, your children born of water and the Spirit,
faithful to our calling.
We ask this . . . for ever and ever. ℟. **Amen.** ↓

OR   **[God Became Man]**

Father,
your only Son revealed himself to us by becoming man.

May we who share his humanity
come to share his divinity,
for he lives and reigns with you and the Holy Spirit,
one God, for ever and ever. **Amen.** ↓

ALTERNATIVE OPENING PRAYER   [Radiating Christ]
Let us pray
   [as we listen to the voice of God's Spirit]
Father in heaven,
you revealed Christ as your Son
by the voice that spoke over the waters of the Jordan.
May all who share in the sonship of Christ
follow in his path of service to man,
and reflect the glory of his kingdom
even to the ends of the earth,
for he is Lord for ever and ever. ℟. **Amen.** ↓

FIRST READING Is 42:1-4, 6-7   [Works of the Messiah]
   **The prophet Isaiah sees the spirit upon the Lord's servant
   who will proclaim the "good news" to the poor, freedom
   to prisoners and joy to those in sorrow.**

   A reading from the Book of the Prophet Isaiah

T HUS says the Lord:
   Here is my servant whom I uphold,
      my chosen one with whom I am pleased,
upon whom I have put my spirit;
      he shall bring forth justice to the nations,
not crying out, not shouting,
      not making his voice heard in the street.
A bruised reed he shall not break,
      and a smoldering wick he shall not quench,
until he establishes justice on the earth;
      the coastlands will wait for his teaching.

I, the LORD, have called you for the victory of justice,
      I have grasped you, by the hand;
I formed you, and set you
      as a covenant of the people,

a light for the nations,
to open the eyes of the blind,
to bring out prisoners from confinement,
and from the dungeon, those who live in darkness.
The word of the Lord. ℟. **Thanks be to God.** ↓

RESPONSORIAL PSALM Ps 29   [Peace for God's People]

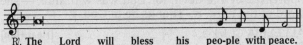

℟. The   Lord   will   bless   his   peo-ple with peace.

Give to the LORD, you sons of God,
give to the LORD glory and praise,
give to the LORD the glory due his name;
adore the LORD in holy attire.

℟. **The Lord will bless his people with peace.**

The voice of the LORD is over the waters,
the LORD, over vast waters.
The voice of the LORD is mighty;
the voice of the LORD is majestic.

℟. **The Lord will bless his people with peace.**

The God of glory thunders,
and in his temple all say, "Glory!"
The LORD is enthroned above the flood;
the LORD is enthroned as king forever.

℟. **The Lord will bless his people with peace.** ↓

SECOND READING Acts 10:34-38   [Anointed to Do Good]

God anointed Jesus the Savior with the Holy Spirit and
power. Jesus is the Lord of all, and he brought healing to
all who were in the grip of the devil.

A reading from the Acts of the Apostles

PETER proceeded to speak to those gathered in the
house of Cornelius, saying: "In truth, I see that God
shows no partiality. Rather, in every nation whoever
fears him and acts uprightly is acceptable to him. You

know the word that he sent to the Israelites as he proclaimed peace through Jesus Christ, who is Lord of all, what has happened all over Judea, beginning in Galilee after the baptism that John preached, how God anointed Jesus of Nazareth with the Holy Spirit and power. He went about doing good and healing all those oppressed by the devil, for God was with him."—The word of the Lord. ℟. **Thanks be to God.** ↓

ALLELUIA Cf. Mk 9:7   [Hear Him]

℟. **Alleluia, alleluia.**

The heavens were opened and the voice of the Father
 thundered:
This is my beloved Son, listen to him.

℟. **Alleluia, alleluia.** ↓

GOSPEL Mt 3:13-17   [Beloved Son]

John objected to baptizing Jesus since he recognized the Messiah. Jesus insisted, and the heavens opened showing God's favor. God also identified his Son, Jesus.

℣. The Lord be with you. ℟. **And also with you.**
✝ A reading from the holy Gospel according to Matthew. ℟. **Glory to you, Lord.**

JESUS came from Galilee to John at the Jordan to be baptized by him. John tried to prevent him, saying, "I need to be baptized by you, and yet you are coming to me?" Jesus said to him in reply, "Allow it now, for thus it is fitting for us to fulfill all righteousness." Then he allowed him. After Jesus was baptized, he came up from the water and behold, the heavens were opened for him, and he saw the Spirit of God descending like a dove and coming upon him. And a voice came from the heavens, saying, "This is my beloved Son, with whom I am well pleased."—The Gospel of the Lord. ℟. **Praise to you, Lord Jesus Christ.**   ➜ No. 14, p. 18

PRAYER OVER THE GIFTS　　　　[Christ's Revelation]

Lord,
we celebrate the revelation of Christ your Son
who takes away the sins of the world.
Accept our gifts
and let them become one with his sacrifice,
for he is Lord for ever and ever. R̶̸. **Amen.** ↓

PREFACE (P 7)　　　　　　　[New Gift of Baptism]

V̶̸. The Lord be with you. R̶̸. **And also with you.**
V̶̸. Lift up your hearts. R̶̸. **We lift them up to the Lord.**
V̶̸. Let us give thanks to the Lord our God. R̶̸. **It is right
to give him thanks and praise.**

Father, all-powerful and ever-living God,
we do well always and everywhere to give you thanks.
You celebrated your new gift of baptism
by signs and wonders at the Jordan.
Your voice was heard from heaven
to awaken faith in the presence among us
of the Word made man.
Your Spirit was seen as a dove,
revealing Jesus as your servant,
and anointing him with joy as the Christ,
sent to bring to the poor
the good news of salvation.
In our unending joy we echo on earth
the song of the angels in heaven
as they praise your glory for ever:　　→ No. 23, p. 23

COMMUNION ANT. Jn 1:32, 34　　[Witness to God's Son]

**This is he of whom John said: I have seen and have
given witness that this is the Son of God.** ↓

PRAYER AFTER COMMUNION　　　　[One in Love]

Lord,
you feed us with bread from heaven.

May we hear your Son with faith
and become your children in name and in fact.
We ask this in the name of Jesus the Lord.
℟. **Amen.**   ➜ No. 32, p. 70

Optional Solemn Blessings, p. 92, and Prayers Over the People, p. 99

*"Behold, the Lamb of God who takes away
the sin of the world."*

JANUARY 16

2nd SUNDAY IN ORDINARY TIME

ENTRANCE ANT. Ps 66:4   [Proclaim His Glory]
**May all the earth give you worship and praise, and
break into song to your name, O God, Most High.**
   ➜ No. 2, p. 10

OPENING PRAYER   [Peace in the World]
Let us pray
   [to our Father for the gift of peace]
Father of heaven and earth,
hear our prayers,
and show us the way to peace in the world.
Grant this through our Lord Jesus Christ, your Son,

who lives and reigns with you and the Holy Spirit,
one God, for ever and ever. ℟. **Amen.** ↓

ALTERNATIVE OPENING PRAYER [Reflecting God's Peace]

Let us pray
   [for the gift of peace]
Almighty and ever-present Father,
your watchful care reaches from end to end
and orders all things in such power
that even the tensions and the tragedies of sin
cannot frustrate your loving plans.
Help us to embrace your will,
give us the strength to follow your call,
so that your truth may live in our hearts
and reflect peace to those who believe in your love.
We ask this in the name of Jesus the Lord. ℟. **Amen.** ↓

FIRST READING Is 49:3, 5-6   [God Is My Strength]

Through Israel the Lord will show forth his glory and
splendor. Israel is to be a light for all nations whereby salvation will come to all people.

A reading from the Book of the Prophet Isaiah

THE LORD said to me: You are my servant,
   Israel, through whom I show my glory.
Now the LORD has spoken
   who formed me as his servant from the womb,
that Jacob may be brought back to him
   and Israel gathered to him;
and I am made glorious in the sight of the LORD,
   and my God is now my strength!
It is too little, the LORD says, for you to be my servant,
   to raise up the tribes of Jacob,
   and restore the survivors of Israel;
I will make you a light to the nations,
   that my salvation may reach to the ends of the
   earth.
The word of the Lord. ℟. **Thanks be to God.** ↓

RESPONSORIAL PSALM Ps 40   [Doing God's Will]

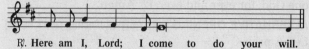

℟. Here am I, Lord; I come to do your will.

I have waited, waited for the LORD,
  and he stooped toward me and heard my cry.
And he put a new song into my mouth,
  a hymn to our God.

℟. **Here am I, Lord; I come to do your will.**

Sacrifice or offering you wished not,
  but ears open to obedience you gave me.
Holocausts or sin-offerings you sought not;
  then said I, "Behold I come."

℟. **Here am I, Lord; I come to do your will.**

"In the written scroll it is prescribed for me,
to do your will, O my God, is my delight,
  and your law is within my heart!"

℟. **Here am I, Lord; I come to do your will.**

I announced your justice in the vast assembly;
  I did not restrain my lips, as you, O LORD, know.

℟. **Here am I, Lord; I come to do your will.**

SECOND READING 1 Cor 1:1-3   [A Holy People]

**Paul and Sosthenes greet the people at Corinth. They are
to be a holy people as are all who call upon the name of
Jesus, acknowledging him as Lord.**

A reading from the first Letter of Saint Paul
to the Corinthians

PAUL, called to be an apostle of Christ Jesus by the
will of God, and Sosthenes our brother, to the
church of God that is in Corinth, to you who have been
sanctified in Christ Jesus, called to be holy, with all
those everywhere who call upon the name of our Lord

Jesus Christ, their Lord and ours. Grace to you and peace from God our Father and the Lord Jesus Christ.—The word of the Lord. ℟. **Thanks be to God.** ↓

ALLELUIA Jn 1:14a, 12a   [Children of God]

℟. **Alleluia, alleluia.**
The Word of God became flesh and dwelt among us.
To those who accepted him,
he gave power to become children of God.
℟. **Alleluia, alleluia.** ↓

In place of the Alleluia given for each Sunday in Ordinary Time, another may be selected.

GOSPEL Jn 1: 29-34   [Encountering Christ]
   John the Baptist recognized Jesus: The Lamb of God who takes away the sins of the world. This is God's chosen one upon whom the Spirit descended and came to rest.

℣. The Lord be with you. ℟. **And also with you.**
✛ A reading from the holy Gospel according to John.
℟. **Glory to you, Lord.**

JOHN the Baptist saw Jesus coming toward him and said, "Behold the Lamb of God, who takes away the sin of the world. He is the one of whom I said, 'A man is coming after me who ranks ahead of me because he existed before me.' I did not know him, but the reason why I came baptizing with water was that he might be made known to Israel." John testified further, saying, "I saw the Spirit come down like a dove from heaven and remain upon him. I did not know him, but the one who sent me to baptize with water told me, 'On whomever you see the Spirit come down and remain, he is the one who will baptize with the Holy Spirit.' Now I have seen and testified that he is the Son of God."—The Gospel of the Lord. ℟. **Praise to you, Lord Jesus Christ.**   → No. 14, p. 18

PRAYER OVER THE GIFTS   [Work of Salvation]

Father,
may we celebrate the eucharist
with reverence and love,
for when we proclaim the death of the Lord
you continue the work of his redemption,
who is Lord for ever and ever.
℞. **Amen.**   → No. 21, p. 22 (Pref. P 29-36)

COMMUNION ANT. Ps 23:5   [A Feast for Me]
The Lord has prepared a feast for me: given wine in plenty for me to drink. ↓

OR 1 Jn 4:16   [God's Love]
We know and believe in God's love for us. ↓

PRAYER AFTER COMMUNION   [One in Love]

Lord,
you have nourished us with bread from heaven.
Fill us with your Spirit,
and make us one in peace and love.
We ask this through Christ our Lord.
℞. **Amen.**   → No. 32, p. 70

Optional Solemn Blessings, p. 92, and Prayers Over the People, p. 99

"Come after me, and I will make you fishers of men."

JANUARY 23

3rd SUNDAY IN ORDINARY TIME

ENTRANCE ANT. Ps 96:1, 6   [Sing to the Lord]

Sing a new song to the Lord! Sing to the Lord, all the earth. Truth and beauty surround him, he lives in holiness and glory.   → No. 2, p. 10

OPENING PRAYER   [Working for Unity]

Let us pray
   [for unity and peace]
All-powerful and ever-living God,
direct your love that is within us,
that our efforts in the name of your Son
may bring mankind to unity and peace.
We ask this through our Lord Jesus Christ, your Son,
who lives and reigns with you and the Holy Spirit,
one God, for ever and ever. ℟. **Amen.** ↓

ALTERNATIVE OPENING PRAYER   [Vision of God]

Let us pray
   [pleading that our vision
   may overcome our weakness]

175

Almighty Father,
the love you offer
always exceeds the furthest expression of our human
    longing,
for you are greater than the human heart.
Direct each thought, each effort of our life,
so that the limits of our faults and weaknesses
may not obscure the vision of your glory
or keep us from the peace you have promised.
We ask this through Christ our Lord. R̰. **Amen.** ↓

FIRST READING Is 8:23—9:3   [Joy and Light]

Isaiah tells of the land in the west where there is no gloom, for the people see a great light. They are to rejoice that the yoke that bound them is to be smashed.

A reading from the Book of the Prophet Isaiah

F IRST the Lord degraded the land of Zebulun and the land of Naphtali; but in the end he has glorified the seaward road, the land west of the Jordan, the District of the Gentiles.

Anguish has taken wing, dispelled is darkness:
    for there is no gloom where but now there was
        distress.
The people who walked in darkness
    have seen a great light;
upon those who dwelt in the land of gloom
    a light has shone.
You have brought them abundant joy
    and great rejoicing,
as they rejoice before you as at the harvest,
    as people make merry when dividing spoils.
For the yoke that burdened them,
    the pole on their shoulder,
and the rod of their taskmaster
    you have smashed, as on the day of Midian.
The word of the Lord. R̰. **Thanks be to God.** ↓

RESPONSORIAL PSALM Ps 27   [Wait With Courage]

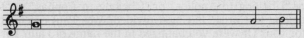

℟. The   Lord   is   my   light   and   my   sal - va - tion.

The LORD is my light and my salvation;
  whom should I fear?
The LORD is my life's refuge;
  of whom should I be afraid?

℟. **The Lord is my light and my salvation.**

One thing I ask of the LORD;
  this I seek:
to dwell in the house of the LORD
  all the days of my life,
that I may gaze on the loveliness of the LORD
  and contemplate his temple.

℟. **The Lord is my light and my salvation.**

I believe that I shall see the bounty of the LORD
  in the land of the living.
Wait for the LORD with courage;
  be stouthearted, and wait for the LORD.

℟. **The Lord is my light and my salvation.** ↓

SECOND READING 1 Cor 1:10-13, 17   [Need for Unity]

Paul warns the people of Corinth that there must be unity among the people of God. There is only one gospel message. Jesus cannot be divided, no matter who preaches about him.

A reading from the first Letter of Saint Paul
to the Corinthians

I URGE you, brothers and sisters, in the name of our
Lord Jesus Christ, that all of you agree in what you say,
and that there be no divisions among you, but that you be
united in the same mind and in the same purpose. For it
has been reported to me about you, my brothers and sisters, by Chloe's people that there are rivalries among

you. I mean that each of you is saying, "I belong to Paul," or "I belong to Apollos," or "I belong to Cephas," or "I belong to Christ." Is Christ divided? Was Paul crucified for you? Or were you baptized in the name of Paul? For Christ did not send me to baptize but to preach the gospel, and not with the wisdom of human eloquence, so that the cross of Christ might not be emptied of its meaning.—The word of the Lord. ℟. **Thanks be to God.** ↓

ALLELUIA Cf. Mt 4:23   [Proclaim the Gospel]
℟. **Alleluia, alleluia.**
Jesus proclaimed the Gospel of the kingdom,
and cured every disease among the people.
℟. **Alleluia, alleluia.** ↓

GOSPEL Mt 4:12-23 or 4:12-17   [Reform Your Lives]
[If the "Shorter Form" is used, the indented text in brackets is omitted.]

Jesus preached reform. At the Sea of Galilee he called Peter and Andrew, James and John, to become fishers of people. At once, they left their nets to follow him. Jesus taught and worked miracles.

℣. The Lord be with you. ℟. **And also with you.**
✢ A reading from the holy Gospel according to Matthew. ℟. **Glory to you, Lord.**

WHEN Jesus heard that John had been arrested, he withdrew to Galilee. He left Nazareth and went to live in Capernaum by the sea, in the region of Zebulun and Naphtali, that what had been said through Isaiah the prophet might be fulfilled:

Land of Zebulun and land of Naphtali,
     the way to the sea, beyond the Jordan,
     Galilee of the Gentiles,
the people who sit in darkness have seen a great
     light,
on those dwelling in a land overshadowed by death
     light has arisen.

From that time on, Jesus began to preach and say, "Repent for the kingdom of heaven is at hand."

[As he was walking by the Sea of Galilee, he saw two brothers, Simon who is called Peter, and his brother Andrew, casting a net into the sea; they were fishermen. He said to them, "Come after me, and I will make you fishers of men." At once they left their nets and followed him. He walked along from there and saw two other brothers, James, the son of Zebedee, and his brother John. They were in a boat, with their father Zebedee, mending their nets. He called them, and immediately they left their boat and their father and followed him. He went around all of Galilee, teaching in their synagogues, proclaiming the gospel of the kingdom, and curing every disease and illness among the people.]

The Gospel of the Lord. ℟. **Praise to you, Lord Jesus Christ.** ➙ No. 14, p. 18

PRAYER OVER THE GIFTS   [Offerings of Salvation]

Lord,
receive our gifts.
Let our offerings make us holy
and bring us salvation.
Grant this through Christ our Lord.
℟. **Amen.**   ➙ No. 21, p. 22 (Pref. P 29-36)

COMMUNION ANT. Ps 34:6   [Gladness]
Look up at the Lord with gladness and smile; your face will never be ashamed. ↓

OR Jn 8:12   [Light of Life]
I am the light of the world, says the Lord; the man who follows me will have the light of life. ↓

PRAYER AFTER COMMUNION   [New Life]

God, all-powerful Father,
may the new life you give us increase our love

and keep us in the joy of your kingdom.
We ask this in the name of Jesus the Lord.
℟. **Amen.**   → No. 32, p. 70

Optional Solemn Blessings, p. 92, and Prayers Over the People, p. 99

"Your reward will be great in heaven."

JANUARY 30

4th SUNDAY IN ORDINARY TIME

ENTRANCE ANT. Ps 106:47   [Save Us]

**Save us, Lord our God, and gather us together from
the nations, that we may proclaim your holy name and
glory in your praise.**   → No. 2, p. 10

OPENING PRAYER   [Christian Love]
Let us pray
   [for a greater love of God
   and of our fellow men]
Lord our God,
help us to love you with all our hearts
and to love all men as you love them.
Grant this through our Lord Jesus Christ, your Son,
who lives and reigns with you and the Holy Spirit,
one God, for ever and ever. ℟. **Amen.** ↓

ALTERNATIVE OPENING PRAYER   [Praise of God]

Let us pray
  [joining in the praise of the living God
  for we are his people]
Father in heaven,
from the days of Abraham and Moses
until this gathering of your Church in prayer,
you have formed a people in the image of your Son.
Bless this people with the gift of your kingdom.
May we serve you with our every desire
and show love for one another
even as you have loved us.
Grant this through Christ our Lord. ℟. **Amen.** ↓

FIRST READING Zep 2:3; 3:12-13   [Seek the Lord]

The Lord is to be found among a people who are humble
and lowly. Those who are humble seek after God. They
shall find repose in him.

A reading from the Book of the Prophet Zephaniah

SEEK the LORD, all you humble of the earth,
  who have observed his law;
seek justice, seek humility;
    perhaps you may be sheltered
    on the day of the LORD's anger.

But I will leave as a remnant in your midst
    a people humble and lowly,
who shall take refuge in the name of the LORD:
    the remnant of Israel.
They shall do no wrong
    and speak no lies;
nor shall there be found in their mouths
    a deceitful tongue;
they shall pasture and couch their flocks
    with none to disturb them.
The word of the Lord. ℟. **Thanks be to God.** ↓

RESPONSORIAL PSALM Ps 146   [Bounty of the Lord]

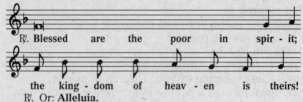

℟. Blessed are the poor in spir - it; the king - dom of heav - en is theirs!
℟. Or: **Alleluia.**

The LORD keeps faith forever,
   secures justice for the oppressed,
   gives food to the hungry.
The Lord sets captives free.—℟.

The LORD give sight to the blind;
   the LORD raises up those who were bowed down.
The LORD loves the just;
   the LORD protects strangers.—℟.

The fatherless and the widow the LORD sustains,
   but the way of the wicked he thwarts.
The LORD shall reign forever;
   your God, O Zion, through all generations. Alleluia.—℟. ↓

SECOND READING 1 Cor 1:26-31   [Boast in the Lord]

**Contrary to worldly standards, God chooses those who are
weak, lowborn and despised. To these God has given his
own Son, Jesus, for sanctification and redemption.**

A reading from the first Letter of Saint Paul
to the Corinthians

CONSIDER your own calling, brothers and sisters.
Not many of you were wise by human standards,
not many were powerful, not many were of noble
birth. Rather, God chose the foolish of the world to
shame the wise, and God chose the weak of the world
to shame the strong, and God chose the lowly and
despised of the world, those who count for nothing, to
reduce to nothing those who are something, so that no

human being might boast before God. It is due to him
that you are in Christ Jesus, who became for us wisdom from God, as well as righteousness, sanctification, and redemption, so that, as it is written, "Whoever
boasts, should boast in the Lord."—The word of the
Lord. ℞. **Thanks be to God.** ↓

ALLELUIA Mt 5:12a   [Rejoice and Be Glad]

℞. **Alleluia, alleluia.**
Rejoice and be glad;
your reward will be great in heaven.
℞. **Alleluia, alleluia.** ↓

GOSPEL Mt 5:1-12a   [A New Teaching]

Jesus says that the poor in spirit, the sorrowing, those
thirsting for holiness, the merciful, the peacemakers, and
those who suffer for holiness' sake are "blessed"—their
reward awaits them in heaven.

℣. The Lord be with you. ℞. **And also with you.**
✛ A reading from the holy Gospel according to
Matthew. ℞. **Glory to you, Lord.**

WHEN Jesus saw the crowds, he went up the
mountain, and after he had sat down, his disci-
ples came to him. He began to teach them, saying:
"Blessed are the poor in spirit,
    for theirs is the kingdom of heaven.
Blessed are they who mourn,
    for they will be comforted.
Blessed are the meek,
    for they will inherit the land.
Blessed are they who hunger and thirst for
        righteousness,
    for they will be satisfied.
Blessed are the merciful,
    for they will be shown mercy.
Blessed are the clean of heart,
    for they will see God.

Blessed are the peacemakers,
     for they will be called children of God.
Blessed are they who are persecuted for the sake
     of righteousness,
     for theirs is the kingdom of heaven.
Blessed are you when they insult you and persecute
you and utter every kind of slander against you
falsely because of me. Rejoice and be glad, for your
reward will be great in heaven."—The Gospel of the
Lord. ℟. **Praise to you, Lord Jesus Christ.**

→ No. 14, p. 18

PRAYER OVER THE GIFTS   [Sacrament of Salvation]

Lord,
be pleased with the gifts we bring to your altar,
and make them the sacrament of our salvation.
We ask this through Christ our Lord.
℟. **Amen.**   → No. 21, p. 22 (Pref. P 29-36)

COMMUNION ANT. Ps 31:17-18   [Save Me]
**Let your face shine on your servant, and save me by
your love. Lord, keep me from shame, for I have
called to you. ↓**

OR Mt 5:3-4   [Poor in Spirit]
**Happy are the poor in spirit; the kingdom of heaven
is theirs! Happy are the lowly; they shall inherit the
land. ↓**

PRAYER AFTER COMMUNION   [True Faith]

Lord,
you invigorate us with this help to our salvation.
By this eucharist give the true faith continued growth
throughout the world.
We ask this in the name of Jesus the Lord.
℟. **Amen.**   → No. 32, p. 70

Optional Solemn Blessings, p. 92, and Prayers Over the People, p. 99

"You are the light of the world."

FEBRUARY 6

5th SUNDAY IN ORDINARY TIME

ENTRANCE ANT. Ps 95:6-7 [Adoration]

Come, let us worship the Lord. Let us bow down in the presence of our maker, for he is the Lord our God. ➜ No. 2, p. 10

OPENING PRAYER [God's Care]

Let us pray
   [that God will watch over us and protect us]
Father,
watch over your family
and keep us safe in your care,
for all our hope is in you.
Grant this through our Lord Jesus Christ, your Son,
who lives and reigns with you and the Holy Spirit,
one God, for ever and ever. ℟. **Amen.** ↓

ALTERNATIVE OPENING PRAYER [God's Presence]

Let us pray
   [with reverence in the presence of the living God]
In faith and love we ask you, Father,
to watch over your family gathered here.

185

In your mercy and loving kindness
no thought of ours is left unguarded,
no tear unheeded, no joy unnoticed.
Through the prayer of Jesus
may the blessings promised to the poor in spirit
lead us to the treasures of your heavenly kingdom.
We ask this in the name of Jesus the Lord. ℟. **Amen.** ↓

FIRST READING Is 58:7-10   [Charity]

**The Lord promises that those who share their food with
the hungry and their clothing with the naked shall find true
favor with him. A light shall shine for them.**

A reading from the Book of the Prophet Isaiah

THUS says the LORD:
Share your bread with the hungry,
    shelter the oppressed and the homeless;
clothe the naked when you see them,
    and do not turn your back on your own.
Then your light shall break forth like the dawn,
    and your wound shall quickly be healed;
your vindication shall go before you,
    and the glory of the LORD shall be your rear guard.
Then you shall call, and the LORD will answer,
    you shall cry for help, and he will say: Here I am!
If you remove from your midst
    oppression, false accusation and malicious speech;
if you bestow your bread on the hungry
    and satisfy the afflicted;
then light shall rise for you in the darkness,
    and the gloom shall become for you like midday.
The word of the Lord. ℟. **Thanks be to God.** ↓

RESPONSORIAL PSALM Ps 112   [The Just Man]

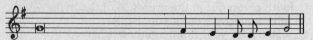

℟. **The just man is a light in dark-ness to the up - right.**

℟. Or: **Alleluia.**

Light shines through the darkness, for the upright;
    he is gracious and merciful and just.
Well for the man who is gracious and lends,
    who conducts his affairs with justice.—℟.

He shall never be moved;
    the just man shall be in everlasting remembrance.
An evil report he shall not fear;
    his heart is firm, trusting in the LORD.—℟.

His heart is steadfast; he shall not fear.
    Lavishly he gives to the poor;
his justice shall endure forever;
    his horn shall be exalted in glory.—℟. ↓

SECOND READING 1 Cor 2:1-5   [Power of the Spirit]

Paul preached to the Corinthians in weakness and fear. He preached Jesus crucified, but through the working of the Holy Spirit, these people came to be believers.

A reading from the first Letter of Saint Paul
to the Corinthians

WHEN I came to you, brothers and sisters, proclaiming the mystery of God, I did not come with sublimity of words or of wisdom. For I resolved to know nothing while I was with you except Jesus Christ, and him crucified. I came to you in weakness and fear and much trembling, and my message and my proclamation were not with persuasive words of wisdom, but with a demonstration of Spirit and power, so that your faith might rest not on human wisdom but on the power of God.—The word of the Lord. ℟. **Thanks be to God.** ↓

ALLELUIA Jn 8:12   [Light of Life]
℟. **Alleluia, alleluia.**
I am the light of the world, says the Lord;

whoever follows me will have the light of life.
℟. **Alleluia, alleluia.** ↓

GOSPEL Mt 5:13-16   [Light of the World]
> The faithful followers of Jesus are the salt of the earth and
> a light to the world. Being true Christ-believers, they
> become an example for others.

℣. The Lord be with you. ℟. **And also with you.**
✠ A reading from the holy Gospel according to
Matthew. ℟. **Glory to you, Lord.**

JESUS said to his disciples: "You are the salt of the
earth. But if salt loses its taste, with what can it be
seasoned? It is no longer good for anything but to be
thrown out and trampled underfoot. You are the light
of the world. A city set on a mountain cannot be hidden. Nor do they light a lamp and then put it under a
bushel basket; it is set on a lampstand, where it gives
light to all in the house. Just so, your light must shine
before others, that they may see your good deeds and
glorify your heavenly Father."—The Gospel of the
Lord. ℟. **Praise to you, Lord Jesus Christ.**

→ No. 14, p. 18

PRAYER OVER THE GIFTS   [Eternal Life]
Lord our God,
may the bread and wine
you give us for our nourishment on earth
become the sacrament of our eternal life.
We ask this through Christ our Lord.
℟. **Amen.**   → No. 21, p. 22 (Pref. P 29-36)

COMMUNION ANT. Ps 107:8-9   [The Lord's Kindness]
**Give praise to the Lord for his kindness, for his won-
derful deeds toward men. He has filled the hungry
with good things, he has satisfied the thirsty.** ↓

OR Mt 5:5-6   [The Sorrowing]

Happy are the sorrowing; they shall be consoled. Happy those who hunger and thirst for what is right; they shall be satisfied. ↓

PRAYER AFTER COMMUNION   [Salvation and Joy]

God our Father,
you give us a share in the one bread and the one cup
and make us one in Christ.
Help us to bring your salvation and joy
to all the world.
We ask this through Christ our Lord.
℟. **Amen.**   ➜ No. 32, p. 70

Optional Solemn Blessings, p. 92, and Prayers Over the People, p. 99

"Go first and be reconciled with your brother."

FEBRUARY 13

6th SUNDAY IN ORDINARY TIME

ENTRANCE ANT. Ps 31:3-4   [Rock of Safety]

Lord, be my rock of safety, the stronghold that saves me. For the honor of your name, lead me and guide me.   ➜ No. 2, p. 10

OPENING PRAYER   [Living in God's Presence]

Let us pray
   [that everything we do
   will be guided by God's law of love]
God our Father,
you have promised to remain for ever
with those who do what is just and right.
Help us to live in your presence.
We ask this through our Lord Jesus Christ, your Son,
who lives and reigns with you and the Holy Spirit,
one God, for ever and ever. ℟. **Amen.** ↓

ALTERNATIVE OPENING PRAYER   [God's Wisdom]

Let us pray
   [for the wisdom that is greater than human words]
Father in heaven,
the loving plan of your wisdom took flesh in Jesus Christ,
and changed mankind's history
by his command of perfect love.
May our fulfillment of his command reflect your wisdom
and bring your salvation to the ends of the earth.
We ask this through Christ our Lord. ℟. **Amen.** ↓

FIRST READING Sir 15:15-20   [Freedom To Do Good]

**God is all-knowing, always aware of everything that we
do. All persons are free to choose to do God's will, for God
uses no force.**

A reading from the Book of Sirach

IF you choose you can keep the commandments, they
   will save you;
   if you trust in God, you too shall live;
he has set before you fire and water;
   to whichever you choose, stretch forth your hand.
Before man are life and death, good and evil,
   whichever he chooses shall be given him.

Immense is the wisdom of the Lord;
  he is mighty in power, and all–seeing.
The eyes of God are on those who fear him;
  he understands man's every deed.
No one does he command to act unjustly,
  to none does he give license to sin.
The word of the Lord. ℟. **Thanks be to God.** ↓

RESPONSORIAL PSALM Ps 119   [Following God's Law]

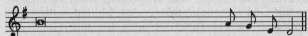

  ℟. **Blessed are they who follow the law of the Lord!**

Blessed are they whose way is blameless,
  who walk in the law of the Lᴏʀᴅ.
Blessed are they who observe his decrees,
  who seek him with all their heart.

℟. **Blessed are they who follow the law of the Lord!**

You have commanded that your precepts
  be diligently kept.
Oh, that I might be firm in the ways
  of keeping your statutes!

℟. **Blessed are they who follow the law of the Lord!**

Be good to your servant, that I may live
  and keep your words.
Open my eyes, that I may consider
  the wonders of your law.

℟. **Blessed are they who follow the law of the Lord!**

Instruct me, O Lᴏʀᴅ, in the way of your statutes,
  that I may exactly observe them.
Give me discernment, that I may observe your law
  and keep it with all my heart.

℟. **Blessed are they who follow the law of the Lord!** ↓

SECOND READING 1 Cor 2:6-10   [God's Wisdom]

Out of wisdom that is beyond our imagination, God has revealed the Divinity through the Holy Spirit. The Spirit knows the inner workings of God.

A reading from the first Letter of Saint Paul
to the Corinthians

BROTHERS and sisters: We speak a wisdom to those who are mature, not a wisdom of this age, nor of the rulers of this age who are passing away. Rather, we speak God's wisdom, mysterious, hidden, which God predetermined before the ages for our glory, and which none of the rulers of this age knew; for, if they had known it, they would not have crucified the Lord of glory. But as it is written:

What eye has not seen, and ear has not heard,
and what has not entered the human heart,
what God has prepared for those who love him,
this God has revealed to us through the Spirit.

For the Spirit scrutinizes everything, even the depths of God.—The word of the Lord. ℟. **Thanks be to God.** ↓

ALLELUIA Cf. Mt 11:25   [The Kingdom]
℟. **Alleluia, alleluia.**
Blessed are you, Father, Lord of heaven and earth;
you have revealed to little ones the mysteries of the
    kingdom.
℟. **Alleluia, alleluia.** ↓

GOSPEL Mt 5:17-37 or 5:20-22a, 27-28, 33-34a, 37 [Holiness]

God revealed the divine law to the Israelites, and Jesus came to bring it to perfection. Those who obey God's laws will become great in the kingdom of God. Jesus explains more fully the laws of God.

[If the "Shorter Form" is used, omit indented text in brackets.]

℣. The Lord be with you. ℟. **And also with you.**
✚ A reading from the holy Gospel according to Matthew. ℟. **Glory to you, Lord.**

JESUS said to his disciples:
[“Do not think that I have come to abolish the law or the prophets. I have come not to abolish but to fulfill. Amen, I say to you, until heaven and earth pass away, not the smallest letter or the smallest part of a letter will pass from the law, until all things have taken place. Therefore, whoever breaks one of the least of these commandments and teaches others to do so will be called least in the kingdom of heaven. But whoever obeys and teaches these commandments will be called greatest in the kingdom of heaven.]

“I tell you, unless your righteousness surpasses that of the scribes and Pharisees, you will not enter the kingdom of heaven.

“You have heard that it was said to your ancestors, *You shall not kill; and whoever kills will be liable to judgment.* But I say to you, whoever is angry with his brother will be liable to judgment;

[and whoever says to his brother, ‘Raqa,’ will be answerable to the Sanhedrin; and whoever says, ‘You fool,’ will be liable to fiery Gehenna. Therefore, if you bring your gift to the altar, and there recall that your brother has anything against you, leave your gift there at the altar, go first and be reconciled with your brother, and then come and offer your gift. Settle with your opponent quickly while on the way to court. Otherwise your opponent will hand you over to the judge, and the judge will hand you over to the guard, and you will be thrown into prison. Amen, I say to you, you will not be released until you have paid the last penny.]

"You have heard that it was said, *You shall not commit adultery.* But I say to you, everyone who looks at a woman with lust has already committed adultery with her in his heart.

["If your right eye causes you to sin, tear it out and throw it away. It is better for you to lose one of your members than to have your whole body thrown into Gehenna. And if your right hand causes you to sin, cut it off and throw it away. It is better for you to lose one of your members than to have your whole body go into Gehenna.

"It was also said, *Whoever divorces his wife must give her a bill of divorce.* But I say to you, whoever divorces his wife—unless the marriage is unlawful—causes her to commit adultery, and whoever marries a divorced woman commits adultery.]

"Again you have heard that it was said to your ancestors, *Do not take a false oath, but make good to the Lord all that you vow.* But I say to you, do not swear at all;

[not by heaven, for it is God's throne; nor by the earth, for it is his footstool; nor by Jerusalem, for it is the city of the great King. Do not swear by your head, for you cannot make a single hair white or black.]

Let your 'Yes' mean 'Yes,' and your 'No' mean 'No.' Anything more is from the evil one." —The Gospel of the Lord. ℟. **Praise to you, Lord Jesus Christ.**

→ No. 14, p. 18

PRAYER OVER THE GIFTS   [Obedience]

Lord,
we make this offering in obedience to your word.
May it cleanse and renew us,
and lead us to our eternal reward.

We ask this in the name of Jesus the Lord.
℟. **Amen.**   ➜ No. 21, p. 22 (Pref. P 29-36)

COMMUNION ANT. Ps 78:29-30   [God's Food]

They ate and were filled; the Lord gave them what they wanted: they were not deprived of their desire. ↓

OR Jn 3:16   [God's Love]

God loved the world so much, he gave his only Son, that all who believe in him might not perish, but might have eternal life. ↓

PRAYER AFTER COMMUNION   [Bread of Life]

Lord,
you give us food from heaven.
May we always hunger
for the bread of life.
Grant this through Christ our Lord.
℟. **Amen.**   ➜ No. 32, p. 70

Optional Solemn Blessings, p. 92, and Prayers Over the People, p. 99

*"If anyone wants to go to law over your shirt,
offer him your coat as well."*

FEBRUARY 20

7th SUNDAY IN ORDINARY TIME

ENTRANCE ANT. Ps 13:6   **[God's Mercy]**
**Lord, your mercy is my hope, my heart rejoices in
your saving power. I will sing to the Lord for his goodness to me.**   → No. 2, p. 10

OPENING PRAYER   **[Imitating Christ]**
Let us pray
    [that God will make us more like Christ, his Son]
Father,
keep before us the wisdom and love
you have revealed in your Son.
Help us to be like him
in word and deed,
for he lives and reigns with you and the Holy Spirit,
one God, for ever and ever. ℟. **Amen.** ↓

ALTERNATIVE OPENING PRAYER   **[God's Life]**
Let us pray
    [to the God of power and might,
    for his mercy is our hope]

Almighty God,
Father of our Lord Jesus Christ,
faith in your word is the way to wisdom,
and to ponder your divine plan is to grow in the truth.
Open our eyes to your deeds,
our ears to the sound of your call,
so that our every act may increase our sharing
in the life you have offered us.
Grant this through Christ our Lord. ℟. **Amen.** ↓

FIRST READING Lev 19:1-2, 17-18   [Love of Neighbor]

Our inner attitude before God has a fraternal dimension. We must be holy because God is holy.

A reading from the Book of Leviticus

THE LORD said to Moses, "Speak to the whole Israelite community and tell them: Be holy, for I, the LORD, your God, am holy.

"You shall not bear hatred for your brother or sister in your heart. Though you may have to reprove your fellow citizen, do not incur sin because of him. Take no revenge and cherish no grudge against any of your people. You shall love your neighbor as yourself. I am the LORD."—The word of the Lord. ℟. **Thanks be to God.** ↓

RESPONSORIAL PSALM Ps 103   [Plea for Pardon]

℟. The Lord is kind and mer - ci - ful.

Bless the LORD, O my soul;
    and all my being, bless his holy name.
Bless the LORD, O my soul,
    and forget not all his benefits.

℟. **The Lord is kind and merciful.**

He pardons all your iniquities,
    he heals all your ills.
He redeems your life from destruction,
    he crowns you with kindness and compassion.

℞. **The Lord is kind and merciful.**

Merciful and gracious is the LORD,
    slow to anger and abounding in kindness.
Not according to our sins does he deal with us,
    nor does he requite us according to our crimes.

℞. **The Lord is kind and merciful.**

As far as the east is from the west,
    so far has he put our transgressions from us.
As a father has compassion on his children,
    so the LORD has compassion on those who fear
        him.

℞. **The Lord is kind and merciful.** ↓

SECOND READING 1 Cor 3:16-23   **[Temple of God]**

   **The Christian community is the temple of God and so is
   each Christian. Hence, respect is owed the community and
   each member.**

A reading from the first Letter of Paul
to the Corinthians

BROTHERS and sisters: Do you not know that you
are the temple of God, and that the Spirit of God
dwells in you? If anyone destroys God's temple, God
will destroy that person; for the temple of God, which
you are, is holy.

   Let no one deceive himself. If any one among you
considers himself wise in this age, let him become a
fool, so as to become wise. For the wisdom of this
world is foolishness in the eyes of God, for it is written:
   God catches the wise in their own ruses,
and again:

*The Lord knows the thoughts of the wise, that they
are vain.*

So let no one boast about human beings, for everything belongs to you, Paul or Apollos or Cephas, or the
world or life or death, or the present or the future: all
belong to you, and you to Christ, and Christ to God.—
The word of the Lord. ℟. **Thanks be to God.** ↓

ALLELUIA 1 Jn 2:5   [Perfected in Love]

℟. **Alleluia, alleluia.**
Whoever keeps the word of Christ,
the love of God is truly perfected in him.
℟. **Alleluia, alleluia.** ↓

GOSPEL Mt 5:38-48   [Love of Enemies]

**We are called not to encourage another's injustice but to
avoid vengeance. We must desire good things for others
in spite of any evil they may do us.**

℣. The Lord be with you. ℟. **And also with you.**
✛   A reading from the holy Gospel according to
Matthew. ℟. **Glory to you, Lord.**

JESUS said to his disciples: "You have heard that it
was said, *An eye for an eye and a tooth for a tooth.*
But I say to you, offer no resistance to one who is evil.
When someone strikes you on your right cheek, turn
the other one as well. If anyone wants to go to law with
you over your tunic, hand over your cloak as well.
Should anyone press you into service for one mile, go
for two miles. Give to the one who asks of you, and do
not turn your back on one who wants to borrow.

    "You have heard that it was said, *You shall love your
neighbor and hate your enemy.* But I say to you, love
your enemies and pray for those who persecute you,
that you may be children of your heavenly Father, for
he makes his sun rise on the bad and the good, and
causes rain to fall on the just and the unjust. For if you

love those who love you, what recompense will you have? Do not the tax collectors do the same? And if you greet your brothers only, what is unusual about that? Do not the pagans do the same? So be perfect, just as your heavenly Father is perfect."—The Gospel of the Lord. ℟. **Praise to you, Lord Jesus Christ.**

→ No. 14, p. 18

PRAYER OVER THE GIFTS   [Spirit and Truth]

Lord,
as we make this offering,
may our worship in Spirit and truth
bring us salvation.
We ask this in the name of Jesus the Lord.
℟. **Amen.**   → No. 21, p. 22 (Pref. P 29-36)

COMMUNION ANT. Ps 9:2-3   [Joy in God]

I will tell all your marvelous works. I will rejoice and be glad in you, and sing to your name, Most High. ↓

OR Jn 11:27   [Belief in Christ]

Lord, I believe that you are the Christ, the Son of God, who was to come into this world. ↓

PRAYER AFTER COMMUNION   [Example of Love]

Almighty God,
help us to live the example of love
we celebrate in this eucharist,
that we may come to its fulfillment in your presence.
We ask this through Christ our Lord.
℟. **Amen.**   → No. 32, p. 70

Optional Solemn Blessings, p. 92, and Prayers Over the People, p. 99

"Learn a lesson from the way the wild flowers grow."

FEBRUARY 27

8th SUNDAY IN ORDINARY TIME

ENTRANCE ANT. Ps 18:19-20   [God Our Strength]
The Lord has been my strength; he has led me into freedom. He saved me because he loves me.

→ No. 2, p. 10

OPENING PRAYER   [Freedom]

Let us pray
 [that God will bring peace to the world
  and freedom to his Church]
Lord,
guide the course of world events
and give your Church the joy and peace
of serving you in freedom.
We ask this through our Lord Jesus Christ, your Son,
who lives and reigns with you and the Holy Spirit,
one God, for ever and ever. ℟. **Amen.** ↓

ALTERNATIVE OPENING PRAYER   [Peace]

Let us pray
 [that the peace of Christ
  may find welcome in the world]

Father in heaven,
form in us the likeness of your Son
and deepen his life within us.
Send us as witnesses of gospel joy
into a world of fragile peace and broken promises.
Touch the hearts of all men with your love
that they in turn may love one another.
We ask this through Christ our Lord. ℟. **Amen.** ↓

FIRST READING Is 49:14-15   [God's Faithfulness]

**Although at times God seems far from us, He is ever near.
No matter what evils may overtake us, God will never forget us.**

A reading from the Book of the Prophet Isaiah

Z ION said, "The LORD has forsaken me;
my LORD has forgotten me."
Can a mother forget her infant,
  be without tenderness for the child of her womb?
Even should she forget,
  I will never forget you.
The word of the Lord. ℟. **Thanks be to God.** ↓

RESPONSORIAL PSALM Ps 62   [Trust in God]

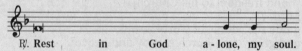

℟. Rest   in   God   a - lone, my   soul.

Only in God is my soul at rest;
  from him comes my salvation.
He only is my rock and my salvation,
  my stronghold; I shall not be disturbed at all.

℟. **Rest in God alone, my soul.**

Only in God be at rest, my soul,
  for from him comes my hope.
He only is my rock and my salvation,
  my stronghold; I shall not be disturbed.

℞. **Rest in God alone, my soul.**

With God is my safety and my glory,
　he is the rock of my strength; my refuge is in God.
Trust in him at all times, O my people!
　Pour out your hearts before him.

℞. **Rest in God alone, my soul.** ↓

SECOND READING 1 Cor 4:1-5　　　　**[God Our Judge]**

It is not for us to pass judgment on others. Christ will
judge all at the time of His second coming.

A reading from the first Letter of Paul
to the Corinthians

BROTHERS and sisters: Thus should one regard us:
as servants of Christ and stewards of the mysteries
of God. Now it is of course required of stewards that
they be found trustworthy. It does not concern me in
the least that I be judged by you or any human tribu-
nal; I do not even pass judgment on myself; I am not
conscious of anything against me, but I do not thereby
stand acquitted; the one who judges me is the Lord.
Therefore do not make any judgment before the
appointed time, until the Lord comes, for he will bring
to light what is hidden in darkness and will manifest
the motives of our hearts, and then everyone will
receive praise from God.—The word of the Lord. ℞.
Thanks be to God. ↓

ALLELUIA Heb 4:12　　　　**[Living Word]**

℞. **Alleluia, alleluia.**
The word of God is living and effective,
discerning reflections and thoughts of the heart.
℞. **Alleluia, alleluia.** ↓

GOSPEL Mt 6:24-34　　　　**[Trust in God]**

Irrational concern for the things of the world hinders our
spiritual good. We must live each day in total trust in God.

℣. The Lord be with you. ℟. **And also with you.**

✝ A reading from the holy Gospel according to Matthew. ℟. **Glory to you, Lord.**

JESUS said to his disciples: "No one can serve two masters. He will either hate one and love the other, or be devoted to one and despise the other. You cannot serve God and mammon.

"Therefore I tell you, do not worry about your life, what you will eat or drink, or about your body, what you will wear. Is not life more than food and the body more than clothing? Look at the birds in the sky; they do not sow or reap, they gather nothing into barns, yet your heavenly Father feeds them. Are not you more important than they? Can any of you by worrying add a single moment to your life-span? Why are you anxious about clothes? Learn from the way the wild flowers grow. They do not work or spin. But I tell you that not even Solomon in all his splendor was clothed like one of them. If God so clothes the grass of the field, which grows today and is thrown into the oven tomorrow, will he not much more provide for you, O you of little faith? So do not worry and say, 'What are we to eat?' or 'What are we to drink?' or 'What are we to wear?' All these things the pagans seek. Your heavenly Father knows that you need them all. But seek first the kingdom of God and his righteousness, and all these things will be given you besides. Do not worry about tomorrow; tomorrow will take care of itself. Sufficient for a day is its own evil."—The Gospel of the Lord. ℟. **Praise to you, Lord Jesus Christ.**   → No. 14, p. 18

PRAYER OVER THE GIFTS   [Sign of Worship]

God our Creator,
may this bread and wine we offer
as a sign of our love and worship

lead us to salvation.
Grant this through Christ our Lord.
℟. **Amen.**   ➙ No. 21, p. 22 (Pref. P 29-36)

COMMUNION ANT. Ps 13:6   [God's Goodness]
I will sing to the Lord for his goodness to me, I will sing the name of the Lord, Most High. ↓

OR Mt 28:20   [Christ's Presence]
I, the Lord, am with you always, until the end of the world. ↓

PRAYER AFTER COMMUNION   [Strength and Life]
God of salvation,
may this sacrament which strengthens us here on earth
bring us to eternal life.
We ask this in the name of Jesus the Lord.
℟. **Amen.**   ➙ No. 32, p. 70

Optional Solemn Blessings, p. 92, and Prayers Over the People, p. 99

"Only the one who does the will of my Father"
will enter the kingdom of heaven.

MARCH 6

9th SUNDAY IN ORDINARY TIME

ENTRANCE ANT. Ps 25:16, 18   [Be Merciful]
**O look at me and be merciful, for I am wretched and
alone. See my hardship and my poverty, and pardon
all my sins.**   → No. 2, p. 10

OPENING PRAYER   [God's Care]

Let us pray
   [for God's care and protection]
Father,
your love never fails.
Hear our call.
Keep us from danger
and provide for all our needs.
Grant this through our Lord Jesus Christ, your Son,
who lives and reigns with you and the Holy Spirit,
one God, for ever and ever.
℟. **Amen.** ↓

ALTERNATIVE OPENING PRAYER   [Increase Our Faith]

Let us pray
   [for the confidence born of faith]

God our Father,
teach us to cherish the gifts that surround us.
Increase our faith in you
and bring our trust to its promised fulfillment
in the joy of your kingdom.
Grant this through Christ our Lord.
℟. **Amen.** ↓

FIRST READING Dt 11:18, 26-28, 32 [Obey the Commandments]

> The Book of Deuteronomy (Second Law) is a series of sermons or meditations on the Law of Moses. It stresses honesty. "You shall put these words of mine into your heart and soul." We should heed honesty when we read the Bible. We know that Scripture never tells a story merely for a story's sake. It always wants to bring out a point, which is God's word to the reader.

A reading from the Book of Deuteronomy

MOSES told the people, "Take these words of mine into your heart and soul. Bind them at your wrist as a sign, and let them be a pendant on your forehead.

"I set before you here, this day, a blessing and a curse: a blessing for obeying the commandments of the LORD, your God, which I enjoin on you today; a curse if you do not obey the commandments of the LORD, your God, but turn aside from the way I ordain for you today, to follow other gods, whom you have not known. Be careful to observe all the statutes and decrees that I set before you today."—The word of the Lord. ℟. **Thanks be to God.** ↓

RESPONSORIAL PSALM Ps 31   [God Our Help]

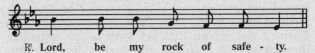

℟. Lord,   be   my   rock   of   safe - ty.

In you, O LORD, I take refuge;
let me never be put to shame.
In your justice rescue me,
incline your ear to me,
make haste to deliver me!

℟. **Lord, be my rock of safety.**

Be my rock of refuge,
a stronghold to give me safety.
You are my rock and my fortress;
for your name's sake you will lead and guide me.

℟. **Lord, be my rock of safety.**

Let your face shine upon your servant;
save me in your kindness.
Take courage and be stouthearted,
all you who hope in the LORD.

℟. **Lord, be my rock of safety.** ↓

SECOND READING Rom 3:21-25, 28 [Justification by Faith]

Faith, like love, is a total surrender of self to God. If you truly love and have real faith in God, you do not ask: "What must I do to avoid trouble?"; you are constantly concerned about what you can do to please the beloved, i.e., God. Paul explains beautifully: "Love is the fulfillment of the law" (Rom 13:10). Keep this in mind also when you read the Gospel.

A reading from the Letter of Saint Paul to the Romans

BROTHERS and sisters: Now the righteousness of God has been manifested apart from the law, though testified to by the law and the prophets, the righteousness of God through faith in Jesus Christ for all who believe. For there is no distinction; all have sinned and are deprived of the glory of God. They are justified freely by his grace through the redemption in Christ Jesus, whom God set forth as an expiation, through faith, by his blood. For we consider that a person is justified by faith apart from works of the law.— The word of the Lord. ℟. **Thanks be to God.** ↓

ALLELUIA Jn 15:5   [Fruitful Union with Christ]

℟. **Alleluia, alleluia.**
I am the vine, you are the branches, says the Lord, whoever remains in me and I in him will bear much fruit.
℟. **Alleluia, alleluia.** ↓

GOSPEL Mt 7:21-27   [Gaining the Kingdom]

Jesus finishes the Sermon on the Mount by warning against hypocrisy. We find it everywhere and not least in religion. This does not mean that we can do without religion. It means that those who practice religion should constantly check whether they are being honest.

℣. The Lord be with you. ℟. **And also with you.**
✝ A reading from the holy Gospel according to Matthew. ℟. **Glory to you, Lord.**

JESUS said to his disciples:"Not everyone who says to me, 'Lord, Lord,' will enter the kingdom of heaven, but only the one who does the will of my Father in heaven. Many will say to me on that day, 'Lord, Lord, did we not prophesy in your name? Did we not drive out demons in your name? Did we not do mighty deeds in your name?' Then I will declare to them solemnly, 'I never knew you. Depart from me, you evildoers.'

"Everyone who listens to these words of mine and acts on them will be like a wise man who built his house on rock. The rain fell, the floods came, and the winds blew and buffeted the house. But it did not collapse; it had been set solidly on rock. And everyone who listens to these words of mine but does not act on them will be like a fool who built his house on sand. The rain fell, the floods came, and the winds blew and buffeted the house. And it collapsed and was completely ruined."—The Gospel of the Lord. R̸. **Praise to you, Lord Jesus Christ.**   → No. 14, p. 18

PRAYER OVER THE GIFTS   [Holiness]

Lord,
as we gather to offer our gifts
confident in your love,
make us holy by sharing your life with us
and by this eucharist forgive our sins.
We ask this through Christ our Lord.
R̸. **Amen.**   → No. 21, p. 22 (Pref. P 29-36)

COMMUNION ANT. Ps 17:6   [Confident Prayer]

I call upon you, God, for you will answer me; bend your ear and hear my prayer. ↓

OR Mk 11:23-24   [Productive Prayer]

I tell you solemnly, whatever you ask for in prayer, believe that you have received it, and it will be yours, says the Lord. ↓

PRAYER AFTER COMMUNION   [Guidance of the Spirit]

Lord,
as you give us the body and blood of your Son,
guide us with your Spirit
that we may honor you
not only with our lips,
but also with the lives we lead,
and so enter your kingdom.
We ask this in the name of Jesus the Lord.
R̸. **Amen.**   → No. 32, p. 70

Optional Solemn Blessings, p. 92, and Prayers Over the People, p. 99

"One does not live on bread alone."

MARCH 13

1st SUNDAY OF LENT

ENTRANCE ANT. Ps 91:15-16 [Long Life]

When he calls to me, I will answer; I will rescue him and give him honor. Long life and contentment will be his. ➡ No. 2, p. 10 (Omit Gloria)

OPENING PRAYER [Christ's Saving Love]

Let us pray
   [that this Lent will help us reproduce in our lives
   the self-sacrificing love of Christ]
Father,
through our observance of Lent,
help us to understand the meaning
of your Son's death and resurrection,
and teach us to reflect it in our lives.
Grant this . . . for ever and ever. ℞. **Amen.** ↓

ALTERNATIVE OPENING PRAYER [Spirit of Repentance]

Let us pray
   [at the beginning of Lent
   for the spirit of repentance]

Lord our God,
you formed man from the clay of the earth
and breathed into him the spirit of life,
but he turned from your face and sinned.
In this time of repentance
we call out for your mercy.
Bring us back to you
and to the life your Son won for us
by his death on the cross,
for he lives and reigns for ever and ever. ℟. **Amen.** ↓

FIRST READING Gn 2:7-9; 3:1-7   [Sin of Our First Parents]

God created Adam and Eve and placed them in the luxurious Garden of Eden. They could eat fruit from every tree except one. After being tempted by the devil, Eve—then Adam—disobeyed God's command. Immediately their lives changed.

A reading from the Book of Genesis

THE LORD God formed man out of the clay of the ground and blew into his nostrils the breath of life, and so man became a living being.

Then the LORD God planted a garden in Eden, in the east, and placed there the man whom he had formed. Out of the ground the LORD God made various trees grow that were delightful to look at and good for food, with the tree of life in the middle of the garden and the tree of the knowledge of good and evil.

Now the serpent was the most cunning of all the animals that the LORD God had made. The serpent asked the woman, "Did God really tell you not to eat from any of the trees in the garden?" The woman answered the serpent: "We may eat of the fruit of the trees in the garden; it is only about the fruit of the tree in the middle of the garden that God said, 'You shall not eat it or even touch it, lest you die.' " But the serpent said to the woman: "You certainly will not die! No, God knows well that the moment you eat of it you will be like gods who

know what is good and what is evil."The woman saw
that the tree was good for food, pleasing to the eyes,
and desirable for gaining wisdom. So she took some of
its fruit and ate it; and she also gave some to her husband, who was with her, and he ate it. Then the eyes of
both of them were opened, and they realized that they
were naked; so they sewed fig leaves together and
made loincloths for themselves.—The word of the
Lord. ℟. **Thanks be to God.** ↓

RESPONSORIAL PSALM Ps 51   [Repentance]

℟. Be   merciful,   O Lord,   for we have sinned.

Have mercy on me, O God, in your goodness;
    in the greatness of your compassion wipe out my
        offense.
Thoroughly wash me from my guilt
    and of my sin cleanse me.

℟. **Be merciful, O Lord, for we have sinned.**

For I acknowledge my offense,
    and my sin is before me always:
"Against you only have I sinned,
    and done what is evil in your sight."

℟. **Be merciful, O Lord, for we have sinned.**

A clean heart create for me, O God,
    and a steadfast spirit renew within me.
Cast me not out from your presence,
    and your Holy Spirit take not from me.

℟. **Be merciful, O Lord, for we have sinned.**

Give me back the joy of your salvation,
    and a willing spirit sustain in me.
O Lord, open my lips,
    and my mouth shall proclaim your praise.

℟. **Be merciful, O Lord, for we have sinned.** ↓

SECOND READING Rom 5:12-19 or 5:12, 17-19

[Saved Through Christ]

From the fall of Adam, sin came into the world. God, however, gave the gift of his Son, Jesus. Through him justice was restored. Through the obedience of Jesus, justice comes to all.

[If the "Shorter Form" is used, the indented text in brackets is omitted.]

A reading from the Letter of Saint Paul to the Romans

BROTHERS and sisters: Through one man sin entered the world, and through sin, death, and thus death came to all men, inasmuch as all sinned —
[for up to the time of the law, sin was in the world, though sin is not accounted when there is no law. But death reigned from Adam to Moses, even over those who did not sin after the pattern of the trespass of Adam, who is the type of the one who was to come.

But the gift is not like the transgression. For if by the transgression of the one, the many died, how much more did the grace of God and the gracious gift of the one man Jesus Christ overflow for the many. And the gift is not like the result of the one who sinned. For after one sin there was the judgment that brought condemnation; but the gift, after many transgressions, brought acquittal.]
For if, by the transgression of the one, death came to reign through that one, how much more will those who receive the abundance of grace and of the gift of justification come to reign in life through the one Jesus Christ. In conclusion, just as through one transgression condemnation came upon all, so, through one righteous act, acquittal and life came to all. For just as through the disobedience of the one man the many were made sinners, so, through the obedience of the

one, the many will be made righteous.—The word of
the Lord. ℞. **Thanks be to God.** ↓

VERSE BEFORE THE GOSPEL Mt 4:4b   [Word of Life]

℞. **Praise to you, Lord Jesus Christ, king of endless
    glory!***
One does not live on bread alone;
but on every word that comes forth from the mouth of
    God.
℞. **Praise to you, Lord Jesus Christ, king of endless
    glory!** ↓

GOSPEL Mt 4:1-11   [Temptation]

> **The devil tempted Adam; he also tempts Jesus three
> times, making lavish promises. Jesus rebukes Satan, for
> only God is to be adored.**

℣. The Lord be with you. ℞. **And also with you.**
✠ A reading from the holy Gospel according to
Matthew. ℞. **Glory to you, Lord.**

AT that time Jesus was led by the Spirit into the
desert to be tempted by the devil. He fasted for
forty days and forty nights, and afterwards he was
hungry. The tempter approached and said to him, "If
you are the Son of God, command that these stones
become loaves of bread." He said in reply,
"It is written:
One does not live on bread alone,
    but on every word that comes forth
    from the mouth of God."
Then the devil took him to the holy city, and made him
stand on the parapet of the temple, and said to him, "If
you are the Son of God, throw yourself down. For it is
written:
He will command his angels concerning you
    and with their hands they will support you,
    lest you dash your foot against a stone."

---

* *See p. 16 for other Gospel Acclamations.*

Jesus answered him, "Again it is written,
You shall not put the Lord, your God, to the test."
Then the devil took him up to a very high mountain,
and showed him all the kingdoms of the world in their
magnificence, and he said to him, "All these I shall give
to you, if you will prostrate yourself and worship me."
At this, Jesus said to him, "Get away, Satan! It is
written:
The Lord, your God, shall you worship
and him alone shall you serve."
Then the devil left him and, behold, angels came and
ministered to him.—The Gospel of the Lord. ℟. **Praise
to you, Lord Jesus Christ.**   ➔ No. 14, p. 18

PRAYER OVER THE GIFTS   [Better Lives]

Lord,
make us worthy to bring you these gifts.
May this sacrifice
help to change our lives.
We ask this in the name of Jesus the Lord. ℟. **Amen.** ↓

PREFACE (P 12)   [Christ's Self-Denial]

℣. The Lord be with you. ℟. **And also with you.**
℣. Lift up your hearts. ℟. **We lift them up to the Lord.**
℣. Let us give thanks to the Lord our God. ℟. **It is right
to give him thanks and praise.**

Father, all-powerful and ever-living God,
we do well always and everywhere to give you thanks
through Jesus Christ our Lord.
His fast of forty days
makes this a holy season of self-denial.
By rejecting the devil's temptations
he has taught us
to rid ourselves of the hidden corruption of evil,
and so to share his paschal meal in purity of heart,
until we come to its fulfillment

in the promised land of heaven.
Now we join the angels and the saints
as they sing their unending hymn of praise:

→ No. 23, p. 23

COMMUNION ANT. Mt 4:4   [Life-Giving Word]

**Man does not live on bread alone, but on every word
that comes from the mouth of God. ↓**

OR Ps 91:4   [Refuge in God]

**The Lord will overshadow you, and you will find
refuge under his wings. ↓**

PRAYER AFTER COMMUNION   [Words and Bread of Life]

Father,
you increase our faith and hope,
you deepen our love in this communion.
Help us to live by your words
and to seek Christ, our bread of life,
who is Lord for ever and ever.
℟. **Amen.**   → No. 32, p. 70

Optional Solemn Blessings, p. 92, and Prayers Over the People, p. 99

"Moses and Elijah appeared to them, conversing with him."

MARCH 20

2nd SUNDAY OF LENT

ENTRANCE ANT. Ps 25:6, 3, 22   [God's Mercies]
Remember your mercies, Lord, your tenderness from ages past. Do not let our enemies triumph over us; O God, deliver Israel from all her distress.

OR Ps 27:8-9   [God's Face]
My heart has prompted me to seek your face; I seek it, Lord; do not hide from me. ➜ No. 2, p. 10 (Omit Gloria)

OPENING PRAYER   [Our Response]
Let us pray
  [for the grace to respond
   to the Word of God]
God our Father,
help us to hear your Son.
Enlighten us with your word,
that we may find the way to your glory.
We ask this through our Lord Jesus Christ, your Son,
who lives and reigns with you and the Holy Spirit,
one God, for ever and ever. ℟. **Amen.** ↓

ALTERNATIVE OPENING PRAYER   [Gift of Integrity]

Let us pray
   [in this season of Lent
   for the gift of integrity]
Father of light,
in you is found no shadow of change
but only the fullness of life and limitless truth.
Open our hearts to the voice of your Word
and free us from the original darkness that shadows
   our vision.
Restore our sight that we may look upon your Son
who calls us to repentance and a change of heart,
for he lives and reigns with you for ever and ever.
℟. **Amen.** ↓

FIRST READING Gn 12:1-4a   [Mission of Abraham]

**God calls Abraham and promises to make him a leader of
a great nation whom all will respect.**

A reading from the Book of Genesis

T HE LORD said to Abram: "Go forth from the land of
your kinsfolk and from your father's house to a
land that I will show you.
   "I will make of you a great nation,
     and I will bless you;
   I will make your name great,
     ·so that you will be a blessing.
   I will bless those who bless you
     and curse those who curse you.
   All the communities of the earth
     shall find blessing in you."
Abram went as the LORD directed him.—The word of
the Lord. ℟. **Thanks be to God.** ↓

RESPONSORIAL PSALM Ps 33   [Trust in God]

℟. Lord, let your mercy be   on us, as we place our trust in you.

Upright is the word of the LORD,
　and all his works are trustworthy.
He loves justice and right;
　of the kindness of the LORD the earth is full.

℟. **Lord, let your mercy be on us,
　as we place our trust in you.**

See, the eyes of the LORD are upon those who fear him,
　upon those who hope for his kindness,
to deliver them from death
　and preserve them in spite of famine.

℟. **Lord, let your mercy be on us,
　as we place our trust in you.**

Our soul waits for the LORD,
　who is our help and our shield.
May your kindness, O LORD, be upon us
　who have put our hope in you.

℟. **Lord, let your mercy be on us,
　as we place our trust in you.** ↓

SECOND READING 2 Tm 1:8b-10   [Design of God]

**God has saved us. He has called us to a holy life. He has
brought life to us through the good news of the gospel.**

A reading from the second Letter of Saint Paul
to Timothy

BELOVED: Bear your share of hardship for the
gospel with the strength that comes from God.
He saved us and called us to a holy life, not according
to our works but according to his own design and the
grace bestowed on us in Christ Jesus before time began,
but now made manifest through the appearance of our
savior Christ Jesus, who destroyed death and brought
life and immortality to light through the gospel.—The
word of the Lord. ℟. **Thanks be to God.** ↓

VERSE BEFORE THE GOSPEL Cf. Mt. 17:5 [Beloved Son]

℟. **Praise and honor to you, Lord Jesus Christ!***

From the shining cloud the Father's voice is heard:
This is my beloved Son, hear him.

℟. **Praise and honor to you, Lord Jesus Christ!** ↓

GOSPEL Mt 17:1-9   [Jesus Transfigured]

> Jesus is transfigured before Peter, James and John. God acknowledges his Son and bids the disciples to listen to him. Jesus asks them not to reveal this vision until after the resurrection.

℣. The Lord be with you. ℟. **And also with you.**
✛ A reading from the holy Gospel according to Matthew. ℟. **Glory to you, Lord.**

JESUS took Peter, James, and John his brother, and led them up a high mountain by themselves. And he was transfigured before them; his face shone like the sun and his clothes became white as light. And behold, Moses and Elijah appeared to them, conversing with him. Then Peter said to Jesus in reply, "Lord, it is good that we are here. If you wish, I will make three tents here, one for you, one for Moses, and one for Elijah." While he was still speaking, behold, a bright cloud cast a shadow over them, then from the cloud came a voice that said, "This is my beloved Son, with whom I am well pleased; listen to him." When the disciples heard this, they fell prostrate and were very much afraid. But Jesus came and touched them, saying, "Rise, and do not be afraid." And when the disciples raised their eyes, they saw no one else but Jesus alone.

As they were coming down from the mountain, Jesus charged them, "Do not tell the vision to anyone until the Son of Man has been raised from the dead."— The Gospel of the Lord. ℟. **Praise to you, Lord Jesus Christ.**   → No. 14, p. 18

---

* *See p. 16 for other Gospel Acclamations.*

PRAYER OVER THE GIFTS　　　　[Holiness]

Lord,
make us holy.
May this eucharist take away our sins
that we may be prepared
to celebrate the resurrection.
We ask this in the name of Jesus the Lord. ℟. **Amen.** ↓

PREFACE (P 13)　　　　[Jesus in Glory]

℣. The Lord be with you. ℟. **And also with you.**
℣. Lift up your hearts. ℟. **We lift them up to the Lord.**
℣. Let us give thanks to the Lord our God. ℟. **It is right to give him thanks and praise.**

Father, all-powerful and ever-living God,
we do well always and everywhere to give you thanks
through Jesus Christ our Lord.
On your holy mountain he revealed himself in glory
in the presence of his disciples.
He had already prepared them for his approaching
　death.
He wanted to teach them through the Law and the
　Prophets
that the promised Christ had first to suffer
and so come to the glory of his resurrection.
In our unending joy we echo on earth
the song of the angels in heaven
as they praise your glory for ever.　　➜ No. 23, p. 23

COMMUNION ANT. Mt 17:5　　　　[Son of God]

This is my Son, my beloved, in whom is all my delight: listen to him. ↓

PRAYER AFTER COMMUNION　　　　[Life To Come]

Lord,
we give you thanks for these holy mysteries
which bring to us here on earth
a share in the life to come through Christ our Lord.
℟. **Amen.**　　　　➜ No. 32, p. 70

Optional Solemn Blessings, p. 92, and Prayers Over the People, p. 99

"I am [the Messiah], the one speaking with you."

MARCH 27

3rd SUNDAY OF LENT

The alternative prayers given below are for the Ritual Mass for the First Scrutiny assigned to this Sunday in the Rite of Christian Initiation of Adults. (The chants and readings are the same as those for the 3rd Sunday of Lent.)

ENTRANCE ANT. Ps 25:15-16   **[Eyes on God]**
My eyes are ever fixed on the Lord, for he releases my feet from the snare. O look at me and be merciful, for I am wretched and alone.

OR Ez 36:23-26   **[A New Spirit]**
[Also for First Scrutiny]
I will prove my holiness through you. I will gather you from the ends of the earth; I will pour clean water on you and wash away all your sins. I will give you a new spirit within you, says the Lord.

→ No. 2, p. 10 (Omit Gloria)

OPENING PRAYER   **[Prayer, Fasting, Works]**
Let us pray
   [for confidence in the love of God
   and the strength to overcome all our weakness]

Father,
you have taught us to overcome our sins
by prayer, fasting and works of mercy.
When we are discouraged by our weakness,
give us confidence in your love.
We ask this through our Lord Jesus Christ, your Son,
who lives and reigns with you and the Holy Spirit,
one God, for ever and ever. R̸. **Amen.** ↓

ALTERNATIVE OPENING PRAYER   [A New Heart]

Let us pray
    [to the Father and ask him
    to form a new heart within us]
God of all compassion, Father of all goodness,
to heal the wounds our sins and selfishness bring upon
    us
you bid us turn to fasting, prayer, and sharing with our
    brothers.
We acknowledge our sinfulness, our guilt is ever
    before us:
when our weakness causes discouragement,
let your compassion fill us with hope
and lead us through a Lent of repentance to the beau-
    ty of Easter joy.
Grant this through Christ our Lord. R̸. **Amen.** ↓

Opening Prayer for First Scrutiny

Lord,   [Growth in Wisdom and Love]
you call these chosen ones
to the glory of a new birth in Christ, the second
    Adam.
Help them grow in wisdom and love
as they prepare to profess their faith in you.
Grant this through our Lord Jesus Christ, your Son,
who lives and reigns with you and the Holy Spirit,
one God, for ever and ever. R̸. **Amen.** ↓

FIRST READING Ex 17:3-7   [Water from Rock]

The Israelites murmured against God in their thirst. God directs Moses to strike a rock with his staff, and water issues forth.

A reading from the Book of Exodus

IN those days, in their thirst for water, the people grumbled against Moses, saying, "Why did you ever make us leave Egypt? Was it just to have us die here of thirst with our children and our livestock?" So Moses cried out to the LORD, "What shall I do with this people? A little more and they will stone me!" The LORD answered Moses, "Go over there in front of the people, along with some of the elders of Israel, holding in your hand, as you go, the staff with which you struck the river. I will be standing there in front of you on the rock in Horeb. Strike the rock, and the water will flow from it for the people to drink." This Moses did, in the presence of the elders of Israel. The place was called Massah and Meribah, because the Israelites quarreled there and tested the LORD, saying, "Is the LORD in our midst or not?"—The word of the Lord. ℟. **Thanks be to God.** ↓

RESPONSORIAL PSALM Ps 95   [The Lord Our Rock]

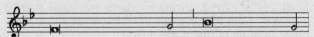

℟. If today you hear his voice, harden not your hearts.

Come, let us sing joyfully to the LORD;
   let us acclaim the Rock of our salvation.
Let us come into his presence with thanksgiving;
   let us joyfully sing psalms to him.

℟. **If today you hear his voice,**
   harden not your hearts.

Come, let us bow down in worship;
  let us kneel before the LORD who made us.
For he is our God,
  and we are the people he shepherds, the flock he
    guides.

℟. **If today you hear his voice,**
  harden not your hearts.

Oh, that today you would hear his voice:
  "Harden not your hearts as at Meribah,
  as in the day of Massah in the desert,
where your fathers tempted me;
  they tested me though they had seen my works."

℟. **If today you hear his voice,**
  harden not your hearts. ↓

SECOND READING Rom 5:1-2, 5-8   [God's Love for Us]

Through Jesus we have received the grace of faith. The
love of God has been poured upon us. Jesus laid down his
life for us while we were still sinners.

A reading from the Letter of Saint Paul to the
Romans

B ROTHERS and sisters: Since we have been justified by faith, we have peace with God through our
Lord Jesus Christ, through whom we have gained
access by faith to this grace in which we stand, and we
boast in hope of the glory of God.

And hope does not disappoint, because the love of
God has been poured out into our hearts through the
Holy Spirit who has been given to us. For Christ, while
we were still helpless, died at the appointed time for
the ungodly. Indeed, only with difficulty does one die
for a just person, though perhaps for a good person
one might even find courage to die. But God proves his
love for us in that while we were still sinners Christ

died for us.—The word of the Lord. ℟. **Thanks be to God.** ↓

VERSE BEFORE THE GOSPEL Cf. Jn 4:42, 15 [Living Water]

℟. **Glory and praise to you, Lord Jesus Christ!***
Lord, you are truly the Savior of the world;
give me living water, that I may never thirst again.
℟. **Glory and praise to you, Lord Jesus Christ!** ↓

GOSPEL Jn 4:5-42 or 4:5-15, 19b-26, 39, 40-42 [Samaritan Woman]
Jesus speaks to the Samaritan woman at the well. He searches her soul, and she recognizes him as a prophet. Jesus speaks of the water of eternal life. He also notes the fields are ready for harvest.

[If the "Shorter Form" is used, the indented text in brackets is omitted.]

℣. The Lord be with you. ℟. **And also with you.**
✛ A reading from the holy Gospel according to John.
℟. **Glory to you, Lord.**

JESUS came to a town of Samaria called Sychar, near the plot of land that Jacob had given to his son Joseph. Jacob's well was there. Jesus, tired from his journey, sat down there at the well. It was about noon.
A woman of Samaria came to draw water. Jesus said to her, "Give me a drink." His disciples had gone into the town to buy food. The Samaritan woman said to him, "How can you, a Jew, ask me, a Samaritan woman, for a drink?"—For Jews use nothing in common with Samaritans.—Jesus answered and said to her, "If you knew the gift of God and who is saying to you, 'Give me a drink,' you would have asked him and he would have given you living water." The woman

---
* *See p. 16 for other Gospel Acclamations.*

said to him, "Sir, you do not even have a bucket and the cistern is deep; where then can you get this living water? Are you greater than our father Jacob, who gave us this cistern and drank from it himself with his children and his flocks?" Jesus answered and said to her, "Everyone who drinks this water will be thirsty again; but whoever drinks the water I shall give will never thirst; the water I shall give will become in him a spring of water welling up to eternal life." The woman said to him, "Sir, give me this water, so that I may not be thirsty or have to keep coming here to draw water."

[Jesus said to her, "Go call your husband and come back." The woman answered and said to him, "I do not have a husband." Jesus answered her, "You are right in saying, 'I do not have a husband.' For you have had five husbands, and the one you have now is not your husband. What you have said is true."]

[The woman said to him,] "[Sir,] I can see that you are a prophet. Our ancestors worshiped on this mountain; but you people say that the place to worship is in Jerusalem." Jesus said to her, "Believe me, woman, the hour is coming when you will worship the Father neither on this mountain nor in Jerusalem. You people worship what you do not understand; we worship what we understand, because salvation is from the Jews. But the hour is coming, and is now here, when true worshippers will worship the Father in Spirit and truth; and indeed the Father seeks such people to worship him. God is Spirit, and those who worship him must worship in Spirit and truth." The woman said to him, "I know that the Messiah is coming, the one called the Christ; when he comes, he will tell us everything." Jesus said to her, "I am he, the one speaking with you."

[At that moment his disciples returned, and were amazed that he was talking with a woman, but still no one said, "What are you looking for?" or "Why are you talking with her?" The woman left her water jar and went into the town and said to the people, "Come see a man who told me everything I have done. Could he possibly be the Christ?" They went out of the town and came to him. Meanwhile, the disciples urged him, "Rabbi, eat." But he said to them, "I have food to eat of which you do not know." So the disciples said to one another, "Could someone have brought him something to eat?" Jesus said to them, "My food is to do the will of the one who sent me and to finish his work. Do you not say, 'In four months the harvest will be here'? I tell you, look up and see the fields ripe for the harvest. The reaper is already receiving payment and gathering crops for eternal life, so that the sower and reaper can rejoice together. For here the saying is verified that 'One sows and another reaps.' I sent you to reap what you have not worked for; others have done the work, and you are sharing the fruits of their work."]

Many of the Samaritans of that town began to believe in him because of the word of the woman who testified, "He told me everything I have done." When the Samaritans came to him, they invited him to stay with them; and he stayed there two days. Many more began to believe in him because of his word, and they said to the woman, "We no longer believe because of your word; for we have heard for ourselves, and we know that this is truly the savior of the world."—The Gospel of the Lord. ℟. **Praise to you, Lord Jesus Christ.**   ➜ No. 14, p. 18

PRAYER OVER THE GIFTS   [Forgiveness]

Lord,
by the grace of this sacrifice
may we who ask forgiveness
be ready to forgive one another.
We ask this through Christ our Lord. ℟. **Amen.** ↓

Prayer Over the Gifts for First Scrutiny

Lord God,   [Faith and Love]
give faith and love to your children
and lead them safely to the banquet
you have prepared for them.
We ask this in the name of Jesus the Lord.
℟. **Amen.** ↓

PREFACE (P 14)   [Gift of Faith]

℣. The Lord be with you. ℟. **And also with you.**
℣. Lift up your hearts. ℟. **We lift them up to the Lord.**
℣. Let us give thanks to the Lord our God. ℟. **It is right to give him thanks and praise.**

Father, all-powerful and ever-living God,
we do well always and everywhere to give you thanks
through Jesus Christ our Lord.
When he asked the woman of Samaria for water to
    drink,
Christ had already prepared for her the gift of faith.
In his thirst to receive her faith
he awakened in her heart the fire of your love.
With thankful praise,
in company with the angels
we glorify the wonders of your power: ➔ No. 23, p. 23

When Eucharistic Prayer I is used, the special Christian Initiation forms of Remember, Lord, your people *and* Father, accept this offering *are said.*

Remember, Lord, these godparents
who will present your chosen men and women for
   baptism.

(the names of the godparents are mentioned).

Lord, remember all of us. . . (p. 24).

Father,
accept this offering
from your whole family.
We offer it especially for the men and women
you call to share your life
through the living waters of baptism.
[Through Christ our Lord, Amen.]

The rest follows the Roman Canon, pp. 25-28.

COMMUNION ANT. Jn 4:13-14   [Water of Eternal Life]

Whoever drinks the water that I shall give him, says the Lord, will have a spring inside him, welling up for eternal life. ↓

PRAYER AFTER COMMUNION   [Unity and Peace]

Lord,
in sharing this sacrament
may we receive your forgiveness
and be brought together in unity and peace.
We ask this through Christ our Lord.
℟. **Amen.**   → No. 32, p. 70

Prayer After Communion for First Scrutiny
Lord,   [God's Protection]
be present in our lives
with your gifts of salvation.
Prepare these men and women for your sacraments
and protect them in your love.
We ask this in the name of Jesus the Lord.
℞. **Amen.**   ➜ No. 32, p. 70

Optional Solemn Blessings, p. 92, and Prayers Over the People, p. 99

"I am the light of the world."

APRIL 3

4th SUNDAY OF LENT

*The alternative chants and prayers given below are for the
Ritual Mass for the Second Scrutiny assigned to this Sunday
in the Rite of Christian Initiation of Adults. (The readings
are the same as those for the 4th Sunday of Lent.)*

ENTRANCE ANT. See Is 66:10-11   [Rejoice]
**Rejoice, Jerusalem! Be glad for her, you who love her;
rejoice with her, you who mourned for her, and you
will find contentment at her consoling breasts.**
                              ➜ No. 2, p. 10 (Omit Gloria)

Entrance Antiphon for Second Scrutiny
                      Ez 36:23-26 [A New Spirit]

I will prove my holiness through you. I will gather you from the ends of the earth; I will pour clean water on you and wash away all your sins. I will give you a new spirit within you, says the Lord.

➔ No. 2, p. 10 (Omit Gloria)

OPENING PRAYER   [Faith and Love]

Let us pray
   [for a greater faith and love]
Father of peace,
we are joyful in your Word,
your Son Jesus Christ,
who reconciles us to you.
Let us hasten toward Easter
with the eagerness of faith and love.
We ask this through our Lord Jesus Christ, your Son,
who lives and reigns with you and the Holy Spirit,
one God, for ever and ever. ℟. **Amen.** ↓

ALTERNATIVE OPENING PRAYER   [Bringing Peace]

Let us pray
[that by growing in love this lenten season
we may bring the peace of Christ to our world]
God our Father,
your Word, Jesus Christ, spoke peace to a sinful world
and brought mankind the gift of reconciliation
by the suffering and death he endured.
Teach us, the people who bear his name,
to follow the example he gave us:
may our faith, hope, and charity
turn hatred to love, conflict to peace, death to eternal
   life.
We ask this through Christ our Lord. ℟. **Amen.** ↓

> **Opening Prayer for Second Scrutiny**   [Rebirth]
>
> Almighty and eternal God,
> may your Church increase in true joy.
> May these candidates for baptism,
> and all the family of man,
> be reborn into the life of your kingdom.
> We ask this . . . for ever and ever. ℟. **Amen.** ↓

FIRST READING 1 Sm 16:1b, 6-7, 10-13a

[The Lord's Anointed]

God directs Samuel to anoint David king. God looks into the heart of each person.

A reading from the first Book of Samuel

THE LORD said to Samuel: "Fill your horn with oil, and be on your way. I am sending you to Jesse of Bethlehem, for I have chosen my king from among his sons."

As Jesse and his sons came to the sacrifice, Samuel looked at Eliab and thought, "Surely the LORD's anointed is here before him." But the LORD said to Samuel: "Do not judge from his appearance or from his lofty stature, because I have rejected him. Not as man sees does God see, because man sees the appearance but the LORD looks into the heart." In the same way Jesse presented seven sons before Samuel, but Samuel said to Jesse, "The LORD has not chosen any one of these." Then Samuel asked Jesse, "Are these all the sons you have?" Jesse replied, "There is still the youngest, who is tending the sheep." Samuel said to Jesse, "Send for him; we will not begin the sacrificial banquet until he arrives here." Jesse sent and had the young man brought to them. He was ruddy, a youth handsome to behold and making a splendid appearance. The LORD said, "There—anoint him, for this is the one!" Then Samuel, with the horn of oil in hand, anointed him in the presence of his brothers; and from that day on, the spirit of the LORD rushed upon David.—The word of the Lord. ℟. **Thanks be to God.** ↓

RESPONSORIAL PSALM Ps 23   [The Lord's Protection]

℟. **The Lord is my shep-herd, there is noth-ing I shall want.**

The LORD is my shepherd, I shall not want.
   In verdant pastures he gives me repose;
beside restful waters he leads me;
   he refreshes my soul.

℟. **The Lord is my shepherd, there is nothing I shall
       want.**

He guides me in right paths
   for his name's sake.
Even though I walk in the dark valley
   I fear no evil; for you are at my side
with your rod and your staff
   that give me courage.

℟. **The Lord is my shepherd, there is nothing I shall
       want.**

You spread the table before me
   in the sight of my foes;
you anoint my head with oil;
   my cup overflows.

℟. **The Lord is my shepherd, there is nothing I shall
       want.**

Only goodness and kindness follow me
   all the days of my life;
and I shall dwell in the house of the LORD
   for years to come.

℟. **The Lord is my shepherd, there is nothing I shall
       want.** ↓

SECOND READING Eph 5:8-14   [Children of Light]

> We are to walk in the light which shows goodness, justice, and truth. Christ gives this light whereby we live.

A reading from the Letter of Saint Paul to the Ephesians

B ROTHERS and sisters: You were once darkness, but now you are light in the Lord. Live as children of light, for light produces every kind of goodness and righteousness and truth. Try to learn what is pleasing to the Lord. Take no part in the fruitless works of darkness; rather expose them, for it is shameful even to mention the things done by them in secret; but everything exposed by the light becomes visible, for everything that becomes visible is light. Therefore, it says:

"Awake, O sleeper,
  and arise from the dead,
  and Christ will give you light."

The word of the Lord. ℟. **Thanks be to God.** ↓

VERSE BEFORE THE GOSPEL Jn 8:12   [Light of Life]

℟. **Glory to you, Word of God, Lord Jesus Christ!***
I am the light of the world, says the Lord;
whoever follows me will have the light of life.
℟. **Glory to you, Word of God, Lord Jesus Christ!** ↓

GOSPEL Jn 9:1-41 or 9:1, 6-9, 13-17, 34-38 [Cure of Blind Man]

> Jesus is the light. He cures a man born blind by bringing him to see. Jesus identifies himself as the Son of Man.

[If the "Shorter Form" is used, the indented text in brackets is omitted.]

℣. The Lord be with you. ℟. **And also with you.**
✛ A reading from the holy Gospel according to John.
℟. **Glory to you, Lord.**

A S Jesus passed by he saw a man blind from birth. [His disciples asked him, "Rabbi, who sinned, this man or his parents, that he was born blind?" Jesus answered, "Neither he nor his parents

---

* *See p. 16 for other Gospel Acclamations.*

sinned; it is so that the works of God might be made visible through him.We have to do the works of the one who sent me while it is day. Night is coming when no one can work. While I am in the world, I am the light of the world." When he had said this,]

he spat on the ground and made clay with the saliva, and smeared the clay on his eyes, and said to him,"Go wash in the Pool of Siloam"—which means Sent—. So he went and washed, and came back able to see.

His neighbors and those who had seen him earlier as a beggar said,"Isn't this the one who used to sit and beg?" Some said, "It is," but others said, "No, he just looks like him."He said,"I am."

[So they said to him, "How were your eyes opened?" He replied,"The man called Jesus made clay and anointed my eyes and told me, 'Go to Siloam and wash.' So I went there and washed and was able to see."And they said to him,"Where is he?" He said,"I don't know."]

They brought the one who was once blind to the Pharisees. Now Jesus had made clay and opened his eyes on a sabbath. So then the Pharisees also asked him how he was able to see. He said to them,"He put clay on my eyes, and I washed, and now I can see." So some of the Pharisees said,"This man is not from God, because he does not keep the sabbath."But others said, "How can a sinful man do such signs?" And there was a division among them. So they said to the blind man again, "What do you have to say about him, since he opened your eyes?" He said,"He is a prophet."

[Now the Jews did not believe that he had been blind and gained his sight until they summoned the parents of the one who had gained his sight. They asked them,"Is this your son, who you say was born blind? How does he now see?" His parents answered and said, "We know that this is our son and that he was born blind. We do not know how he sees now, nor do we know who opened his eyes. Ask him, he is of age; he can speak for himself." His parents said this because they were afraid of the Jews, for the Jews had already agreed that if anyone acknowledged him as the Christ, he would be expelled from the synagogue. For this reason his parents said, "He is of age; question him."

So a second time they called the man who had been blind and said to him, "Give God the praise! We know that this man is a sinner." He replied, "If he is a sinner, I do not know. One thing I do know is that I was blind and now I see." So they said to him, "What did he do to you? How did he open your eyes?" He answered them, "I told you already and you did not listen. Why do you want to hear it again? Do you want to become his disciples, too?" They ridiculed him and said, "You are that man's disciple; we are disciples of Moses! We know that God spoke to Moses, but we do not know where this one is from." The man answered and said to them, "This is what is so amazing, that you do not know where he is from, yet he opened my eyes. We know that God does not listen to sinners, but if one is devout and does his will, he listens to him. It is unheard of that anyone ever opened the eyes of a person born blind. If this man were not from God, he would not be able to do anything."]

They answered and said to him, "You were born totally in sin, and are you trying to teach us?" Then they threw him out.

When Jesus heard that they had thrown him out, he found him and said, "Do you believe in the Son of Man?" He answered and said, "Who is he, sir, that I may believe in him?" Jesus said to him, "You have seen him, and the one speaking with you is he." He said, "I do believe, Lord," and he worshiped him.

[Then Jesus said, "I came into this world for judgment, so that those who do not see might see, and those who do see might become blind."

Some of the Pharisees who were with him heard this and said to him, "Surely we are not also blind, are we?" Jesus said to them, "If you were blind, you would have no sin; but now you are saying, 'We see,' so your sin remains."]

The Gospel of the Lord. ℟. **Praise to you, Lord Jesus Christ.**   → No. 14, p. 18

PRAYER OVER THE GIFTS   [Increased Reverence]

Lord,
we offer you these gifts
which bring us peace and joy.
Increase our reverence by this eucharist,
and bring salvation to the world.
We ask this through Christ our Lord. ℟. **Amen.** ↓

Prayer Over the Gifts for Second Scrutiny

Lord,   [Faith and Love]
we offer these gifts
in joy and thanksgiving for our salvation.
May the example of our faith and love
help your chosen ones on their way to salvation.
Grant this through Christ our Lord. ℟. **Amen.** ↓

PREFACE (P 15)   [From Darkness to Light]

℣. The Lord be with you. ℟. **And also with you.**
℣. Lift up your hearts. ℟. **We lift them up to the Lord.**
℣. Let us give thanks to the Lord our God. ℟. **It is right to give him thanks and praise.**

Father, all-powerful and ever-living God,
we do well always and everywhere to give you thanks,

through Jesus Christ our Lord.
He came among us as a man,
to lead mankind from darkness
into the light of faith.
Through Adam's fall we were born as slaves of sin,
but now through baptism in Christ
we are reborn as your adopted children.
Earth unites with heaven
to sing the new song of creation,
as we adore and praise you for ever: ➔ No. 23, p. 23

---

*When Eucharistic Prayer I is used, the special Christian
Initiation forms of* Remember, Lord, your people *and*
Father, accept this offering *are said.*

Remember, Lord, these godparents
who will present your chosen men and women for
   baptism.

(the names of the godparents are mentioned).

Lord, remember all of us. . . (p. 24).

Father,
accept this offering
from your whole family.
We offer it especially for the men and women
you call to share your life
through the living waters of baptism.

[Through Christ our Lord, Amen.]

The rest follows the Roman Canon, pp. 25-28.

COMMUNION ANT. See Jn 9:11   [Spiritual Sight]

**The Lord rubbed my eyes: I went away and washed;
then I could see, and I believed in God.** ↓

PRAYER AFTER COMMUNION   [Light of Gospel]

Father,
you enlighten all who come into the world.

Fill our hearts with the light of your gospel,
that our thoughts may please you,
and our love be sincere.
Grant this through Christ our Lord.
℟. **Amen.**   ➜ No. 32, p. 70

Prayer After Communion for Second Scrutiny
Lord,   [Joy of Salvation]
be close to your family.
Rule and guide us on our way to your kingdom
and bring us to the joy of salvation.
Grant this through Christ our Lord.
℟. **Amen.**   ➜ No. 32, p. 70

Optional Solemn Blessings, p. 92, and Prayers Over the People, p. 99

"The dead man came out, tied hand and foot."

APRIL 10

5th SUNDAY OF LENT

*The alternative chants and prayers given below are for the
Ritual Mass for the Third Scrutiny assigned to this Sunday
in the Rite of Christian Initiation of Adults. (The readings
are the same as those for the 5th Sunday of Lent.)*

ENTRANCE ANT. Ps 43:1-2   [Rescue Me]

Give me justice, O God, and defend my cause against the wicked; rescue me from deceitful and unjust men. You, O God, are my refuge.

→ No. 2, p. 10 (Omit Gloria)

Entrance Antiphon for Third Scrutiny
Ez 36:23-26 [A New Spirit]

I will prove my holiness through you. I will gather you from the ends of the earth; I will pour clean water on you and wash away all your sins. I will give you a new spirit within you, says the Lord.

→ No. 2, p. 10 (Omit Gloria)

OPENING PRAYER   [Courage To Follow Christ]

Let us pray
  [for the courage to follow Christ]
Father,
help us to be like Christ your Son,
who loved the world and died for our salvation.
Inspire us by his love,
guide us by his example,
who lives and reigns with you and the Holy Spirit,
one God, for ever and ever. ℟. **Amen.** ↓

ALTERNATIVE OPENING PRAYER
[Transforming the World]

Let us pray
  [for the courage to embrace the world
  in the name of Christ]
Father in heaven,
the love of your Son led him to accept the suffering of the cross
that his brothers might glory in new life.
Change our selfishness into self-giving.
Help us to embrace the world you have given us,
that we may transform the darkness of its pain

into the life and joy of Easter.
Grant this through Christ our Lord. ℟. **Amen.** ↓

> ### Opening Prayer for Third Scrutiny
>
> Lord,   [Members of the Church]
> enlighten your chosen ones with the word of life.
> Give them a new birth
> in the waters of baptism
> and make them living members of the Church.
> Grant this . . . for ever and ever. ℟. **Amen.** ↓

FIRST READING Ez 37:12-14   [The Lord's Promise]

The Lord promises to bring his people back to their home-land. He will be with them and they will know him.

A reading from the Book of the Prophet Ezekiel

THUS says the LORD God: O my people, I will open your graves and have you rise from them, and bring you back to the land of Israel. Then you shall know that I am the LORD, when I open your graves and have you rise from them, O my people! I will put my spirit in you that you may live, and I will settle you upon your land; thus you shall know that I am the LORD. I have promised, and I will do it, says the LORD.—The word of the Lord. ℟. **Thanks be to God.** ↓

RESPONSORIAL PSALM Ps 130 [Mercy and Redemption]

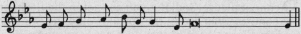

℟. With the Lord there is mer-cy and fullness of redemp - tion.

Out of the depths I cry to you, O LORD;
  LORD, hear my voice!
Let your ears be attentive
  to my voice in supplication.

℟. **With the Lord there is mercy and fullness of redemption.**

If you, O Lord, mark iniquities,
  Lord, who can stand?
But with you is forgiveness,
  that you may be revered.

℟. **With the Lord there is mercy and fullness of redemption.**

I trust in the Lord;
  my soul trusts in his word.
More than sentinels wait for the dawn,
  let Israel wait for the Lord.

℟. **With the Lord there is mercy and fullness of redemption.**

For with the Lord is kindness
  and with him is plenteous redemption;
and he will redeem Israel
  from all their iniquities.

℟. **With the Lord there is mercy and fullness of redemption.** ↓

SECOND READING Rom 8:8-11   [Indwelling of Christ's Spirit]
The followers of Jesus live in the Spirit of God. The same Spirit who brought Jesus back to life will bring mortal bodies to life since God's Spirit dwells in them.

A reading from the Letter of Saint Paul to the Romans

BROTHERS and sisters: Those who are in the flesh cannot please God. But you are not in the flesh; on the contrary, you are in the spirit, if only the Spirit of God dwells in you. Whoever does not have the Spirit of Christ does not belong to him. But if Christ is in you, although the body is dead because of sin, the spirit is alive because of righteousness. If the Spirit of the one who raised Jesus from the dead dwells in you, the one who raised Christ from the dead will give life to your mortal bodies also, through his Spirit dwelling in you.—The word of the Lord. ℟. **Thanks be to God.** ↓

VERSE BEFORE THE GOSPEL Jn 11:25a, 26   [Resurrection]

℟. **Praise and honor to you, Lord Jesus Christ!***
I am the resurrection and the life, says the Lord;
whoever believes in me will never die.
℟. **Praise and honor to you, Lord Jesus Christ!** ↓

GOSPEL Jn 11:1-45 or 11:3-7, 17, 20-27, 33b-45   [Lazarus]

Lazarus, the brother of Martha and Mary, died and was buried. When Jesus came, he assured them that he was the resurrection and the life. Jesus gave life back to Lazarus.

[If the "Shorter Form" is used, the indented text in brackets is omitted.]

℣. The Lord be with you. ℟. **And also with you.**
✚ A reading from the holy Gospel according to John.
℟. **Glory to you, Lord.**

[NOW a man was ill, Lazarus from Bethany, the village of Mary and her sister Martha. Mary was the one who had anointed the Lord with perfumed oil and dried his feet with her hair; it was her brother Lazarus who was ill.]
[So] the sisters sent word to Jesus saying, "Master, the one you love is ill." When Jesus heard this he said, "This illness is not to end in death, but is for the glory of God, that the Son of God may be glorified through it." Now Jesus loved Martha and her sister and Lazarus. So when he heard that he was ill, he remained for two days in the place where he was. Then after this he said to his disciples, "Let us go back to Judea."

[The disciples said to him, "Rabbi, the Jews were just trying to stone you, and you want to go back there?" Jesus answered, "Are there not twelve hours in a day? If one walks during the day, he does not stumble, because he sees the light of this

---

* See p. 16 for other Gospel Acclamations.

world. But if one walks at night, he stumbles, because the light is not in him." He said this, and then told them, "Our friend Lazarus is asleep, but I am going to awaken him." So the disciples said to him, "Master, if he is asleep, he will be saved." But Jesus was talking about his death, while they thought that he meant ordinary sleep. So then Jesus said to them clearly, "Lazarus has died. And I am glad for you that I was not there, that you may believe. Let us go to him." So Thomas, called Didymus, said to his fellow disciples, "Let us also go to die with him."]

When Jesus arrived, he found that Lazarus had already been in the tomb for four days.

[Now Bethany was near Jerusalem, only about two miles away. And many of the Jews had come to Martha and Mary to comfort them about their brother.]

When Martha heard that Jesus was coming, she went to meet him; but Mary sat at home. Martha said to Jesus, "Lord, if you had been here, my brother would not have died. But even now I know that whatever you ask of God, God will give you." Jesus said to her, "Your brother will rise." Martha said to him, "I know he will rise, in the resurrection on the last day." Jesus told her, "I am the resurrection and the life; whoever believes in me, even if he dies, will live, and everyone who lives and believes in me will never die. Do you believe this?" She said to him, "Yes, Lord. I have come to believe that you are the Christ, the Son of God, the one who is coming into the world."

[When she had said this, she went and called her sister Mary secretly, saying, "The teacher is here and is asking for you." As soon as she heard this, she rose quickly and went to him. For Jesus had not yet come into the village, but was still where Martha had met him. So when the Jews who were with her in the house comforting her saw Mary get up quickly and go out, they followed her, presuming that she was going to the tomb to weep there. When Mary came to where Jesus was and saw him, she fell at his feet and said to him, "Lord, if you had been here, my brother would not have died." When Jesus saw her weeping and the Jews who had come with her weeping,]

he became perturbed and deeply troubled, and said, "Where have you laid him?" They said to him, "Sir, come and see." And Jesus wept. So the Jews said, "See how he loved him." But some of them said, "Could not the one who opened the eyes of the blind man have done something so that this man would not have died?"

So Jesus, perturbed again, came to the tomb. It was a cave, and a stone lay across it. Jesus said, "Take away the stone." Martha, the dead man's sister, said to him, "Lord, by now there will be a stench; he has been dead for four days." Jesus said to her, "Did I not tell you that if you believe you will see the glory of God?" So they took away the stone. And Jesus raised his eyes and said, "Father, I thank you for hearing me. I know that you always hear me; but because of the crowd here I have said this, that they may believe that you sent me." And when he had said this, he cried out in a loud voice, "Lazarus, come out!" The dead man came out, tied hand and foot with burial bands, and his face was wrapped in a cloth. So Jesus said to them, "Untie him and let him go."

Now many of the Jews who had come to Mary and seen what he had done began to believe in him.—The Gospel of the Lord. ℟. **Praise to you, Lord Jesus Christ.**   ➔ No. 14, p. 18

PRAYER OVER THE GIFTS   [Take Away Sins]

Almighty God,
may the sacrifice we offer
take away the sins of those
whom you enlighten with the Christian faith.
We ask this in the name of Jesus the Lord.
℟. **Amen.** ↓

> **Prayer Over the Gifts for Third Scrutiny**
> Almighty God,   [Preparing for Baptism]
> hear our prayers for these men and women
> who have begun to learn the Christian faith,
> and by this sacrifice prepare them for baptism.
> We ask this through Christ our Lord. ℟. **Amen.** ↓

PREFACE (P 16)   [Christ Raised Lazarus]

℣. The Lord be with you. ℟. **And also with you.**
℣. Lift up your hearts. ℟. **We lift them up to the Lord.**
℣. Let us give thanks to the Lord our God. ℟. **It is right
to give him thanks and praise.**

Father, all-powerful and ever-living God,
we do well always and everywhere to give you thanks
through Jesus Christ our Lord.
As a man like us, Jesus wept for Lazarus his friend.
As the eternal God, he raised Lazarus from the dead.
In his love for us all,
Christ gives us the sacraments
to lift us up to everlasting life.
Through him the angels of heaven offer their prayer of
    adoration
as they rejoice in your presence for ever.
May our voices be one with theirs
in their triumphant hymn of praise: ➜ No. 23, p. 23

When Eucharistic Prayer I is used, the special Christian Initiation forms of Remember, Lord, your people *and* Father, accept this offering *are said.*

Remember, Lord, these godparents
who will present your chosen men and women for
    baptism.

(the names of the godparents are mentioned).

Lord, remember all of us. . . (p. 24).

Father,
accept this offering
from your whole family.
We offer it especially for the men and women
you call to share your life
through the living waters of baptism.

[Through Christ our Lord. Amen.]

The rest follows the Roman Canon, pp. 25-28.

COMMUNION ANT. Jn 11:26   [Eternal Life]

**He who lives and believes in me will not die for ever,
said the Lord.** ↓

PRAYER AFTER COMMUNION   [Union with Jesus]

Almighty Father,
by this sacrifice
may we always remain one with your Son, Jesus
    Christ,
whose body and blood we share,
for he is Lord for ever and ever.
℟. **Amen.**   ➙ No. 32, p. 70

Prayer After Communion for Third Scrutiny

Lord,   [Joy of Salvation]
may your people be one in spirit
and serve you with all their heart.
Free them from all fear.
Give them joy in your gifts
and love for those
who are to be reborn as your children.
We ask this through Christ our Lord.
℟. **Amen.**   ➜ No. 32, p. 70

Optional Solemn Blessings, p. 92, and Prayers Over the People, p. 99

*"Blessed are you who have come to us
so rich in love and mercy."*

APRIL 17

PALM SUNDAY OF THE LORD'S PASSION

On this day the Church celebrates Christ's entrance into Jerusalem to accomplish his paschal mystery. Accordingly, the memorial of this event is included in every Mass, with the procession or the solemn entrance before the principal Mass, with the simple entrance before the other Masses.

Commemoration of the Lord's Entrance into Jerusalem

FIRST FORM: THE PROCESSION

The following antiphon or any other appropriate song is sung.

ANTIPHON Mt 21:9   [Hosanna]

**Hosanna to the Son of David,
the King of Israel.
Blessed is he who comes
in the name of the Lord.
Hosanna in the highest.**

The priest then greets the people in the usual way and gives a brief introduction, inviting them to take a full part in the celebration, using these or similar words:

Dear friends in Christ, for five weeks of Lent we have been preparing, by works of charity and self-sacrifice, for the celebration of our Lord's paschal mystery. Today we come together to begin this solemn celebration in union with the whole Church throughout the world. Christ entered in triumph into his own city, to complete his work as our Messiah: to suffer, to die, and to rise again. Let us remember with devotion this entry which began his saving work and follow him with a lively faith. United with him in his suffering on the cross, may we share his resurrection and new life.

Afterwards the priest, with hands joined, says one of the following prayers:

PRAYER   **[Following Christ]**

Let us pray.
Almighty God,
we pray you
bless ✛ these branches
and make them holy.
Today we joyfully acclaim Jesus our Messiah and King.
May we reach one day the happiness of the new and
    everlasting Jerusalem
by faithfully following him
who lives and reigns for ever and ever. ℞. **Amen.** ↓

OR   **[Christ Our King]**

Let us pray.
Lord,
increase the faith of your people
and listen to our prayers.
Today we honor Christ our triumphant King
by carrying these branches.

May we honor you every day
by living always in him,
for he is Lord for ever and ever. ℟. **Amen.** ↓

The priest sprinkles the branches with holy water in silence.

Then the account of the Lord's entrance is proclaimed from one of the four gospels. This is done in the usual way or, if there is no deacon, by the priest.

GOSPEL Mt 21:1-11   [Jesus' Triumphal Entry]

In triumphant glory Jesus comes into Jerusalem. The people spread their cloaks on the ground for him, wave olive branches and sing in his honor.

℣. The Lord be with you. ℟. **And also with you.**

✚ A reading from the holy Gospel according to Matthew. ℟. **Glory to you, Lord.**

WHEN Jesus and the disciples drew near Jerusalem and came to Bethphage on the Mount of Olives, Jesus sent two disciples, saying to them, "Go into the village opposite you, and immediately you will find an ass tethered, and a colt with her. Untie them and bring them here to me. And if anyone should say anything to you, reply, 'The master has need of them.' Then he will send them at once." This happened so that what had been spoken through the prophet might be fulfilled:

Say to daughter Zion,
"Behold, your king comes to you,
    meek and riding on an ass,
    and on a colt, the foal of a beast of burden."

The disciples went and did as Jesus had ordered them. They brought the ass and the colt and laid their cloaks over them, and he sat upon them. The very large crowd spread their cloaks on the road, while others cut branches from the trees and strewed them on the road. The crowds preceding him and those following kept crying out and saying:

"Hosanna to the Son of David;
blessed is he who comes in the name of the
Lord;
hosanna in the highest."

And when he entered Jerusalem the whole city was shaken and asked, "Who is this?" And the crowds replied, "This is Jesus the prophet, from Nazareth in Galilee."—The Gospel of the Lord. ℟. **Praise to you, Lord Jesus Christ.**

After the Gospel, a brief homily may be given. Before the procession begins, the celebrant or other suitable minister may address the people in these or similar words:

Let us go forth in peace,
praising Jesus our Messiah,
as did the crowds who welcomed him to Jerusalem.

The procession to the church where Mass will be celebrated then begins.

If incense is used, the thurifer goes first with a lighted censer, followed by the cross-bearer (with the cross suitably decorated) between two ministers with lighted candles, then the priest with the ministers, and finally the congregation carrying branches.

During the procession, the choir and people sing the following or other appropriate songs:

ANTIPHON 1   [Hosanna]

**The children of Jerusalem
welcomed Christ the King.
They carried olive branches
and loudly praised the Lord:
Hosanna in the highest.**

The above antiphon may be repeated between verses of Psalm 24.

PSALM 24   [The King of Glory]

**The LORD'S are the earth and its fullness;
the world and those who dwell in it.**

For he founded it upon the seas
 and established it upon the rivers.

Repeat antiphon 1

Who can ascend the mountain of the LORD?
 or who may stand in his holy place?
He whose hands are sinless, whose heart is clean,
 who desires not what is vain,
 nor swears deceitfully to his neighbor.

Repeat antiphon 1

He shall receive a blessing from the LORD,
 a reward from God his savior.
Such is the race that seeks for him,
 that seeks the face of the God of Jacob.

Repeat antiphon 1

Lift up, O gates, your lintels;
 reach up, you ancient portals,
 that the king of glory may come in!
Who is this king of glory?
 The LORD, strong and mighty,
 the LORD, mighty in battle.   *Repeat antiphon 1*

Lift up, O gates, your lintels;
 reach up, you ancient portals,
 that the king of glory may come in!
Who is this king of glory?
 The LORD of hosts; he is the king of glory.

Repeat antiphon 1

ANTIPHON 2   [Hosanna]

The children of Jerusalem
welcomed Christ the King.
They spread their cloaks before him
and loudly praised the Lord:
Hosanna to the Son of David!
Blessed is he who comes
in the name of the Lord!

The above antiphon may be repeated between the verses of Psalm 47.

PSALM 47   [The Great King]

All you peoples, clap your hands,
  shout to God with cries of gladness.
For the LORD the Most High, the awesome,
  is the great king over all the earth.

Repeat antiphon 2

He brings peoples under us;
  nations under our feet.
He chooses for us our inheritance,
  the glory of Jacob, whom he loves.

Repeat antiphon 2

God mounts his throne amid shouts of joy;
  the LORD, amid trumpet blasts.
Sing praise to God, sing praise;
  sing praise to our king, sing praise.

Repeat antiphon 2

For king of all the earth is God;
  sing hymns of praise.
God reigns over the nations,
  God sits upon his holy throne.

Repeat antiphon 2

The princes of the peoples are gathered together
  with the people of the God of Abraham.
For God's are the guardians of the earth;
  he is supreme.

Repeat antiphon 2

A hymn in honor of Christ the King, such as All Glory,
Laud and Honor, *is sung during the procession.*

HYMN TO CHRIST THE KING

1. All   glo – ry, laud, and   hon – or   To
3. The   com – pa – ny   of   an – gels Are
5. To   thee be – fore thy   Pas – sion They

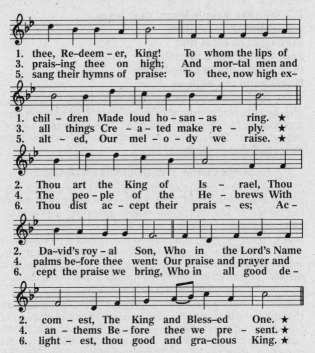

1. thee, Re-deem-er, King! To whom the lips of
3. prais-ing thee on high; And mor-tal men and
5. sang their hymns of praise: To thee, now high ex-

1. chil-dren Made loud ho-san-as ring. ★
3. all things Cre-a-ted make re-ply. ★
5. alt-ed, Our mel-o-dy we raise. ★

2. Thou art the King of Is-rael, Thou
4. The peo-ple of the He-brews With
6. Thou dist ac-cept their prais-es; Ac-

2. Da-vid's roy-al Son, Who in the Lord's Name
4. palms be-fore thee went: Our praise and prayer and
6. cept the praise we bring, Who in all good de-

2. com-est, The King and Bless-ed One. ★
4. an-thems Be-fore thee we pre-sent. ★
6. light-est, thou good and gra-cious King. ★

★ The first stanza is repeated wherever the star occurs.

As the procession enters the church, the following responsory
or another song which refers to the Lord's entrance is sung.

OPENING PRAYER   [Hosanna]

℞. **The children of Jerusalem**
welcomed Christ the King.
They proclaimed the resurrection of life,
and, waving olive branches,
they loudly praised the Lord:
Hosanna in the highest.

℣. **When the people heard that Jesus**
was entering Jerusalem,
they went to meet him
and, waving olive branches,
they loudly praised the Lord:
Hosanna in the highest.

When the priest comes to the altar he venerates it and may
also incense it. Then he goes to his chair (removes the cope
and puts on the chasuble) and begins immediately the open-
ing prayer of Mass, which concludes the procession. Mass
then continues in the usual way.

SECOND FORM: THE SOLEMN ENTRANCE

If the procession cannot be held outside the church, the com-
memoration of the Lord's entrance may be celebrated before
the principal Mass with the solemn entrance, which takes
place within the church.

The faithful, holding the branches, assemble either in front
of the church door or inside the church. The priest and min-
isters, with a representative group of the faithful, go to a
suitable place in the church outside the sanctuary, so that
most of the people will be able to see the rite.

While the priest goes to the appointed place, the antiphon
Hosanna *or other suitable song is sung. Then the blessing of*
branches and proclamation of the gospel about the Lord's
entrance into Jerusalem take place, as above. After the gospel
the priest, with the ministers and the group of the faithful,
moves solemnly through the church to the sanctuary, while
the responsory The Children of Jerusalem *or other appro-*
priate song is sung.

When the priest comes to the altar he venerates it, goes to his
chair, and immediately begins the opening prayer of Mass,
which then continues in the usual way.

THIRD FORM: THE SIMPLE ENTRANCE

At all other Masses on this Sunday, if the solemn entrance is
not held, the Lord's entrance is commemorated with the fol-
lowing simple entrance.

While the priest goes to the altar, the entrance antiphon with its psalm or another song with the same theme is sung.

ENTRANCE ANT. [Praise the Lord]

Six days before the solemn passover the Lord came to Jerusalem, and children waving palm branches ran out to welcome him. They loudly praised the Lord: Blessed are you who have come to us so rich in love and mercy.

PSALM 24:9-10 [The King of Glory]

**Open wide the doors and gates.
Lift high the ancient portals.
The King of glory enters.
Who is this King of glory?
He is God the mighty Lord.
Hosanna in the highest.
Blessed are you who have come to us
so rich in love and mercy.
Hosanna in the highest.**

Where neither the procession nor the solemn entrance can be celebrated, there should be a bible service on the theme of the Lord's messianic entrance and passion, either on Saturday evening or on Sunday at a convenient time.

MASS

After the procession or solemn entrance the priest begins the Mass with the Opening Prayer.

OPENING PRAYER [Union with Christ]

Let us pray
[for a closer union with Christ
during this holy season]
Almighty, ever-living God,
you have given the human race Jesus Christ our Savior
as a model of humility.
He fulfilled your will

by becoming man and giving his life on the cross.
Help us to bear witness to you
by following his example of suffering
and make us worthy to share in his resurrection.
We ask this through our Lord Jesus Christ, your Son,
who lives and reigns with you and the Holy Spirit,
one God, for ever and ever. ℞. **Amen.** ↓

ALTERNATIVE OPENING PRAYER

[Guided by Christ's Truth]

Let us pray
   [as we accompany our King to Jerusalem]
Almighty Father of our Lord Jesus Christ,
you sent your Son
to be born of woman and to die on a cross,
so that through the obedience of one man,
estrangement might be dissolved for all men.
Guide our minds by his truth
and strengthen our lives by the example of his death,
that we may live in union with you
in the kingdom of your promise.
Grant this through Christ our Lord. ℞. **Amen.** ↓

FIRST READING Is 50:4-7   [Christ's Suffering]

**The servant was persecuted and struck by his own people;
he was spit upon and beaten. He proclaims the true faith
and suffers to atone for the sins of his people. Here we see
a foreshadowing of the true servant of God.**

A reading from the Book of the Prophet Isaiah

THE Lord GOD has given me
   a well-trained tongue,
that I might know how to speak to the weary
   a word that will rouse them.
Morning after morning
   he opens my ear that I may hear;
and I have not rebelled,
   have not turned back.

I gave my back to those who beat me,
　　my cheeks to those who plucked my beard;
my face I did not shield
　　from buffets and spitting.
The Lord GOD is my help,
　　therefore I am not disgraced;
I have set my face like flint,
　　knowing that I shall not be put to shame.
The word of the Lord. ℟. **Thanks be to God.** ↓

RESPONSORIAL PSALM Ps 22   [Christ's Abandonment]

　　℟. **My God, my God, why have you a-ban-doned me?**

All who see me scoff at me;
　　they mock me with parted lips, they wag their
　　　　heads:
"He relied on the LORD; let him deliver him,
　　let him rescue him, if he loves him."

℟. **My God, my God, why have you abandoned me?**

Indeed, many dogs surround me,
　　a pack of evildoers closes in upon me;
they have pierced my hands and my feet;
　　I can count all my bones.

℟. **My God, my God, why have you abandoned me?**

They divide my garments among them,
　　and for my vesture they cast lots.
But you, O LORD, be not far from me;
　　O my help, hasten to aid me.

℟. **My God, my God, why have you abandoned me?**

I will proclaim your name to my brethren;
　　in the midst of the assembly I will praise you:
"You who fear the LORD, praise him;
　　all you descendants of Jacob, give glory to him,
　　revere him, all you descendants of Israel."

℟. **My God, my God, why have you abandoned me?** ↓

SECOND READING Phil 2:6-11   [Humility]

Paul urges us to humility by which we are made like Christ our Lord. He put off the majesty of his divinity and became man and humbled himself in obedience to the ignominious death on the cross.

A reading from the Letter of Saint Paul to the Philippians

CHRIST Jesus, though he was in the form of God,
   did not regard equality with God
      something to be grasped.
Rather, he emptied himself,
      taking the form of a slave,
      coming in human likeness;
      and found human in appearance,
      he humbled himself,
      becoming obedient to the point of death,
      even death on a cross.
Because of this, God greatly exalted him
      and bestowed on him the name
      which is above every name,
      that at the name of Jesus
      every knee should bend,
         of those in heaven and on earth and under the
            earth,
      and every tongue confess that
      Jesus Christ is Lord,
      to the glory of God the Father.
The word of the Lord. ℟. **Thanks be to God.** ↓

VERSE BEFORE THE GOSPEL   [Obedient to Death]

℟. **Praise to you, Lord Jesus Christ, king of endless glory!***
Christ became obedient to the point of death,
even death on a cross.
Because of this, God greatly exalted him
and bestowed on him the name which is above every
   name.

* *See p. 16 for other Gospel Acclamations.*

℞. **Praise to you, Lord Jesus Christ, king of endless glory!** ↓

GOSPEL Mt 26:14—27:66 or 27:11-54 [Christ's Passion]

Matthew portrays the passion and death of Jesus. Jesus gives his disciples his body and blood. Judas betrays him. Jesus is condemned to die on the cross.

When the Shorter Form is read, the Passion begins at no. 9 below and ends after no. 13, pp. 242-245.

The Passion may be read by lay readers, with the part of Christ, if possible, read by a priest. The Narrator is noted by N, the words of Jesus by a ✚ *and the words of others by V(Voice) and C (Crowd). The part of the Crowd (C) printed in boldface type may be recited by the people.*

We participate in the passion narrative in several ways: by reading it and reflecting on it during the week ahead; by listening with faith as it is proclaimed; by respectful posture during the narrative; by reverent silence after the passage about Christ's death. We do not hold the palms during the reading on Passion Sunday.

Who caused the death of Jesus? In listening to God's word today, we must remember that our Lord died to save every human person. By our sins we have contributed to his suffering and death. The authorities of his time bear responsibility for carrying out his execution; this charge must not be laid against all the Jewish people of Jesus' day or of our own. We are all responsible for sin and for our Lord's suffering.

This week we are challenged by the passion narrative to reflect on the way we are living up to our baptismal promises of dying with Christ to sin and living with him for God.

N. THE Passion of our Lord Jesus Christ according to Matthew

1. THE BETRAYER

N. ONE of the Twelve, who was called Judas Iscariot, went to the chief priests and said,

V. "What are you willing to give me if I hand him over to you?" **N.** They paid him thirty pieces of silver, and from that time on he looked for an opportunity to hand him over.

On the first day of the Feast of Unleavened Bread, the disciples approached Jesus and said, **V.** "Where do you want us to prepare for you to eat the Passover?" **N.** He said, ✛ *"Go into the city to a certain man and tell him, 'The teacher says, "My appointed time draws near; in your house I shall celebrate the Passover with my disciples."'"* **N.** The disciples then did as Jesus had ordered, and prepared the Passover.

When it was evening, he reclined at table with the Twelve. And while they were eating, he said, ✛ *"Amen, I say to you, one of you will betray me."* **N.** Deeply distressed at this, they began to say to him one after another, **V.** "Surely it is not I, Lord?" **N.** He said in reply, ✛ *"He who has dipped his hand into the dish with me is the one who will betray me. The Son of Man indeed goes, as it is written of him, but woe to that man by whom the Son of Man is betrayed. It would be better for that man if he had never been born."* **N.** Then Judas, his betrayer, said in reply, **V.** "Surely it is not I, Rabbi?" **N.** He answered, ✛ *"You have said so."*

2. THE HOLY EUCHARIST

N. WHILE they were eating, Jesus took bread, said the blessing, broke it, and giving it to his disciples said, ✛ *"Take and eat; this is my body."* **N.** Then he took a cup, gave thanks, and gave it to them, saying, ✛ *"Drink from it, all of you, for this is my blood of the covenant, which will be shed on behalf of many for the forgiveness of sins. I tell you, from now on I shall not drink this fruit of the vine until the day when I drink it with you new in the kingdom of my Father."* **N.** Then, after singing a hymn, they went out to the Mount of Olives.

3. PETER'S DENIAL FORETOLD

N. **T**HEN Jesus said to them, ✠ *"This night all of you will have your faith in me shaken, for it is written:*

I will strike the shepherd,
   and the sheep of the flock will be dispersed;
but after I have been raised up, I shall go before you to Galilee." **N.** Peter said to him in reply, **V.** "Though all may have their faith in you shaken, mine will never be." **N.** Jesus said to him, ✠ *"Amen, I say to you, this very night before the cock crows, you will deny me three times."* **N.** Peter said to him, **V.** "Even though I should have to die with you, I will not deny you." **N.** And all the disciples spoke likewise.

4. THE AGONY IN THE GARDEN

N. **T**HEN Jesus came with them to a place called Gethsemane, and he said to his disciples, ✠ *"Sit here while I go over there and pray."* **N.** He took along Peter and the two sons of Zebedee, and began to feel sorrow and distress. Then he said to them, ✠ *"My soul is sorrowful even to death. Remain here and keep watch with me."* **N.** He advanced a little and fell prostrate in prayer, saying, ✠ *"My Father, if it is possible, let this cup pass from me; yet, not as I will, but as you will."* **N.** When he returned to his disciples he found them asleep. He said to Peter, ✠ *"So you could not keep watch with me for one hour? Watch and pray that you may not undergo the test. The spirit is willing, but the flesh is weak."* **N.** Withdrawing a second time, he prayed again, ✠ *"My Father, if it is not possible that this cup pass without my drinking it, your will be done!"* **N.** Then he returned once more and found them asleep, for they could not keep their eyes open. He left them and withdrew again and prayed a third time, saying the same thing again. Then he returned to his disciples and said to them,

✠ *"Are you still sleeping and taking your rest? Behold, the hour is at hand when the Son of Man is to be handed over to sinners. Get up, let us go. Look, my betrayer is at hand."*

5. JESUS ARRESTED

N. WHILE he was still speaking, Judas, one of the Twelve, arrived, accompanied by a large crowd, with swords and clubs, who had come from the chief priests and the elders of the people. His betrayer had arranged a sign with them, saying, **V.** "The man I shall kiss is the one; arrest him." **N.** Immediately he went over to Jesus and said, **V.** "Hail, Rabbi!" **N.** and he kissed him. Jesus answered him, ✠ *"Friend, do what you have come for."* **N.** Then stepping forward they laid hands on Jesus and arrested him. And behold, one of those who accompanied Jesus put his hand to his sword, drew it, and struck the high priest's servant, cutting off his ear. Then Jesus said to him, ✠ *"Put your sword back into its sheath, for all who take the sword will perish by the sword. Do you think that I cannot call upon my Father and he will not provide me at this moment with more than twelve legions of angels? But then how would the Scriptures be fulfilled which say that it must come to pass in this way?"* **N.** At that hour Jesus said to the crowds, ✠ *"Have you come out as against a robber, with swords and clubs to seize me? Day after day I sat teaching in the temple area, yet you did not arrest me. But all this has come to pass that the writings of the prophets may be fulfilled."* **N.** Then all the disciples left him and fled.

6. JESUS BEFORE THE SANHEDRIN

N. THOSE who had arrested Jesus led him away to Caiaphas the high priest, where the scribes and the elders were assembled. Peter was following him at a distance as far as the high priest's courtyard, and going inside he sat down with the servants to see the outcome. The chief priests and the entire Sanhedrin kept trying to obtain false testimony against Jesus in order to put him to death, but they found none, though many false witnesses came forward. Finally two came forward who stated, **C. "This man said, 'I can destroy the temple of God and within three days rebuild it.' "** N. The high priest rose and addressed him, **V.** "Have you no answer? What are these men testifying against you?" N. But Jesus was silent. Then the high priest said to him, **V.** "I order you to tell us under oath before the living God whether you are the Christ, the Son of God." N. Jesus said to him in reply, ✠ *"You have said so. But I tell you:*

> *From now on you will see 'the Son of Man*
> *seated at the right hand of the Power' and 'coming on the clouds of heaven.' "*

N. Then the high priest tore his robes and said, **V.** "He has blasphemed! What further need have we of witnesses? You have now heard the blasphemy; what is your opinion?" **N.** They said in reply, **C.** "He deserves to die!" **N.** Then they spat in his face and struck him, while some slapped him, saying, **C. "Prophesy for us, Christ: who is it that struck you?"**

7. PETER'S DENIAL

N. NOW Peter was sitting outside in the courtyard. One of the maids came over to him and said, **C. "You too were with Jesus the Galilean."** N. But he denied it in front of everyone, saying, **V.** "I do not know what you are talking about!" N. As he went out to the gate, another girl saw him and said to those who were there, **C. "This man was with Jesus the Nazorean."** N. Again he denied it with an oath, **V.** "I do not know the man!" N. A little later the bystanders came over and said to Peter, **C. "Surely you too are one of them; even your speech gives you away."** N. At that he began to curse and to swear, **V.** "I do not know the man." **N.** And immediately a cock crowed. Then Peter remembered the word that Jesus had spoken: "Before the cock crows you will deny me three times." He went out and began to weep bitterly.

8. JESUS HANDED OVER TO PILATE

N. WHEN it was morning, all the chief priests and the elders of the people took counsel against Jesus to put him to death. They bound him, led him away, and handed him over to Pilate, the governor.

Then Judas, his betrayer, seeing that Jesus had been condemned, deeply regretted what he had done. He returned the thirty pieces of silver to the chief priests and elders, saying, **V.** "I have sinned in betraying innocent blood." **N.** They said, **C.** "What is that to us? Look to it yourself." **N.** Flinging the money into the temple, he departed and went off and hanged himself. The chief priests gathered up the money, but said, **C.** "It is not lawful to deposit this in the temple treasury, for it is the price of blood." **N.** After consultation, they used it to buy the potter's field as a burial place for foreigners. That is why that field even today is called the Field of Blood. Then was fulfilled what had been said through Jeremiah the prophet, *And they took the thirty pieces of silver, the value of a man with a price on his head, a price set by some of the Israelites, and they paid it out for the potter's field just as the Lord had commanded me.*

[Beginning of Shorter Form]

9. JESUS BEFORE PILATE

N. [NOW] Jesus stood before the governor, and he questioned him, **V.** "Are you the king of the Jews?" **N.** Jesus said, ✝ *"You say so."* **N.** And when he was accused by the chief priests and elders, he made no answer. Then Pilate said to him, **V.** "Do you not hear how many things they are testifying against you?" **N.** But he did not answer him one word, so that the governor was greatly amazed.

Now on the occasion of the feast the governor was accustomed to release to the crowd one prisoner whom they wished. And at that time they had a notorious prisoner called Barabbas. So when they had assembled, Pilate said to them, **V.** "Which one do you want me to release to you, Barabbas, or Jesus called Christ?" **N.** For he knew that it was out of envy that they had handed him over. While he was still seated on the bench, his wife sent him a message, **V.** "Have nothing to do with that righteous man. I suffered much in a dream today because of him." **N.** The chief priests and the elders persuaded the crowds to ask for Barabbas but to destroy Jesus. The governor said to them in reply, **V.** "Which of the two do you want me to release to you?" **N.** They answered, **C. "Barabbas!" N.** Pilate said to them, **V.** "Then what shall I do with Jesus called Christ?" **N.** They all said, **C. "Let him be crucified!" N.** But he said, **V.** "Why? What evil has he done?" **N.** They only shouted the louder, **C. "Let him be crucified!" N.** When Pilate saw that he was not succeeding at all, but that a riot was breaking out instead, he took water and washed his hands in the sight of the crowd, saying, **V.** "I am innocent of this man's blood. Look to it yourselves." **N.** And the whole people said in reply, **C. "His blood be upon us and upon our children." N.** Then he released Barabbas to them, but after he had Jesus scourged, he handed him over to be crucified.

10. THE CROWNING WITH THORNS

N. THEN the soldiers of the governor took Jesus inside the praetorium and gathered the whole cohort around him. They stripped off his clothes and threw a scarlet military cloak about him. Weaving a crown out of thorns, they placed it on his head, and a reed in his right hand. And kneeling before him, they mocked him, saying, **N. "Hail, King of the Jews!"** They spat upon him and took the reed and kept striking him on the head. And when they had mocked him, they stripped him of the cloak, dressed him in his own clothes, and led him off to crucify him.

11. THE WAY OF THE CROSS

N. AS they were going out, they met a Cyrenian named Simon; this man they pressed into service to carry his cross.

And when they came to a place called Golgotha— which means Place of the Skull—, they gave Jesus wine to drink mixed with gall. But when he had tasted it, he refused to drink.

12. THE CRUCIFIXION

N. AFTER they had crucified him, they divided his garments by casting lots; then they sat down and kept watch over him there. And they placed over his head the written charge against him: This is Jesus, the King of the Jews. Two revolutionaries were cruci- fied with him, one on his right and the other on his left. Those passing by reviled him, shaking their heads and saying, **C. "You who would destroy the temple and rebuild it in three days, save yourself, if you are the Son of God, and come down from the cross!" N.** Likewise the chief priests with the scribes and elders mocked him and said, **C. "He saved others; he cannot save himself. So he is the king of Israel! Let him come down from the cross now, and we will believe in him. He trusted in God; let him deliver him now if he wants him. For he said, 'I am the Son of God.' " N.** The revolu- tionaries who were crucified with him also kept abus- ing him in the same way.

13. THE DEATH OF JESUS

N. FROM noon onward, darkness came over the whole land until three in the afternoon. And about three o'clock Jesus cried out in a loud voice, ✚ *"Eli, Eli, lema sabachthani?"* **N.** which means, ✚ *"My God, my God, why have you forsaken me?"* **N.** Some of the bystanders who heard it said, **C. "This one is calling for Elijah." N.** Immediately one of them ran to get a sponge; he soaked it in wine, and putting it on a reed, gave it to him to drink. But the rest said, **C. "Wait, let us see if Elijah comes to save him." N.** But Jesus cried out again in a loud voice, and gave up his spirit.

Here all kneel and pause for a short time.

And behold, the veil of the sanctuary was torn in two from top to bottom. The earth quaked, rocks were split, tombs were opened, and the bodies of many saints who had fallen asleep were raised. And coming forth from their tombs after his resurrection, they entered the holy city and appeared to many. The centurion and the men with him who were keeping watch over Jesus feared greatly when they saw the earthquake and all that was happening, and they said, **C. "Truly, this was the Son of God!"**

[End of Shorter Form]

N. There were many women there, looking on from a distance, who had followed Jesus from Galilee, ministering to him. Among them were Mary Magdalene and Mary the mother of James and Joseph, and the mother of the sons of Zebedee.

14. THE BURIAL

N. WHEN it was evening, there came a rich man from Arimathea named Joseph, who was himself a disciple of Jesus. He went to Pilate and asked for the body of Jesus; then Pilate ordered it to be handed over. Taking the body, Joseph wrapped it in clean linen and laid it in his new tomb that he had hewn in the rock. Then he rolled a huge stone across the entrance to the tomb and departed. But Mary Magdalene and the other Mary remained sitting there, facing the tomb.

The next day, the one following the day of preparation, the chief priests and the Pharisees gathered before Pilate and said, **C. "Sir, we remember that this impostor while still alive said, 'After three days I will be raised up.' Give orders, then, that the grave be secured until the third day, lest his disciples come and steal him and say to the people, 'He has been raised from the dead.' This last imposture would be worse than the first." N.** Pilate said to them, **V. "The guard is yours; go, secure it as best you can." N.** So they went and secured the tomb by fixing a seal to the stone and setting the guard.—The Gospel of the Lord. ℟. **Praise to you, Lord Jesus Christ.** → No. 14, p. 18

PRAYER OVER THE GIFTS [Pleasing to God]

Lord,
may the suffering and death of Jesus, your only Son,
make us pleasing to you.
Alone we can do nothing,
but may this perfect sacrifice
win us your mercy and love.
We ask this in the name of Jesus the Lord. ℟. **Amen.** ↓

PREFACE (P 19) [Raised to Holiness of Life]

℣. The Lord be with you. ℟. **And also with you.** ℣. Lift up your hearts. ℟. **We lift them up to the Lord.** ℣. Let us give thanks to the Lord our God. ℟. **It is right to give him thanks and praise.**

Father, all-powerful and ever-living God,
we do well always and everywhere to give you thanks

through Jesus Christ our Lord.
Though he was sinless, he suffered willingly for sinners.
Though innocent, he accepted death to save the guilty.
By his dying he has destroyed our sins.
By his rising he has raised us up to holiness of life.
We praise you, Lord, with all the angels
in their song of joy: → No. 23, p. 23

COMMUNION ANT. Mt 26:42 **[God's Will]**

Father, if this cup may not pass, but I must drink it, then your will be done. ↓

PRAYER AFTER COMMUNION **[Perseverance]**

Lord,
you have satisfied our hunger with this eucharistic food.
The death of your Son gives us hope and strengthens our faith.
May his resurrection give us perseverance
and lead us to salvation.
We ask this through Christ our Lord.
℟. **Amen.** → No. 32, p. 70

Optional Solemn Blessings, p. 92, and Prayers Over the People, p. 99

"The Spirit of the Lord is upon me."

APRIL 21

HOLY THURSDAY

CHRISM MASS

This Mass, which the bishop concelebrates with his presbyterium and at which the oils are blessed, manifests the communion of the priests with their bishop. It is thus desirable that, if possible, all the priests take part in it, together with parish representatives, and receive communion under both kinds. This day also is dedicated to the renewal of priestly ministry.

ENTRANCE ANT. Rv 1:6   [Kingdom of Priests]

Jesus Christ has made us a kingdom of priests to serve his God and Father: glory and kingship be his for ever and ever. Amen.   ➔ No. 2, p. 10

The Gloria is sung or said.

OPENING PRAYER   [Faithful Witnesses]

Father,
by the power of the Holy Spirit
you anointed your only Son Messiah and Lord of cre-
    ation;
you have given us a share in his consecration
to priestly service in your Church.
Help us to be faithful witnesses in the world

274

to the salvation Christ won for all mankind.
We ask this . . . for ever and ever. ℟. **Amen.** ↓

FIRST READING Is 61:1-3ab, 6a, 8b-9 [The Lord's Anointed]

The prophet, anointed by God to bring the Good News to the poor, proclaims a message filled with hope. It is one that replaces mourning with gladness.

A reading from the Book of the Prophet Isaiah

THE spirit of the Lord GOD is upon me,
   because the LORD has anointed me;
he has sent me to bring glad tidings to the poor,
   to heal the brokenhearted,
to proclaim liberty to the captives
   and release to the prisoners,
to announce a year of favor from the LORD
   and a day of vindication by our God,
   to comfort all who mourn;
to place on those who mourn in Zion
   a diadem instead of ashes,
to give them oil of gladness in place of mourning,
   a glorious mantle instead of a listless spirit.
You yourselves shall be named priests of the LORD,
   ministers of our God you shall be called.
I will give them their recompense faithfully,
   a lasting covenant I will make with them.
Their descendants shall be renowned among the
      nations,
   and their offspring among the peoples;
all who see them shall acknowledge them
   as a race the LORD has blessed.
The word of the Lord. ℟. **Thanks be to God.** ↓

RESPONSORIAL PSALM Ps 89   [God the Savior]

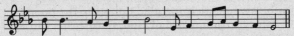

℟. For ev - er I will sing the good-ness of the Lord.

I have found David, my servant;
  with my holy oil I have anointed him,
that my hand may be always with him,
  and that my arm may make him strong.—℟.

My faithfulness and my kindness shall be with him,
  and through my name shall his horn be exalted.
"He shall say of me, 'You are my father,
  my God, the Rock my savior.' "—℟. ↓

SECOND READING Rv 1:5-8   [The Alpha and the Omega]

God says, "I am the Alpha and the Omega, the one who is
and who was and who is to come, the almighty!" All shall
see God as he comes amid the clouds.

A reading from the Book of Revelation

JESUS Christ is the faithful witness, the firstborn of
the dead and ruler of the kings of earth. To him who
loves us and has freed us from our sins by his blood,
who has made us into a kingdom, priests for his God
and Father, to him be glory and power forever and
ever! Amen.

  Behold, he is coming amid the clouds,
    and every eye will see him,
    even of those who pierced him.
  All the peoples of the earth will lament him.
    Yes. Amen.
"I am the Alpha and the Omega," says the Lord God,
"the one who is and who was and who is to come, the
almighty!"—The word of the Lord. ℟. **Thanks be to
God.** ↓

VERSE BEFORE THE GOSPEL Is 61:1 (cited in Lk 4:18)
                                            [Glad Tidings]
℟. **Glory to you, Word of God, Lord Jesus Christ!***
The Spirit of the Lord is upon me
for he sent me to bring glad tidings to the poor.
℟. **Glory to you, Word of God, Lord Jesus Christ!** ↓

* See p. 16 for other Gospel Acclamations.

GOSPEL Lk 4:16-21   [Christ the Messiah]

Jesus reads in the synagogue at Nazareth the words of Isaiah quoted in the first reading. Jesus is the Anointed One. He tells the people that today Isaiah's prophecy is fulfilled.

℣. The Lord be with you. ℟. **And also with you.**

✤ A reading from the holy Gospel according to Luke.

℟. **Glory to you, Lord.**

JESUS came to Nazareth, where he had grown up, and went according to his custom into the synagogue on the sabbath day. He stood up to read and was handed a scroll of the prophet Isaiah. He unrolled the scroll and found the passage where it was written:

The Spirit of the Lord is upon me,
because he has anointed me
   to bring glad tidings to the poor.
He has sent me to proclaim liberty to captives
   and recovery of sight to the blind,
   to let the oppressed go free,
and to proclaim a year acceptable to the Lord.

Rolling up the scroll, he handed it back to the attendant and sat down, and the eyes of all in the synagogue looked intently at him. He said to them, "Today this Scripture passage is fulfilled in your hearing."— The Gospel of the Lord. ℟. **Praise to you, Lord Jesus Christ.**   → No. 14, p. 18

Renewal of Commitment to Priestly Service

After the homily the bishop speaks to the priests:

My brothers,
today we celebrate the memory of the first eucharist,
at which our Lord Jesus Christ
shared with his apostles and with us
his call to the priestly service of his Church.
Now, in the presence of your bishop and God's holy
   people,

are you ready to renew your own dedication to Christ
as priests of his new covenant?
Priests: I am.

Bishop: At your ordination
you accepted the responsibilities of the priesthood
out of love for the Lord Jesus and his Church.
Are you resolved to unite yourselves more closely to
    Christ
and to try to become more like him
by joyfully sacrificing your own pleasure and ambition
to bring his peace and love to your brothers and sis-
    ters?
Priests: I am.

Bishop: Are you resolved
to be faithful ministers of the mysteries of God,
to celebrate the eucharist and the other liturgical serv-
    ices
with sincere devotion?
Are you resolved to imitate Jesus Christ,
the head and shepherd of the Church,
by teaching the Christian faith
without thinking of your own profit,
solely for the well-being of the people
you were sent to serve?
Priests: I am.

Then the bishop addresses the people:
My brothers and sisters,
pray for your priests.
Ask the Lord to bless them with the fullness of his love,
to help them be faithful ministers of Christ the High
    Priest,
so that they will be able to lead you to him,
the fountain of your salvation.
**People: Lord Jesus Christ, hear us and answer our
    prayer.**

Bishop: Pray also for me
that despite my own unworthiness
I may faithfully fulfill the office of apostle
which Jesus Christ, has entrusted to me.
Pray that I may become more like
our High Priest and Good Shepherd,
the teacher and servant of all,
and so be a genuine sign
of Christ's loving presence among you.

**People: Lord Jesus Christ, hear us and answer our
prayer.**

Bishop: May the Lord in his love
keep you close to him always,
and may he bring all of us,
his priests and people,
to eternal life.
All: **Amen.**

*The Profession of Faith and General Intercessions are omit-
ted.*　➜ *No. 17, p. 20*

PRAYER OVER THE GIFTS　　　　　　　　　[New Life]

Lord God,
may the power of this sacrifice
cleanse the old weakness of our human nature.
Give us a newness of life
and bring us to salvation.
Grant this through Christ our Lord. ℟. **Amen.** ↓

PREFACE (P 20)　　　[Continuation of Christ's Priesthood]

℣. The Lord be with you. ℟. **And also with you.**
℣. Lift up your hearts. ℟. **We lift them up to the Lord.**
℣. Let us give thanks to the Lord our God. ℟. **It is right
to give him thanks and praise.**

Father, all-powerful and ever-living God,
we do well always and everywhere to give you thanks.

By your Holy Spirit
you anointed your only Son
High Priest of the new and eternal covenant.
With wisdom and love you have planned
that this one priesthood should continue in the Church.
Christ gives the dignity of a royal priesthood
to the people he has made his own.
From these, with a brother's love,
he chooses men to share his sacred ministry
by the laying on of hands.
He appoints them to renew in his name
the sacrifice of our redemption
as they set before your family his paschal meal.
He calls them to lead your holy people in love,
nourish them by your word,
and strengthen them through the sacraments.
Father, they are to give their lives in your service
and for the salvation of your people
as they strive to grow in the likeness of Christ
and honor you by their courageous witness of faith
    and love.
We praise you Lord, with all the angels and saints
in their song of joy: → No. 23, p. 23

Communion Ant. Ps 89:2   [The Lord's Faithfulness]

**For ever I will sing the goodness of the Lord; I will
proclaim your faithfulness to all generations. ↓**

Prayer After Communion   [Renewed in Christ]

Lord God almighty,
you have given us fresh strength
in these sacramental gifts.
Renew in us the image of Christ's goodness.
We ask this in the name of Jesus the Lord.
℟. **Amen.**   → No. 32, p. 70

Optional Solemn Blessings, p. 92, and Prayers Over the People, p. 99

"Do this in remembrance of me."

APRIL 21

HOLY THURSDAY

EVENING MASS OF THE LORD'S SUPPER

The Evening Mass of the Lord's Supper commemorates the institution of the Holy Eucharist and the sacrament of Holy Orders. It was at this Mass that Jesus changed bread and wine into his Body and Blood. He then directed his disciples to carry out this same ritual: "Do this in remembrance of me."

Introductory Rites and Liturgy of the Word

Entrance Ant. See Gal 6:14   [Glory in the Cross]

We should glory in the cross of our Lord Jesus Christ, for he is our salvation, our life and our resurrection; through him we are saved and made free.   → No. 2, p. 10

During the singing of the Gloria, the church bells are rung and then remain silent until the Easter Vigil, unless the conference of bishops or the Ordinary decrees otherwise.

OPENING PRAYER   [Fullness of Love]

God our Father,
we are gathered here to share in the supper
which your only Son left to his Church to reveal his
   love.

He gave it to us when he was about to die
and commanded us to celebrate it as the new and eternal sacrifice.
We pray that in this eucharist
we may find the fullness of love and life.
Grant this through our Lord Jesus Christ, your Son,
who lives and reigns with you and the Holy Spirit,
one God, for ever and ever. ℟. **Amen.** ↓

FIRST READING Ex 12:1-8, 11-14   [The First Passover]

For the protection of the Jewish people, strict religious and
dietary instructions are given to Moses by God. The law of
the Passover meal requires that the doorposts and lintels
of each house be marked with the blood of the sacrificial
animal so that the Lord can "go through Egypt striking
down every firstborn of the land, both man and beast."

A reading from the Book of Exodus

THE LORD said to Moses and Aaron in the land of
Egypt, "This month shall stand at the head of your
calendar; you shall reckon it the first month of the
year. Tell the whole community of Israel: On the tenth
of this month every one of your families must procure
for itself a lamb, one apiece for each household. If a
family is too small for a whole lamb, it shall join the
nearest household in procuring one and shall share in
the lamb in proportion to the number of persons who
partake of it. The lamb must be a year-old male and
without blemish. You may take it from either the sheep
or the goats. You shall keep it until the fourteenth day
of this month, and then, with the whole assembly of
Israel present, it shall be slaughtered during the
evening twilight. They shall take some of its blood and
apply it to the two doorposts and the lintel of every
house in which they partake of the lamb. That same
night they shall eat its roasted flesh with unleavened
bread and bitter herbs.

"This is how you are to eat it: with your loins girt, sandals on your feet and your staff in hand, you shall eat like those who are in flight. It is the Passover of the LORD. For on this same night I will go through Egypt, striking down every firstborn of the land, both man and beast, and executing judgment on all the gods of Egypt—I, the LORD! But the blood will mark the houses where you are. Seeing the blood, I will pass over you; thus, when I strike the land of Egypt, no destructive blow will come upon you.

"This day shall be a memorial feast for you, which all your generations shall celebrate with pilgrimage to the LORD, as a perpetual institution."—The word of the Lord. ℟. **Thanks be to God.** ↓

RESPONSORIAL PSALM Ps 116   [Thanksgiving]

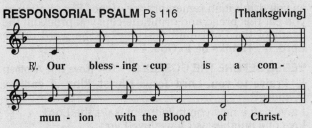

℟. Our bless - ing - cup is a com - mun - ion with the Blood of Christ.

How shall I make a return to the LORD
    for all the good he has done for me?
The cup of salvation I will take up,
    and I will call upon the name of the LORD.—℟.

Precious in the eyes of the LORD
    is the death of his faithful ones.
I am your servant, the son of your handmaid;
    you have loosed my bonds.—℟.

To you will I offer sacrifice of thanksgiving,
    and I will call upon the name of the LORD.
My vows to the LORD I will pay
    in the presence of all his people.—℟. ↓

SECOND READING 1 Cor 11:23-26   [The Lord's Supper]

Paul recounts the events of the Last Supper which were handed down to him. The changing of bread and wine into the Body and Blood of the Lord proclaimed again his death. It was to be a sacrificial meal.

A reading from the first Letter of Saint Paul
to the Corinthians

BROTHERS and sisters: I received from the Lord what I also handed on to you, that the Lord Jesus, on the night he was handed over, took bread, and, after he had given thanks, broke it and said, "This is my body that is for you. Do this in remembrance of me." In the same way also the cup, after supper, saying, "This cup is the new covenant in my blood. Do this, as often as you drink it, in remembrance of me." For as often as you eat this bread and drink the cup, you proclaim the death of the Lord until he comes.—The word of the Lord. ℟. **Thanks be to God.** ↓

VERSE BEFORE THE GOSPEL Jn 13:34 [Love One Another]

℟. **Praise to you, Lord Jesus Christ, king of endless glory!***

I give you a new commandment, says the Lord:
love one another as I have loved you.

℟. **Praise to you, Lord Jesus Christ, king of endless glory!** ↓

GOSPEL Jn 13:1-15   [Love and Service]

Jesus washes the feet of his disciples to prove to them his sincere love and great humility which they should imitate. He teaches them that, although free from sin and not unworthy to receive his most holy body and blood, they should be purified of all evil inclinations.

℣. The Lord be with you. ℟. **And also with you.**
✛ A reading from the holy Gospel according to John.
℟. **Glory to you, Lord.**

---

* See p. 16 for other Gospel Acclamations.

B EFORE the feast of Passover, Jesus knew that his hour had come to pass from this world to the Father. He loved his own in the world and he loved them to the end. The devil had already induced Judas, son of Simon the Iscariot, to hand him over. So, during supper, fully aware that the Father had put everything into his power and that he had come from God and was returning to God, he rose from supper and took off his outer garments. He took a towel and tied it around his waist. Then he poured water into a basin and began to wash the disciples' feet and dry them with the towel around his waist. He came to Simon Peter, who said to him, "Master, are you going to wash my feet?" Jesus answered and said to him, "What I am doing, you do not understand now, but you will understand later." Peter said to him, "You will never wash my feet." Jesus answered him, "Unless I wash you, you will have no inheritance with me." Simon Peter said to him, "Master, then not only my feet, but my hands and head as well." Jesus said to him, "Whoever has bathed has no need except to have his feet washed, for he is clean all over; so you are clean, but not all." For he knew who would betray him; for this reason, he said, "Not all of you are clean."

So when he had washed their feet and put his garments back on and reclined at table again, he said to them, "Do you realize what I have done for you? You call me 'teacher' and 'master,' and rightly so, for indeed I am. If I, therefore, the master and teacher, have washed your feet, you ought to wash one another's feet. I have given you a model to follow, so that as I have done for you, you should also do."—The Gospel of the Lord. ℟. **Praise to you, Lord Jesus Christ.**

➜ No. 14, p. 18

The homily should explain the principal mysteries which are commemorated in this Mass: the institution of the eucharist, the institution of the priesthood, and Christ's commandment of brotherly love.

Washing of Feet

Depending on pastoral circumstances, the washing of feet follows the homily.

The men who have been chosen are led by the ministers to chairs prepared in a suitable place. Then the priest (removing his chasuble if necessary) goes to each man. With the help of the ministers, he pours water over each one's feet and dries them.

Meanwhile some of the following antiphons or other appropriate songs are sung.

ANTIPHON 1 See Jn 13:4, 5, 15   [Jesus' Example]

The Lord Jesus,
when he had eaten with his disciples,
poured water into a basin
and began to wash their feet, saying:
This example I leave you.

ANTIPHON 2 Jn 13:6, 7, 8   [Peter's Understanding]

Lord, do you wash my feet?
Jesus said to him:
If I do not wash your feet,
you can have no part with me.

℣. So he came to Simon Peter,
who said to him:
Lord, do you wash my feet?

℣. Now you do not know what I am doing,
but later you will understand.
Lord, do you wash my feet?

ANTIPHON 3 See Jn 13:14   [Service]

If I, your Lord and Teacher, have washed your feet,
then surely you must wash one another's feet.

ANTIPHON 4 Jn 13:35   [Identified by Love]

If there is this love among you,
all will know that you are my disciples.

℣. Jesus said to his disciples:
If there is this love among you,
all will know that you are my disciples.

ANTIPHON 5 Jn 13:34   [New Commandment]

I give you a new commandment:
love one another as I have loved you, says the Lord.

ANTIPHON 6 1 Cor 13:13   [Greatest Is Love]

Faith, hope, and love,
let these endure among you;
and the greatest of these is love.

*The general intercessions follow the washing of feet, or, if
this does not take place, they follow the homily. The profession of faith is not said in this Mass.*

The Liturgy of the Eucharist

*At the beginning of the liturgy of the eucharist, there may be
a procession of the faithful with gifts for the poor. During the
procession the following may be sung, or another appropriate
song.*

[Christ's Love]

Ant. ℣. Where charity and love are found, there is
     God.
℣. The love of Christ has gathered us together into
     one.
℣. Let us rejoice and be glad in him.
℣. Let us fear and love the living God,
℣. and love each other from the depths of our heart.
Ant. Where charity and love are found, there is God.
℣. Therefore when we are together,
℣. let us take heed not to be divided in mind.
℣. Let there be an end to bitterness and quarrels, an
     end to strife,

℣. **and in our midst be Christ our God.**
Ant. **Where charity and love are found, there is God.**
℣. **And, in company with the blessed, may we see**
℣. **your face in glory, Christ our God,**
℣. **pure and unbounded joy**
℣. **for ever and ever.**
Ant. **Where charity and love are found, there is God.**

➜ No. 17, p. 20

PRAYER OVER THE GIFTS   [Work of Redemption]
Lord,
make us worthy to celebrate these mysteries.
Each time we offer this memorial sacrifice
the work of our redemption is accomplished.
We ask this in the name of Jesus the Lord.
℞. **Amen.**   ➜ No. 21, p. 22 (Pref. P 47)

*When Eucharistic Prayer I is used, the special Holy Thursday
forms of* In union with the whole Church, Father, accept
this offering, *and* The day before he suffered *are said:*

In union with the whole Church
we celebrate that day
when Jesus Christ, our Lord,
was betrayed for us.
We honor Mary,
the ever-virgin mother of Jesus Christ our Lord and God.
We honor Joseph, her husband,
the apostles and martyrs
Peter and Paul, Andrew,
(James, John, Thomas,
James, Philip,
Bartholomew, Matthew, Simon and Jude;
we honor Linus, Cletus, Clement, Sixtus,
Cornelius, Cyprian, Lawrence, Chrysogonus,
John and Paul, Cosmas and Damian)
and all the saints.
May their merits and prayers

gain us your constant help and protection.
(Through Christ our Lord. Amen.)

Father, accept this offering
from your whole family
in memory of the day when Jesus Christ, our Lord,
gave the mysteries of his body and blood
for his disciples to celebrate.
Grant us your peace in this life,
save us from final damnation,
and count us among those you have chosen.
(Through Christ our Lord. Amen.)

Bless and approve our offering;
make it acceptable to you,
an offering in spirit and in truth.
Let it become for us
the body and blood of Jesus Christ,
your only Son, our Lord.

The day before he suffered
to save us and all men,
that is, today,
he took bread in his sacred hands
and looking up to heaven,
to you, his almighty Father,
he gave you thanks and praise.
He broke the bread,
gave it to his disciples, and said:

Take this, all of you, and eat it:
this is my body which will be given up for you.

The rest follows the Roman canon, pp. 26-28.

Communion Ant. 1 Cor 11:24-25   [In Remembrance of Christ]
This body will be given for you. This is the cup of the new covenant in my blood; whenever you receive them, do so in remembrance of me. ↓

*After the distribution of communion, the ciborium with hosts
for Good Friday is left on the altar.*

*A period of silence may be observed after communion, or a
psalm or song of praise may be sung.*

PRAYER AFTER COMMUNION   [New Life]

Almighty God,
we receive new life
from the supper your Son gave us in this world.
May we find full contentment
in the meal we hope to share
in your eternal kingdom.
We ask this through Christ our Lord. ℟. **Amen.**

The Mass concludes with this prayer.

Transfer of the Holy Eucharist

*After the prayer the priest stands before the altar and puts
incense in the thurible. Kneeling, he incenses the Blessed
Sacrament three times. Then he receives the humeral veil,
takes the ciborium, and covers it with the ends of the veil.*

*The Blessed Sacrament is carried through the church in pro-
cession, led by a cross-bearer and accompanied by candles
and incense, to the place of reposition prepared in a chapel
suitably decorated for the occasion. During the procession
the hymn* Pange, lingua *(exclusive of the last two stanzas) or
some other eucharistic song is sung.*

PANGE LINGUA   [Adoring the Lord]

Sing my tongue, the Savior's glory,
Of his flesh the mystery sing;
Of his blood all price exceeding,
Shed by our immortal king,
Destined for the world's redemption,
From a noble womb to spring.

Of a pure and spotless Virgin
Born for us on earth below,
He, as man with man conversing,

Stayed the seeds of truth to sow;
Then he closed in solemn order
Wondrously his life of woe.

On the night of that Last Supper,
Seated with his chosen band,
He, the paschal victim eating,
First fulfills the law's command;
Then as food to all his brethren
Gives himself with his own hand.

Word made Flesh, the bread of nature,
By his word to flesh he turns;
Wine into his blood he changes:
What though sense no change discerns,
Only be the heart in earnest,
Faith her lesson quickly learns.

When the procession reaches the place of reposition, the priest sets the ciborium down. Then he puts incense in the thurible and, kneeling, incenses the Blessed Sacrament, while Tantum ergo Sacramentum *is sung. The tabernacle of reposition is then closed.*

Down in adoration falling,
Lo! the sacred host we hail,
Lo! o'er ancient forms departing
Newer rites of grace prevail;
Faith for all defects supplying,
Where the feeble senses fail.

To the everlasting Father,
And the Son who reigns on high
With the Holy Spirit proceeding
Forth from each eternally,
Be salvation, honor, blessing,
Might and endless majesty. Amen.

After a period of silent adoration, the priest and ministers genuflect and return to the sacristy.

Then the altar is stripped and, if possible, the crosses are removed from the church. It is desirable to cover any crosses which remain in the church.

The faithful should be encouraged to continue adoration before the Blessed Sacrament for a suitable period of time during the night.

"And bowing his head, [Jesus] handed over the spirit."

APRIL 22

GOOD FRIDAY

CELEBRATION OF THE LORD'S PASSION

The liturgy of Good Friday recalls graphically the passion and death of Jesus. The reading of the passion describes the suffering and death of Jesus. Today we show great reverence for the crucifix, the sign of our redemption.

According to the Church's ancient tradition, the sacraments, except for Penance and the Anointing of the Sick, are not celebrated today or tomorrow. The celebration of the Lord's passion takes place in the afternoon, about three o'clock, unless pastoral reasons suggest a later hour.

The priest and deacon, wearing red Mass vestments, go to the altar. There they make a reverence and prostrate themselves, or they may kneel. All pray silently for a while. Then the priest goes to the chair with the ministers. He faces the people and, with hands joined, sings or says one of the following prayers.

PRAYER [Make Us Holy]

Lord,
by shedding his blood for us,
your Son, Jesus Christ,
established the paschal mystery.

In your goodness, make us holy
and watch over us always.
We ask this through Christ our Lord. ℟. **Amen.** ↓

OR   [Likeness of Christ]

Lord,
by the suffering of Christ your Son
you have saved us all from the death
we inherited from sinful Adam.
By the law of nature
we have borne the likeness of his manhood.
May the sanctifying power of grace
help us to put on the likeness of our Lord in heaven,
who lives and reigns for ever and ever. ℟. **Amen.** ↓

PART ONE: LITURGY OF THE WORD

FIRST READING Is 52:13—53:12   [Suffering and Glory]

The suffering Servant shall be raised up and exalted. The Servant remains one with all people in sorrow and yet distinct from each of them in innocence of life and total service to God. The doctrine of expiatory suffering finds supreme expression in these words.

A reading from the Book of the Prophet Isaiah

S EE, my servant shall prosper,
he shall be raised high and greatly exalted.
Even as many were amazed at him—
        so marred was his look beyond human semblance
        and his appearance beyond that of the sons of
            man—
so shall he startle many nations,
        because of him kings shall stand speechless;
for those who have not been told shall see,
        those who have not heard shall ponder it.

Who would believe what we have heard?
        To whom has the arm of the LORD been revealed?
He grew up like a sapling before him,
like a shoot from the parched earth;

there was in him no stately bearing to make us look
    at him,
      nor appearance that would attract us to him.
He was spurned and avoided by people,
      a man of suffering, accustomed to infirmity,
one of those from whom people hide their faces,
      spurned, and we held him in no esteem.

Yet it was our infirmities that he bore,
      our sufferings that he endured,
while we thought of him as stricken,
      as one smitten by God and afflicted.
But he was pierced for our offenses,
      crushed for our sins;
upon him was the chastisement that makes us whole,
      by his stripes we were healed.
We had all gone astray like sheep,
      each following his own way;
but the LORD laid upon him
      the guilt of us all.

Though he was harshly treated, he submitted
      and opened not his mouth;
like a lamb led to the slaughter
      or a sheep before the shearers,
      he was silent and opened not his mouth.
Oppressed and condemned, he was taken away,
      and who would have thought any more of his
        destiny?
When he was cut off from the land of the living,
      and smitten for the sin of his people,
a grave was assigned him among the wicked
      and a burial place with evildoers,
though he had done no wrong
      nor spoken any falsehood.
But the Lord was pleased
      to crush him in infirmity.

If he gives his life as an offering for sin,
      he shall see his descendants in a long life,

and the will of the LORD shall be accomplished
through him.
Because of his affliction
he shall see the light in fullness of days;
through his suffering, my servant shall justify many,
and their guilt he shall bear.
Therefore I will give him his portion among the great,
and he shall divide the spoils with the mighty,
because he surrendered himself to death
and was counted among the wicked;
and he shall take away the sins of many,
and win pardon for their offenses.
The word of the Lord. ℟. **Thanks be to God.** ↓

RESPONSORIAL PSALM Ps 31   [Trust in God]

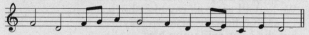

℟. Fa - ther, in -to your hands I com - mend my spir - it.

In you, O LORD, I take refuge;
let me never be put to shame.
In your justice rescue me.
Into your hands I commend my spirit;
you will redeem me, O LORD, O faithful God.

℟. **Father, into your hands I commend my spirit.**

For all my foes I am an object of reproach,
a laughingstock to my neighbors, and a dread to my
friends;
they who see me abroad flee from me.
I am forgotten like the unremembered dead;
I am like a dish that is broken.

℟. **Father, into your hands I commend my spirit.**

But my trust is in you, O LORD;
I say, "You are my God."

In your hands is my destiny; rescue me
   from the clutches of my enemies and my persecutors.

℟. **Father, into your hands I commend my spirit.**

Let your face shine upon your servant;
   save me in your kindness.
Take courage and be stouthearted,
   all you who hope in the LORD.

℟. **Father, into your hands I commend my spirit.** ↓

SECOND READING Heb 4:14-16; 5:7-9   [Access to Christ]

The theme of the compassionate high priest appears again
in this passage. In him the Christian can approach God
confidently and without fear. Christ learned obedience
from his sufferings whereby he became the source of eternal life for all.

A reading from the Letter to the Hebrews

BROTHERS and sisters: Since we have a great high
priest who has passed through the heavens, Jesus,
the Son of God, let us hold fast to our confession. For
we do not have a high priest who is unable to sympa-
thize with our weaknesses, but one who has similarly
been tested in every way, yet without sin. So let us confidently approach the throne of grace to receive mercy
and to find grace for timely help.

   In the days when Christ was in the flesh, he offered
prayers and supplications with loud cries and tears to
the one who was able to save him from death, and he
was heard because of his reverence. Son though he
was, he learned obedience from what he suffered; and
when he was made perfect, he became the source of
eternal salvation for all who obey him.—The word of
the Lord. ℟. **Thanks be to God.** ↓

VERSE BEFORE THE GOSPEL Phil 2:8-9   [Obedient for Us]

℟. **Praise and honor to you, Lord Jesus Christ!***
Christ became obedient to the point of death,
even death on a cross.
Because of this, God greatly exalted him
and bestowed on him the name which is above every
   other name.
℟. **Praise and honor to you, Lord Jesus Christ!** ↓

GOSPEL Jn 18:1—19:42   [Christ's Passion]

Finally the passion is read in the same way as on the preceding Sunday. The narrator is noted by N, the words of Jesus by a ✠ and the words of others by V (Voice) and C (Crowd). The parts of the Crowd (C) printed in boldface type may be recited by the people.

It is important for us to understand the meaning of Christ's sufferings today. See the note on p. 237.

The beginning scene is Christ's agony in the garden. Our Lord knows what is to happen. The Scriptures recount the betrayal, the trial, the condemnation, and the crucifixion of Jesus.

N. THE Passion of our Lord Jesus Christ according to John

1. JESUS IS ARRESTED

N. JESUS went out with his disciples across the Kidron valley to where there was a garden, into which he and his disciples entered. Judas his betrayer also knew the place, because Jesus had often met there with his disciples. So Judas got a band of soldiers and guards from the chief priests and the Pharisees and went there with lanterns, torches, and weapons. Jesus, knowing everything that was going to happen to him, went out and said to them, ✠ *"Whom are you looking for?"* **N.** They answered him, **C. "Jesus the Nazorean."** **N.** He said to them, ✠ *"I AM."* **N.** Judas his betrayer was also with them. When he said

---

* *See p. 16 for other Gospel Acclamations.*

to them, "I AM," they turned away and fell to the ground. So he again asked them, ✚ *"Whom are you looking for?"* **N.** They said, **C.** **"Jesus the Nazorean."** **N.** Jesus answered, ✚ *"I told you that I AM. So if you are looking for me, let these men go."* **N.** This was to fulfill what he had said, "I have not lost any of those you gave me." Then Simon Peter, who had a sword, drew it, struck the high priest's slave, and cut off his right ear. The slave's name was Malchus. Jesus said to Peter, ✚ *"Put your sword into its scabbard. Shall I not drink the cup that the Father gave me?"*

N. So the band of soldiers, the tribune, and the Jewish guards seized Jesus, bound him, and brought him to Annas first. He was the father-in-law of Caiaphas, who was high priest that year. It was Caiaphas who had counseled the Jews that it was better that one man should die rather than the people.

2. PETER'S FIRST DENIAL

N. **S**IMON Peter and another disciple followed Jesus. Now the other disciple was known to the high priest, and he entered the courtyard of the high priest with Jesus. But Peter stood at the gate outside. So the other disciple, the acquaintance of the high priest, went out and spoke to the gatekeeper and brought Peter in. Then the maid who was the gatekeeper said to Peter, **C.** **"You are not one of this man's disciples, are you?"** **N.** He said, **V.** "I am not." **N.** Now the slaves and the guards were standing around a charcoal fire that they had made, because it was cold, and were warming themselves. Peter was also standing there keeping warm.

3. THE INQUIRY BEFORE ANNAS

N. **T**HE high priest questioned Jesus about his disciples and about his doctrine. Jesus answered him, ✚ *"I have spoken publicly to the world. I have always taught in a synagogue or in the temple area* *where all the Jews gather, and in secret I have said nothing. Why ask me? Ask those who heard me what I said to them. They know what I said."* **N.** When he had said this, one of the temple guards standing there struck Jesus and said, **V.** "Is this the way you answer the high priest?" **N.** Jesus answered him, ✠ *"If I have spoken wrongly, testify to the wrong; but if I have spoken rightly, why do you strike me?"* **N.** Then Annas sent him bound to Caiaphas the high priest.

4. THE FURTHER DENIALS

N. **N**OW Simon Peter was standing there keeping warm. And they said to him, **C.** **"You are not one of his disciples, are you?"** **N.** He denied it and said, **V.** "I am not." **N.** One of the slaves of the high priest, a relative of the one whose ear Peter had cut off, said, **C.** **"Didn't I see you in the garden with him?"** **N.** Again Peter denied it. And immediately the cock crowed.

5. JESUS BROUGHT BEFORE PILATE

N. **T**HEN they brought Jesus from Caiaphas to the praetorium. It was morning. And they themselves did not enter the praetorium, in order not to be defiled so that they could eat the Passover. So Pilate came out to them and said, **V.** "What charge do you bring against this man?" **N.** They answered and said to him, **C.** **"If he were not a criminal, we would not have handed him over to you."** **N.** At this, Pilate said to them, **V.** "Take him yourselves, and judge him according to your law." **N.** The Jews answered him, **C.** **"We do not have the right to execute anyone,"** **N.** in order that the word of Jesus might be fulfilled that he said indicating the kind of death he would die.

6. JESUS QUESTIONED BY PILATE

N. **S**O Pilate went back into the praetorium and summoned Jesus and said to him, **V.** "Are you the King of the Jews?"**N.** Jesus answered, ✠ *"Do you say this on your own or have others told you about me?"* **N.** Pilate answered, **V.** "I am not a Jew, am I? Your own nation and the chief priests handed you over to me. What have you done?" **N.** Jesus answered, ✠ *"My kingdom does not belong to this world. If my kingdom did belong to this world, my attendants would be fighting to keep me from being handed over to the Jews. But as it is, my kingdom is not here."* **N.** So Pilate said to him, **V.** "Then you are a king?" **N.** Jesus answered, ✠ *"You say I am a king. For this I was born and for this I came into the world, to testify to the truth. Everyone who belongs to the truth listens to my voice."* **N.** Pilate said to him, **V.** "What is truth?"

7. BARABBAS CHOSEN OVER JESUS

N. WHEN he had said this, he again went out to the Jews and said to them, **V.** "I find no guilt in him. But you have a custom that I release one prisoner to you at Passover. Do you want me to release to you the King of the Jews?" **N.** They cried out again, **C.** "Not this one but Barabbas!" **N.** Now Barabbas was a revolutionary.

8. JESUS IS SCOURGED

N. THEN Pilate took Jesus and had him scourged. And the soldiers wove a crown out of thorns and placed it on his head, and clothed him in a purple cloak, and they came to him and said, **C.** "Hail, King of the Jews!" **N.** And they struck him repeatedly.

9. JESUS IS PRESENTED TO THE CROWD

N. ONCE more Pilate went out and said to them, **V.** "Look, I am bringing him out to you, so that you may know that I find no guilt in him." **N.** So Jesus came out, wearing the crown of thorns and the purple cloak. And Pilate said to them, **V.** "Behold, the man!" **N.** When the chief priests and the guards saw him they cried out, **C. "Crucify him, crucify him!"** N. Pilate said to them, **V.** "Take him yourselves and crucify him. I find no guilt in him." N. The Jews answered, **C. "We have a law, and according to that law he ought to die, because he made himself the Son of God."**

10. JESUS AGAIN QUESTIONED BY PILATE

N. **N**OW when Pilate heard this statement, he became even more afraid, and went back into the praetorium and said to Jesus, **V.** "Where are you from?" **N.** Jesus did not answer him. So Pilate said to him, **V.** "Do you not speak to me? Do you not know that I have power to release you and I have power to crucify you?" [**N.** Jesus answered him,] ✠ *"You would have no power over me if it had not been given to you from above. For this reason the one who handed me over to you has the greater sin."*

11. JESUS SENTENCED TO BE CRUCIFIED

N. **C**ONSEQUENTLY, Pilate tried to release him; but the Jews cried out, **C. "If you release him, you are not a Friend of Caesar. Everyone who makes himself a king opposes Caesar."** N. When Pilate heard these words he brought Jesus out and seated him on the judge's bench in the place called Stone Pavement, in Hebrew, Gabbatha. It was preparation day for Passover, and it was about noon. And he said to the Jews, **V.** "Behold, your king!" N. They cried out, **C. "Take him away, take him away! Crucify him!"** N. Pilate said to them, **V.** "Shall I crucify your king?" **N.** The chief priests answered, **C. "We have no king but Caesar."** N. Then he handed him over to them to be crucified.

12. CRUCIFIXION AND DEATH

N. **S**O they took Jesus, and, carrying the cross himself, he went out to what is called the Place of the Skull, in Hebrew, Golgotha. There they crucified him, and with him two others, one on either side, with Jesus in the middle. Pilate also had an inscription written and put on the cross. It read, "Jesus the Nazorean, the King of the Jews." Now many of the Jews read this inscription, because the place where Jesus was crucified was near the city; and it was written in Hebrew, Latin, and Greek. So the chief priests of the Jews said to Pilate, **C. "Do not write 'The King of the Jews,' but that he said, 'I am the King of the Jews.' "** N. Pilate answered, **V.** "What I have written, I have written."

N. When the soldiers had crucified Jesus, they took his clothes and divided them into four shares, a share for each soldier. They also took his tunic, but the tunic was seamless, woven in one piece from the top down. So they said to one another, **C. "Let's not tear it, but cast lots for it to see whose it will be,"** N. in order that the passage of Scripture might be fulfilled that says:

They divided my garments among them,
and for my vesture they cast lots.

This is what the soldiers did. Standing by the cross of Jesus were his mother and his mother's sister, Mary the wife of Clopas, and Mary of Magdala. When Jesus saw his mother and the disciple there whom he loved he said to his mother, ✠ *"Woman, behold, your son."* **N.** Then he said to the disciple, ✠ *"Behold, your mother."* **N.** And from that hour the disciple took her into his home.

After this, aware that everything was now finished, in order that the Scripture might be fulfilled, Jesus said, ✠ *"I thirst."* **N.** There was a vessel filled with common wine. So they put a sponge soaked in wine on a sprig of hyssop and put it up to his mouth. When Jesus had taken the wine, he said, ✠ *"It is finished."* And bowing his head, he handed over the spirit.

Here all kneel and pause for a short time.

13. THE BLOOD AND WATER

N. **N**OW since it was preparation day, in order that the bodies might not remain on the cross on the sabbath, for the sabbath day of that week was a solemn one, the Jews asked Pilate that their legs be broken and that they be taken down. So the soldiers came and broke the legs of the first and then of the other one who was crucified with Jesus. But when they came to Jesus and saw that he was already dead, they did not break his legs, but one soldier thrust his lance into his side, and immediately blood and water flowed out. An eyewitness has testified, and his testimony is true; he knows that he is speaking the truth, so that you also may come to believe. For this happened so that the Scripture passage might be fulfilled:

Not a bone of it will be broken.

And again another passage says:

They will look upon him whom they have pierced.

14. BURIAL OF JESUS

N. **A**FTER this, Joseph of Arimathea, secretly a disciple of Jesus for fear of the Jews, asked Pilate if he could remove the body of Jesus. And Pilate permitted it. So he came and took his body. Nicodemus, the one who had first come to him at night, also came bringing a mixture of myrrh and aloes weighing about one hundred pounds. They took the body of Jesus and bound it with burial cloths along with the spices, according to the Jewish burial custom. Now in the place where he had been crucified there was a garden, and in the garden a new tomb, in which no one had yet been buried. So they laid Jesus there because of the Jewish preparation day; for the tomb was close by.— The Gospel of the Lord. ℟. **Praise to you, Lord Jesus Christ.** ➜ No. 14, p. 18

GENERAL INTERCESSIONS

*The general intercessions conclude the liturgy of the word.
The deacon, standing at the ambo, sings or says the introduction in which each intention is stated. All kneel and pray
silently for some period of time, and then the priest, with
hands outstretched, standing either at the chair or at the
altar, sings or says the prayer. The people may either kneel or
stand throughout the entire period of the general intercessions.*

I. For the Church

Let us pray, dear friends,
for the holy Church of God throughout the world,
that God the almighty Father
guide it and gather it together
so that we may worship him
in peace and tranquility.

Silent prayer. Then the priest sings or says:

Almighty and eternal God,
you have shown your glory to all nations
in Christ, your Son.
Guide the work of your Church.
Help it to persevere in faith,
proclaim your name,
and bring your salvation to people everywhere.
We ask this through Christ our Lord. R̸. **Amen.** ↓

II. For the Pope

Let us pray
for our Holy Father, Pope N.,
that God who chose him to be bishop
may give him health and strength
to guide and govern God's holy people.

Silent prayer. Then the priest sings or says:

Almighty and eternal God,
you guide all things by your word,
you govern all Christian people.

In your love protect the Pope you have chosen for us.
Under his leadership deepen our faith
and make us better Christians.
We ask this through Christ our Lord. R̰. **Amen.** ↓

III. For the clergy and laity of the Church

Let us pray
for N., our bishop,
for all bishops, priests and deacons,
for all who have a special ministry in the Church
and for all God's people.

Silent prayer. Then the priest sings or says:

Almighty and eternal God,
your Spirit guides the Church
and makes it holy.
Listen to our prayers
and help each of us
in his own vocation
to do your work more faithfully.
We ask this through Christ our Lord. R̰. **Amen.** ↓

IV. For those preparing for baptism

Let us pray
for those [among us] preparing for baptism,
that God in his mercy
make them responsive to his love,
forgive their sins through the waters of new birth,
and give them life in Jesus Christ our Lord.

Silent prayer. Then the priest sings or says:

Almighty and eternal God,
you continually bless your Church with new members.
Increase the faith and understanding
of those [among us] preparing for baptism.
Give them a new birth in these living waters
and make them members of your chosen family.
We ask this through Christ our Lord. R̰. **Amen.** ↓

V. For the unity of Christians

Let us pray
for all our brothers and sisters
who share our faith in Jesus Christ,
that God may gather and keep together in one Church
all those who seek the truth with sincerity.

Silent prayer. Then the priest sings or says:

Almighty and eternal God,
you keep together those you have united.
Look kindly on all who follow Jesus your Son.
We are all consecrated to you by our common baptism.
Make us one in the fullness of faith,
and keep us one in the fellowship of love.
We ask this through Christ our Lord. ℟. **Amen.** ↓

VI. For the Jewish people

Let us pray
for the Jewish people,
the first to hear the word of God,
that they may continue to grow in the love of his name
and in faithfulness to his covenant.

Silent prayer. Then the priest sings or says:

Almighty and eternal God,
long ago you gave your promise to Abraham and his
    posterity.
Listen to your Church as we pray
that the people you first made your own
may arrive at the fullness of redemption.
We ask this through Christ our Lord. ℟. **Amen.** ↓

VII. For those who do not believe in Christ

Let us pray
for those who do not believe in Christ,
that the light of the Holy Spirit
may show them the way to salvation.

Silent prayer. Then the priest sings or says:

Almighty and eternal God,
enable those who do not acknowledge Christ
to find the truth
as they walk before you in sincerity of heart.
Help us to grow in love for one another,
to grasp more fully the mystery of your godhead,
and to become more perfect witnesses of your love
in the sight of men.
We ask this through Christ our Lord. ℟. **Amen.** ↓

VIII. For those who do not believe in God

Let us pray
for those who do not believe in God,
that they may find him
by sincerely following all that is right.

Silent prayer. Then the priest sings or says:

Almighty and eternal God,
you created mankind
so that all might long to find you
and have peace when you are found.
Grant that, in spite of the hurtful things
that stand in their way,
they may all recognize in the lives of Christians
the tokens of your love and mercy,
and gladly acknowledge you
as the one true God and Father of us all.
We ask this through Christ our Lord. ℟. **Amen.** ↓

IX. For all in public office

Let us pray
for those who serve us in public office,
that God may guide their minds and hearts,
so that all men may live in true peace and freedom.

Silent prayer. Then the priest sings or says:

Almighty and eternal God,
you know the longings of men's hearts

and you protect their rights.
In your goodness
watch over those in authority,
so that people everywhere may enjoy
religious freedom, security, and peace.
We ask this through Christ our Lord. ℟. **Amen.** ↓

X. For those in special need

Let us pray, dear friends,
that God the almighty Father
may heal the sick,
comfort the dying,
give safety to travelers,
free those unjustly deprived of liberty,
and rid the world of falsehood,
hunger, and disease.

Silent prayer. Then the priest sings or says:

Almighty, ever-living God,
you give strength to the weary
and new courage to those who have lost heart.
Hear the prayers of all who call on you in any trouble
that they may have the joy of receiving your help in their
   need.
We ask this through Christ our Lord. ℟. **Amen.** ↓

PART TWO: VENERATION OF THE CROSS

*After the general intercessions, the veneration of the
cross takes place. Pastoral demands will determine which
of the two forms is more effective and should be chosen.*

First Form of Showing the Cross

*The veiled cross is carried to the altar, accompanied by two
ministers with lighted candles. Standing at the altar, the
priest takes the cross, uncovers the upper part of it, then ele-
vates it and begins the invitation* This is the wood of the
cross. *He is assisted in the singing by the deacon or, if convenient, by the choir. All respond:* Come, let us worship. *At the
end of the singing all kneel and venerate the cross briefly in
silence; the priest remains standing and holds the cross high.*

Then the priest uncovers the right arm of the cross, lifts it up, and again begins the invitation This is the wood of the cross, *and the rite is repeated as before.*

Finally he uncovers the entire cross, lifts it up, and begins the invitation This is the wood of the cross *a third time, and the rite is repeated as before.*

Accompanied by two ministers with lighted candles, the priest then carries the cross to the entrance of the sanctuary or to another suitable place. There he lays the cross down or hands it to the ministers to hold. Candles are placed on either side of the cross, and the veneration follows as below.

Second Form of Showing the Cross

The priest or deacon, accompanied by the ministers or by another suitable minister, goes to the church door. There he takes the (uncovered) cross, and the ministers take lighted candles. They go in procession through the church to the sanctuary. Near the entrance of the church, in the middle of the church, and at the entrance to the sanctuary, the one carrying the cross stops, lifts it up and sings the invitation This is the wood of the cross. *All respond:* Come, let us worship. *After each response all kneel and venerate the cross briefly in silence as above.*

Then the cross and candles are placed at the entrance to the sanctuary.

INVITATION

℣. This is the wood of the cross, on which hung the Savior of the world.

℟. **Come, let us worship.**

Veneration of the Cross

The priest, clergy, and faithful approach to venerate the cross in a kind of procession. They make a simple genuflection or perform some other appropriate sign of reverence according to local custom, for example, kissing the cross.

During the veneration the antiphon We worship you, Lord, *the reproaches or other suitable songs are sung. All who have venerated the cross return to their places and sit.*

Only one cross should be used for the veneration. If the number of people makes it impossible for everyone to venerate the cross individually, the priest may take the cross, after some of the faithful have venerated it, and stand in the center in front of the altar. In a few words he invites the people to venerate the cross and then holds it up briefly for them to worship in silence.

In the United States, if pastoral reasons suggest that there be individual veneration even though the number of people is very large, a second or third cross may be used.

After the veneration, the cross is carried to its place at the altar, and the lighted candles are placed around the altar or near the cross.

Songs at the Veneration of the Cross

Individual parts are indicated by no. 1 (first choir) and no. 2 (second choir); parts sung by both choirs together are indicated by nos. 1 and 2.

ANTIPHON   [Holy Cross]

1 and 2: Antiphon
We worship you, Lord,
we venerate your cross,
we praise your resurrection.
Through the cross you brought joy to the world.

1: Psalm 67:2
May God be gracious and bless us;
and let his face shed its light upon us.

1 and 2: Antiphon
We worship you, Lord,
we venerate your cross,
we praise your resurrection.
Through the cross you brought joy to the world.

REPROACHES

If these optional "Reproaches" are used, it is important to note that the Church intends them to be a rebuke for Christian faithlessness and ingratitude.

I

1 and 2: **My people, what have I done to you?**
  how have I offended you? Answer me!

1: I led you out of Egypt, from slavery to freedom,
but you led your Savior to the cross.

2: My people, what have I done to you?
How have I offended you? Answer me!

1: Holy is God!

2: Holy and strong!

1: Holy immortal One,
have mercy on us!

1 and 2: For forty years I led you safely through the
desert.
I fed you with manna from heaven,
and brought you to a land of plenty;
but you led your Savior to the cross.

1: Holy is God!

2: Holy and strong!

1: Holy immortal One,
have mercy on us!

1 and 2: What more could I have done for you?
I planted you as my fairest vine,
but you yielded only bitterness:
when I was thirsty you gave me vinegar to drink,
and you pierced your Savior with a lance.

1: Holy is God!

2: Holy and strong!

1: Holy immortal One,
have mercy on us!

II

1: For your sake I scourged your captors and their
firstborn sons,
but you brought your scourges down on me.

2: My people, what have I done to you?
How have I offended you? Answer me!

1: I led you from slavery to freedom

and drowned your captors in the sea,
but you handed me over to your high priests.

2: My people, what have I done to you?
How have I offended you? Answer me!

1: I opened the sea before you,
but you opened my side with a spear.

2: My people, what have I done to you?
How have I offended you? Answer me!

1: I led you on your way in a pillar of cloud,
but you led me to Pilate's court.

2: My people, what have I done to you?
How have I offended you? Answer me!

1: I bore you up with manna in the desert,
but you struck me down and scourged me.

2: My people, what have I done to you?
How have I offended you? Answer me!

1: I gave you saving water from the rock,
but you gave me gall and vinegar to drink.

2: My people, what have I done to you?
How have I offended you? Answer me!

1: For you I struck down the kings of Canaan,
but you struck my head with a reed.

2: My people, what have I done to you?
How have I offended you? Answer me!

1: I gave you a royal scepter,
but you gave me a crown of thorns.

2: My people, what have I done to you?
How have I offended you? Answer me!

1: I raised you to the height of majesty,
but you have raised me high on a cross.

2: My people, what have I done to you?
How have I offended you? Answer me!

HYMN: PANGE LINGUA   [Sing to the Lord]

Sing, my tongue, the Savior's glory;
  tell his triumph far and wide;
Tell aloud the famous story
  of his body crucified;
How upon the cross a victim,
  vanquishing in death, he died.

Eating of the tree forbidden,
  man had sunk in Satan's snare,
When our pitying Creator did
  this second tree prepare;
Destined, many ages later,
  that first evil to repair.

Such the order God appointed
  when for sin he would atone;
To the serpent thus opposing
  schemes yet deeper than his own;
Thence the remedy procuring,
  when the fatal wound had come.

So when now at length the fullness
  of the sacred time drew nigh,
Then the Son, the world's Creator,
  left his Father's throne on high;
From a virgin's womb appearing,
  clothed in our mortality.

All within a lowly manger,
  lo, a tender babe he lies!
See his gentle Virgin Mother
  lull to sleep his infant cries!
While the limbs of God incarnate
  round with swathing bands she ties.

Thus did Christ to perfect manhood
  in our mortal flesh attain:
Then of his free choice he goeth
  to a death of bitter pain;

And as a lamb, upon the altar of the cross,
   for us is slain.

Lo, with gall his thirst he quenches!
   See the thorns upon his brow!
Nails his tender flesh are rending!
   See, his side is opened now!
Whence, to cleanse the whole creation,
   streams of blood and water flow.

Lofty tree, bend down thy branches,
   to embrace thy sacred load;
Oh, relax the native tension
   of that all too rigid wood;
Gently, gently bear the members
   of thy dying King and God.

Tree, which solely wast found worthy
   the world's great Victim to sustain.
Harbor from the raging tempest!
   Ark, that saved the world again!
Tree, with sacred blood anointed
   of the Lamb for sinners slain.

Blessing, honor everlasting,
   to the immortal Deity;
To the Father, Son, and Spirit,
   equal praises ever be;
Glory through the earth and heaven
   to Trinity in Unity. Amen.

PART THREE: HOLY COMMUNION

The altar is covered with a cloth and the corporal and book are placed on it. Then the deacon or, if there is no deacon, the priest brings the ciborium with the Blessed Sacrament from the place of reposition to the altar without any procession, while all stand in silence.

The priest comes from his chair, genuflects, and goes up to the altar. With hands joined, he says aloud:

Let us pray with confidence to the Father
in the words our Savior gave us:

He extends his hands and continues, with all present:

Our Father . . .

With hands extended, the priest continues alone:

Deliver us, Lord, from every evil,
and grant us peace in our day.
In your mercy keep us free from sin
and protect us from all anxiety
as we wait in joyful hope
for the coming of our Savior, Jesus Christ.

The people end the prayer with the acclamation:

**For the kingdom, the power, and the glory are yours,
now and for ever.**

Then the priest says quietly:

Lord Jesus Christ, with faith in your love and mercy
   I eat your body and drink your blood.
Let it not bring me condemnation, but health in mind
   and body.

Taking the host, the priest says aloud:

This is the Lamb of God
who takes away the sins of the world.
Happy are those who are called to his supper.

He adds, once only, with the people:

**Lord, I am not worthy to receive you,
but only say the word and I shall be healed.**

Facing the altar, he reverently consumes the body of Christ.

Then communion is distributed to the faithful. Any appropriate song may be sung during communion.

When the communion has been completed, a suitable minister may take the ciborium to a place prepared outside the church or, if circumstances require, may place it in the tabernacle.

A period of silence may now be observed. The priest then says the following prayer:

Let us pray.   [Serving God]
Almighty and eternal God,
you have restored us to life
by the triumphant death and resurrection of Christ.
Continue this healing work within us.
May we who participate in this mystery
never cease to serve you.
We ask this through Christ our Lord. ℟. **Amen.** ↓

For the dismissal the priest faces the people, extends his
hands toward them, and says the following prayer:

PRAYER OVER THE PEOPLE   [Salvation Assured]

Lord,
send down your abundant blessing
upon your people who have devoutly recalled the
    death of your Son
in the sure hope of the resurrection.
Grant them pardon; bring them comfort.
May their faith grow stronger
and their eternal salvation be assured.
We ask this through Christ our Lord. ℟. **Amen.** ↓

All depart in silence. The altar is stripped at a convenient
time.

APRIL 23

HOLY SATURDAY

On Holy Saturday the Church waits at the Lord's tomb, med-
itating on his suffering and death. The altar is left bare, and
the sacrifice of the Mass is not celebrated. Only after the
solemn vigil during the night, held in anticipation of the res-
urrection, does the Easter celebration begin, with a spirit of
joy that overflows into the following period of fifty days.

"He is not here, for he has been raised."

APRIL 23

EASTER VIGIL

In accord with ancient tradition, this night is one of vigil for the Lord (Ex 12:42). The Gospel of Luke (12:35ff) is a reminder to the faithful to have their lamps burning ready, to be like men awaiting their master's return so that when he arrives he will find them wide awake and will seat them at his table.

The night vigil is arranged in four parts: (a) a brief service of light; (b) the liturgy of the word, when the Church meditates on all the wonderful things God has done for his people from the beginning; (c) the liturgy of baptism, when new members of the Church are reborn as the day of resurrection approaches; and (d) the liturgy of the eucharist, when the whole Church is called to the table which the Lord has prepared for his people through his death and resurrection.

PART ONE
SOLEMN BEGINNING OF THE VIGIL:
THE SERVICE OF LIGHT
Blessing of the Fire and Lighting the Candle

All the lights in the church are put out.

A large fire is prepared in a suitable place outside the church. When the people have assembled, the priest goes there with the ministers, one of whom carries the Easter candle.

*If it is not possible to light the fire outside the church, the rite
is carried out as below, p. 320.*

*The priest greets the congregation in the usual manner and
briefly instructs them about the vigil in these or similar
words:*

Dear friends in Christ,   **[Honoring Christ's Memory]**
on this most holy night,
when our Lord Jesus Christ passed from death to life,
the Church invites her children throughout the world
to come together in vigil and prayer.
This is the passover of the Lord:
if we honor the memory of his death and resurrection
by hearing his word and celebrating his mysteries,
then we may be confident
that we shall share his victory over death
and live with him for ever in God.

Then the fire is blessed.

[Light of the World]

Let us pray.
Father,
we share in the light of your glory
through your Son, the light of the world.
Make this new fire ✠ holy, and inflame us with new
    hope.
Purify our minds by this Easter celebration
and bring us one day to the feast of eternal light.
We ask this through Christ our Lord. ℟. **Amen.** ↓

The Easter candle is lighted from the new fire.

Preparation of the Candle

*Depending on the nature of the congregation, it may seem
appropriate to stress the dignity and significance of the
Easter candle with other symbolic rites. This may be done as
follows:*

*After the blessing of the new fire, an acolyte or one of the
ministers brings the Easter candle to the celebrant, who cuts*

*a cross in the wax with a stylus. Then he traces the Greek let-
ter alpha above the cross, the letter omega below, and the
numerals of the current year between the arms of the cross.
Meanwhile he says:*

1. Christ yesterday and today *(as he traces the verti-
   cal arm of the cross),*
2. the beginning and the end *(the horizontal arm),*
3. Alpha *(alpha, above the cross),*
4. and Omega *(omega, below the cross);*
5. all time belongs to him *(the first numeral, in the
   upper left corner of the cross),*
6. and all the ages *(the second numeral in
   the upper right corner);*
7. to him be glory and power *(the third
   numeral in the lower left corner),*
8. through every age for ever. Amen.
   (the last numeral in the lower right corner).

```
      A
   2  |  0
      |
   1
      Ω
```

*When the cross and other marks have been made, the priest
may insert five grains of incense in the candle. He does this in
the form of a cross, saying:*

1. By his holy
2. and glorious wounds
3. may Christ our Lord
4. guard us
5. and keep us. Amen.

```
        1
   4  2  5
        3
```

The priest lights the candle from the new fire, saying:

May the light of Christ, rising in glory,
dispel the darkness of our hearts and minds.

*Any or all of the preceding rites may be used, depending on
local pastoral circumstances. The conferences of bishops may
also determine other rites better adapted to the culture of the
people.*

_____

*Where it may be difficult to have a large fire, the blessing of
the fire is adapted to the circumstances. When the people
have assembled in the church as on other occasions, the*

priest goes with the ministers (carrying the Easter candle) to the church door. If possible, the people turn to face the priest.

The greeting and brief instruction take place as above, p. 319. Then the fire is blessed and, if desired, the candle is prepared and lighted as above.

Procession

Then the deacon or, if there is no deacon, the priest takes the Easter candle, lifts it high, and sings alone:

Christ our light.

All answer:

Thanks be to God.

The conferences of bishops may determine a richer acclamation.

Then all enter the church, led by the deacon with the Easter candle. If incense is used, the thurifer goes before the deacon.

At the church door the deacon lifts the candle high and sings a second time:

Christ our light.

All answer:

Thanks be to God.

All light their candles from the Easter candle and continue in the procession.

When the deacon arrives before the altar, he faces the people and sings a third time:

Christ our light.

All answer:

Thanks be to God.

Then the lights in the church are put on.

Easter Proclamation (Exsultet)

When he comes to the altar, the priest goes to his chair. The deacon places the Easter candle on a stand in the middle of the sanctuary or near the lectern. If incense is used, the priest puts some in the censer, as at the gospel of Mass. Then the deacon asks the blessing of the priest, who says in a low voice:

The Lord be in your heart and on your lips,
that you may worthily proclaim his Easter praise.
In the name of the Father, and of the Son ✝ and of the Holy Spirit. ℞. **Amen.** ↓

The book and candle may be incensed. Then the deacon or, if there is no deacon, the priest sings the Easter proclamation at the lectern or pulpit. All stand and hold lighted candles.

If necessary, the Easter proclamation may be sung by one who is not a deacon. In this case the bracketed words are omitted.

[When the short form is used, omit the italicized parts.]

Rejoice, heavenly powers! Sing, choirs of angels!
　　Exult, all creation around God's throne!
　　Jesus Christ, our King, is risen!
　　Sound the trumpet of salvation!

Rejoice, O earth, in shining splendor,
　　radiant in the brightness of your King!
　　Christ has conquered! Glory fills you!
　　Darkness vanishes for ever!

Rejoice, O Mother Church! Exult in glory!
　　The risen Savior shines upon you!
　　Let this place resound with joy,
　　echoing the mighty song of all God's people!

　　[My dearest friends, standing with me in this holy light,
　　　　join me in asking God for mercy,
　　　　that he may give his unworthy minister
　　　　grace to sing his Easter praises.]

[℣. The Lord be with you. ℞. **And also with you.**]
℣. Lift up your hearts. ℞. **We lift them up to the Lord.**
℣. Let us give thanks to the Lord our God. ℞. **It is right to give him thanks and praise.**

It is truly right
that with full hearts and minds and voices
we should praise the unseen God, the all-powerful
    Father,
and his only Son, our Lord Jesus Christ.
For Christ has ransomed us with his blood,
    and paid for us the price of Adam's sin
    to our eternal Father!
This is our passover feast,
    when Christ, the true Lamb, is slain,
    whose blood consecrates the homes of all believers.
This is the night when first you saved our fathers:
    you freed the people of Israel from their slavery
    and led them dry-shod through the sea.
This is the night when the pillar of fire
    destroyed the darkness of sin!
This is the night when Christians everywhere,
    washed clean of sin
    and freed from all defilement,
    are restored to grace and grow together in holiness.
This is the night when Jesus Christ
    broke the chains of death
    and rose triumphant from the grave.
What good would life have been to us,
    had Christ not come as our Redeemer?
Father, how wonderful your care for us!
    How boundless your merciful love!
    To ransom a slave
    you gave away your Son.
O happy fault, O necessary sin of Adam,
    which gained for us so great a Redeemer!
Most blessed of all nights, chosen by God
    to see Christ rising from the dead!
Of this night scripture says:
    "The night will be as clear as day:
    it will become my light, my joy."

The power of this holy night
   dispels all evil, washes guilt away,
   restores lost innocence, brings mourners joy;
   it casts out hatred, brings us peace, and humbles
     earthly pride.
Night truly blessed when heaven is wedded to earth
   and man is reconciled with God!
Therefore, heavenly Father, in the joy of this night,
   receive our evening sacrifice of praise,
   your Church's solemn offering.
Accept this Easter candle,
   a flame divided but undimmed,
   a pillar of fire that glows to the honor of God.

Short form only:
  May it always dispel the darkness of this night!

Let it mingle with the lights of heaven
   and continue bravely burning
   to dispel the darkness of this night!
May the Morning Star which never sets find this flame
     still burning:
   Christ, that Morning Star, who came back from the
     dead,
   and shed his peaceful light on all mankind,
   your Son who lives and reigns for ever and ever.
℞. **Amen.** ↓

PART TWO

LITURGY OF THE WORD

In this vigil, the mother of all vigils, nine readings are provided, seven from the Old Testament and two from the New Testament (the epistle and gospel).

The number of readings from the Old Testament may be reduced for pastoral reasons, but it must always be borne in mind that the reading of the word of God is the fundamental element of the Easter Vigil. At least three readings from the Old Testament should be read, although for more serious reasons the number may be reduced to two. The reading of Exodus 14 (reading 3), however, is never to be omitted.

After the Easter proclamation, the candles are put aside and all sit down. Before the readings begin, the priest speaks to the people in these or similar words:

Dear friends in Christ,   **[Attentive Listening]**
we have begun our solemn vigil.
Let us now listen attentively to the word of God,
recalling how he saved his people throughout history
and, in the fullness of time,
sent his own Son to be our Redeemer.
Through this Easter celebration,
may God bring to perfection
the saving work he has begun in us.

The readings follow. A reader goes to the lectern and proclaims the first reading. Then the cantor leads the psalm and the people respond. All rise and the priest sings or says Let us pray. *When all have prayed silently for a while, he sings or says the prayer.*

Instead of the responsorial psalm a period of silence may be observed. In this case the pause after Let us pray *is omitted.*

FIRST READING Gn 1:1—2:2 or 1:1, 26-31a **[God Our Creator]**
God created the world and all that is in it. He saw that it was good. This reading from the first book of the Bible shows that God loved all that he made.

[If the "Shorter Form" is used, the indented text in brackets is omitted.]

A reading from the Book of Genesis

IN the beginning, when God created the heavens and the earth,
        [the earth was a formless wasteland, and darkness covered the abyss, while a mighty wind swept over the waters.

Then God said, "Let there be light," and there was light. God saw how good the light was. God then separated the light from the darkness. God called the light "day," and the darkness he called "night." Thus evening came, and morning followed—the first day.

Then God said, "Let there be a dome in the middle of the waters, to separate one body of water from the other." And so it happened: God made the dome, and it separated the water above the dome from the water below it. God called the dome "the sky." Evening came, and morning followed—the second day.

Then God said, "Let the water under the sky be gathered into a single basin, so that the dry land may appear." And so it happened: the water under the sky was gathered into its basin, and the dry land appeared. God called the dry land "the earth," and the basin of the water he called "the sea." God saw how good it was. Then God said, "Let the earth bring forth vegetation: every kind of plant that bears seed and every kind of fruit tree on earth that bears fruit with its seed in it." And so it happened: the earth brought forth every kind of plant that bears seed and every kind of fruit tree on earth that bears fruit with its seed in it. God saw how good it was. Evening came, and morning followed—the third day.

Then God said: "Let there be lights in the dome of the sky, to separate day from night. Let them mark the fixed times, the days and the years, and serve as luminaries in the dome of the sky, to shed light upon the earth." And so it happened: God made the two great lights, the greater one to govern the day, and the lesser one to govern the night; and he made the stars. God set them in the dome of the sky, to shed light upon the earth, to govern the day and the night, and to separate the light from the darkness. God saw how good it was. Evening came, and morning followed—the fourth day.

Then God said, "Let the water teem with an abundance of living creatures, and on the earth let birds fly beneath the dome of the sky." And so it happened: God created the great sea monsters and all kinds of swimming creatures with which the water teems, and all kinds of winged birds. God saw how good it was, and God blessed them, saying, "Be fertile, multiply, and fill the water of the seas; and let the birds multiply on the earth." Evening came, and morning followed—the fifth day.

Then God said, "Let the earth bring forth all kinds of living creatures: cattle, creeping things, and wild animals of all kinds." And so it happened: God made all kinds of wild animals, all kinds of cattle, and all kinds of creeping things of the earth. God saw how good it was. Then]

God said: "Let us make man in our image, after our likeness. Let them have dominion over the fish of the sea, the birds of the air, and the cattle, and over all the wild animals and all the creatures that crawl on the ground."

God created man in his image;
in the divine image he created him;
male and female he created them.

God blessed them, saying: "Be fertile and multiply; fill the earth and subdue it. Have dominion over the fish of the sea, the birds of the air, and all the living things that move on the earth." God also said: "See, I give you every seed-bearing plant all over the earth and every tree that has seed-bearing fruit on it to be your food; and to all the animals of the land, all the birds of the air, and all the living creatures that crawl on the ground, I give all the green plants for food." And so it happened. God looked at everything he had made, and he found it very good.

[Evening came, and morning followed—the sixth day.

Thus the heavens and the earth and all their array were completed. Since on the seventh day God was finished with the work he had been doing, he rested on the seventh day from all the work he had undertaken.]

The word of the Lord. ℟. **Thanks be to God.** ↓

RESPONSORIAL PSALM Ps 104   [Come, Holy Spirit]

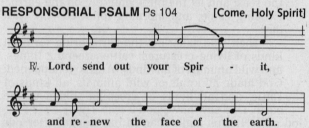

℟. Lord, send out your Spir - it,

and re - new the face of the earth.

Bless the LORD, O my soul!
   O LORD, my God, you are great indeed!
You are clothed with majesty and glory,
   robed in light as with a cloak.

℟. **Lord, send out your Spirit,**
   and renew the face of the earth.

You fixed the earth upon its foundation,
   not to be moved forever;
with the ocean, as with a garment, you covered it;
   above the mountains the waters stood.

℟. **Lord, send out your Spirit,**
   and renew the face of the earth.

You send forth springs into the watercourses
   that wind among the mountains.

Beside them the birds of heaven dwell;
  from among the branches they send forth their song.

℟. **Lord, send out your Spirit,**
  and renew the face of the earth.

You water the mountains from your palace;
  the earth is replete with the fruit of your works.
You raise grass for the cattle,
  and vegetation for men's use,
producing bread from the earth.

℟. **Lord, send out your Spirit,**
  and renew the face of the earth.

How manifold are your works, O LORD!
  In wisdom you have wrought them all—
the earth is full of your creatures.
  Bless the Lord, O my soul! Alleluia.

℟. **Lord, send out your Spirit,**
  and renew the face of the earth. ↓

OR

RESPONSORIAL PSALM Ps 33   [The Lord's Goodness]

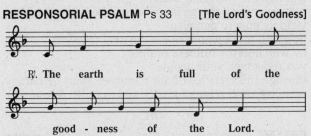

℟. The earth is full of the good - ness of the Lord.

Upright is the word of the LORD,
  and all his works are trustworthy.
He loves justice and right;
  of the kindness of the LORD the earth is full.

℟. **The earth is full of the goodness of the Lord.**

By the word of the LORD the heavens were made;
  by the breath of his mouth all their host.
He gathers the waters of the sea as in a flask;
  in cellars he confines the deep.

℟. **The earth is full of the goodness of the Lord.**

Blessed the nation whose God is the LORD,
  the people he has chosen for his own inheritance.
From heaven the LORD looks down;
  he sees all mankind.

℟. **The earth is full of the goodness of the Lord.**

Our soul waits for the LORD,
  who is our help and our shield.
May your kindness, O LORD, be upon us
  who have put our hope in you.

℟. **The earth is full of the goodness of the Lord.** ↓

PRAYER   [New Creation]
Let us pray.
Almighty and eternal God,
you created all things in wonderful beauty and order.
Help us now to perceive
how still more wonderful is the new creation
by which in the fullness of time
you redeemed your people
through the sacrifice of our passover, Jesus Christ,
who lives and reigns for ever and ever. ℟. **Amen.** ↓

OR

PRAYER (on the creation of man)   [Our Redemption]
Let us pray.
Lord God,
the creation of man was a wonderful work,
his redemption still more wonderful.
May we persevere in right reason
against all that entices to sin

and so attain to everlasting joy.
We ask this through Christ our Lord. ℟. **Amen.** ↓

SECOND READING Gn 22:1-18 or 22:1-2, 9, 10-13, 15-18

[Obedience to God]

Abraham is obedient to the will of God. Because God asks him, without hesitation he prepares to sacrifice his son Isaac. In the new order, God sends his Son to redeem man by his death on the cross.

[If the "Shorter Form" is used, the indented text in brackets is omitted.]

A reading from the Book of Genesis

GOD put Abraham to the test. He called to him, "Abraham!" "Here I am," he replied. Then God said: "Take your son Isaac, your only one, whom you love, and go to the land of Moriah. There you shall offer him up as a holocaust on a height that I will point out to you."

[Early the next morning Abraham saddled his donkey, took with him his son Isaac, and two of his servants as well, and with the wood that he had cut for the holocaust, set out for the place of which God had told him.

On the third day Abraham got sight of the place from afar. Then he said to his servants: "Both of you stay here with the donkey, while the boy and I go on over yonder. We will worship and then come back to you." Thereupon Abraham took the wood for the holocaust and laid it on his son Isaac's shoulders, while he himself carried the fire and the knife. As the two walked on together, Isaac spoke to his father Abraham. "Father!" Isaac said. "Yes, son," he replied. Isaac continued, "Here are the fire and the wood, but where is the sheep for the holocaust?" "Son," Abraham answered, "God himself will provide the sheep for the holocaust." Then the two continued going forward.]

When they came to the place of which God had told him, Abraham built an altar there and arranged the wood on it.

[Next he tied up his son Isaac, and put him on top of the wood on the altar.]

Then he reached out and took the knife to slaughter his son. But the LORD's messenger called to him from heaven, "Abraham, Abraham!" "Here I am," he answered. "Do not lay your hand on the boy," said the messenger. "Do not do the least thing to him. I know now how devoted you are to God, since you did not withhold from me your own beloved son." As Abraham looked about, he spied a ram caught by its horns in the thicket. So he went and took the ram and offered it up as a holocaust in place of his son.

[Abraham named the site Yahweh-yireh; hence people now say, "On the mountain the LORD will see."]

Again the LORD's messenger called to Abraham from heaven and said: "I swear by myself, declares the LORD, that because you acted as you did in not withholding from me your beloved son, I will bless you abundantly and make your descendants as countless as the stars of the sky and the sands of the seashore; your descendants shall take possession of the gates of their enemies, and in your descendants all the nations of the earth shall find blessing—all this because you obeyed my command."—The word of the Lord. ℟. **Thanks be to God.** ↓

RESPONSORIAL PSALM Ps 16   [God Our Hope]

℟. You   are   my   in- her - i -tance, O   Lord.

O Lord, my allotted portion and my cup,
  you it is who hold fast my lot.
I set the Lord ever before me;
  with him at my right I shall not be disturbed.

℟. **You are my inheritance, O Lord.**

Therefore my heart is glad and my soul rejoices,
  my body, too, abides in confidence;
because you will not abandon my soul to the nether-
    world,
  nor will you suffer your faithful one to undergo cor-
    ruption.

℟. **You are my inheritance, O Lord.**

You will show me the path to life,
  fullness of joys in your presence,
    the delights at your right hand forever.

℟. **You are my inheritance, O Lord.** ↓

PRAYER   [Response to God's Call]

Let us pray.
God and Father of all who believe in you,
you promised Abraham that he would become the
    father of all nations,
and through the death and resurrection of Christ
you fulfill that promise:
everywhere throughout the world you increase your
    chosen people.
May we respond to your call
by joyfully accepting your invitation to the new life of
    grace.
We ask this through Christ our Lord. ℟. **Amen.** ↓

THIRD READING Ex 14:15—15:1   [Exodus]

  **Moses leads the Israelites out of Egypt. He opens a path of
  escape through the Red Sea. God protects his people.
  Through the waters of baptism, human beings are freed
  from sin.**

A reading from the Book of Exodus

THE LORD said to Moses, "Why are you crying out to me? Tell the Israelites to go forward. And you, lift up your staff and, with hand outstretched over the sea, split the sea in two, that the Israelites may pass through it on dry land. But I will make the Egyptians so obstinate that they will go in after them. Then I will receive glory through Pharaoh and all his army, his chariots and charioteers. The Egyptians shall know that I am the LORD, when I receive glory through Pharaoh and his chariots and charioteers."

The angel of God, who had been leading Israel's camp, now moved and went around behind them. The column of cloud also, leaving the front, took up its place behind them, so that it came between the camp of the Egyptians and that of Israel. But the cloud now became dark, and thus the night passed without the rival camps coming any closer together all night long. Then Moses stretched out his hand over the sea, and the LORD swept the sea with a strong east wind throughout the night and so turned it into dry land. When the water was thus divided, the Israelites marched into the midst of the sea on dry land, with the water like a wall to their right and to their left.

The Egyptians followed in pursuit; all Pharaoh's horses and chariots and charioteers went after them right into the midst of the sea. In the night watch just before dawn the LORD cast through the column of the fiery cloud upon the Egyptian force a glance that threw it into a panic; and he so clogged their chariot wheels that they could hardly drive. With that the Egyptians sounded the retreat before Israel, because the LORD was fighting for them against the Egyptians.

Then the LORD told Moses, "Stretch out your hand over the sea, that the water may flow back upon the Egyptians, upon their chariots and their charioteers." So Moses stretched out his hand over the sea, and at dawn the sea flowed back to its normal depth. The Egyptians were fleeing head on toward the sea, when the LORD hurled them into its midst. As the water flowed back, it covered the chariots and the charioteers of Pharaoh's whole army which had followed the Israelites into the sea. Not a single one of them escaped. But the Israelites had marched on dry land through the midst of the sea, with the water like a wall to their right and to their left. Thus the LORD saved Israel on that day from the power of the Egyptians. When Israel saw the Egyptians lying dead on the seashore and beheld the great power that the LORD had shown against the Egyptians, they feared the LORD and believed in him and in his servant Moses.

Then Moses and the Israelites sang this song to the LORD:

    I will sing to the LORD, for he is gloriously triumphant;
      horse and chariot he has cast into the sea.

The word of the Lord. ℞. **Thanks be to God.** ↓

RESPONSORIAL PSALM Ex 15   [God the Savior]

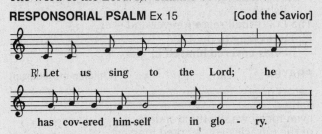

℞. Let us sing to the Lord; he has cov-ered him-self in glo - ry.

I will sing to the LORD, for he is gloriously triumphant;
    horse and chariot he has cast into the sea.
My strength and my courage is the LORD,
    and he has been my savior.
He is my God, I praise him;
    the God of my father, I extol him.

℟. **Let us sing to the Lord;**
  he has covered himself in glory.

The LORD is a warrior,
  LORD is his name!
Pharaoh's chariots and army he hurled into the sea;
  the elite of his officers were submerged into the Red
    Sea.

℟. **Let us sing to the Lord;**
  he has covered himself in glory.

The flood waters covered them,
  they sank into the depths like a stone.
Your right hand, O LORD, magnificent in power,
  your right hand, O LORD, has shattered the enemy.

℟. **Let us sing to the Lord;**
  he has covered himself in glory.

You brought in the people you redeemed
  and planted them on the mountain of your inheri-
    tance—
the place where you made your seat, O LORD,
  the sanctuary, O LORD, which your hands estab-
    lished.
The LORD shall reign forever and ever.

℟. **Let us sing to the Lord;**
  he has covered himself in glory. ↓

PRAYER   [Children of Abraham]

Let us pray.
Father,
even today we see the wonders
of the miracles you worked long ago.
You once saved a single nation from slavery,
and now you offer that salvation to all through baptism.
May the peoples of the world become true sons of
  Abraham
and prove worthy of the heritage of Israel.
We ask this through Christ our Lord. ℟. **Amen.** ↓

OR

PRAYER [New Birth]

Let us pray.
Lord God,
in the new covenant
you shed light on the miracles you worked in ancient
     times:
the Red Sea is a symbol of our baptism,
and the nation you freed from slavery
is a sign of your Christian people.
May every nation
share the faith and privilege of Israel
and come to new birth in the Holy Spirit.
We ask this through Christ our Lord. ℟. **Amen.** ↓

FOURTH READING Is 54:5-14 [God's Love]

For a time, God hid from his people, but his love for them
is everlasting. He takes pity on them and promises them
prosperity.

A reading from the Book of the Prophet Isaiah

THE One who has become your husband is your
     Maker; his name is the LORD of hosts;
your redeemer is the Holy One of Israel,
     called God of all the earth.
The LORD calls you back,
     like a wife forsaken and grieved in spirit,
a wife married in youth and then cast off,
     says your God.
For a brief moment I abandoned you,
     but with great tenderness I will take you back.
In an outburst of wrath, for a moment
     I hid my face from you;
but with enduring love I take pity on you,
     says the LORD, your redeemer.
This is for me like the days of Noah,
     when I swore that the waters of Noah
     should never again deluge the earth;

so I have sworn not to be angry with you,
   or to rebuke you.
Though the mountains leave their place
   and the hills be shaken,
my love shall never leave you
   nor my covenant of peace be shaken,
    says the LORD, who has mercy on you.
O afflicted one, storm-battered and unconsoled,
   I lay your pavements in carnelians,
   and your foundations in sapphires;
I will make your battlements of rubies,
   your gates of carbuncles,
   and all your walls of precious stones.
All your sons shall be taught by the LORD,
   and great shall be the peace of your children.
In justice shall you be established,
   far from the fear of oppression,
   where destruction cannot come near you.
The word of the Lord. ℟. **Thanks be to God.** ↓

RESPONSORIAL PSALM Ps 30   [God Our Help]

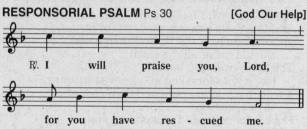

℟. I will praise you, Lord,
for you have res - cued me.

I will extol you, O LORD, for you drew me clear
   and did not let my enemies rejoice over me.
O LORD, you brought me up from the netherworld;
   you preserved me from among those going down
     into the pit.

℟. **I will praise you, Lord,**
   for you have rescued me.

Sing praise to the LORD, you his faithful ones,
  and give thanks to his holy name.
For his anger lasts but a moment;
  a lifetime, his good will.
At nightfall, weeping enters in,
  but with the dawn, rejoicing.

R̶. **I will praise you, Lord,**
  for you have rescued me.

Hear, O LORD, and have pity on me;
  O LORD, be my helper.
You changed my mourning into dancing;
  O LORD, my God, forever will I give you thanks.

R̶. **I will praise you, Lord,**
  for you have rescued me. ↓

PRAYER   [Fulfillment of God's Promise]

Let us pray.
Almighty and eternal God,
glorify your name by increasing your chosen people
as you promised long ago.
In reward for their trust,
may we see in the Church the fulfillment of your promise.
We ask this through Christ our Lord. R̶. **Amen.** ↓

*Prayers may also be chosen from those given after the follow-
ing readings, if the readings are omitted.*

FIFTH READING Is 55:1-11   [God of Forgiveness]

  **God is a loving Father and he calls his people back. He
  promises an everlasting covenant with them. God is merciful, generous, and forgiving.**

  A reading from the Book of the Prophet Isaiah

THUS says the LORD:
  All you who are thirsty,
    come to the water!

You who have no money,
    come, receive grain and eat;
come, without paying and without cost,
    drink wine and milk!
Why spend your money for what is not bread;
    your wages for what fails to satisfy?
Heed me, and you shall eat well,
    you shall delight in rich fare.
Come to me heedfully,
    listen, that you may have life.
I will renew with you the everlasting covenant,
    the benefits assured to David.
As I made him a witness to the peoples,
    a leader and commander of nations,
so shall you summon a nation you knew not,
    and nations that knew you not shall run to you,
because of the LORD, your God,
    the Holy One of Israel, who has glorified you.

Seek the LORD while he may be found,
    call him while he is near.
Let the scoundrel forsake his way,
    and the wicked man his thoughts;
let him turn to the LORD for mercy;
    to our God, who is generous in forgiving.
For my thoughts are not your thoughts,
    nor are your ways my ways, says the LORD.
As high as the heavens are above the earth,
    so high are my ways above your ways,
    and my thoughts above your thoughts.

For just as from the heavens
    the rain and snow come down
and do not return there
    till they have watered the earth,
    making it fertile and fruitful,
giving seed to the one who sows
    and bread to the one who eats,

so shall my word be
  that goes forth from my mouth;
my word shall not return to me void,
  but shall do my will,
    achieving the end for which I sent it.
The word of the Lord. ℟. **Thanks be to God.** ↓

RESPONSORIAL PSALM Is 12 [Make Known God's Deeds]

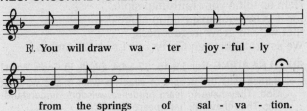

℟. You will draw wa - ter joy - ful - ly
from the springs of sal - va - tion.

God indeed is my savior;
  I am confident and unafraid.
My strength and my courage is the LORD,
  and he has been my savior.
With joy you will draw water
  at the fountain of salvation.

℟. **You will draw water joyfully from the springs of salvation.**

Give thanks to the LORD, acclaim his name;
  among the nations make known his deeds,
    proclaim how exalted is his name.

℟. **You will draw water joyfully from the springs of salvation.**

Sing praise to the LORD for his glorious achievement;
  let this be known throughout all the earth.
Shout with exultation, O city of Zion,
  for great in your midst
    is the Holy One of Israel!

℟. **You will draw water joyfully from the springs of salvation.** ↓

PRAYER   [Growth in Goodness]
Let us pray.
Almighty, ever-living God,
only hope of the world,
by the preaching of the prophets
you proclaimed the mysteries we are celebrating
   tonight.
Help us to be your faithful people,
for it is by your inspiration alone
that we can grow in goodness.
We ask this through Christ our Lord. ℟. **Amen.** ↓

SIXTH READING Bar 3:9-15, 32—4:4 [Walk in God's Ways]
   Baruch tells the people of Israel to walk in the ways of
   God. They have to learn prudence, wisdom, understand-
   ing. Then they will have peace forever.

A reading from the Book of the Prophet Baruch

HEAR, O Israel, the commandments of life:
   listen, and know prudence!
How is it, Israel,
      that you are in the land of your foes,
      grown old in a foreign land,
defiled with the dead,
      accounted with those destined for the netherworld?
You have forsaken the fountain of wisdom!
      Had you walked in the way of God,
      you would have dwelt in enduring peace.
Learn where prudence is,
      where strength, where understanding;
that you may know also
      where are length of days, and life,
      where light of the eyes, and peace.
Who has found the place of wisdom,
      who has entered into her treasuries?

The One who knows all things knows her;
      he has probed her by his knowledge—

the One who established the earth for all time,
  and filled it with four-footed beasts;
he who dismisses the light, and it departs,
  calls it, and it obeys him trembling;
before whom the stars at their posts
  shine and rejoice;
when he calls them, they answer, "Here we are!"
  shining with joy for their Maker.
Such is our God;
  no other is to be compared to him:
he has traced out all the way of understanding,
  and has given her to Jacob, his servant,
  to Israel, his beloved son.

Since then she has appeared on earth,
  and moved among people.
She is the book of the precepts of God,
  the law that endures forever;
all who cling to her will live,
  but those will die who forsake her.
Turn, O Jacob, and receive her:
  walk by her light toward splendor.
Give not your glory to another,
  your privileges to an alien race.
Blessed are we, O Israel;
  for what pleases God is known to us!
The word of the Lord. ℟. **Thanks be to God.** ↓

RESPONSORIAL PSALM Ps 19   [Words of Eternal Life]

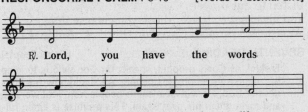

℟. Lord, you have the words of ev-er-last-ing life.

The law of the LORD is perfect,
  refreshing the soul;
the decree of the LORD is trustworthy,
  giving wisdom to the simple.

℟. **Lord, you have the words of everlasting life.**

The precepts of the LORD are right,
  rejoicing the heart;
the command of the LORD is clear,
  enlightening the eye.

℟. **Lord, you have the words of everlasting life.**

The fear of the LORD is pure,
  enduring forever;
the ordinances of the LORD are true,
  all of them just.

℟. **Lord, you have the words of everlasting life.**

They are more precious than gold,
  than a heap of purest gold;
sweeter also than syrup
  or honey from the comb.

℟. **Lord, you have the words of everlasting life.** ↓

PRAYER   [Hear Our Prayer]

Let us pray.
Father,
you increase your Church
by continuing to call all people to salvation.
Listen to our prayers
and always watch over those you cleanse in baptism.
We ask this through Christ our Lord. ℟. **Amen.** ↓

SEVENTH READING Ez 36:16-28   [God's People]
Ezekiel, as God's prophet, speaks for God who is to keep
his name holy among his people. All shall know the holiness of God. He will cleanse his people from idol worship
and make them his own again. This promise is again fulfilled in baptism in the restored order of redemption.

A reading from the Book of the Prophet Ezekiel

THE word of the LORD came to me, saying: Son of man, when the house of Israel lived in their land, they defiled it by their conduct and deeds. Therefore I poured out my fury upon them because of the blood that they poured out on the ground, and because they defiled it with idols. I scattered them among the nations, dispersing them over foreign lands; according to their conduct and deeds I judged them. But when they came among the nations wherever they came, they served to profane my holy name, because it was said of them: "These are the people of the LORD, yet they had to leave their land." So I have relented because of my holy name which the house of Israel profaned among the nations where they came. Therefore say to the house of Israel: Thus says the Lord GOD: Not for your sakes do I act, house of Israel, but for the sake of my holy name, which you profaned among the nations to which you came. I will prove the holiness of my great name, profaned among the nations, in whose midst you have profaned it. Thus the nations shall know that I am the LORD, says the Lord GOD, when in their sight I prove my holiness through you. For I will take you away from among the nations, gather you from all the foreign lands, and bring you back to your own land. I will sprinkle clean water upon you to cleanse you from all your impurities, and from all your idols I will cleanse you. I will give you a new heart and place a new spirit within you, taking from your bodies your stony hearts and giving you natural hearts. I will put my spirit within you and make you live by my statutes, careful to observe my decrees. You shall live in the land I gave your fathers; you shall be my people, and I will be your God.—The word of the Lord. ℟. **Thanks be to God.** ↓

When baptism is celebrated, responsorial psalm 42 is used; when baptism is not celebrated, Is 12 or Ps 51 is used.

RESPONSORIAL PSALM Ps 42   **[Longing for God]**

℟. Like a deer that longs for run - ning streams, my soul longs for you, my God.

Athirst is my soul for God, the living God.
When shall I go and behold the face of God?

℟. **Like a deer that longs for running streams,
my soul longs for you, my God.**

I went with the throng
and led them in procession to the house of God,
amid loud cries of joy and thanksgiving,
with the multitude keeping festival.

℟. **Like a deer that longs for running streams,
my soul longs for you, my God.**

Send forth your light and your fidelity;
they shall lead me on
and bring me to your holy mountain,
to your dwelling-place.

℟. **Like a deer that longs for running streams,
my soul longs for you, my God.**

Then will I go into the altar of God,
the God of my gladness and joy;
then will I give you thanks upon the harp,
O God, my God!

℟. **Like a deer that longs for running streams,
my soul longs for you, my God.** ↓

OR

*When baptism is not celebrated, the responsorial psalm after
the Fifth Reading (Is 12:2-3, 4bcd, 5-6) as above, p. 341, may
be used; or the following:*

RESPONSORIAL PSALM Ps 51   [A Clean Heart]

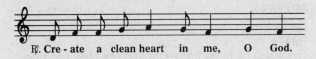

℟. Cre - ate a clean heart in me, O God.

A clean heart create for me, O God,
    and a steadfast spirit renew within me.
Cast me not out from your presence,
    and your Holy Spirit take not from me.

℟. **Create a clean heart in me, O God.**

Give me back the joy of your salvation,
    and a willing spirit sustain in me.
I will teach transgressors your ways,
    and sinners shall return to you.

℟. **Create a clean heart in me, O God.**

For you are not pleased with sacrifices;
    should I offer a holocaust, you would not accept it.
My sacrifice, O God, is a contrite spirit;
    a heart contrite and humbled, O God, you will not
      spurn.

℟. **Create a clean heart in me, O God.** ↓

PRAYER   [Lasting Salvation]

Let us pray.
God of unchanging power and light,
look with mercy and favor on your entire Church.
Bring lasting salvation to mankind,
so that the world may see
the fallen lifted up,
the old made new,
and all things brought to perfection,
through him who is their origin,
our Lord Jesus Christ,
who lives and reigns for ever and ever. ℟. **Amen.** ↓

OR

PRAYER   [Confirm Our Hope]

Let us pray.
Father,
you teach us in both the Old and the New Testament
to celebrate this passover mystery.
Help us to understand your great love for us.
May the goodness you now show us
confirm our hope in your future mercy.
We ask this through Christ our Lord. ℟. **Amen.** ↓

*After the last reading from the Old Testament with its
responsory and prayer, the altar candles are lighted, and the
priest intones the* Gloria, *which is taken up by all present.
The church bells are rung, according to local custom.*

*At the end of the hymn, the priest sings or says the opening
prayer in the usual way.*

OPENING PRAYER   [Renewed in Mind and Body]

Let us pray.
Lord God,
you have brightened this night
with the radiance of the risen Christ.
Quicken the spirit of sonship in your Church;
renew us in mind and body
to give you whole-hearted service.
Grant this through our Lord Jesus Christ, your Son,
who lives and reigns with you and the Holy Spirit,
one God, for ever and ever. ℟. **Amen.** ↓

Then a reader proclaims the reading from the Apostle Paul.

EPISTLE Rom 6:3-11   [Alive in Christ]
   By Baptism the Christian is not merely identified with the
   dying Christ, who has won a victory over sin, but is introduced into the very act by which Christ died to sin.

A reading from the Letter of Saint Paul to the Romans

BROTHERS and sisters: Are you unaware that we who were baptized into Christ Jesus were baptized into his death? We were indeed buried with him through baptism into death, so that, just as Christ was raised from the dead by the glory of the Father, we too might live in newness of life.

For if we have grown into union with him through a death like his, we shall also be united with him in the resurrection. We know that our old self was crucified with him, so that our sinful body might be done away with, that we might no longer be in slavery to sin. For a dead person has been absolved from sin. If, then, we have died with Christ, we believe that we shall also live with him. We know that Christ, raised from the dead, dies no more; death no longer has power over him. As to his death, he died to sin once and for all; as to his life, he lives for God. Consequently, you too must think of yourselves as being dead to sin and living for God in Christ Jesus.—The word of the Lord. ℟. **Thanks be to God.** ↓

After the Epistle all rise, and the priest solemnly intones the alleluia, *which is repeated by all present.*

RESPONSORIAL PSALM Ps 118   [God's Mercy]

℟. **Al -le -lu -ia. Al - le - lu -ia.   Al - le - lu - ia.**

Give thanks to the LORD, for he is good,
    for his mercy endures forever.
Let the house of Israel say,
    "His mercy endures forever."
℟. **Alleluia. Alleluia. Alleluia.**
The right hand of the LORD has struck with power;
    the right hand of the LORD is exalted.

I shall not die, but live,
    and declare the works of the LORD.

℞. **Alleluia. Alleluia. Alleluia.**

The stone which the builders rejected
    has become the cornerstone.
By the LORD has this been done;
    it is wonderful in our eyes.

℞. **Alleluia. Alleluia. Alleluia.** ↓

Incense may be used at the Gospel, but candles are not carried.

GOSPEL Mt 28:1-10   [The Resurrection]

Jesus has risen; he is not here. The cross has yielded to the empty tomb. The Easter message is first announced to the faithful, devoted women who followed Jesus.

℣. The Lord be with you. ℞. **And also with you.**
✤ A reading from the holy Gospel according to Matthew. ℞. **Glory to you, Lord.**

AFTER the sabbath, as the first day of the week was dawning, Mary Magdalene and the other Mary came to see the tomb. And behold, there was a great earthquake; for an angel of the Lord descended from heaven, approached, rolled back the stone, and sat upon it. His appearance was like lightning and his clothing was white as snow. The guards were shaken with fear of him and became like dead men. Then the angel said to the women in reply, "Do not be afraid! I know that you are seeking Jesus the crucified. He is not here, for he has been raised just as he said. Come and see the place where he lay. Then go quickly and tell his disciples, 'He has been raised from the dead, and he is going before you to Galilee; there you will see him.' Behold, I have told you." Then they went away quickly from the tomb, fearful yet overjoyed, and ran to announce this to his disciples. And behold,

Jesus met them on their way and greeted them. They approached, embraced his feet, and did him homage. Then Jesus said to them, "Do not be afraid. Go tell my brothers to go to Galilee, and there they will see me."— The Gospel of the Lord. ℟. **Praise to you, Lord Jesus Christ.**

➔ No. 14, p. 18

PART THREE

LITURGY OF SACRAMENTS OF INITIATION

The following is taken from the Rite of Christian Initiation of Adults.

Celebration of Baptism

PRESENTATION OF THE CANDIDATES

An assisting deacon or other minister calls the candidates for baptism forward and their godparents present them. The invitation to prayer and the Litany of the Saints follow.

INVITATION TO PRAYER   [Supportive Prayer]

The celebrant addresses the following or a similar invitation for the assembly to join in prayer for the candidates for baptism.

Dear friends, let us pray to almighty God for our brothers and sisters, N. and N., who are asking for baptism. He has called them and brought them to this moment; may he grant them light and strength to follow Christ with resolute hearts and to profess the faith of the Church. May he give them the new life of the Holy Spirit, whom we are about to call down on this water.

LITANY OF THE SAINTS   [Petitioning the Saints]

The singing of the Litany of the Saints is led by cantors and may include, at the proper place, names of other saints (for example, the titular of the church, the patron saints of the place or of those to be baptized) or petitions suitable to the occasion.

Lord, have mercy.
Lord, have mercy.

Christ, have mercy.
Christ, have mercy.

Lord, have mercy.
Lord, have mercy.

Holy Mary, Mother of God, **pray for us.**

Saint Michael, **pray for us.**

Holy angels of God, **pray for us.**

Saint John the Baptist, **pray for us.**

Saint Joseph, **pray for us.**

Saint Peter and Saint Paul, **pray for us.**

Saint Andrew, **pray for us.**

Saint John, **pray for us.**

Saint Mary Magdalene, **pray for us.**

Saint Stephen, **pray for us.**

Saint Ignatius, **pray for us.**

Saint Lawrence, **pray for us.**

Saint Perpetua and Saint Felicity, **pray for us.**

Saint Agnes, **pray for us.**

Saint Gregory, **pray for us.**

Saint Augustine, **pray for us.**

Saint Athanasius, **pray for us.**

Saint Basil, **pray for us.**

Saint Martin, **pray for us.**

Saint Benedict, **pray for us.**

Saint Francis and Saint Dominic, **pray for us.**

Saint Francis Xavier, **pray for us.**

Saint John Vianney, **pray for us.**

Saint Catherine, **pray for us.**

Saint Teresa, **pray for us.**

All holy men and women, **pray for us.**

Lord, be merciful, **Lord, save your people.**

From all evil, **Lord, save your people.**

From every sin, **Lord, save your people.**

From everlasting death, **Lord, save your people.**

By your coming as man, **Lord, save your people.**

By your death and rising to new life, **Lord, save your people.**

By your gift of the Holy Spirit, **Lord, save your people.**

Be merciful to us sinners, **Lord, hear our prayer.**

Give new life to these chosen ones by the grace of baptism, **Lord, hear our prayer.**

Jesus, Son of the living God, **Lord, hear our prayer.**

Christ, hear us.
Christ, hear us.

Lord Jesus, hear our prayer.
Lord Jesus, hear our prayer.

Blessing of the Water   [Grace-Filled Water]

Facing the font (or vessel) containing the water, the celebrant sings or says the following:

Father,
you give us grace through sacramental signs,
which tell us the wonders of your unseen power.
In baptism we use your gift of water,
which you have made a rich symbol of the grace
you give us in this sacrament.
At the very dawn of creation
your Spirit breathed on the waters,
making them the wellspring of all holiness.
The waters of the great flood
you made a sign of the waters of baptism,
that make an end of sin
and a new beginning of goodness.
Through the waters of the Red Sea
you led Israel out of slavery,
to be an image of God's holy people,
set free from sin by baptism.
In the waters of the Jordan
your Son was baptized by John
and anointed with the Spirit.
Your Son willed that water and blood should flow from
his side
as he hung upon the cross.
After his resurrection he told his disciples:
"Go out and teach all nations,

baptizing them in the name of the Father and of the
Son and of the Holy Spirit."
Father,
look now with love upon your Church,
and unseal for it the fountain of baptism.
By the power of the Spirit
give to this water the grace of your Son,
so that in the sacrament of baptism
all those whom you have created in your likeness may
be cleansed from sin
and rise to a new birth of innocence
by water and the Holy Spirit.

*Here, if this can be done conveniently, the celebrant before
continuing lowers the Easter candle into the water once or
three times, then holds it there until the acclamation at the
end of the blessing.*

We ask you, Father, with your Son
to send the Holy Spirit upon the waters of this font.
May all who are buried with Christ in the death of baptism
rise also with him to newness of life.
We ask this through Christ our Lord.
All: **Amen.**

*The celebrant then raises it and the people sing the following
or another suitable acclamation:*

Springs of water, bless the Lord.
Give him glory and praise for ever.

PROFESSION OF FAITH   [Witnessing to Our Faith]

*After the blessing of the water, the celebrant continues with
the profession of faith, which includes the renunciation of
sin and the profession itself.*

RENUNCIATION OF SIN   [Reject Evil]

*Using one of the following formularies, the celebrant ques-
tions all the elect together; or, after being informed of each
candidate's name by the godparents, he may use the same
formularies to question the candidates individually.*

A

Do you reject sin so as to live in the freedom of God's children? **I do.**

Do you reject the glamor of evil, and refuse to be mastered by sin? **I do.**

Do you reject Satan, father of sin and prince of darkness? **I do.**

B

Do you reject Satan, and all his works, and all his empty promises? **I do.**

C

Do you reject Satan? **I do.**
And all his works? **I do.**
And all his empty promises? **I do.**

PROFESSION OF FAITH   **[We Do Believe]**

Then the celebrant, informed again of each candidate's name by the godparents, questions each candidate individually. Each candidate is baptized immediately after his or her profession of faith.

Celebrant: N., do you believe in God, the Father almighty,
    creator of heaven and earth?
Candidate: **I do.**
Celebrant: Do you believe in Jesus Christ, his only Son, our Lord,
    who was born of the Virgin Mary,
    was crucified, died and was buried,
    rose from the dead,
    and is now seated at the right hand of the Father?
Candidate: **I do.**
Celebrant: Do you believe in the Holy Spirit,
    the holy Catholic Church, the communion of saints,
    the forgiveness of sins, the resurrection of the body,
    and the life everlasting?
Candidate: **I do.**

Baptism   [Children of God]

The celebrant baptizes each candidate either by immersion or by the pouring of water.

N., I baptize you in the name of the Father, and of the Son, and of the Holy Spirit.

EXPLANATORY RITES

The celebration of baptism continues with the explanatory rites, after which the celebration of confirmation normally follows.

ANOINTING AFTER BAPTISM   [Chrism of Salvation]

If the confirmation of those baptized is separated from their baptism, the celebrant anoints them with chrism immediately after baptism.

The God of power and Father of our Lord Jesus Christ
has freed you from sin
and brought you to new life
through water and the Holy Spirit.

He now anoints you with the chrism of salvation,
so that, united with his people,
you may remain for ever a member of Christ
who is Priest, Prophet, and King.

Newly baptized: **Amen.**

In silence each of the newly baptized is anointed with chrism on the crown of the head.

CLOTHING WITH A BAPTISMAL GARMENT
                                        [Clothed in Christ]

The garment used in this rite may be white or of a color that conforms to local custom. If circumstances suggest, this rite may be omitted.

N. and N., you have become a new creation
and have clothed yourselves in Christ.

Receive this baptismal garment
and bring it unstained to the judgment seat of our Lord
    Jesus Christ,
so that you may have everlasting life.

Newly baptized: **Amen.**

PRESENTATION OF A LIGHTED CANDLE [Light of Christ]

The celebrant takes the Easter candle in his hands or touches it, saying:

Godparents, please come forward to give to the newly
baptized the light of Christ.

A godparent of each of the newly baptized goes to the celebrant, lights a candle from the Easter candle, then presents it to the newly baptized.

You have been enlightened by Christ.
Walk always as children of the light
and keep the flame of faith alive in your hearts.
When the Lord comes, may you go out to meet him
with all the saints in the heavenly kingdom.

Newly baptized: **Amen.**

Renewal of Baptismal Promises

INVITATION   [Call to Renewal]

After the celebration of baptism, the celebrant addresses the community, in order to invite those present to the renewal of their baptismal promises; the candidates for reception into full communion join the rest of the community in this renunciation of sin and profession of faith. All stand and hold lighted candles. The celebrant may use the following or similar words.

Dear friends, through the paschal mystery we have
been buried with Christ in baptism, so that we may
rise with him to newness of life. Now that we have
completed our Lenten observance, let us renew the
promises we made in baptism when we rejected Satan

and his works, and promised to serve God faithfully
in his holy Catholic Church.

RENEWAL OF BAPTISMAL PROMISES

RENUNCIATION OF SIN   [Reject Evil]

A

Celebrant: Do you reject sin so as to live in the freedom of God's children?
All: **I do.**

Celebrant: Do you reject the glamor of evil,
   and refuse to be mastered by sin?
All: **I do.**

Celebrant: Do you reject Satan, father of sin and
   prince of darkness?
All: **I do.**

B

Celebrant: Do you reject Satan?
All: **I do.**
Celebrant: And all his works?
All: **I do.**
Celebrant: And all his empty promises?
All: **I do.**

PROFESSION OF FAITH   [We Do Believe]

Then the celebrant continues:

Celebrant: Do you believe in God, the Father almighty,
   creator of heaven and earth?
All: **I do.**
Celebrant: Do you believe in Jesus Christ, his only
   Son, our Lord,
   who was born of the Virgin Mary,
   was crucified, died and was buried,
   rose from the dead,
   and is now seated at the right hand of the Father?
All: **I do.**

Celebrant: Do you believe in the Holy Spirit,
the holy Catholic Church, the communion of saints,
the forgiveness of sins, the resurrection of the body,
and the life everlasting?

All: **I do.**

SPRINKLING WITH BAPTISMAL WATER   [Water of Life]

The celebrant sprinkles all the people with the blessed baptismal water, while all sing the following song or any other that is baptismal in character.

ANTIPHON See Ez 47:1-2, 9

**I saw water flowing
from the right side of the temple, alleluia.
It brought God's life and his salvation,
and the people sang in joyful praise:
alleluia, alleluia.**

The celebrant then concludes with the following prayer.

God, the all-powerful Father of our Lord Jesus Christ,
has given us a new birth by water and the Holy Spirit
and forgiven all our sins.
May he also keep us faithful to our Lord Jesus Christ
for ever and ever.

All: **Amen.**

Celebration of Reception

INVITATION   [Call To Come Forward]

If baptism has been celebrated at the font, the celebrant, the assisting ministers, and the newly baptized with their godparents proceed to the sanctuary. As they do so the assembly may sing a suitable song.

Then in the following or similar words the celebrant invites the candidates for reception, along with their sponsors, to come into the sanctuary and before the community to make a profession of faith.

N. and N., of your own free will you have asked to be received into the full communion of the Catholic

Church. You have made your decision after careful thought under the guidance of the Holy Spirit. I now invite you to come forward with your sponsors and in the presence of this community to profess the Catholic faith. In this faith you will be one with us for the first time at the eucharistic table of the Lord Jesus, the sign of the Church's unity.

PROFESSION BY THE CANDIDATES   [Belief in Church]

When the candidates for reception and their sponsors have taken their places in the sanctuary, the celebrant asks the candidates to make the following profession of faith. The candidates say:

I believe and profess all that the holy Catholic Church believes, teaches, and proclaims to be revealed by God.

ACT OF RECEPTION   [Full Communion]

Then the candidates with their sponsors go individually to the celebrant, who says to each candidate (laying his right hand on the head of any candidate who is not to receive confirmation):

N., the Lord receives you into the Catholic Church.
His loving kindness has led you here,
so that in the unity of the Holy Spirit
you may have full communion with us
in the faith that you have professed in the presence of
   his family.

Celebration of Confirmation

INVITATION   [Strength in the Spirit]

The newly baptized with their godparents and, if they have not received the sacrament of confirmation, the newly received with their sponsors, stand before the celebrant. He first speaks briefly to the newly baptized and the newly received in these or similar words.

My dear candidates for confirmation, by your baptism you have been born again in Christ and you have become members of Christ and of his priestly people. Now you are to share in the outpouring of the Holy Spirit among us, the Spirit sent by the Lord upon his apostles at Pentecost and given by them and their successors to the baptized.

The promised strength of the Holy Spirit, which you are to receive, will make you more like Christ and help you to be witnesses to his suffering, death, and resurrection. It will strengthen you to be active members of the Church and to build up the Body of Christ in faith and love.

My dear friends, let us pray to God our Father, that he will pour out the Holy Spirit on these candidates for confirmation to strengthen them with his gifts and anoint them to be more like Christ, the Son of God.

All pray briefly in silence.

LAYING ON OF HANDS   [Gifts of the Spirit]

The celebrant holds his hands outstretched over the entire group of those to be confirmed and says the following prayer.

All-powerful God, Father of our Lord Jesus Christ,
by water and the Holy Spirit
you freed your sons and daughters from sin
and gave them new life.
Send your Holy Spirit upon them
to be their helper and guide.
Give them the spirit of wisdom and understanding,
the spirit of right judgment and courage,
the spirit of knowledge and reverence.
Fill them with the spirit of wonder and awe in your
    presence.
We ask this through Christ our Lord.
R̷. **Amen.**

ANOINTING WITH CHRISM   [Sealed in the Spirit]

Either or both godparents and sponsors place the right hand on the shoulder of the candidate; and a godparent or a sponsor of the candidate gives the candidate's name to the minister of the sacrament. During the conferral of the sacrament an appropriate song may be sung.

The minister of the sacrament dips his right thumb in the chrism and makes the sign of the cross on the forehead of the one to be confirmed as he says:

N., be sealed with the Gift of the Holy Spirit.
Newly confirmed: **Amen.**
Minister: Peace be with you.
Newly confirmed: **And also with you.**

After all have received the sacrament, the newly confirmed as well as the godparents and sponsors are led to their places in the assembly.

[Since the profession of faith is not said, the general intercessions (no. 15, p. 19) begin immediately and for the first time the neophytes take part in them.]

PART FOUR

LITURGY OF THE EUCHARIST

The priest goes to the altar and begins the liturgy of the eucharist in the usual way.

It is fitting that the bread and wine be brought forward by the newly baptized.

PRAYER OVER THE GIFTS   [God's Saving Work]

Lord,
accept the prayers and offerings of your people.
With your help
may this Easter mystery of our redemption
bring to perfection the saving work you have begun in
    us.
We ask this through Christ our Lord. ℟. **Amen.** ↓

Preface of Easter I (P 21: on this Easter day), p. 81.

When Eucharistic Prayer I is used, the special Easter forms of In union with the whole Church, *and* Father, accept this offering *are said.*

Communion Ant. 1 Cor 5:7-8   [Sincerity and Truth]

Christ has become our paschal sacrifice; let us feast with the unleavened bread of sincerity and truth, alleluia. ↓

PRAYER AFTER COMMUNION   [Peace and Love]

Lord,
you have nourished us with your Easter sacraments.
Fill us with your Spirit,
and make us one in peace and love.
We ask this through Christ our Lord. ℟. **Amen.**

The deacon (or the priest) sings or says the dismissal as follows:

Go in the peace of Christ, alleluia, alleluia.

OR

The Mass is ended, go in peace, alleluia, alleluia.

OR

Go in peace to love and serve the Lord, alleluia, alleluia.

℟. **Thanks be to God, alleluia, alleluia.**

"I have risen: I am with you once more."

APRIL 24

EASTER SUNDAY

ENTRANCE ANT. Ps 139:18, 5-6   [Christ's Resurrection]

I have risen: I am with you once more; you placed your hand on me to keep me safe. How great is the depth of your wisdom, alleluia!

OR Lk 24:34; see Rv 1:6   [King and Lord]

The Lord has indeed risen, alleluia. Glory and king-ship be his for ever and ever.   → No. 2, p. 10

OPENING PRAYER   [Renewal]

Let us pray
   [that the risen Christ will raise us up
   and renew our lives]
God our Father,
by raising Christ your Son
you conquered the power of death
and opened for us the way to eternal life.
Let our celebration today
raise us up and renew our lives
by the Spirit that is within us.
Grant this . . . for ever and ever. ℟. **Amen.** ↓

ALTERNATIVE OPENING PRAYER   [God's Life]

Let us pray
  [on this Easter morning for the life
  that never again shall see darkness]
God our Father, creator of all,
today is the day of Easter joy.
This is the morning on which the Lord appeared to
    men
who had begun to lose hope
and opened their eyes to what the scriptures foretold:
that first he must die, and then he would rise
and ascend into his Father's glorious presence.
May the risen Lord
breathe on our minds and open our eyes
that we may know him in the breaking of bread,
and follow him in his risen life.
Grant this through Christ our Lord. ℟. **Amen.** ↓

FIRST READING Acts 10:34a, 37-43   [Salvation in Christ]

**In his sermon Peter sums up the "good news," the Gospel.
Salvation comes through Christ, the beloved Son of the
Father, the anointed of the Holy Spirit.**

A reading from the Acts of the Apostles

PETER proceeded to speak and said: "You know
what has happened all over Judea, beginning in
Galilee after the baptism that John preached, how God
anointed Jesus of Nazareth with the Holy Spirit and
power. He went about doing good and healing all those
oppressed by the devil, for God was with him. We are
witnesses of all that he did both in the country of the
Jews and in Jerusalem. They put him to death by hang-
ing him on a tree. This man God raised on the third day
and granted that he be visible, not to all the people, but
to us, the witnesses chosen by God in advance, who ate
and drank with him after he rose from the dead. He
commissioned us to preach to the people and testify

that he is the one appointed by God as judge of the living and the dead. To him all the prophets bear witness, that everyone who believes in him will receive forgiveness of sins through his name.—The word of the Lord. ℟. **Thanks be to God.** ↓

RESPONSORIAL PSALM Ps 118   [The Day of the Lord]

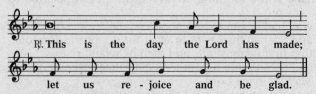

℟. This is the day the Lord has made; let us re - joice and be glad.

℟. Or: **Alleluia**.

Give thanks to the LORD, for he is good,
    for his mercy endures forever.
Let the house of Israel say,
    "His mercy endures forever."—℟.

The right hand of the LORD has struck with power;
    the right hand of the LORD is exalted.
I shall not die, but live,
    and declare the works of the LORD.—℟.

The stone which the builders rejected
    has become the cornerstone.
By the LORD has this been done;
    it is wonderful in our eyes.—℟. ↓

One of the following texts may be chosen as the Second Reading.

SECOND READING Col 3:1-4   [Seek Heavenly Things]
Look to the glory of Christ in which we share because our lives are hidden in him (through baptism) and we are destined to share in the glory.

A reading from the Letter of Saint Paul to the Colossians

BROTHERS and sisters: If then you were raised with Christ, seek what is above, where Christ is seated at the right hand of God. Think of what is above, not of what is on earth. For you have died, and your life is hidden with Christ in God. When Christ your life appears, then you too will appear with him in glory.— The word of the Lord. ℞. **Thanks be to God.** ↓

OR

SECOND READING 1 Cor 5:6b-8   [Change of Heart]

Turn away from your old ways, from sin. Have a change of heart; be virtuous.

A reading from the first Letter of Saint Paul
to the Corinthians

BROTHERS and sisters: Do you not know that a little yeast leavens all the dough? Clear out the old yeast, so that you may become a fresh batch of dough, inasmuch as you are unleavened. For our paschal lamb, Christ, has been sacrificed. Therefore, let us celebrate the feast, not with the old yeast, the yeast of malice and wickedness, but with the unleavened bread of sincerity and truth.—The word of the Lord. ℞. **Thanks be to God.** ↓

SEQUENCE *(Victimae paschali laudes)*   [Hymn to the Victor]

Christians, to the Paschal Victim
    Offer your thankful praises!
A Lamb the sheep redeems;
    Christ, Who only is sinless,
    Reconciles sinners to the Father.
Death and life have contended in that combat stupendous:
    The Prince of life, who died, reigns immortal.

Speak, Mary, declaring
    What you saw, wayfaring.

"The tomb of Christ, who is living,
    The glory of Jesus' resurrection;
Bright angels attesting,
    The shroud and napkin resting.
Yes, Christ my hope is arisen;
    To Galilee he goes before you."
Christ indeed from death is risen, our new life obtain-
    ing.
    Have mercy, victor King, ever reigning!
    Amen. Alleluia. ↓

ALLELUIA Cf. 1 Cor 5:7b-8a   [Joy in the Lord]

℟. **Alleluia, alleluia.**
Christ, our paschal lamb, has been sacrificed;
let us then feast with joy in the Lord.
℟. **Alleluia, alleluia.** ↓

(For Morning Mass)

GOSPEL Jn 20:1-9   [Renewed Faith]

Let us discover the empty tomb and ponder this mystery,
and like Christ's first followers be strengthened in our
faith.

℣. The Lord be with you. ℟. **And also with you.**
✠ A reading from the holy Gospel according to John.
℟. **Glory to you, Lord.**

ON the first day of the week, Mary of Magdala came
to the tomb early in the morning, while it was still
dark, and saw the stone removed from the tomb. So she
ran and went to Simon Peter and to the other disciple
whom Jesus loved, and told them, "They have taken the
Lord from the tomb, and we don't know where they put
him." So Peter and the other disciple went out and came
to the tomb. They both ran, but the other disciple ran
faster than Peter and arrived at the tomb first; he bent
down and saw the burial cloths there, but did not go in.

When Simon Peter arrived after him, he went into the tomb and saw the burial cloths there, and the cloth that had covered his head, not with the burial cloths but rolled up in a separate place. Then the other disciple also went in, the one who had arrived at the tomb first, and he saw and believed. For they did not yet understand the Scripture that he had to rise from the dead.— The Gospel of the Lord. ℟. **Praise to you, Lord Jesus Christ.**   → No. 14, p. 18

OR

GOSPEL Mt 28:1-10   [The Resurrection]
See p. 350.   _____

(For an Afternoon or Evening Mass)

GOSPEL Lk 24:13-35   [The Messiah's Need To Suffer]
Let us accept the testimony of these two witnesses that our hearts may burn with the fire of faith.

℣. The Lord be with you. ℟. **And also with you.**
✤ A reading from the holy Gospel according to Luke.
℟. **Glory to you, Lord.**

THAT very day, the first day of the week, two of Jesus' disciples were going to a village seven miles from Jerusalem called Emmaus, and they were conversing about all the things that had occurred. And it happened that while they were conversing and debating, Jesus himself drew near and walked with them, but their eyes were prevented from recognizing him. He asked them, "What are you discussing as you walk along?" They stopped, looking downcast. One of them, named Cleopas, said to him in reply, "Are you the only visitor to Jerusalem who does not know of the things that have taken place there in these days?" And he replied to them, "What sort of things?" They said to him, "The things that happened to Jesus the Nazarene, who was a prophet mighty in deed and word before God and all the people, how our chief priests and rulers both handed him over to a sentence of death and crucified him. But we were hoping that he would be the one to redeem Israel; and besides all this, it is now the third day since this took place. Some women from our group, however, have astounded us: they were at the tomb early in the morning and did not find his body; they came back and reported that they had indeed seen a vision of angels who announced that he was alive. Then some of those with us went to the tomb and found things just as the women had described, but him they did not see."

And he said to them, "Oh, how foolish you are! How slow of heart to believe all that the prophets spoke! Was is not necessary that the Christ should suffer these things and enter into his glory?" Then beginning with Moses and all the prophets, he interpreted to them what referred to him in all the Scriptures. As they approached the village to which they were going, he gave the impression that he was going farther. But they urged him, "Stay with us, for it is nearly evening and the day is almost over." So he went in to stay with them.

And it happened that, while he was with them at table, he took bread, said the blessing, broke it, and gave it to them. With that their eyes were opened and they recognized him, but he vanished from their sight. They said to each other, "Were not our hearts burning within us while he spoke to us on the way and opened the Scriptures to us?" So they set out at once and returned to Jerusalem where they found gathered together the eleven and those with them who were saying, "The Lord has truly been raised and has appeared to Simon!" Then the two recounted what had taken place on the way and how he was made known

to them in the breaking of bread.—The Gospel of the
Lord. ℟. **Praise to you, Lord Jesus Christ.**

➜ No. 14, p. 18

Renewal of Baptismal Promises, p. 357 (omit Creed).

PRAYER OVER THE GIFTS   [Renewing Sacrifice]

Lord,
with Easter joy we offer you the sacrifice
by which your Church is reborn and nourished
through Christ our Lord. ℟. **Amen.**

➜ No. 21, p. 22 (Pref. P 21: on this Easter Day)

*When Eucharistic Prayer I is used, the special Easter forms
of* In union with the whole Church *and* Father, accept this
offering *are said.*

COMMUNION ANT. 1 Cor 5:7-8   [Sincerity and Truth]

**Christ has become our paschal sacrifice; let us feast
with the unleavened bread of sincerity and truth,
alleluia.** ↓

PRAYER AFTER COMMUNION   [Glory of Resurrection]

Father of love,
watch over your Church
and bring us to the glory of the resurrection
promised by this Easter sacrament.
We ask this in the name of Jesus the Lord.
℟. **Amen.**

➜ No. 32, p. 70

Optional Solemn Blessings, p. 92, and Prayers Over the People, p. 99

"Thomas . . . said to him, 'My Lord and my God!' "

MAY 1

2nd SUNDAY OF EASTER

ENTRANCE ANT. 1 Pt 2:2   [Thirst for Spiritual Milk]

Like newborn children you should thirst for milk, on which your spirit can grow to strength, alleluia.

OR 4 Ezr 2:36-37   [Give Thanks]

Rejoice to the full in the glory that is yours, and give thanks to God who called you to his kingdom, alleluia.

→ No. 2, p. 10

OPENING PRAYER   [Renewed Gift of Life]

Let us pray
  [for a deeper awareness of our Christian baptism]
God of mercy,
you wash away our sins in water,
you give us new birth in the Spirit,
and redeem us in the blood of Christ.
As we celebrate Christ's resurrection
increase our awareness of these blessings,
and renew your gift of life within us.

We ask this through our Lord Jesus Christ, your Son,
who lives and reigns with you and the Holy Spirit,
one God, for ever and ever. ℟. **Amen.** ↓

ALTERNATIVE OPENING PRAYER   [God's People]
Let us pray
   [as Christians thirsting for the risen life]
Heavenly Father and God of mercy,
we no longer look for Jesus among the dead,
for he is alive and has become the Lord of life.
From the waters of death you raise us with him
and renew your gift of life within us.
Increase in our minds and hearts
the risen life we share with Christ
and help us to grow as your people
toward the fullness of eternal life with you.
We ask this through Christ our Lord. ℟. **Amen.** ↓

FIRST READING Acts 2:42-47   [True Christian Fellowship]
**The faithful lived a common life, sharing all their goods.
The apostles worked many miracles. They prayed together
and broke bread. Daily their numbers increased.**

A reading from the Acts of the Apostles

THEY devoted themselves to the teaching of the
apostles and to the communal life, to the breaking
of bread and to the prayers. Awe came upon everyone,
and many wonders and signs were done through the
apostles. All who believed were together and had all
things in common; they would sell their property and
possessions and divide them among all according to
each one's need. Every day they devoted themselves to
meeting together in the temple area and to breaking
bread in their homes. They ate their meals with exultation and sincerity of heart, praising God and enjoying
favor with all the people. And every day the Lord
added to their number those who were being saved.—
The word of the Lord. ℟. **Thanks be to God.** ↓

RESPONSORIAL PSALM Ps 118   [The Lord's Goodness]

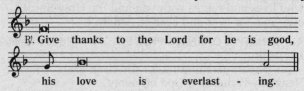

℟. **Give** thanks to the Lord for he is good,
his love is everlast - ing.

℟. Or: **Alleluia.**

Let the house of Israel say,
"His mercy endures forever."
Let the house of Aaron say,
"His mercy endures forever."
Let those who fear the LORD say,
"His mercy endures forever."—℟.

I was hard pressed and was falling,
but the LORD helped me.
My strength and my courage is the LORD,
and he has been my savior.
The joyful shout of victory
in the tents of the just:—℟.

The stone which the builders rejected
has become the cornerstone.
By the LORD has this been done;
it is wonderful in our eyes.
This is the day the LORD has made;
let us be glad and rejoice in it.—℟. ↓

SECOND READING 1 Pt 1:3-9   [Love in Practice]

God, our Father, has given us a new hope in Jesus, a birthright kept in heaven. Although there may be suffering, this is at the same time a cause for rejoicing. Faith in Jesus will bring salvation.

A reading from the first Letter of Saint Peter

BLESSED be the God and Father of our Lord Jesus Christ, who in his great mercy gave us a new birth to a living hope through the resurrection of Jesus Christ from the dead, to an inheritance that is imperishable, undefiled, and unfading, kept in heaven for you who by the power of God are safeguarded through faith, to a salvation that is ready to be revealed in the final time. In this you rejoice, although now for a little while you may have to suffer through various trials, so that the genuineness of your faith, more precious than gold that is perishable even though tested by fire, may prove to be for praise, glory, and honor at the revelation of Jesus Christ. Although you have not seen him you love him; even though you do not see him now yet believe in him, you rejoice with an indescribable and glorious joy, as you attain the goal of your faith, the salvation of your souls.—The word of the Lord. ℟. **Thanks be to God.** ↓

ALLELUIA Jn 20:29   [Blind Faith]

℟. **Alleluia, alleluia.**
You believe in me, Thomas, because you have seen me, says the Lord;
blessed are they who have not seen me, but still believe!
℟. **Alleluia, alleluia.**

GOSPEL Jn 20:19-31   [Living Faith]
Jesus appears to the disciples, coming through locked doors. He shows them his hands and side. He greets them in peace and gives them the power to forgive sin. A week later Jesus appears again directly to Thomas who now professes his belief.

℣. The Lord be with you. ℟. **And also with you.**
✣ A reading from the holy Gospel according to John.
℟. **Glory to you, Lord.**

ON the evening of that first day of the week, when the doors were locked, where the disciples were, for fear of the Jews, Jesus came and stood in their midst and said to them, "Peace be with you." When he had said this, he showed them his hands and his side. The disciples rejoiced when they saw the Lord. Jesus said to them again, "Peace be with you. As the Father has sent me, so I send you." And when he had said this, he breathed on them and said to them, "Receive the Holy Spirit. Whose sins you forgive are forgiven them, and whose sins you retain are retained."

Thomas, called Didymus, one of the Twelve, was not with them when Jesus came. So the other disciples said to him, "We have seen the Lord." But he said to them, "Unless I see the mark of the nails in his hands and put my finger into the nailmarks and put my hand into his side, I will not believe."

Now a week later his disciples were again inside and Thomas was with them. Jesus came, although the doors were locked, and stood in their midst and said, "Peace be with you." Then he said to Thomas, "Put your finger here and see my hands, and bring your hand and put it into my side, and do not be unbelieving, but believe." Thomas answered and said to him, "My Lord and my God!" Jesus said to him, "Have you come to believe because you have seen me? Blessed are those who have not seen and have believed."

Now, Jesus did many other signs in the presence of his disciples that are not written in this book. But these are written that you may come to believe that Jesus is the Christ, the Son of God, and that through this belief you may have life in his name.—The Gospel of the Lord. ℟. **Praise to you, Lord Jesus Christ.**

→ No. 14, p. 18

PRAYER OVER THE GIFTS   [Offerings Yielding Eternal Bliss]

Lord,
through faith and baptism
we have become a new creation.

Accept the offerings of your people
(and of those born again in baptism)
and bring us to eternal happiness.
Grant this through Christ our Lord.
℟. **Amen.**   ➜ No. 21, p. 22 (Pref. P 21)

When Eucharistic Prayer I is used, the special Easter forms
of In union with the whole Church *and* Father, accept this
offering *are said.*

COMMUNION ANT. See Jn 20:27   [Believe]

Jesus spoke to Thomas: Put your hand here, and see
the place of the nails. Doubt no longer, but believe,
alleluia. ↓

PRAYER AFTER COMMUNION   [Devout Reception]

Almighty God,
may the Easter sacraments we have received
live for ever in our minds and hearts.
We ask this through Christ our Lord.
℟. **Amen.**   ➜ No. 32, p. 70

Optional Solemn Blessings, p. 92, and Prayers Over the People, p. 99

"Their eyes were opened and they recognized him."

MAY 8

3rd SUNDAY OF EASTER

ENTRANCE ANT. Ps 66:1-2 [Praise the Lord]

Let all the earth cry out to God with joy; praise the glory of his name; proclaim his glorious praise, alleluia. → No. 2, p. 10

OPENING PRAYER [Hope of Resurrection]

Let us pray
　[that Christ will give us
　a share in the glory of his unending life]
God our Father,
may we look forward with hope to our resurrection,
for you have made us your sons and daughters,
and restored the joy of our youth.
We ask this through our Lord Jesus Christ, your Son,
who lives and reigns with you and the Holy Spirit,
one God, for ever and ever. ℞. **Amen.** ↓

ALTERNATIVE OPENING PRAYER [Eternal Light]

Let us pray
　[in confident peace and Easter hope]

Father in heaven, author of all truth,
a people once in darkness has listened to your Word,
and followed your Son as he rose from the tomb.
Hear the prayer of this newborn people
and strengthen your Church to answer your call.
May we rise and come forth into the light of day
to stand in your presence until eternity dawns.
We ask this through Christ our Lord. ℟. **Amen.** ↓

FIRST READING Acts 2:14, 22-33   [Reform Your Lives]

Peter proposes in short summary the name, work, death, and resurrection of our Lord. The Church teaches that although some of the authorities of Christ's time bear responsibility for carrying out his execution, this charge must not be laid against all the Jewish people of Jesus' day or of our own. We are all responsible for sin and for our Lord's suffering.

A reading from the Acts of the Apostles

THEN Peter stood up with the Eleven, raised his voice, and proclaimed: "You who are Jews, indeed all of you staying in Jerusalem. Let this be known to you, and listen to my words. You who are Israelites, hear these words. Jesus the Nazarene was a man commended to you by God with mighty deeds, wonders, and signs, which God worked through him in your midst, as you yourselves know. This man, delivered up by the set plan and foreknowledge of God, you killed, using lawless men to crucify him. But God raised him up, releasing him from the throes of death, because it was impossible for him to be held by it. For David says of him:

I saw the Lord ever before me,
    with him at my right hand I shall not be disturbed.
*Therefore my heart has been glad and my tongue
        has exulted;*
    my flesh, too, will dwell in hope,
*because you will not abandon my soul to the nether-
        world,*

nor will you suffer your holy one to see corruption.

You have made known to me the paths of life;
you will fill me with joy in your presence.

"My brothers, one can confidently say to you about the patriarch David that he died and was buried, and his tomb is in our midst to this day. But since he was a prophet and knew that God had sworn an oath to him that he would set one of his descendants upon his throne, he foresaw and spoke of the resurrection of the Christ, that neither was he abandoned to the netherworld nor did his flesh see corruption. God raised this Jesus; of this we are all witnesses. Exalted at the right hand of God, he received the promise of the Holy Spirit from the Father and poured him forth, as you see and hear."—The word of the Lord. ℟. **Thanks be to God.** ↓

RESPONSORIAL PSALM Ps 16   [Divine Security]

℟. **Lord, you will show us the path of life.**

℟. Or: **Alleluia.**

Keep me, O God, for in you I take refuge;
  I say to the LORD, "My LORD are you."
O LORD, my allotted portion and my cup,
  you it is who hold fast my lot.—℟.

I bless the LORD who counsels me;
  even in the night my heart exhorts me.
I set the LORD ever before me;
  with him at my right hand I shall not be disturbed.—℟.

Therefore my heart is glad and my soul rejoices,
  my body, too, abides in confidence;
because you will not abandon my soul to the netherworld,

nor will you suffer your faithful one to undergo corruption.—℟.

You will show me the path to life,
  abounding joy in your presence,
  the delights at your right hand forever.—℟. ↓

SECOND READING 1 Pt 1:17-21   [Love in Practice]

As followers of Jesus we have been ransomed by his blood. Through him we are believers in God who raised Jesus from the dead. Our faith and hope is in him.

A reading from the first Letter of Saint Peter

Bᴇʟᴏᴠᴇᴅ: If you invoke as Father him who judges impartially according to each one's works, conduct yourselves with reverence during the time of your sojourning, realizing that you were ransomed from your futile conduct, handed on by your ancestors, not with perishable things like silver or gold but with the precious blood of Christ as of a spotless unblemished lamb.

He was known before the foundation of the world but revealed in the final time for you, who through him believe in God who raised him from the dead and gave him glory, so that your faith and hope are in God.—The word of the Lord. ℟. **Thanks be to God.** ↓

ALLELUIA Cf. Lk 24:32   [Ardent Word]

℟. **Alleluia, alleluia.**
Lord Jesus, open the Scriptures to us;
make our hearts burn while you speak to us.
℟. **Alleluia, alleluia.** ↓

GOSPEL Lk 24:13-35   [Christ Is Lord]

Two disciples who do not recognize Jesus walk with him. Cleopas tells about Jesus—his miracles, passion, death and resurrection, and the hope Israel had in him. Finally, in the breaking of bread they see that Jesus is with them, truly risen.

℣. The Lord be with you. ℟. **And also with you.**

✚ A reading from the holy Gospel according to Luke.
℟. **Glory to you, Lord.**

THAT very day, the first day of the week, two of
Jesus' disciples were going to a village seven miles
from Jerusalem called Emmaus, and they were conversing about all the things that had occurred. And it
happened that while they were conversing and debating, Jesus himself drew near and walked with them,
but their eyes were prevented from recognizing him.
He asked them, "What are you discussing as you walk
along?" They stopped, looking downcast. One of them,
named Cleopas, said to him in reply, "Are you the only
visitor to Jerusalem who does not know of the things
that have taken place there in these days?" And he
replied to them, "What sort of things?" They said to
him, "The things that happened to Jesus the Nazarene,
who was a prophet mighty in deed and word before
God and all the people, how our chief priests and
rulers both handed him over to a sentence of death
and crucified him. But we were hoping that he would
be the one to redeem Israel; and besides all this, it is
now the third day since this took place. Some women
from our group, however, have astounded us: they
were at the tomb early in the morning and did not find
his body; they came back and reported that they had
indeed seen a vision of angels who announced that he
was alive. Then some of those with us went to the tomb
and found things just as the women had described, but
him they did not see."

And he said to them, "Oh, how foolish you are! How
slow of heart to believe all that the prophets spoke!
Was it not necessary that the Christ should suffer
these things and enter into his glory?" Then beginning
with Moses and all the prophets, he interpreted to
them what referred to him in all the Scriptures. As
they approached the village to which they were going,

he gave the impression that he was going on farther. But they urged him, "Stay with us, for it is nearly evening and the day is almost over." So he went in to stay with them.

And it happened that, while he was with them at table, he took bread, said the blessing, broke it, and gave it to them. With that their eyes were opened and they recognized him, but he vanished from their sight. Then they said to each other, "Were not our hearts burning within us while he spoke to us on the way and opened the Scriptures to us?" So they set out at once and returned to Jerusalem where they found gathered together the eleven and those with them who were saying, "The Lord has truly been raised and has appeared to Simon!" Then the two recounted what had taken place on the way and how he was made known to them in the breaking of bread.—The Gospel of the Lord. ℞. **Praise to you, Lord Jesus Christ.**

➔ No. 14, p. 18

PRAYER OVER THE GIFTS   [Perfect Joy]

Lord,
receive these gifts from your Church.
May the great joy you give us
come to perfection in heaven.
Grant this through Christ our Lord.
℞. **Amen.**   ➔ No. 21, p. 22 (Pref. P 21-25)

COMMUNION ANT. Lk 24:35   [Christ's Presence]

The disciples recognized the Lord Jesus in the breaking of bread, alleluia. ↓

PRAYER AFTER COMMUNION   [The Lord's Kindness]

Lord,
look on your people with kindness
and by these Easter mysteries
bring us to the glory of the resurrection.

We ask this in the name of Jesus the Lord.
℟. **Amen.**　　　　　　　　　　　→ No. 32, p. 70

Optional Solemn Blessings, p. 92, and Prayers Over the People, p. 99

"The sheep follow him, because they recognize his voice."

MAY 15

4th SUNDAY OF EASTER

ENTRANCE ANT. Ps 33:5-6　　　　　[God the Creator]

The earth is full of the goodness of the Lord; by the word of the Lord the heavens were made, alleluia.
→ No. 2, p. 10

OPENING PRAYER　　　　　　[Strengthened in Christ]

Let us pray
　[that Christ our shepherd
　will lead us through the difficulties of this life]
Almighty and ever-living God,
give us new strength
from the courage of Christ our shepherd,
and lead us to join the saints in heaven,
where he lives and reigns with you and the Holy Spirit,
one God for ever and ever. ℟. **Amen.** ↓

ALTERNATIVE OPENING PRAYER   [God Our Helper]

Let us pray
  [to God our helper in time of distress]
God and Father of our Lord Jesus Christ,
though your people walk in the valley of darkness,
no evil should they fear;
for they follow in faith the call of the shepherd
whom you have sent for their hope and strength.
Attune our minds to the sound of his voice,
lead our steps in the path he has shown,
that we may know the strength of his outstretched arm
and enjoy the light of your presence for ever.
We ask this in the name of Jesus the Lord. ℟. **Amen.** ↓

FIRST READING Acts 2:14a, 36-41   [Salvation in Jesus]
  **Peter states that Jesus is the Messiah who was crucified.
  Peter admonishes the people to reform and be baptized to
  receive the Holy Spirit. (See introduction to First Reading
  on p. 353.)**

A reading from the Acts of the Apostles

THEN Peter stood up with the Eleven, raised his
voice, and proclaimed: "Let the whole house of
Israel know for certain that God has made both Lord
and Christ, this Jesus whom you crucified."

Now when they heard this, they were cut to the
heart, and they asked Peter and the other apostles,
"What are we to do, my brothers?" Peter said to them,
"Repent and be baptized, every one of you, in the name
of Jesus Christ for the forgiveness of your sins; and you
will receive the gift of the Holy Spirit. For the promise
is made to you and to your children and to all those far
off, whomever the Lord our God will call." He testified
with many other arguments, and was exhorting them,
"Save yourselves from this corrupt generation." Those

who accepted his message were baptized, and about three thousand persons were added that day.—The word of the Lord. ℟. **Thanks be to God.** ↓

RESPONSORIAL PSALM Ps 23   [Refuge in God]

℟. **The Lord is my shep-herd; there is noth-ing I shall want.**

℟. Or: **Alleluia.**

The LORD is my shepherd; I shall not want.
  In verdant pastures he gives me repose;
beside restful waters he leads me;
  he refreshes my soul.—℟.

He guides me in right paths
  for his name's sake.
Even though I walk in the dark valley
  I fear no evil; for you are at my side
with your rod and your staff
  that give me courage.—℟.

You spread the table before me
  in the sight of my foes;
you anoint my head with oil;
  my cup overflows.—℟.

Only goodness and kindness follow me
  all the days of my life;
and I shall dwell in the house of the LORD
  for years to come.—℟. ↓

SECOND READING 1 Pt 2:20b-25   [Christ Our Savior]

Jesus gave an example. He suffered for us. He did no wrong; he did not answer with insults or threats. He died for our sins. By his wounds we are healed.

A reading from the first Letter of Saint Peter

BELOVED: If you are patient when you suffer for doing what is good, this is a grace before God. For to this you have been called, because Christ also suffered for you, leaving you an example that you should follow in his footsteps.

He committed no sin,
*   and no deceit was found in his mouth.*

When he was insulted, he returned no insult; when he suffered, he did not threaten; instead, he handed himself over to the one who judges justly. He himself bore our sins in his body upon the cross, so that, free from sin, we might live for righteousness. By his wounds you have been healed. For you had gone astray like sheep, but you have now returned to the shepherd and guardian of your souls.—The word of the Lord. ℟. **Thanks be to God.** ↓

ALLELUIA Jn 10:14   [God's Sheep]

℟. **Alleluia, alleluia.**
I am the good shepherd, says the Lord;
I know my sheep, and mine know me.
℟. **Alleluia, alleluia.** ↓

GOSPEL Jn 10:1-10   [The Good Shepherd]
    Jesus is the "Good Shepherd." He knows his sheep and
    they know him. Whoever enters his sheepfold will be safe.

℣. The Lord be with you. ℟. **And also with you.**
✝ A reading from the holy Gospel according to John.
℟. **Glory to you, Lord.**

JESUS said: "Amen, amen, I say to you, whoever does not enter a sheepfold through the gate but climbs over elsewhere is a thief and a robber. But whoever enters through the gate is the shepherd of the sheep. The gatekeeper opens it for him, and the sheep hear his voice, as the shepherd calls his own sheep by name and leads them out. When he has driven out all his own, he walks ahead of them, and the sheep follow him, because they recognize his voice. But they will not follow a stranger; they will run away from him, because they do not recognize the voice of strangers." Although Jesus used this figure of speech, the Pharisees did not realize what he was trying to tell them.

So Jesus said again, "Amen, amen, I say to you, I am the gate for the sheep. All who came before me are thieves and robbers, but the sheep did not listen to them. I am the gate. Whoever enters through me will be saved, and will come in and go out and find pasture. A thief comes only to steal and slaughter and destroy; I came so that they might have life and have it more abundantly."—The Gospel of the Lord. ℟. **Praise to you, Lord Jesus Christ.**   ➜ No. 14, p. 18

PRAYER OVER THE GIFTS   [Eternal Joy]

Lord,
restore us by these Easter mysteries.
May the continuing work of our redeemer
bring us eternal joy.
We ask this through Christ our Lord.
℟. **Amen.**   ➜ No. 21, p. 22 (Pref. P 21-25)

COMMUNION ANT.   [The Risen Shepherd]

The Good Shepherd is risen! He who laid down his life for his sheep, who died for his flock, he is risen, alleluia. ↓

PRAYER AFTER COMMUNION   [Eternal Shepherd]

Father, eternal shepherd,
watch over the flock redeemed by the blood of Christ
and lead us to the promised land.
Grant this through Christ our Lord.
℟. **Amen.**   ➜ No. 32, p. 70

Optional Solemn Blessings, p. 92, and Prayers Over the People, p. 99

"In my Father's house there are many dwelling places."

MAY 22

5th SUNDAY OF EASTER

ENTRANCE ANT. Ps 98:1, 2   **[Marvelous Deeds]**

Sing to the Lord a new song, for he has done marvelous deeds; he has revealed to the nations his saving power, alleluia. → No. 2, p. 10

OPENING PRAYER   **[True Freedom]**

Let us pray
  [that we may enjoy true freedom]
God our Father,
look upon us with love.
You redeem us and make us your children in Christ.
Give us true freedom
and bring us to the inheritance you promised.
We ask this through our Lord Jesus Christ, your Son,
who lives and reigns with you and the Holy Spirit,
one God, for ever and ever. ℟. **Amen.** ↓

ALTERNATIVE OPENING PRAYER   **[God's Praise]**

Let us pray
  [in the freedom of the sons of God]

Father of our Lord Jesus Christ,
you have revealed to the nations your saving power
and filled all ages with the words of a new song.
Hear the echo of this hymn.
Give us voice to sing your praise
throughout this season of joy.
We ask this through Christ our Lord. ℟. **Amen.** ↓

FIRST READING Acts 6:1-7   [Spiritual and Material Tasks]

Since the number of faithful was growing, seven men were proposed as ministers to help in the work of the Church. The apostles prayed over them and imposed hands on them.

A reading from the Acts of the Apostles

AS the number of disciples continued to grow, the Hellenists complained against the Hebrews because their widows were being neglected in the daily distribution. So the Twelve called together the community of the disciples and said, "It is not right for us to neglect the word of God to serve at table. Brothers, select from among you seven reputable men, filled with the Spirit and wisdom, whom we shall appoint to this task, whereas we shall devote ourselves to prayer and to the ministry of the word." The proposal was acceptable to the whole community, so they chose Stephen, a man filled with faith and the Holy Spirit, also Philip, Prochorus, Nicanor, Timon, Parmenas, and Nicholas of Antioch, a convert to Judaism. They presented these men to the apostles who prayed and laid hands on them. The word of God continued to spread, and the number of the disciples in Jerusalem increased greatly; even a large group of priests were becoming obedient to the faith.—The word of the Lord. ℟. **Thanks be to God.** ↓

RESPONSORIAL PSALM Ps 33   [Exult in the Lord]

℟. **Lord, let your mercy be   on us,   as we place our trust in you.**

℟. Or: **Alleluia.**

Exult, you just, in the LORD;
  praise from the upright is fitting.
Give thanks to the LORD on the harp;
  with the ten-stringed lyre chant his praises.—℟.

Upright is the word of the LORD,
  and all his works are trustworthy.
He loves justice and right;
  of the kindness of the LORD the earth is full.—℟.

See, the eyes of the LORD are upon those who fear him,
  upon those who hope for his kindness,
to deliver them from death
  and preserve them in spite of famine.—℟. ↓

SECOND READING 1 Pt 2:4-9   [A Royal Priesthood]

**Jesus is the cornerstone of the Church. The people of God
are living stones. We are a royal priesthood, a consecrated
nation, a people set apart to proclaim Jesus' good works.**

A reading from the first Letter of Saint Peter

BELOVED: Come to him, a living stone, rejected by
human beings but chosen and precious in the sight
of God, and, like living stones, let yourselves be built
into a spiritual house to be a holy priesthood to offer
spiritual sacrifices acceptable to God through Jesus
Christ. For it says in Scripture:
  Behold, I am laying a stone in Zion,
  a cornerstone, chosen and precious,
  and whoever believes in it shall not be put to shame.
Therefore, its value is for you who have faith, but for
those without faith:

*The stone that the builders rejected
has become the cornerstone, and
A stone that will make people stumble,
and a rock that will make them fall.*

They stumble by disobeying the word, as is their destiny.

You are "a chosen race, a royal priesthood, a holy nation, a people of his own, so that you may announce the praises" of him who called you out of darkness into his wonderful light.—The word of the Lord. ℟. **Thanks be to God.** ↓

ALLELUIA Jn 14:6 [Christ the Way]

℟. **Alleluia, alleluia.**
I am the way, the truth and the life, says the Lord;
no one comes to the Father, except through me.
℟. **Alleluia, alleluia.** ↓

GOSPEL Jn 14:1-12 [Faith in God]

Jesus assures his apostles that he is the way, the truth, and the life. The Father lives in him and he in the Father. Whoever has faith in Jesus will do the works of God.

℣. The Lord be with you. ℟. **And also with you.**
✜ A reading from the holy Gospel according to John.
℟. **Glory to you, Lord.**

JESUS said to his disciples: "Do not let your hearts be troubled. You have faith in God; have faith also in me. In my Father's house there are many dwelling places. If there were not, would I have told you that I am going to prepare a place for you? And if I go and prepare a place for you, I will come back again and take you to myself, so that where I am you also may be. Where I am going you know the way." Thomas said to him, "Master, we do not know where you are going; how can we know the way?" Jesus said to him, "I am the way and the truth and the life. No one comes to the Father except through me. If you know me, then you will also know my Father. From now on you do know him and have seen him." Philip said to him, "Master, show us the Father, and that will be enough for us." Jesus said to him, "Have I been with you for so long a time and you still do not know me, Philip? Whoever has seen me has seen the Father. How can you say, 'Show us the Father'? Do you not believe that I am in the Father and the Father is in me? The words that I speak to you I do not speak on my own. The Father who dwells in me is doing his works. Believe me that I am in the Father and the Father is in me, or else, believe because of the works themselves. Amen, amen, I say to you, whoever believes in me will do the works that I do, and will do greater ones than these, because I am going to the Father."—The Gospel of the Lord. ℟. **Praise to you, Lord Jesus Christ.**   ➜ No. 14, p. 18

PRAYER OVER THE GIFTS   [Guided by God's Truth]

Lord God,
by this holy exchange of gifts
you share with us your divine life.
Grant that everything we do
may be directed by the knowledge of your truth.
We ask this in the name of Jesus the Lord.
℟. **Amen.**   ➜ No. 21, p. 22 (Pref. P 21-25)

COMMUNION ANT. Jn 15:5   [Union with Christ]

I am the vine and you are the branches, says the Lord; he who lives in me, and I in him, will bear much fruit, alleluia. ↓

PRAYER AFTER COMMUNION   [New Life]

Merciful Father,
may these mysteries give us new purpose
and bring us to a new life in you.
Grant this through Christ our Lord.
℟. **Amen.**   ➜ No. 32, p. 70

Optional Solemn Blessings, p. 92, and Prayers Over the People, p. 99

"I will ask the Father, and he will give you another Advocate."

MAY 29

6th SUNDAY OF EASTER

When the Ascension of the Lord is celebrated the following Sunday, the second reading and Gospel from the 7th Sunday of Easter (pp. 406-407) may be read on the 6th Sunday of Easter.

ENTRANCE ANT. Is 48:20   [Spiritual Freedom]

Speak out with a voice of joy; let it be heard to the ends of the earth: The Lord has set his people free, alleluia.   → No. 2, p. 10

OPENING PRAYER   [Operative Faith]

Let us pray
    [that we may practice in our lives
     the faith we profess]
Ever-living God,
help us to celebrate our joy
in the resurrection of the Lord
and to express in our lives
the love we celebrate.
Grant this through our Lord Jesus Christ, your Son,
who lives and reigns with you and the Holy Spirit,
one God, for ever and ever. ℟. **Amen.** ↓

ALTERNATIVE OPENING PRAYER   [Resurrection]

Let us pray
  [in silence, reflecting on the joy of Easter]
God our Father, maker of all,
the crown of your creation was the Son of Man,
born of a woman, but without beginning;
he suffered for us but lives for ever.
May our mortal lives be crowned with the ultimate joy
of rising with him,
who is Lord for ever and ever. ℟. **Amen.** ↓

FIRST READING Acts 8:5-8, 14-17 [Reception of Holy Spirit]

**Philip carried the good news to Samaria. He performed
many miracles. Peter and John laid hands on these people
in Samaria and they received the Holy Spirit.**

A reading from the Acts of the Apostles

PHILIP went down to the city of Samaria and proclaimed the Christ to them. With one accord, the
crowds paid attention to what was said by Philip when
they heard it and saw the signs he was doing. For
unclean spirits, crying out in a loud voice, came out of
many possessed people, and many paralyzed or crip-
pled people were cured. There was great joy in that
city.

  Now when the apostles in Jerusalem heard that
Samaria had accepted the word of God, they sent them
Peter and John, who went down and prayed for them,
that they might receive the Holy Spirit, for it had not
yet fallen upon any of them; they had only been baptized in the name of the Lord Jesus. Then they laid
hands on them and they received the Holy Spirit.—The
word of the Lord. ℟. **Thanks be to God.** ↓

RESPONSORIAL PSALM Ps 66   [Glorious Deeds]

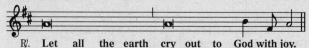

℞. **Let all the earth cry out to God with joy.**

℞. Or: **Alleluia.**

Shout joyfully to God, all the earth,
  sing praise to the glory of his name;
  proclaim his glorious praise.
Say to God, "How tremendous are your deeds!—℞.

Let all on earth worship and sing praise to you,
  sing praise to your name!"
Come and see the works of God,
  his tremendous deeds among the children of
  men.—℞.

He has changed the sea into dry land;
  through the river they passed on foot;
  therefore let us rejoice in him.
He rules by his might forever.—℞.

Hear now, all you who fear God, while I declare
  what he has done for me.
Blessed be God who refused me not
  my prayer or his kindness! —℞. ↓

SECOND READING 1 Pt 3:15-18   [Life in the Spirit]
    **Always worship God in your hearts. Jesus died for sins just
    once for all who are sinners to lead us to God.**

    A reading from the first Letter of Saint Peter

BELOVED: Sanctify Christ as Lord in your hearts.
Always be ready to give an explanation to anyone
who asks you for a reason for your hope, but do it with
gentleness and reverence, keeping your conscience
clear, so that, when you are maligned, those who
defame your good conduct in Christ may themselves
be put to shame. For it is better to suffer for doing

good, if that be the will of God, than for doing evil. For Christ also suffered for sins once, the righteous for the sake of the unrighteous, that he might lead you to God. Put to death in the flesh, he was brought to life in the Spirit.—The word of the Lord. ℟. **Thanks be to God.** ↓

ALLELUIA Jn 14:23   [Divine Love]

℟. **Alleluia, alleluia.**
Whoever loves me will keep my word, says the Lord, and my Father will love him and we will come to him.
℟. **Alleluia, alleluia.** ↓

GOSPEL Jn 14:15-21   [Eternal Presence]

Jesus promises to ask for a Paraclete for those who love him. The world will not accept or understand the Paraclete. All who obey the commandments show their love for God and will be loved in return.

℣. The Lord be with you. ℟. **And also with you.**
✝ A reading from the holy Gospel according to John. ℟. **Glory to you, Lord.**

JESUS said to his disciples: "If you love me, you will keep my commandments. And I will ask the Father, and he will give you another Advocate to be with you always, the Spirit of truth, whom the world cannot accept, because it neither sees nor knows him. But you know him, because he remains with you, and will be in you. I will not leave you orphans; I will come to you. In a little while the world will no longer see me, but you will see me, because I live and you will live. On that day you will realize that I am in my Father and you are in me and I in you. Whoever has my commandments and observes them is the one who loves me. And whoever loves me will be loved by my Father, and I will love him and reveal myself to him."—The Gospel of the Lord. ℟. **Praise to you, Lord Jesus Christ.**   ➔ No. 14, p. 18

PRAYER OVER THE GIFTS　　　　　[Forgiveness]

Lord,
accept our prayers and offerings.
Make us worthy of your sacraments of love
by granting us your forgiveness.
We ask this in the name of Jesus the Lord.
℟. **Amen.**　　　　➜ No. 21, p. 22 (Pref. P 21-25)

COMMUNION ANT. Jn 14:15-16　　[Role of the Spirit]

**If you love me, keep my commandments, says the
Lord. The Father will send you the Holy Spirit, to be
with you for ever, alleluia. ↓**

PRAYER AFTER COMMUNION　　[Eucharistic Strength]

Almighty and ever-living Lord,
you restored us to life
by raising Christ from death.
Strengthen us by this Easter sacrament;
may we feel its saving power in our daily life.
We ask this through Christ our Lord.
℟. **Amen.**　　　　➜ No. 32, p. 70

Optional Solemn Blessings, p. 92, and Prayers Over the People, p. 99

"Go, therefore, and make disciples of all nations."

In the states of Alaska, California, Hawaii, Idaho, Montana, Nevada, Oregon, Utah, and Washington (and others if applicable), the following Mass of the Ascension is celebrated on June 5, in place of the Mass of the 7th Sunday of Easter that appears on p. 404.

JUNE 2

ASCENSION OF THE LORD

ENTRANCE ANT. Acts 1:11   [The Lord Will Return]

Men of Galilee, why do you stand looking in the sky? The Lord will return, just as you have seen him ascend, alleluia. → No. 2, p. 10

OPENING PRAYER   [Joy in the Ascension]

Let us pray
  [that the risen Christ
  will lead us to eternal life]
God our Father,
make us joyful in the ascension of your Son Jesus Christ.
May we follow him into the new creation,
for his ascension is our glory and our hope.
We ask this through our Lord Jesus Christ, your Son,
who lives and reigns with you and the Holy Spirit,
one God, for ever and ever. ℟. **Amen.** ↓

ALTERNATIVE OPENING PRAYER   [Following Jesus]

Let us pray
[on this day of Ascension
as we watch and wait for Jesus' return]
Father in heaven,
our minds were prepared for the coming of your king-
    dom
when you took Christ beyond our sight
so that we might seek him in his glory.
May we follow where he has led
and find our hope in his glory,
for he is Lord for ever. ℟. **Amen.** ↓

FIRST READING Acts 1:1-11   [Christ's Ascension]

Christ is divine! He will come again! Our faith affirms this for us. We live in the era of the Holy Spirit.

A reading from the the Acts of the Apostles

IN the first book, Theophilus, I dealt with all that Jesus did and taught until the day he was taken up, after giving instructions through the Holy Spirit to the apostles whom he had chosen. He presented himself alive to them by many proofs after he had suffered, appearing to them during forty days and speaking about the kingdom of God. While meeting with them, he enjoined them not to depart from Jerusalem, but to wait for "the promise of the Father about which you have heard me speak; for John baptized with water, but in a few days you will be baptized with the Holy Spirit."

When they had gathered together they asked him, "Lord, are you at this time going to restore the king-dom to Israel?" He answered them, "It is not for you to know the times or seasons that the Father has estab-lished by his own authority. But you will receive power when the Holy Spirit comes upon you, and you will be my witnesses in Jerusalem, throughout Judea and

Samaria, and to the ends of the earth." When he had said this, as they were looking on, he was lifted up, and a cloud took him from their sight. While they were looking intently at the sky as he was going, suddenly two men dressed in white garments stood beside them. They said, "Men of Galilee, why are you standing there looking at the sky? This Jesus who has been taken up from you into heaven will return in the same way as you have seen him going into heaven."—The word of the Lord. ℟. **Thanks be to God.** ↓

RESPONSORIAL PSALM Ps 47   [Praise to the Lord]

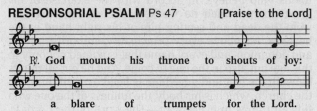

℟. God mounts his throne to shouts of joy:
a blare of trumpets for the Lord.

℟. Or: **Alleluia.**

All you peoples, clap your hands,
    shout to God with cries of gladness.
For the LORD, the Most High, the awesome,
    is the great king over all the earth.—℟.

God mounts his throne amid shouts of joy;
    the LORD, amid trumpet blasts.
Sing praise to God, sing praise;
    sing praise to our king, sing praise.—℟.

For king of all the earth is God;
    sing hymns of praise.
God reigns over the nations,
    God sits upon his holy throne.—℟. ↓

SECOND READING Eph 1:17-23   [Glorification of Jesus]
    Our hope is in God. He is our strength. With Christ our
    head, we his people will receive the gift of wisdom and
    insight.

A reading from the Letter of Saint Paul to the
Ephesians

BROTHERS and sisters: May the God of our Lord
Jesus Christ, the Father of glory, give you a Spirit of
wisdom and revelation resulting in knowledge of him.
May the eyes of your hearts be enlightened, that you
may know what is the hope that belongs to his call, what
are the riches of glory in his inheritance among the holy
ones, and what is the surpassing greatness of his power
for us who believe, in accord with the exercise of his
great might, which he worked in Christ, raising him
from the dead and seating him at his right hand in the
heavens, far above every principality, authority, power,
and dominion, and every name that is named not only in
this age but also in the one to come. And he put all things
beneath his feet and gave him as head over all things to
the church, which is his body, the fullness of the one who
fills all things in every way.—The word of the Lord. ℟.
Thanks be to God. ↓

ALLELUIA Mt 28:19a, 20b   [Christ's Abiding Presence]

℟. **Alleluia, alleluia.**
Go and teach all nations, says the Lord;
I am with you always, until the end of the world.
℟. **Alleluia, alleluia.** ↓

GOSPEL Mt 28:16-20   [Commission of the Apostles]

**Jesus speaks to the eleven admitting his full authority. He
commissions them to make disciples of all people, to baptize them. Jesus also promises to be with them to the end
of the world.**

℣. The Lord be with you. ℟. **And also with you.**
✛ A reading from the holy Gospel according to
Matthew. ℟. **Glory to you, Lord.**

THE eleven disciples went to Galilee, to the mountain to which Jesus had ordered them. When they

saw him, they worshiped, but they doubted. Then Jesus approached and said to them, "All power in heaven and on earth has been given to me. Go, therefore, and make disciples of all nations, baptizing them in the name of the Father, and of the Son, and of the Holy Spirit, teaching them to observe all that I have commanded you. And behold, I am with you always, until the end of the age."—The Gospel of the Lord. ℟. **Praise to you, Lord Jesus Christ.**   ➜ No. 14, p. 18

PRAYER OVER THE GIFTS   [Rising with Christ]

Lord,
receive our offering
as we celebrate the ascension of Christ your Son.
May his gifts help us rise with him
to the joys of heaven,
where he lives and reigns for ever and ever.
℟. **Amen.**   ➜ No. 21, p. 22 (Pref. P 26-27)

When Eucharistic Prayer I is used, the special Ascension form of In union with the whole Church *is said.*

COMMUNION ANT. Mt 28:20   [Christ's Presence]

I, the Lord, am with you always, until the end of the world, alleluia. ↓

PRAYER AFTER COMMUNION   [Divine Life]

Father,
in this eucharist
we touch the divine life you give to the world.
Help us to follow Christ with love
to eternal life where he is Lord for ever and ever.
℟. **Amen.**   ➜ No. 32, p. 70

Optional Solemn Blessings, p. 92, and Prayers Over the People, p. 99

"Father, the hour has come. Give glory to your Son."

In the following states of Alaska, California, Hawaii, Idaho, Montana, Nevada, Oregon, Utah, and Washington (and others if applicable), the Mass of the Ascension that appears on p. 399 is celebrated today in place of the following Mass of the 7th Sunday of Easter.

JUNE 5

7th SUNDAY OF EASTER

ENTRANCE ANT. Ps 27:7-9   [Seeking the Lord]

Lord, hear my voice when I call to you. My heart has prompted me to seek your face; I seek it, Lord; do not hide from me, alleluia. → No. 2, p. 10

OPENING PRAYER   [Recognizing Christ Among Us]

Let us pray
  [that we may recognize
  the presence of Christ in our midst]
Father,
help us keep in mind that Christ our Savior
lives with you in glory
and promised to remain with us until the end of time.
We ask this through our Lord Jesus Christ, your Son,
who lives and reigns with you and the Holy Spirit,
one God, for ever and ever. ℟. **Amen.** ↓

ALTERNATIVE OPENING PRAYER   [Christ's Presence]

Let us pray
  [to our Father
  who has raised us to life in Christ]
Eternal Father,
reaching from end to end of the universe,
and ordering all things with your mighty arm:
for you, time is the unfolding of truth that already is,
the unveiling of beauty that is yet to be.
Your Son has saved us in history
by rising from the dead,
so that transcending time he might free us from death.
May his presence among us
lead to the vision of unlimited truth
and unfold the beauty of your love.
We ask this in the name of Jesus the Lord. ℞. **Amen.** ↓

FIRST READING Acts 1:12-14   [Constant Prayer]

After the ascension the apostles returned to pray in the upper room at Jerusalem. Mary and some other women were with them. They prayed continuously for nine days.

A reading from the Acts of the Apostles

AFTER Jesus had been taken up to heaven the apostles returned to Jerusalem from the mount called Olivet, which is near Jerusalem, a sabbath day's journey away. When they entered the city they went to the upper room where they were staying, Peter and John and James and Andrew, Philip and Thomas, Bartholomew and Matthew, James son of Alphaeus, Simon the Zealot, and Judas son of James. All these devoted themselves with one accord to prayer, together with some women, and Mary the mother of Jesus, and his brothers.—The word of the Lord. ℞. **Thanks be to God.** ↓

RESPONSORIAL PSALM Ps 27   [The House of the Lord]

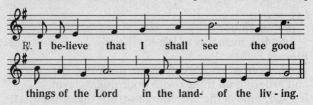

℟. I be-lieve that I shall see the good things of the Lord in the land- of the liv-ing.

℟. Or: **Alleluia.**

The LORD is my light and my salvation;
  whom should I fear?
The LORD is my life's refuge;
  of whom should I be afraid?—℟.

One thing I ask of the LORD;
  this I seek;
to dwell in the house of the LORD
  all the days of my life,
that I may gaze on the loveliness of the LORD
  and contemplate his temple.—℟.

Hear, O LORD, the sound of my call;
  have pity on me, and answer me.
Of you my heart speaks; you my glance seeks.—℟. ↓

SECOND READING 1 Pt 4:13-16   [Joy in Suffering]

We should rejoice in sharing in the suffering of Jesus; for this we should not be ashamed. Beware, however, not to violate the rights of others.

A reading from the first Letter of Saint Peter

BELOVED: Rejoice to the extent that you share in the sufferings of Christ, so that when his glory is revealed you may also rejoice exultantly. If you are insulted for the name of Christ, blessed are you, for the Spirit of glory and of God rests upon you. But let no one among you be made to suffer as a murderer, a thief, an evildoer, or as an intriguer. But whoever is made to suffer as a Christian should not be ashamed but glorify God because of the name.—The word of the Lord. ℟. **Thanks be to God.** ↓

ALLELUIA Cf. Jn 14:18   [Come, Lord Jesus]

℟. **Alleluia, alleluia.**
I will not leave you orphans, says the Lord.
I will come back to you, and your hearts will rejoice.
℟. **Alleluia, alleluia.** ↓

GOSPEL Jn 17:1-11a   [Eternal Life]

Jesus prays to his Father noting that the work given him is finished. The Father is known on earth. Jesus prays for his apostles to whom he entrusted the "good news" of salvation.

℣. The Lord be with you. ℟. **And also with you.**
✚ A reading from the holy Gospel according to John.
℟. **Glory to you, Lord.**

JESUS raised his eyes to heaven and said, "Father, the hour has come. Give glory to your son, so that your son may glorify you, just as you gave him authority over all people, so that your son may give eternal life to all you gave him. Now this is eternal life, that they should know you, the only true God, and the one whom you sent, Jesus Christ. I glorified you on earth by accomplishing the work you gave me to do. Now glorify me, Father, with you, with the glory that I had with you before the world began.

"I revealed your name to those whom you gave me out of the world. They belonged to you, and you gave them to me, and they have kept your word. Now they know that everything you gave me is from you, because the words you gave to me I have given to them, and they accepted them and truly understood that I came from you, and they have believed that you sent me. I pray for them. I do not pray for the world but for the ones you have given me, because they are yours, and everything of mine is yours and everything of yours is mine, and I have been glorified in them. And now I will no longer be in the world, but they are in the world, while I am coming to you."—The Gospel of the Lord. R̶⁄. **Praise to you, Lord Jesus Christ.**

➜ No. 14, p. 18

PRAYER OVER THE GIFTS   [Gifts of Love]

Lord,
accept the prayers and gifts
we offer in faith and love.
May this eucharist
bring us to your glory.
Grant this through Christ our Lord.
R̶⁄. **Amen.**   ➜   No. 21, p. 22 (Pref. P 21-25 or P 26-27)

COMMUNION ANT. Jn 17:22   [Christian Unity]

This is the prayer of Jesus: that his believers may become one as he is one with the Father, alleluia. ↓

PRAYER AFTER COMMUNION   [Glory of Christ's Body]

God our Savior,
hear us,
and through this holy mystery give us hope
that the glory you have given Christ
will be given to the Church, his body,
for he is Lord for ever and ever.
R̶⁄. **Amen.**   ➜ No. 32, p. 70

Optional Solemn Blessings, p. 92, and Prayers Over the People, p. 99

"They were all filled with the Holy Spirit."

JUNE 12

PENTECOST SUNDAY

VIGIL MASS

ENTRANCE ANT. See Rom 5:5; 8:11 [Love-Imparting Spirit]

The love of God has been poured into our hearts by his Spirit living in us, alleluia.　　→ No. 2, p. 10

OPENING PRAYER　　　　　　　　[Spirit of Peace]

Let us pray
　[that the Holy Spirit
　may bring peace and unity to all mankind]
Almighty and ever-living God,
you fulfilled the Easter promise
by sending us your Holy Spirit.
May that Spirit unite the races and nations on earth
to proclaim your glory.
Grant this through our Lord Jesus Christ, your Son,
who lives and reigns with you and the Holy Spirit,
one God, for ever and ever. ℞. **Amen.** ↓

OR　　　　　　　　　　　[New Birth in the Spirit]

God our Father,
you have given us new birth.

409

Strengthen us with your Holy Spirit
and fill us with your light.
Grant this through our Lord Jesus Christ, your Son,
who lives and reigns with you and the Holy Spirit,
one God, for ever and ever. ℟. **Amen.** ↓

ALTERNATIVE OPENING PRAYER   [Eliminate Division]

Let us pray
  [that the flame of the Spirit will descend upon us]
Father in heaven,
fifty days have celebrated the fullness
of the mystery of your revealed love.
See your people gathered in prayer,
open to receive the Spirit's flame.
May it come to rest in our hearts
and disperse the divisions of word and tongue.
With one voice and one song
may we praise your name in joy and thanksgiving.
Grant this through Christ our Lord. ℟. **Amen.** ↓

FIRST READING

A Gn 11:1-9   [Dangers of Human Pride]
Those who put their trust in pride, and human ability, are bound to fail.

A reading from the Book of Genesis

THE whole world spoke the same language, using the same words. While the people were migrating in the east, they came upon a valley in the land of Shinar and settled there. They said to one another, "Come, let us mold bricks and harden them with fire." They used bricks for stone, and bitumen for mortar. Then they said, "Come, let us build ourselves a city and a tower with its top in the sky, and so make a name for ourselves; otherwise we shall be scattered all over the earth."

The LORD came down to see the city and the tower that the people had built. Then the LORD said: "If now, while they are one people, all speaking the same language, they have started to do this, nothing will later stop them from doing whatever they presume to do. Let us then go down there and confuse their language, so that one will not understand what another says." Thus the LORD scattered them from there all over the earth, and they stopped building the city. That is why it was called Babel, because there the LORD confused the speech of all the world. It was from that place that he scattered them all over the earth.—The word of the Lord. ℟. **Thanks be to God.** ↓

OR

B Ex 19:3-8a, 16-20b   [The Lord on Mount Sinai]

The Lord God covenants with the Israelites—they are to be a holy nation, a princely Kingdom.

A reading from the Book of Exodus

MOSES went up the mountain to God. Then the LORD called to him and said, "Thus shall you say to the house of Jacob; tell the Israelites: You have seen for your-selves how I treated the Egyptians and how I bore you up on eagle wings and brought you here to myself. Therefore, if you hearken to my voice and keep my covenant, you shall be my special possession, dearer to me than all other people, though all the earth is mine. You shall be to me a kingdom of priests, a holy nation. That is what you must tell the Israelites." So Moses went and summoned the elders of the people. When he set before them all that the LORD had ordered him to tell them, the people all answered together, "Everything the LORD has said, we will do."

On the morning of the third day there were peals of thunder and lightning, and a heavy cloud over the mountain, and a very loud trumpet blast, so that all the people in the camp trembled. But Moses led the people

out of the camp to meet God, and they stationed themselves at the foot of the mountain. Mount Sinai was all
wrapped in smoke, for the LORD came down upon it in
fire. The smoke rose from it as though from a furnace,
and the whole mountain trembled violently. The trumpet
blast grew louder and louder, while Moses was speaking
and God answering him with thunder.

When the LORD came down to the top of Mount
Sinai, he summoned Moses to the top of the mountain.—The word of the Lord. ℟. **Thanks be to God.** ↓

OR

C Ez 37:1-14   [Life-Giving Spirit]

**The prophet, in a vision, sees the power of God—the band
of the living and the dead, as he describes the resurrection
of the dead.**

A reading from the Book of the Prophet Ezekiel

THE hand of the LORD came upon me, and he led me
out in the spirit of the LORD and set me in the center of the plain, which was now filled with bones. He
made me walk among the bones in every direction so
that I saw how many they were on the surface of the
plain. How dry they were! He asked me: Son of man,
can these bones come to life? I answered, "LORD God,
you alone know that." Then he said to me: Prophesy
over these bones, and say to them: Dry bones, hear the
word of the LORD! Thus says the Lord GOD to these
bones: See! I will bring spirit into you, that you may
come to life. I will put sinews upon you, make flesh
grow over you, cover you with skin, and put spirit in
you so that you may come to life and know that I am
the LORD. I, Ezekiel, prophesied as I had been told, and
even as I was prophesying I heard a noise; it was a rat-
tling as the bones came together, bone joining bone. I
saw the sinews and the flesh come upon them, and the
skin cover them, but there was no spirit in them. Then
the LORD said to me: Prophesy to the spirit, prophesy,

son of man, and say to the spirit: Thus says the Lord GOD: From the four winds come, O spirit, and breathe into these slain that they may come to life. I prophesied as he told me, and the spirit came into them; they came alive and stood upright, a vast army. Then he said to me: Son of man, these bones are the whole house of Israel. They have been saying, "Our bones are dried up, our hope is lost, and we are cut off." Therefore, prophesy and say to them: Thus says the Lord GOD: O my people, I will open your graves and have you rise from them, and bring you back to the land of Israel. Then you shall know that I am the LORD, when I open your graves and have you rise from them, O my people! I will put my spirit in you that you may live, and I will settle you upon your land; thus you shall know that I am the LORD. I have promised, and I will do it, says the LORD.—The word of the Lord. ℟. **Thanks be to God.** ↓

OR

D Jl 3:1-5   **[Signs of the Spirit]**

At the end of time, the Day of the Lord, Judgment Day, those who persevere in faith will be saved.

A reading from the Book of the Prophet Joel

THUS says the LORD:
I will pour out my spirit upon all flesh.
Your sons and daughters shall prophesy,
    your old men shall dream dreams,
    your young men shall see visions;
even upon the servants and the handmaids,
    in those days, I will pour out my spirit.
And I will work wonders in the heavens and on the
        earth,
    blood, fire, and columns of smoke;
the sun will be turned to darkness,
    and the moon to blood,

at the coming of the day of the LORD,
    the great and terrible day.
Then everyone shall be rescued
    who calls on the name of the LORD;
for on Mount Zion there shall be a remnant,
    as the LORD has said,
and in Jerusalem survivors
    whom the LORD shall call.
The word of the Lord. ℟. **Thanks be to God.** ↓

RESPONSORIAL PSALM Ps 104   [Send Out Your Spirit]

℟. **Lord, send out your Spir - it, and re-new the face of the earth.**

℟. Or: **Alleluia.**

Bless the LORD, O my soul!
    O LORD, my God, you are great indeed!
You are clothed with majesty and glory,
    robed in light as with a cloak.—℟.

How manifold are your works, O LORD!
    In wisdom you have wrought them all—
the earth is full of your creatures;
    bless the LORD, O my soul! Alleluia.—℟.

Creatures all look to you
    to give them food in due time.
When you give it to them, they gather it;
    when you open your hand, they are filled with good
        things.—℟.

If you take away their breath, they perish
    and return to their dust.
When you send forth your spirit, they are created,
    and you renew the face of the earth.—℟. ↓

SECOND READING Rom 8:22-27   [The Spirit Our Helper]
    Be patient and have hope. The Spirit intercedes for us.

A reading from the Letter of Saint Paul to the Romans

BROTHERS and sisters: We know that all creation is groaning in labor pains even until now; and not only that, but we ourselves, who have the firstfruits of the Spirit, we also groan within ourselves as we wait for adoption, the redemption of our bodies. For in hope we were saved. Now hope that sees is not hope. For who hopes for what one sees? But if we hope for what we do not see, we wait with endurance.

In the same way, the Spirit too comes to the aid of our weakness; for we do not know how to pray as we ought, but the Spirit himself intercedes with inexpressible groanings. And the one who searches hearts knows what is the intention of the Spirit, because he intercedes for the holy ones according to God's will.— The word of the Lord. ℟. **Thanks be to God.** ↓

ALLELUIA   [Fire of God's Love]
℟. **Alleluia, alleluia.**
Come, Holy Spirit, fill the hearts of the faithful
and kindle in them the fire of your love.
℟. **Alleluia, alleluia.** ↓

GOSPEL Jn 7:37-39   [Prediction of the Spirit]
   The Spirit is the source of life for those who have faith and believe.

℣. The Lord be with you. ℟. **And also with you.**
✤ A reading from the holy Gospel according to John.
℟. **Glory to you, Lord**.

ON the last and greatest day of the feast, Jesus stood up and exclaimed, "Let anyone who thirsts come to me and drink. As scripture says:
   Rivers of living water will flow from within him
who believes in me." He said this in reference to the Spirit that those who came to believe in him were to receive. There was, of course, no Spirit yet, because Jesus had not

yet been glorified.—The Gospel of the Lord. ℞. **Praise to you, Lord Jesus Christ.**   ➜ No. 14, p. 18

PRAYER OVER THE GIFTS   [Manifestation of Salvation]

Lord,
send your Spirit on these gifts
and through them help the Church you love
to show your salvation to all the world.
We ask this in the name of Jesus the Lord.
℞. **Amen.**   ➜ Pref. (P 28), p. 399

When Eucharistic Prayer I is used, the special Pentecost form of In union with the whole Church *is said.*

COMMUNION ANT. Jn 7:37   [Thirst for the Spirit]

On the last day of the festival, Jesus stood up and cried aloud: If anyone is thirsty, let him come to me and drink, alleluia. ↓

PRAYER AFTER COMMUNION   [Eucharistic Love]

Lord,
through this eucharist,
send the Holy Spirit of Pentecost into our hearts
to keep us always in your love.
We ask this through Christ our Lord.
℞. **Amen.**   ➜ No. 32, p. 70

Optional Solemn Blessings, p. 92, and Prayers Over the People, p. 99

MASS DURING THE DAY

ENTRANCE ANT. Wis 1:7   [The Spirit in the World]

The Spirit of the Lord fills the whole world. It holds all things together and knows every word spoken by man, alleluia.

OR See Rom 5:5; 8:11   [God's Love for Us]

The love of God has been poured into our hearts by his Spirit living in us, alleluia.   ➜ No. 2, p. 10

OPENING PRAYER   [Work of the Spirit]

Let us pray
  [that the Spirit will work through our lives
  to bring Christ to the world]
God our Father,
let the Spirit you sent on your Church
to begin the teaching of the gospel
continue to work in the world
through the hearts of all who believe.
We ask this through our Lord Jesus Christ, your Son,
who lives and reigns with you and the Holy Spirit,
one God, for ever and ever. R̶. **Amen.** ↓

ALTERNATIVE OPENING PRAYER   [Power of the Spirit]

Let us pray
  [in the Spirit who dwells within us]
Father of light, from whom every good gift comes,
send your Spirit into our lives
with the power of a mighty wind,
and by the flame of your wisdom
open the horizons of our minds.
Loosen our tongues to sing your praise
in words beyond the power of speech,
for without your Spirit
man could never raise his voice in words of peace
or announce the truth that Jesus is Lord,
who lives and reigns with you and the Holy Spirit,
one God, for ever and ever. R̶. **Amen.** ↓

FIRST READING Acts 2:1-11   [Coming of the Spirit]

As promised by Jesus, the Holy Spirit fills the faithful and, inspired, they proclaim the good news.

A reading from the Acts of the Apostles

WHEN the time for Pentecost was fulfilled, they were
all in one place together. And suddenly there came
from the sky a noise like a strong driving wind, and it

filled the entire house in which they were. Then there appeared to them tongues as of fire, which parted and came to rest on each of them. And they were all filled with the Holy Spirit and began to speak in different tongues, as the Spirit enabled them to proclaim.

Now there were devout Jews from every nation under heaven staying in Jerusalem. At this sound, they gathered in a large crowd, but they were confused because each one heard them speaking in his own language. They were astounded, and in amazement asked, "Are not all these people who are speaking Galileans? Then how does each of us hear them in his native language? We are Parthians, Medes, and Elamites, inhabitants of Mesopotamia, Judea and Cappadocia, Pontus and Asia, Phrygia and Pamphylia, Egypt, and the districts of Libya near Cyrene, as well as travelers from Rome, both Jews and converts to Judaism, Cretans and Arabs, yet we hear them speaking in our own tongues of the mighty acts of God."—The word of the Lord. ℟. **Thanks be to God.** ↓

RESPONSORIAL PSALM Ps 104   [Renewal by the Spirit]

℟. **Lord, send out your Spir - it,   and re-new the face of the earth.**

℟. Or: **Alleluia.**

Bless the Lord, O my soul!
   O Lord, my God, you are great indeed!
How manifold are your works, O Lord!
   the earth is full of your creatures.—℟.

May the glory of the Lord endure forever,
   may the Lord be glad in his works!
Pleasing to him be my theme;
   I will be glad in the Lord.—℟.

If you take away their breath, they perish
   and return to their dust.

When you send forth your spirit, they are created,
and you renew the face of the earth.—R̸.↓

SECOND READING 1 Cor 12:3b-7, 12-13   [Grace of the Spirit]

The gifts of the Spirit are not exclusive but for all. The Spirit brings a radical uniting that overcomes all destructions.

A reading from the first Letter of Saint Paul
to the Corinthians

BROTHERS and sisters: No one can say: "Jesus is Lord," except by the Holy Spirit. There are different kinds of spiritual gifts but the same Spirit; there are different forms of service but the same Lord; there are different workings but the same God who produces all of them in everyone. To each individual the manifestation of the Spirit is given for some benefit.

As a body is one though it has many parts, all the parts of the body, though many, are one body, so also Christ. For in one Spirit we were all baptized into one body, whether Jews or Greeks, slaves or free persons, and we are all given to drink of one Spirit.—The word of the Lord. R̸. **Thanks be to God.** ↓

SEQUENCE (Veni, Sancte Spiritus)   [Come, Holy Spirit]

Come, Holy Spirit, come!
And from your celestial home
Shed a ray of light divine!
Come, Father of the poor!
Come, source of all our store!
Come, within our bosoms shine!
You, of comforters the best;
You, the soul's most welcome guest;
Sweet refreshment here below;
In our labor, rest most sweet;
Grateful coolness in the heat;
Solace in the midst of woe.
O most blessed Light divine,
Shine within these hearts of yours,
And our inmost being fill!

Where you are not, we have naught,
Nothing good in deed or thought,
  Nothing free from taint of ill.
Heal our wounds, our strength renew;
On our dryness pour your dew;
  Wash the stains of guilt away:
Bend the stubborn heart and will;
Melt the frozen, warm the chill;
  Guide the steps that go astray.
On the faithful, who adore
And confess you, evermore
  In your sevenfold gift descend;
Give them virtue's sure reward;
Give them your salvation, Lord;
  Give them joys that never end. Amen.
  Alleluia. ↓

ALLELUIA   **[Fire of God's Love]**
℞. **Alleluia, alleluia.**
Come, Holy Spirit, fill the hearts of your faithful
and kindle in them the fire of your love.
℞. **Alleluia, alleluia.** ↓

GOSPEL Jn 20:19-23   **[Christ Imparts the Spirit]**
   Jesus gives the blessing of peace, and bestows his author-
   ity on the disciples as he confers on them the Holy Spirit.

℣. The Lord be with you. ℞. **And also with you.**
✠ A reading from the holy Gospel according to John. ℞.
Glory to you, Lord.

O N the evening of that first day of the week, when the
  doors were locked, where the disciples were, for fear
of the Jews, Jesus came and stood in their midst and said
to them, "Peace be with you." When he had said this, he
showed them his hands and his side. The disciples
rejoiced when they saw the Lord. Jesus said to them
again, "Peace be with you. As the Father has sent me, so
I send you." And when he had said this, he breathed on

them and said to them, "Receive the Holy Spirit. Whose sins you forgive are forgiven them, and whose sins you retain are retained."—The Gospel of the Lord. ℟. **Praise to you, Lord Jesus Christ.**   ➔ No. 14, p. 18

PRAYER OVER THE GIFTS   [Spirit of Jesus]

Lord,
may the Spirit you promised
lead us into all truth
and reveal to us the full meaning of this sacrifice.
Grant this through Christ our Lord. ℟. **Amen.** ↓

PREFACE (P 28)   [Coming of the Spirit]

℣. The Lord be with you. ℟. **And also with you.** ℣. Lift up your hearts. ℟. **We lift them up to the Lord.** ℣. Let us give thanks to the Lord our God. ℟. **It is right to give him thanks and praise.**

Father, all-powerful and ever-living God,
we do well always and everywhere to give you thanks.
Today you sent the Holy Spirit
on those marked out to be your children
by sharing the life of your only Son,
and so you brought the paschal mystery to its completion.
Today we celebrate the great beginning of your Church
when the Holy Spirit made known to all peoples the one true God,
and created from the many languages of man
one voice to profess one faith.
The joy of the resurrection renews the whole world,
while the choirs of heaven sing for ever to your glory:
                    ➔ No. 23, p. 23

When Eucharistic Prayer I is used, the special Pentecost form of In union with the whole Church *is said.*

COMMUNION ANT. Acts 2:4, 11   [Filled with the Spirit]

They were all filled with the Holy Spirit, and they spoke of the great things God had done, alleluia. ↓

PRAYER AFTER COMMUNION   [Vigor of the Spirit]

Father,
may the food we receive in the eucharist
help our eternal redemption.
Keep within us the vigor of your Spirit
and protect the gifts you have given to your Church.
We ask this in the name of Jesus the Lord.

℞. **Amen.**   → No. 32, p. 70

*The Blessing, p. 70 is given as usual. (At the end of the
Dismissal the people answer: "Thanks be to God, alleluia,
alleluia.")*

Optional Solemn Blessings, p. 92, and Prayers Over the People, p. 99

*"Blessed be God the Father and his only-begotten Son
and the Holy Spirit."*

JUNE 19

TRINITY SUNDAY

ENTRANCE ANT.   [Blessed Trinity]

**Blessed be God the Father and his only-begotten Son
and the Holy Spirit: for he has shown that he loves us.**
→ No. 2, p. 10

OPENING PRAYER   [Witnessing to the Trinity]

Let us pray
  [to the one God, Father, Son and Spirit,
  that our lives may bear witness to our faith]

Father,
you sent your Word to bring us truth
and your Spirit to make us holy.
Through them we come to know the mystery of your
    life.
Help us to worship you, one God in three Persons,
by proclaiming and living our faith in you.
Grant this through our Lord Jesus Christ, your Son,
who lives and reigns with you and the Holy Spirit,
one God, for ever and ever. ℟. **Amen.** ↓

ALTERNATIVE OPENING PRAYER

Let us pray   [Praise to the Triune God]
    [to our God who is Father, Son, and Holy Spirit]
God, we praise you:
Father all-powerful, Christ Lord and Savior, Spirit of
    love.
You reveal yourself in the depths of our being,
drawing us to share in your life and your love.
One God, three Persons,
be near to the people formed in your image,
close to the world your love brings to life.
We ask you this, Father, Son, and Holy Spirit,
one God, true and living, for ever and ever. ℟. **Amen.** ↓

FIRST READING Ex 34:4b-6, 8-9   [The One God]

**Moses takes two stone tablets up on Mount Sinai. Moses
bows down in worship asking the Lord to be with his people and pardon their sins and offenses.**

A reading from the Book of Exodus

EARLY in the morning Moses went up Mount Sinai
as the LORD had commanded him, taking along the
two stone tablets.

Having come down in a cloud, the LORD stood with
him there and proclaimed his name, "LORD." Thus the
LORD passed before him and cried out, "The LORD, the
LORD, a merciful and gracious God, slow to anger and

rich in kindness and fidelity." Moses at once bowed down to the ground in worship. Then he said, "If I find favor with you, O LORD, do come along in our company. This is indeed a stiff-necked people; yet pardon our wickedness and sins, and receive us as your own." —The word of the Lord. ℟. **Thanks be to God.** ↓

RESPONSORIAL PSALM Dn 3   [Praise the Lord]

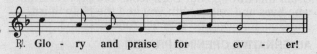

℟. Glo - ry and praise for ev - er!

Blessed are you, O Lord, the God of our fathers,
    praiseworthy and exalted above all forever;
and blessed is your holy and glorious name,
    praiseworthy and exalted above all for all ages.

℟. **Glory and praise for ever!**

Blessed are you in the temple of your holy glory,
    praiseworthy and glorious above all forever.

℟. **Glory and praise for ever!**

Blessed are you on the throne of your kingdom,
    praiseworthy and exalted above all forever.

℟. **Glory and praise for ever!**

Blessed are you who look into the depths
    from your throne upon the cherubim,
    praiseworthy and exalted above all forever.

℟. **Glory and praise for ever!** ↓

SECOND READING 2 Cor 13:11-13
                    [God's Grace, Love, and Fidelity]
Paul encourages the Corinthians to live showing the love of God among them—to live in harmony, peace, and love in the fellowship of the Holy Spirit.

A reading from the second Letter of Saint Paul
to the Corinthians

Brothers and sisters, rejoice. Mend your ways, encourage one another, agree with one another, live in peace, and the God of love and peace will be with you. Greet one another with a holy kiss. All the holy ones greet you.

The grace of the Lord Jesus Christ and the love of God and the fellowship of the Holy Spirit be with all of you.—The word of the Lord. ℟. **Thanks be to God.** ↓

ALLELUIA Cf. Rv 1:8   [Triune God]

℟. **Alleluia, alleluia.**
Glory to the Father, the Son, and the Holy Spirit:
to God who is, who was, and who is to come.
℟. **Alleluia, alleluia.** ↓

GOSPEL Jn 3:16-18   [God's Love]

God sent his Son into the world that whoever would believe would therefore have eternal life.

℣. The Lord be with you. ℟. **And also with you.**
✛ A reading from the holy Gospel according to John.
℟. **Glory to you, Lord.**

God so loved the world that he gave his only Son, so that everyone who believes in him might not perish but might have eternal life. For God did not send his Son into the world to condemn the world, but that the world might be saved through him. Whoever believes in him will not be condemned, but whoever does not believe has already been condemned, because he has not believed in the name of the only Son of God.—The Gospel of the Lord. ℟. **Praise to you, Lord Jesus Christ.**   → No. 14, p. 18

PRAYER OVER THE GIFTS   [Perfect Offering]

Lord our God,
make these gifts holy,
and through them

make us a perfect offering to you.
We ask this in the name of Jesus the Lord. ℟. **Amen.** ↓

PREFACE (P 43)   [Mystery of the One Godhead]
℣. The Lord be with you. ℟. **And also with you.** ℣. Lift
up your hearts. ℟. **We lift them up to the Lord.** ℣. Let
us give thanks to the Lord our God. ℟. **It is right to
give him thanks and praise.**

Father, all-powerful and ever-living God,
we do well always and everywhere to give you thanks.
We joyfully proclaim our faith
in the mystery of your Godhead.
You have revealed your glory
as the glory also of your Son
and of the Holy Spirit:
three Persons equal in majesty,
undivided in splendor,
yet one Lord, one God,
ever to be adored in your everlasting glory.
And so, with all the choirs of angels in heaven
we proclaim your glory
and join in their unending hymn of praise:

→ No. 23, p. 23

COMMUNION ANT. Gal 4:6   [Abba, Father]
**You are the sons of God, so God has given you the
Spirit of his Son to form your hearts and make you cry
out: Abba, Father.** ↓

PRAYER AFTER COMMUNION   [Eternal God]
Lord God,
we worship you, a Trinity of Persons, one eternal God.
May our faith and the sacrament we receive
bring us health of mind and body.
We ask this through Christ our Lord.
℟. **Amen.**

→ No. 32, p. 70

Optional Solemn Blessings, p. 92, and Prayers Over the People, p. 99

"This is my body. . . ."

JUNE 26

BODY AND BLOOD OF CHRIST
(CORPUS CHRISTI)

ENTRANCE ANT. Ps 81:17   [Finest Wheat and Honey]

The Lord fed his people with the finest wheat and honey; their hunger was satisfied.   → No. 2, p. 10

OPENING PRAYER   [Memorial of Christ]

Let us pray
  [to the Lord who gives himself in the eucharist,
    that this sacrament may bring us salvation and
      peace]
Lord Jesus Christ,
you gave us the eucharist
as the memorial of your suffering and death.
May our worship of this sacrament of your body and
   blood
help us to experience the salvation you won for us
and the peace of the kingdom
where you live with the Father and the Holy Spirit,
one God, for ever and ever. ℟. **Amen.** ↓

ALTERNATIVE OPENING PRAYER   [Eucharistic Love]

Let us pray
 [for the willingness to make present in our world
  the love of Christ shown to us in the eucharist]
Lord Jesus Christ,
we worship you living among us
in the sacrament of your body and blood.
May we offer to our Father in heaven
a solemn pledge of undivided love.
May we offer to our brothers and sisters
a life poured out in loving service of that kingdom
where you live with the Father and the Holy Spirit,
one God, for ever and ever. ℟. **Amen.** ↓

FIRST READING Dt 8:2-3, 14b-16a   [Manna in the Desert]

**Moses reminds the Israelites that although God let them
hunger, still he fed them with manna, a food unknown. He
brought them out of the slavery of Egypt and cared for them.**

A reading from the Book of Deuteronomy

MOSES said to the people: "Remember how for
forty years now the LORD, your God, has directed
all your journeying in the desert, so as to test you by
affliction and find out whether or not it was your
intention to keep his commandments. He therefore let
you be afflicted with hunger, and then fed you with
manna, a food unknown to you and your fathers, in
order to show you that not by bread alone does one
live, but by every word that comes forth from the
mouth of the LORD.

"Do not forget, the LORD, your God, who brought you
out of the land of Egypt, that place of slavery; who
guided you through the vast and terrible desert with its
saraph serpents and scorpions, its parched and water-
less ground; who brought forth water for you from the
flinty rock and fed you in the desert with manna, a

food unknown to your fathers."—The word of the Lord. ℟. **Thanks be to God.** ↓

RESPONSORIAL PSALM Ps 147　　　[The Best of Wheat]

℟. **Praise　　the Lord,　Je - ru - sa - lem.**

℟. Or: **Alleluia.**

Glorify the LORD, O Jerusalem;
　praise your God, O Zion.
For he has strengthened the bars of your gates;
　he has blessed your children within you.—℟.

He has granted peace in your borders;
　with the best of wheat he fills you.
He sends forth his command to the earth;
　swiftly runs his word!—℟.

He has proclaimed his word to Jacob,
　his statutes and his ordinances to Israel.
He has not done thus for any other nation;
　his ordinances he has not made known to them.
　　Alleluia.—℟. ↓

SECOND READING 1 Cor 10:16-17　　　[Body and Blood]

In the one bread and sharing the one cup, we are united in the body and blood of Jesus. We, though many, are still one body in Jesus.

A reading from the first Letter of Saint Paul
to the Corinthians

BROTHERS and sisters: The cup of blessing that we bless, is it not a participation in the blood of Christ? The bread that we break, is it not a participation in the body of Christ? Because the loaf of bread is one, we, though many, are one body, for we all partake of the one loaf.—The word of the Lord. ℟. **Thanks be to God.** ↓

SEQUENCE (*Lauda Sion*)   [Praise of the Eucharist]

The sequence Laud, O Zion (Lauda Sion), *or the shorter form beginning with the verse* Lo! the angel's food is given, *may be sung optionally before the Alleluia.*

Laud, O Zion, your salvation,
Laud with hymns of exultation,
  Christ, your king and shepherd true:
Bring him all the praise you know,
He is more than you bestow.
  Never can you reach his due.

Special theme for glad thanksgiving
Is the quick'ning and the living
  Bread today before you set:
From his hands of old partaken,
As we know, by faith unshaken,
  Where the Twelve at supper met.

Full and clear ring out your chanting,
Joy nor sweetest grace be wanting,
  From your heart let praises burst:
For today the feast is holden,
When the institution olden
  Of that supper was rehearsed.

Here the new law's new oblation,
By the new king's revelation,
  Ends the form of ancient rite:
Now the new the old effaces,
Truth away the shadow chases,
  Light dispels the gloom of night.

What he did at supper seated,
Christ ordained to be repeated,
  His memorial ne'er to cease:
And his rule for guidance taking,
Bread and wine we hallow, making
  Thus our sacrifice of peace.

This truth each Christian learns,
Bread into his flesh he turns,
  To his precious blood the wine:
Sight has fail'd, nor thought conceives,
But a dauntless faith believes,
  Resting on a pow'r divine.

Here beneath these signs are hidden
Priceless things to sense forbidden;
  Signs, not things are all we see:
Blood is poured and flesh is broken,
Yet in either wondrous token
  Christ entire we know to be.

Whoso of this food partakes,
Does not rend the Lord nor breaks;
  Christ is whole to all that taste:
Thousands are, as one, receivers,
One, as thousands of believers,
  Eats of him who cannot waste.

Bad and good the feast are sharing,
Of what divers dooms preparing,
  Endless death, or endless life.
Life to these, to those damnation,
See how like participation
  Is with unlike issues rife.

When the sacrament is broken,
Doubt not, but believe 'tis spoken,
  That each sever'd outward token
doth the very whole contain.
Nought the precious gift divides,
Breaking but the sign betides,
  Jesus still the same abides,
  still unbroken does remain.

The shorter form of the sequence begins here.

Lo! the angel's food is given
To the pilgrim who has striven;
  See the children's bread from heaven,
  which on dogs may not be spent.
Truth the ancient types fulfilling,
Isaac bound, a victim willing,
  Paschal lamb, its lifeblood spilling,
  manna to the fathers sent.

Very bread, good shepherd, tend us,

Jesu, of your love befriend us,
  You refresh us, you defend us,
  Your eternal goodness send us
In the land of life to see.

You who all things can and know,
Who on earth such food bestow,
  Grant us with your saints, though lowest,
  Where the heav'nly feast you show,
Fellow heirs and guests to be.
  Amen. Alleluia. ↓

ALLELUIA Jn 6:51   [Bread from Heaven]

℞. **Alleluia, alleluia.**
I am the living bread that came down from heaven,
   says the Lord;
whoever eats this bread will live for ever.
℞. **Alleluia, alleluia.** ↓

GOSPEL Jn 6:51-58   [Living Bread]

**Jesus speaks of his body and blood in the holy eucharist.
Whoever receives the holy eucharist will be raised up on
the last day; whoever eats this bread will live forever.**

℣. The Lord be with you. ℞. **And also with you.**
✚ A reading from the holy Gospel according to John.
℞. **Glory to you, Lord.**

JESUS said to the Jewish crowds: "I am the living
bread that came down from heaven; whoever eats
this bread will live forever; and the bread that I will
give is my flesh for the life of the world."

   The Jews quarreled among themselves, saying, "How
can this man give us his flesh to eat?" Jesus said to them,
"Amen, amen, I say to you, unless you eat the flesh of the
Son of Man and drink his blood, you do not have life
within you. Whoever eats my flesh and drinks my blood
has eternal life, and I will raise him on the last day. For
my flesh is true food, and my blood is true drink.
Whoever eats my flesh and drinks my blood remains in
me, and I in him. Just as the living Father sent me and I
have life because of the Father, so also the one who feeds
on me will have life because of me. This is the bread that
came down from heaven. Unlike your ancestors who ate
and still died, whoever eats this bread will live forever."—
The Gospel of the Lord. ℞. **Praise to you, Lord Jesus
Christ.**   ➜ No. 14, p. 18

PRAYER OVER THE GIFTS   [Unity and Peace]
Lord,
may the bread and cup we offer

bring your Church the unity and peace they signify.
We ask this in the name of Jesus the Lord.
℟. **Amen.**   ➜ No. 21, p. 22 (Pref. P 47-48)

COMMUNION ANT. Jn 6:57   [Eucharistic Life]
**Whoever eats my flesh and drinks my blood will live
in me and I in him, says the Lord.** ↓

PRAYER AFTER COMMUNION   [Divine Life]
Lord Jesus Christ,
you give us your body and blood in the eucharist
as a sign that even now we share your life.
May we come to possess it completely in the kingdom
where you live for ever and ever.
℟. **Amen.**   ➜ No. 32, p. 70

Optional Solemn Blessings, p. 92, and Prayers Over the People, p. 99

"Come to me, all you who labor and are burdened, and I will give you rest."

JULY 3

14th SUNDAY IN ORDINARY TIME

ENTRANCE ANT. Ps 48:10-11 [God's Kindness and Justice]

Within your temple, we ponder your loving kindness, O God. As your name, so also your praise reaches to the ends of the earth; your right hand is filled with justice. → No. 2, p. 10

OPENING PRAYER [Forgiveness]

Let us pray
   [for forgiveness through the grace of Jesus Christ]
Father,
through the obedience of Jesus,
your servant and your Son,
you raised a fallen world.
Free us from sin
and bring us the joy that lasts for ever.
We ask this through our Lord Jesus Christ, your Son,
who lives and reigns with you and the Holy Spirit,
one God, for ever and ever. ℟. **Amen.** ↓

ALTERNATIVE OPENING PRAYER

[Serving God and Others]

Let us pray
  [for greater willingness
  to serve God and our fellow man]
Father,
in the rising of your Son
death gives birth to new life.
The sufferings he endured restored hope to a fallen
  world.
Let sin never ensnare us
with empty promises of passing joy.
Make us one with you always,
so that our joy may be holy,
and our love may give life.
We ask this through Christ our Lord. ℟. **Amen.** ↓

FIRST READING Zec 9:9-10   [Portrait of the Messiah]

Zechariah foretells the coming of the Messiah. Rejoicing
shall come to Jerusalem. He shall bring peace to all
nations and he shall rule over them.

A reading from the Book of the Prophet Zechariah

THUS says the LORD:
  rejoice heartily, O daughter Zion,
shout for joy, O daughter Jerusalem!
See, your king shall come to you;
  a just savior is he,
meek, and riding on an ass,
  on a colt, the foal of an ass.
He shall banish the chariot from Ephraim,
  and the horse from Jerusalem;
the warrior's bow shall be banished,
  and he shall proclaim peace to the nations.
His dominion shall be from sea to sea,
  and from the River to the ends of the earth.

The word of the Lord. ℟. **Thanks be to God.** ↓

RESPONSORIAL PSALM Ps 145   [God's Mercy]

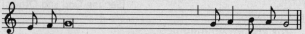

℟. **I will praise your name for ever,   my king and my God.**

℟. Or: **Alleluia.**

I will extol you, O my God and King,
    and I will bless your name forever and ever.
Every day will I bless you,
    and I will praise your name forever and ever.—℟.

The Lord is gracious and merciful,
    slow to anger and of great kindness.
The Lord is good to all
    and compassionate toward all his works.—℟.

Let all your works give you thanks, O Lord,
    and let your faithful ones bless you.
Let them discourse of the glory of your kingdom
    and speak of your might.—℟.

The Lord is faithful in all his words
    and holy in all his works.
The Lord lifts up all who are falling
    and raises up all who are bowed down.—℟. ↓

SECOND READING Rom 8:9, 11-13   [The Spirit of Christ]

Although we are both flesh and spirit, we must live
according to the Spirit of God who dwells in us. This is a
pledge for life if we die to sin and live by the Spirit.

A reading from the Letter of Saint Paul to the Romans

BROTHERS and sisters: You are not in the flesh; on
the contrary, you are in the spirit, if only the Spirit
of God dwells in you. Whoever does not have the
Spirit of Christ does not belong to him. If the Spirit of
the one who raised Jesus from the dead dwells in you,
the one who raised Christ from the dead will give life
to your mortal bodies also, through his Spirit that
dwells in you. Consequently, brothers and sisters, we

are not debtors to the flesh, to live according to the flesh. For if you live according to the flesh, you will die, but if by the Spirit you put to death the deeds of the body, you will live.—The word of the Lord. ℟. **Thanks be to God.** ↓

ALLELUIA Cf. Mt 11:25   [Revealed to Little Ones]

℟. **Alleluia, alleluia.**

Blessed are you, Father, Lord of heaven and earth;
you have revealed to little ones the mysteries of the
    kingdom.

℟. **Alleluia, alleluia.** ↓

GOSPEL Mt 11:25-30   [Solace in Christ]

Jesus gives praise to his Father. No one knows the Son but the Father and those to whom the Father reveals this truth. Jesus calls to himself those who are troubled and weary that they may find refreshment.

℣. The Lord be with you. ℟. **And also with you.**
✠ A reading from the holy Gospel according to Matthew. ℟. **Glory to you, Lord**.

AT that time Jesus exclaimed: "I give praise to you, Father, Lord of heaven and earth, for although you have hidden these things from the wise and the learned you have revealed them to little ones. Yes, Father, such has been your gracious will. All things have been handed over to me by my Father. No one knows the Son except the Father, and no one knows the Father except the Son and anyone to whom the Son wishes to reveal him.

   "Come to me, all you who labor and are burdened, and I will give you rest. Take my yoke upon you and learn from me, for I am meek and humble of heart; and you will find rest for yourselves. For my yoke is easy, and my burden light."—The Gospel of the Lord. ℟. **Praise to you, Lord Jesus Christ.**   → No. 14, p. 18

PRAYER OVER THE GIFTS   [God's Glory]

Lord,
let this offering to the glory of your name
purify us and bring us closer to eternal life.
We ask this in the name of Jesus the Lord.
℟. **Amen.**   ➔ No. 21, p. 22 (Pref. P 29-36)

COMMUNION ANT. Ps 34:9   [The Lord's Goodness]

**Taste and see the goodness of the Lord; blessed is he
who hopes in God. ↓**

OR Mt 11:28   [Refuge in God]

**Come to me, all you that labor and are burdened, and
I will give you rest, says the Lord. ↓**

PRAYER AFTER COMMUNION   [Life and Salvation]

Lord,
may we never fail to praise you
for the fullness of life and salvation
you give us in this eucharist.
We ask this through Christ our Lord.
℟. **Amen.**   ➔ No. 32, p. 70

Optional Solemn Blessings, p. 92, and Prayers Over the People, p. 99

"A sower went out to sow. . . ."

JULY 10

15th SUNDAY IN ORDINARY TIME

ENTRANCE ANT. Ps 7:15   [God's Face]

In my justice I shall see your face, O Lord; when your glory appears, my joy will be full.   → No. 2, p. 10

OPENING PRAYER   [Rule of Life]

Let us pray
   [that the gospel may be our rule of life]
God our Father,
your light of truth
guides us to the way of Christ.
May all who follow him
reject what is contrary to the gospel.
We ask this through our Lord Jesus Christ, your Son,
who lives and reigns with you and the Holy Spirit,
one God, for ever and ever. ℟. **Amen.** ↓

ALTERNATIVE OPENING PRAYER   [Fidelity]

Let us pray
   [to be faithful to the light we have received,
   to the name we bear]

Father,
let the light of your truth
guide us to your kingdom
through a world filled with lights contrary to your own.
Christian is the name and the gospel we glory in.
May your love make us what you have called us to be.
We ask this through Christ our Lord. ℟. **Amen.** ↓

FIRST READING Is 55:10-11   [God's Fruitful Word]

Isaiah uses the example of rain and snow seeping into the ground to make it fertile to show how the word of God filters into the hearts of men. It shall not be void and empty.

A reading from the Book of the Prophet Isaiah

T HUS says the LORD:
Just as from the heavens
the rain and snow come down
and do not return there
    till they have watered the earth,
        making it fertile and fruitful,
giving seed to the one who sows
    and bread to the one who eats,
so shall my word be
    that goes forth from my mouth;
my word shall not return to me void,
    but shall do my will,
        achieving the end for which I sent it.
The word of the Lord. ℟. **Thanks be to God.** ↓

RESPONSORIAL PSALM Ps 65   [A Fruitful Harvest]

℟. **The seed that falls on good ground will yield a fruitful harvest.**

You have visited the land and watered it;
    greatly have you enriched it.
God's watercourses are filled;
    you have prepared the grain.

℟. **The seed that falls on good ground**
    will yield a fruitful harvest.

Thus have you prepared the land: drenching its furrows,
    breaking up its clods,
softening it with showers,
    blessing its yield.

℟. **The seed that falls on good ground**
    will yield a fruitful harvest.

You have crowned the year with your bounty,
    and your paths overflow with a rich harvest;
the untilled meadows overflow with it,
    and rejoicing clothes the hills.

℟. **The seed that falls on good ground**
    will yield a fruitful harvest.

The fields are garmented with flocks
    and the valleys blanketed with grain.
    They shout and sing for joy.

℟. **The seed that falls on good ground**
    will yield a fruitful harvest. ↓

SECOND READING Rom 8:18-23

[Future Redemption of the Body]

The sufferings and trials of the present are destined to be only a prelude to the glorious future of the children of God. During this life we await the redemption of our bodies.

A reading from the Letter of Saint Paul to the Romans

BROTHERS and sisters: I consider that the sufferings of this present time are as nothing compared with the glory to be revealed for us. For creation awaits with eager expectation the revelation of the children of God; for creation was made subject to futility, not of its own accord but because of the one who subjected it, in hope that creation itself would be set free from slavery to corruption and share in the glorious freedom of the children of God. We know that all creation is groaning in labor pains even until now; and not only that, but we ourselves, who have the firstfruits of the Spirit, we also groan within ourselves as we wait for adoption, the redemption of our bodies.—The word of the Lord. ℟. **Thanks be to God. ↓**

ALLELUIA

℟. **Alleluia, alleluia.**
The seed is the word of God, Christ is the sower.
All who come to him have life for ever.
℟. **Alleluia, alleluia. ↓**

GOSPEL Mt 13:1-23 or 13:1-9   [Parable of the Sower]

Jesus teaches in parables that can be easily understood. He speaks of sowing the message of salvation which by some is heeded for a while, or ignored. Others, however, listen intently and try to live according to the will of God. Jesus explains this parable in detail.

[If the "Shorter Form" is used, the indented text in brackets is omitted.]

℣. The Lord be with you. ℟. **And also with you.**
✠ A reading from the holy Gospel according to Matthew. ℟. **Glory to you, Lord.**

ON that day, Jesus went out of the house and sat down by the sea. Such large crowds gathered around him that he got into a boat and sat down, and the whole crowd stood along the shore. And he spoke to them at length in parables, saying: "A sower went out to sow. And as he sowed, some seed fell on the path, and birds came and ate it up. Some fell on rocky ground, where it had little soil. It sprang up at once because the soil was not deep, and when the sun rose it was scorched, and it withered for lack of roots. Some seed fell among thorns, and the thorns grew up and choked it. But some seed fell on rich soil, and produced fruit, a hundred or sixty or thirtyfold. Whoever has ears ought to hear."

[The disciples approached him and said, "Why do you speak to them in parables?" He said to them in reply, "Because knowledge of the mysteries of the kingdom of heaven has been granted to you, but to them it has not been granted. To anyone who has, more will be given and he will grow rich; from anyone who has not, even what he has will be taken away. This is why I speak to them in parables, because *they look but do not see and hear but do not listen or understand.* Isaiah's prophecy is fulfilled in them, which says:

You shall indeed hear but not understand,
you shall indeed look but never see.
Gross is the heart of this people,
they will hardly hear with their ears,
they have closed their eyes,
lest they see with their eyes
and hear with their ears
and understand with their hearts and be converted,
and I heal them.

"But blessed are your eyes, because they see, and your ears, because they hear. Amen, I say to you, many prophets and righteous people longed to see what you see but did not see it, and to hear what you hear but did not hear it.

"Hear then the parable of the sower. The seed sown on the path is the one who hears the word of the kingdom without understanding it, and the evil one comes and steals away what was sown in his heart. The seed sown on rocky ground is the one who hears the word and receives it at once with joy. But he has no root and lasts only for a time. When some tribulation or persecution comes because of the word, he immediately falls away. The seed sown among thorns is the one who hears the word, but then worldly anxiety and the lure of riches choke the word and it bears no fruit. But the seed sown on rich soil is the one who hears the word and understands it, who indeed bears fruit and yields a hundred or sixty or thirtyfold."]

The Gospel of the Lord. ℟. **Praise to you, Lord Jesus Christ.**   ➤ No. 14, p. 18

PRAYER OVER THE GIFTS   [Growth in Faith]

Lord,
accept the gifts of your Church.
May this eucharist
help us grow in holiness and faith.
We ask this in the name of Jesus the Lord.
℟. **Amen.**   ➤ No. 21, p. 22 (Pref. P 29-36)

COMMUNION ANT. Ps 84:4-5   [The Lord's House]

The sparrow even finds a home, the swallow finds a nest wherein to place her young, near to your altars, Lord of hosts, my King, my God! How happy they who dwell in your house! For ever they are praising you. ↓

OR Jn 6:57   [Life in Jesus]

Whoever eats my flesh and drinks my blood will live in me and I in him, says the Lord. ↓

PRAYER AFTER COMMUNION   [God's Love]

Lord,
by our sharing in the mystery of this eucharist,
let your saving love grow within us.
Grant this through Christ our Lord.
℟. **Amen.**   ➤ No. 32, p. 70

Optional Solemn Blessings, p. 92, and Prayers Over the People, p. 99

"His enemy came and sowed weeds all through the wheat."

JULY 17

16th SUNDAY IN ORDINARY TIME

ENTRANCE ANT. Ps 54:6, 8   **[God Our Help]**

God himself is my help. The Lord upholds my life. I will offer you a willing sacrifice; I will praise your name, O Lord, for its goodness.   ➜ No. 2, p. 10

OPENING PRAYER   **[Faithful Service]**

Let us pray
  [to be kept faithful in the service of God]
Lord,
be merciful to your people.
Fill us with your gifts
and make us always eager to serve you
in faith, hope, and love.
Grant this . . . for ever and ever. ℟. **Amen.** ↓

ALTERNATIVE OPENING PRAYER   **[God's Blessing]**

Let us pray
  [that God will continue to bless us
  with his compassion and love]
Father,
let the gift of your life

445

continue to grow in us,
drawing us from death to faith, hope, and love.
Keep us alive in Christ Jesus.
Keep us watchful in prayer
and true to his teaching
till your glory is revealed in us.
Grant this through Christ our Lord. ℟. **Amen.** ↓

FIRST READING Wis 12:13, 16-19   [God's Mercy]

The real source of might and power is justice. Through justice a man becomes master of his power. He can become lenient and kind and encourage repentance for sin.

A reading from the Book of Wisdom

T HERE is no god besides you who have the care
of all,
    that you need show you have not unjustly con-
        demned.
For your might is the source of justice;
    your mastery over all things makes you lenient
        to all.
For you show your might when the perfection of
        your power is disbelieved;
    and in those who know you, you rebuke temerity.
But though you are master of might, you judge
        with clemency,
    and with much lenience you govern us;
    for power, whenever you will, attends you.
And you taught your people, by these deeds,
    that those who are just must be kind;
and you gave your children good ground for hope
    that you would permit repentance for their sins.
The word of the Lord. ℟. **Thanks be to God.** ↓

RESPONSORIAL PSALM Ps 86   [Kindness and Fidelity]

℟. **Lord, you are good and for - giv - ing.**

You, O LORD, are good and forgiving,
   abounding in kindness to all who call upon you.
Hearken, O LORD, to my prayer
   and attend to the sound of my pleading.
R̸. **Lord, you are good and forgiving.**
All the nations you have made shall come
   and worship you, O LORD,
   and glorify your name.
For you are great, and you do wondrous deeds;
   you alone are God.
R̸. **Lord, you are good and forgiving.**
You, O LORD, are a God merciful and gracious,
   slow to anger, abounding in kindness and fidelity.
Turn toward me, and have pity on me;
   give your strength to your servant.
R̸. **Lord, you are good and forgiving.** ↓

SECOND READING Rom 8:26-27 [Intercession of the Spirit]
   Through the Spirit our weakness in prayer is overcome. He
   searches our hearts and makes true intercessions in our
   behalf.

A reading from the Letter of Saint Paul to the Romans

B ROTHERS and sisters: The Spirit comes to the aid
   of our weakness; for we do not know how to pray
as we ought, but the Spirit himself intercedes with inexpressible groanings. And the one who searches hearts
knows what is the intention of the Spirit, because he
intercedes for the holy ones according to God's will.—
The word of the Lord. R̸. **Thanks be to God.** ↓

ALLELUIA Cf. Mt 11:25   [Revealed to Little Ones]
R̸. **Alleluia, alleluia.**
Blessed are you, Father, Lord of heaven and earth;
you have revealed to little ones the mysteries of the
   kingdom.
R̸. **Alleluia, alleluia.** ↓

GOSPEL Mt 13:24-43 or 13:24-30   [Parable of the Weeds]

Jesus teaches about God's kingdom in parables. His kingdom is like a field in which good grain and weeds grow. At harvest time the good will be sorted from the bad. God's kingdom is also like a mustard plant reaching out to embrace all as it grows.

[If the "Shorter Form" is used, the indented text in brackets is omitted.]

℣. The Lord be with you. ℟. **And also with you.**
✛ A reading from the holy Gospel according to Matthew. ℟. **Glory to you, Lord.**

JESUS proposed another parable to the crowds, saying: "The kingdom of heaven may be likened to a man who sowed good seed in his field. While everyone was asleep his enemy came and sowed weeds all through the wheat, and then went off. When the crop grew and bore fruit, the weeds appeared as well. The slaves of the householder came to him and said, 'Master, did you not sow good seed in your field? Where have the weeds come from?' He answered, 'An enemy has done this.' His slaves said to him, 'Do you want us to go and pull them up?' He replied, 'No, if you pull up the weeds you might uproot the wheat along with them. Let them grow together until harvest; then at harvest time I will say to the harvesters, "First collect the weeds and tie them in bundles for burning; but gather the wheat into my barn."'"

[He proposed another parable to them. "The kingdom of heaven is like a mustard seed that a person took and sowed in a field. It is the smallest of all the seeds, yet when full-grown it is the largest of plants. It becomes a large bush, and the 'birds of the sky come and dwell in its branches.'"

He spoke to them another parable. "The kingdom of heaven is like yeast that a woman took and mixed with three measures of wheat flour until the whole batch was leavened." All these things Jesus spoke to the crowds in parables. He spoke to them only in parables, to fulfill what had been said through the prophet:

"I will open my mouth in parables,
I will announce what has lain hidden from
   the foundation
of the world."

Then, dismissing the crowds, he went into the house. His disciples approached him and said, "Explain to us the parable of the weeds in the field." He said in reply, "He who sows good seed is the Son of Man, the field is the world, the good seed the children of the kingdom. The weeds are the children of the evil one, and the enemy who sows them is the devil. The harvest is the end of the age, and the harvesters are angels. Just as weeds are collected and burned up with fire, so will it be at the end of the age. The Son of Man will send his angels, and they will collect out of his kingdom all who cause others to sin and all evildoers. They will throw them into the fiery furnace, where there will be wailing and grinding of teeth. Then the righteous will shine like the sun in the kingdom of their Father. Whoever has ears ought to hear."]

The Gospel of the Lord. ℟. **Praise to you, Lord Jesus Christ.**   ➜ No. 14, p. 18

PRAYER OVER THE GIFTS   [Saving Gifts]

Lord,
bring us closer to salvation
through these gifts which we bring in your honor.
Accept the perfect sacrifice you have given us,
bless it as you blessed the gifts of Abel.

We ask this through Christ our Lord.
℟. **Amen.**   ➙ No. 21, p. 22 (Pref. P 29-36)

COMMUNION ANT. Ps 111:4-5   [Jesus Provides]
**The Lord keeps in our minds the wonderful things he
has done. He is compassion and love; he always provides for his faithful.** ↓

OR Rv 3:20   [Jesus Knocks]
**I stand at the door and knock, says the Lord. If anyone
hears my voice and opens the door, I will come in and
sit down to supper with him, and he with me.** ↓

PRAYER AFTER COMMUNION   [New Life]
Merciful Father,
may these mysteries
give us new purpose
and bring us to a new life in you.
We ask this in the name of Jesus the Lord.
℟. **Amen.**   ➙ No. 32, p. 70

Optional Solemn Blessings, p. 92, and Prayers Over the People, p. 99

"The kingdom of heaven is like a treasure buried in a field. . . ."

JULY 24

17th SUNDAY IN ORDINARY TIME

ENTRANCE ANT. Ps 68:6-7, 36   [God Our Strength]
God is in his holy dwelling; he will give a home to the lonely, he gives power and strength to his people.

→ No. 2, p. 10

OPENING PRAYER   [Wise Use of Gifts]

Let us pray
  [that we will make good use of the gifts
  that God has given us]
God our Father and protector,
without you nothing is holy,
nothing has value.
Guide us to everlasting life
by helping us to use wisely
the blessings you have given to the world.
We ask . . . for ever and ever. ℟. **Amen.** ↓

ALTERNATIVE OPENING PRAYER   [God in the World]

Let us pray
  [for the faith to recognize God's presence
  in our world]

451

God our Father,
open our eyes to see your hand at work
in the splendor of creation,
in the beauty of human life.
Touched by your hand our world is holy.
Help us to cherish the gifts that surround us,
to share your blessings with our brothers and sisters,
and to experience the joy of life in your presence.
We ask this through Christ our Lord. ℟. **Amen.** ↓

FIRST READING 1 Kgs 3:5, 7-12   [The Gift of Understanding]

Solomon prays for wisdom to lead the people of God. God is pleased that Solomon asked above all else to know right from wrong. God promises him wisdom and understanding that will be unequalled either in times past or in the future.

A reading from the first Book of Kings

THE LORD appeared to Solomon in a dream at night. God said, "Ask something of me and I will give it to you." Solomon answered: "O LORD, my God, you have made me, your servant, king to succeed my father David; but I am a mere youth, not knowing at all how to act. I serve you in the midst of the people whom you have chosen, a people so vast that it cannot be numbered or counted. Give your servant, therefore, an understanding heart to judge your people and to distinguish right from wrong. For who is able to govern this vast people of yours?"

The LORD was pleased that Solomon made this request. So God said to him: "Because you have asked for this—not for a long life for yourself, nor for riches, nor for the life of your enemies, but for understanding so that you may know what is right—I do as you requested. I give you a heart so wise and understanding that there has never been anyone like you up to now, and after you there will come no one to equal you."—The word of the Lord. ℟. **Thanks be to God.** ↓

RESPONSORIAL PSALM Ps 119   [The Lord's Decrees]

℟. Lord,   I love   your com - mands.

I have said, O LORD, that my part
  is to keep your words.
The law of your mouth is to me more precious
  than thousands of gold and silver pieces.

℟. **Lord, I love your commands.**

Let your kindness comfort me
  according to your promise to your servants.
Let your compassion come to me that I may live,
  for your law is my delight.

℟. **Lord, I love your commands.**

For I love your commands
  more than gold, however fine.
For in all your precepts I go forward;
  every false way I hate.

℟. **Lord, I love your commands.**

Wonderful are your decrees;
  therefore I observe them.
The revelation of your words sheds light,
  giving understanding to the simple.

℟. **Lord, I love your commands.** ↓

SECOND READING Rom 8:28-30 [All Things Work for Good]

**God makes all his works of creation fit into his divine plan.
He planned to share the image of his Son with us so that
we might be justified and thereby enter into eternal glory.**

A reading from the Letter of Saint Paul to the Romans

BROTHERS and sisters: We know that all things
work for good for those who love God, who are
called according to his purpose. For those he
foreknew he also predestined to be conformed to the

image of his Son, so that he might be the firstborn among many brothers and sisters. And those he pre-destined he also called; and those he called he also justified; and those he justified he also glorified.— The word of the Lord. ℟. **Thanks be to God.** ↓

ALLELUIA Cf. Mt 11:25   [Revealed to Little Ones]
℟. **Alleluia, alleluia.** ·
Blessed are you, Father, Lord of heaven and earth;
for you have revealed to little ones the mysteries of the
   kingdom.
℟. **Alleluia, alleluia.** ↓

GOSPEL Mt 13:44-52 or 13:44-46   [The Kingdom of God]
   Jesus compares the value of the kingdom of God to a hidden treasure, to a most valuable pearl, to a dragnet. It is
   beyond human comprehension but in the end God's angels
   will sort out those who have lived good lives from the
   unrepentant sinners.

*[If the "Shorter Form" is used, the indented text in brackets is
omitted.]*

℣. The Lord be with you. ℟. **And also with you.**
✛ A reading from the holy Gospel according to
Matthew. ℟. **Glory to you, Lord**.

JESUS said to his disciples: "The kingdom of heav-en is like a treasure buried in a field, which a per-son finds and hides again, and out of joy goes and sells all that he has and buys that field. Again, the kingdom of heaven is like a merchant searching for fine pearls. When he finds a pearl of great price, he goes and sells all that he has and buys it.

   ["Again, the kingdom of heaven is like a net thrown into the sea, which collects fish of every kind. When it is full they haul it ashore and sit down to put what is good into buckets. What is bad they throw away. Thus it will be at the end of the age. The angels will go out and separate the wicked from the righteous and throw them into the fiery furnace, where there will be wailing and grinding of teeth.

"Do you understand all these things?" They answered, "Yes." And he replied, "Then every scribe who has been instructed in the kingdom of heaven is like the head of a household who brings from his storeroom both the new and the old."]

The Gospel of the Lord. ℟. **Praise to you, Lord Jesus Christ.**   → No. 14, p. 18

PRAYER OVER THE GIFTS   [Sanctifying Mysteries]

Lord,
receive these offerings
chosen from your many gifts.
May these mysteries make us holy
and lead us to eternal joy.
Grant this through Christ our Lord.
℟. **Amen.**   → No. 21, p. 22 (Pref. P 29-36)

COMMUNION ANT. Ps 103:2   [Bless the Lord]

O bless the Lord, my soul, and remember all his kindness. ↓

OR Mt 5:7-8   [Happy the Pure of Heart]

Happy are those who show mercy; mercy shall be theirs. Happy are the pure of heart, for they shall see God. ↓

PRAYER AFTER COMMUNION   [Memorial of Christ]

Lord,
we receive the sacrament
which celebrates the memory
of the death and resurrection of Christ your Son.
May this gift bring us closer to our eternal salvation.
We ask this through Christ our Lord.
℟. **Amen.**   → No. 32, p. 70

Optional Solemn Blessings, p. 92, and Prayers Over the People, p. 99

*"Taking the five loaves and two fish, . . .
he said the blessing. . . ."*

JULY 31

18th SUNDAY IN ORDINARY TIME

ENTRANCE ANT. Ps 70:2, 6   **[God's Help]**
**God, come to my help. Lord, quickly give me assis-
tance. You are the one who helps me and sets me
free: Lord, do not be long in coming.**   → No. 2, p. 10

OPENING PRAYER   **[God's Forgiveness]**

Let us pray
   [for the gift of God's forgiveness and love]
Father of everlasting goodness,
our origin and guide,
be close to us
and hear the prayers of all who praise you.
Forgive our sins and restore us to life.
Keep us safe in your love.
Grant this through our Lord Jesus Christ, your Son,
who lives and reigns with you and the Holy Spirit,
one God, for ever and ever. ℟. **Amen.** ↓

ALTERNATIVE OPENING PRAYER   **[God's Kindness]**

Let us pray
   [to the Father whose kindness never fails]

God our Father,
gifts without measure flow from your goodness
to bring us your peace.
Our life is your gift.
Guide our life's journey,
for only your love makes us whole.
Keep us strong in your love.
We ask this through Christ our Lord. ℟. **Amen.** ↓

FIRST READING Is 55:1-3   [Receive God's Bread]

Sharing in the happiness of the kingdom is God's free gift to all who thirst for God.

A reading from the Book of the Prophet Isaiah

T HUS says the LORD:
   All you who are thirsty,
come to the water!
You who have no money,
    come, receive grain and eat;
come, without paying and without cost,
    drink wine and milk!
Why spend your money for what is not bread;
    your wages for what fails to satisfy?
Heed me, and you shall eat well,
    you shall delight in rich fare.
Come to me heedfully,
    listen, that you may have life.
I will renew with you the everlasting covenant,
    the benefits assured to David.
The word of the Lord. ℟. **Thanks be to God.** ↓

RESPONSORIAL PSALM Ps 145   [God's Bounty]

℟. **The hand of the Lord feeds us;   he answers all our needs.**

The LORD is gracious and merciful,
    slow to anger and of great kindness.

The Lord is good to all
and compassionate toward all his works.

℞. **The hand of the Lord feeds us;**
he answers all our needs.

The eyes of all look hopefully to you,
and you give them their food in due season;
You open your hand
and satisfy the desire of every living thing.

℞. **The hand of the Lord feeds us;**
he answers all our needs.

The Lord is just in all his ways
and holy in all his works.
The Lord is near to all who call upon him,
to all who call upon him in truth.

℞. **The hand of the Lord feeds us;**
he answers all our needs. ↓

SECOND READING Rom 8:35, 37-39   [The Love of Christ]
We should have a firm hope of sharing in the messianic
banquet, the happiness promised to us by our God.
Nothing can separate us from the love of God that comes
to us in Christ Jesus.

A reading from the Letter of Saint Paul to the Romans

BROTHERS and sisters: What will separate us
from the love of Christ? Will anguish, or distress,
or persecution, or famine, or nakedness, or peril, or
the sword? No, in all these things we conquer over-
whelmingly through him who loved us. For I am con-
vinced that neither death, nor life, nor angels, nor
principalities, nor present things, nor future things,
nor powers, nor height, nor depth, nor any other creature will be able to separate us from the love of God
in Christ Jesus our Lord.——The word of the Lord. ℞.
Thanks be to God. ↓

ALLELUIA Mt 4:4b   [Words of Life]

℞. **Alleluia, alleluia.**
One does not live on bread alone,
but on every word that comes from the mouth of God.
℞. **Alleluia, alleluia.** ↓

GOSPEL Mt 14:13-21   [Multiplication of the Loaves]
The event of this passage (feeding the people) is a messianic sign that will find its fulfillment in the true messianic banquet, the eucharist, which contains the promise of everlasting life in God's kingdom.

℣. The Lord be with you. ℞. **And also with you.**
✣   A reading from the holy Gospel according to Matthew. ℞. **Glory to you, Lord**.

WHEN Jesus heard of the death of John the Baptist, he withdrew in a boat to a deserted place by himself. The crowds heard of this and followed him on foot from their towns. When he disembarked and saw the vast crowd, his heart was moved with pity for them, and he cured their sick. When it was evening, the disciples approached him and said, "This is a deserted place and it is already late; dismiss the crowds so that they can go to the villages and buy food for themselves." Jesus said to them, "There is no need for them to go away; give them some food yourselves." But they said to him, "Five loaves and two fish are all we have here." Then he said, "Bring them here to me," and he ordered the crowds to sit down on the grass. Taking the five loaves and the two fish, and looking up to heaven, he said the blessing, broke the loaves, and gave them to the disciples, who in turn gave them to the crowds. They all ate and were satisfied, and they picked up the fragments left over—twelve wicker baskets full. Those who ate were about five thousand men, not counting women and children.—The Gospel of the Lord. ℟. **Praise to you, Lord Jesus Christ.**

➙ No. 14, p. 18

PRAYER OVER THE GIFTS   [Spiritual Sacrifice]

Merciful Lord,
make holy these gifts,
and let our spiritual sacrifice
make us an everlasting gift to you.
We ask this in the name of Jesus the Lord.
℟. **Amen.**   ➙ No. 21, p. 22 (Pref. P 29-36)

COMMUNION ANT. Wis 16:20   [Bread from Heaven]

You gave us bread from heaven, Lord: a sweet-tasting bread that was very good to eat. ↓

OR Jn 6:35   [Bread of Life]

The Lord says: I am the bread of life. A man who comes to me will not go away hungry, and no one who believes in me will thirst. ↓

PRAYER AFTER COMMUNION   [Strength of New Life]

Lord,
you give us the strength of new life
by the gift of the eucharist.
Protect us with your love
and prepare us for eternal redemption.
We ask this through Christ our Lord.
℟. **Amen.**   ➙ No. 32, p. 70

Optional Solemn Blessings, p. 92, and Prayers Over the People, p. 99

"It is I; do not be afraid."

AUGUST 7

19th SUNDAY IN ORDINARY TIME

ENTRANCE ANT. Ps 74:20, 19, 22, 23   [Rise Up, O God]
**Lord, be true to your covenant, forget not the life of
your poor ones for ever. Rise up, O God, and defend
your cause; do not ignore the shouts of your enemies.**

→ No. 2, p. 10

OPENING PRAYER   [Growth in God's Love]
Let us pray
  [in the Spirit
  that we may grow in the love of God]
Almighty and ever-living God,
your Spirit made us your children,
confident to call you Father.
Increase your Spirit within us
and bring us to our promised inheritance.
Grant this . . . for ever and ever. ℟. **Amen.** ↓

ALTERNATIVE OPENING PRAYER   [Witnesses for Christ]
Let us pray
  [that through us
  others may find the way to life in Christ]

461

Father,
we come, reborn in the Spirit,
to celebrate our sonship in the Lord Jesus Christ.
Touch our hearts,
help them grow toward the life you have promised.
Touch our lives,
make them signs of your love for all men.
Grant this through Christ our Lord. ℟. **Amen.** ↓

FIRST READING 1 Kgs 19:9a, 11-13a [Coming of the Lord]

> The Lord tells Elijah to await him on the mountain. Elijah's faith is tried as he witnesses a devastating wind, an earthquake, and a fire. After these the Lord speaks to Elijah in the sound of a gentle breeze.

A reading from the first Book of Kings

AT the mountain of God, Horeb, Elijah came to a cave where he took shelter. Then the LORD said to him, "Go outside and stand on the mountain before the LORD; the LORD will be passing by." A strong and heavy wind was rending the mountains and crushing rocks before the LORD—but the LORD was not in the wind. After the wind there was an earthquake—but the LORD was not in the earthquake. After the earthquake there was fire—but the LORD was not in the fire. After the fire there was a tiny whispering sound. When he heard this, Elijah hid his face in his cloak and went and stood at the entrance of the cave.—The word of the Lord. ℟. **Thanks be to God.** ↓

RESPONSORIAL PSALM Ps 85   [Truth and Justice]

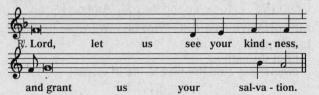

℟. Lord, let us see your kind-ness, and grant us your sal-va-tion.

I will hear what God proclaims;
  the LORD—for he proclaims peace.
Near indeed is his salvation to those who fear him,
  glory dwelling in our land.

℟. **Lord, let us see your kindness,**
  and grant us your salvation.

Kindness and truth shall meet;
  justice and peace shall kiss.
Truth shall spring out of the earth,
  and justice shall look down from heaven.

℟. **Lord, let us see your kindness,**
  and grant us your salvation.

The LORD himself will give his benefits;
  our land shall yield its increase.
Justice shall walk before him,
  and prepare the way of his steps.

℟. **Lord, let us see your kindness,**
  and grant us your salvation. ↓

SECOND READING Rom 9:1-5   [Blessed Be God]

> Paul admits that grief is in his heart. He would even accept
> separation from Jesus if it would help his brothers and sis-
> ters who have been privileged to know the revelation of
> God through the ages. Blessed be God forever.

A reading from the Letter of Saint Paul to the Romans

BROTHERS and sisters: I speak the truth in Christ,
I do not lie; my conscience joins with the Holy
Spirit in bearing me witness that I have great sorrow
and constant anguish in my heart. For I could wish
that I myself were accursed and cut off from Christ
for the sake of my own people, my kindred according
to the flesh. They are Israelites; theirs the adoption,
the glory, the covenants, the giving of the law, the
worship, and the promises; theirs the patriarchs, and
from them, according to the flesh, is the Christ, who

is over all, God blessed forever. Amen. —The word of
the Lord. ℟. **Thanks be to God.** ↓

ALLELUIA Cf. Ps 130:5   [Hope and Trust]

℟. **Alleluia, alleluia.**
I wait for the Lord;
my soul waits for his word.
℟. **Alleluia, alleluia.** ↓

GOSPEL Mt 14:22-33   [Jesus Walks on Water]
Jesus feeds the crowds and then withdraws to pray. His
disciples want to cross the lake but a threatening storm
arises. Jesus appears and Peter gets out of the boat to walk
to Jesus, but because Peter doubts, he begins to sink.
Jesus saves him, and admonishes him for his little faith.
Then Jesus calms the storm.

℣. The Lord be with you. ℟. **And also with you.**
✠ A reading from the holy Gospel according to
Matthew. ℟. **Glory to you, Lord**.

AFTER he had fed the people, Jesus made the disciples get into a boat and precede him to the
other side, while he dismissed the crowds. After
doing so, he went up on the mountain by himself to
pray. When it was evening he was there alone.
Meanwhile the boat, already a few miles offshore,
was being tossed about by the waves, for the wind
was against it. During the fourth watch of the night,
he came toward them walking on the sea. When the
disciples saw him walking on the sea they were terri-
fied. "It is a ghost," they said, and they cried out in
fear. At once Jesus spoke to them, "Take courage, it is
I; do not be afraid." Peter said to him in reply, "Lord, if
it is you, command me to come to you on the water."
He said, "Come." Peter got out of the boat and began
to walk on the water toward Jesus. But when he saw
how strong the wind was he became frightened; and,

beginning to sink, he cried out, "Lord, save me!"
Immediately Jesus stretched out his hand and caught
Peter, and said to him, "O you of little faith, why did
you doubt?" After they got into the boat, the wind died
down. Those who were in the boat did him homage,
saying, "Truly, you are the Son of God."—The Gospel
of the Lord. R̶/. **Praise to you, Lord Jesus Christ.**

➜ No. 14, p. 18

PRAYER OVER THE GIFTS   [Sacrament of Salvation]

God of power,
giver of the gifts we bring,
accept the offering of your Church
and make it the sacrament of our salvation.
We ask this through Christ our Lord.
R̶/. **Amen.**   ➜ No. 21, p. 22 (Pref. P 29-36)

COMMUNION ANT. Ps 147:12, 14   [Praise the Lord]

**Praise the Lord, Jerusalem; he feeds you with the
finest wheat.** ↓

OR Jn 6:52   [The Flesh of Jesus]

**The bread I shall give is my flesh for the life of the
world, says the Lord.** ↓

PRAYER AFTER COMMUNION   [Faithful to God's Truth]

Lord,
may the eucharist you give us
bring us to salvation
and keep us faithful to the light of your truth.
We ask this in the name of Jesus the Lord.
R̶/. **Amen.**   ➜ No. 32, p. 70

Optional Solemn Blessings, p. 92, and Prayers Over the People, p. 99

———

"O woman, great is your faith! Let it be done for you as you wish."

AUGUST 14

20th SUNDAY IN ORDINARY TIME

ENTRANCE ANT. Ps 84:10-11   [God Our Strength]
God, our protector, keep us in mind; always give strength to your people. For if we can be with you even one day, it is better than a thousand without you. → No. 2, p. 10

OPENING PRAYER   [Joy Beyond Imagining]
Let us pray
  [that the love of God
  may raise us beyond what we see
  to the unseen glory of his kingdom]
God our Father,
may we love you in all things and above all things
and reach the joy you have prepared for us
beyond all our imagining.
We ask this through our Lord Jesus Christ, your Son,
who lives and reigns with you and the Holy Spirit,
one God, for ever and ever. ℟. **Amen.** ↓

ALTERNATIVE OPENING PRAYER   [Avoiding Prejudice]

Let us pray
  [with humility and persistence]
Almighty God, ever-loving Father,
your care extends beyond the boundaries of race and
    nation
to the hearts of all who live.
May the walls, which prejudice raises between us,
crumble beneath the shadow of your outstretched arm.
We ask this through Christ our Lord. ℟. **Amen.** ↓

FIRST READING Is 56:1, 6-7   [Justice and Salvation for All]

The prophet warns his people that for salvation they must
do what is just, love the Lord, and keep the sabbath. God
will then lead them to his mountain and accept their sacrifices.

A reading from the Book of the Prophet Isaiah

THUS says the Lord:
  Observe what is right, do what is just;
    for my salvation is about to come,
    my justice, about to be revealed.
The foreigners who join themselves to the Lord,
    ministering to him,
Loving the name of the Lord,
    and becoming his servants—
All who keep the sabbath free from profanation
    and hold to my covenant,
Them I will bring to my holy mountain
    and make joyful in my house of prayer;
Their holocausts and sacrifices
    will be acceptable on my altar,
For my house shall be called
    a house of prayer for all peoples.
The word of the Lord. ℟. **Thanks be to God.** ↓

RESPONSORIAL PSALM Ps 67   [Praise for the Lord]

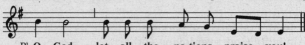

℟. O God,   let all the na-tions praise you!

May God have pity on us and bless us;
   may he let his face shine upon us.
So may your way be known upon earth;
   among all nations, your salvation.

℟. **O God, let all the nations praise you!**

May the nations be glad and exult
   because you rule the peoples in equity;
   the nations on the earth you guide.

℟. **O God, let all the nations praise you!**

May the peoples praise you, O God;
   may all the peoples praise you!
May God bless us,
   and may all the ends of the earth fear him!

℟. **O God, let all the nations praise you!** ↓

SECOND READING Rom 11:13-15, 29-32
                    [Irrevocable Gifts and Call]

**Paul is proud of his ministry and he is anxious to lead his
Jewish brothers and sisters to reconciliation with God. In
spite of their disobedience, God has been merciful toward
them.**

A reading from the Letter of Paul to the Romans

BROTHERS and sisters: I am speaking to you Gentiles. Inasmuch as I am the apostle to the Gentiles,
I glory in my ministry in order to make my race jealous
and thus save some of them. For if their rejection is the
reconciliation of the world, what will their acceptance
be but life from the dead?
   For the gifts and the call of God are irrevocable. Just
as you once disobeyed God but have now received

mercy because of their disobedience, so they have now disobeyed in order that, by virtue of the mercy shown to you, they too may now receive mercy. For God delivered all to disobedience, that he might have mercy upon all.— The word of the Lord. ℟. **Thanks be to God.** ↓

ALLELUIA Cf. Mt 4:23   [The Good News]

℟. **Alleluia, alleluia.**
Jesus proclaimed the Gospel of the kingdom
and cured every disease among the people.
℟. **Alleluia, alleluia.** ↓

GOSPEL Mt 15:21-28   [Reward of Faith]

A Canaanite woman whose daughter is possessed comes to Jesus and asks for a favor with perseverance. Jesus commends her great faith and cures her daughter.

℣. The Lord be with you. ℟. **And also with you.**
✛   A reading from the holy Gospel according to Matthew. ℟. **Glory to you, Lord.**

AT that time, Jesus withdrew to the region of Tyre and Sidon. And behold, a Canaanite woman of that district came and called out, "Have pity on me, Lord, Son of David! My daughter is tormented by a demon." But Jesus did not say a word in answer to her. Jesus' disciples came and asked him, "Send her away, for she keeps calling out after us." He said in reply, "I was sent only to the lost sheep of the house of Israel." But the woman came and did Jesus homage, saying, "Lord, help me." He said in reply, "It is not right to take the food of the children and throw it to the dogs." She said, "Please, Lord, for even the dogs eat the scraps that fall from the table of their masters." Then Jesus said to her in reply, "O woman, great is your faith! Let it be done for you as you wish." And the woman's daughter was healed from that hour.—

The Gospel of the Lord. ℟. **Praise to you, Lord Jesus Christ.**   ➜ No. 14, p. 18

PRAYER OVER THE GIFTS   [Holy Exchange]

Lord,
accept our sacrifice
as a holy exchange of gifts.
By offering what you have given us
may we receive the gift of yourself.
We ask this in the name of Jesus the Lord.
℟. **Amen.**   ➜ No. 21, p. 22 (Pref. P 29-36)

COMMUNION ANT. Ps 130:7   [Fullness of Redemption]
With the Lord there is mercy, and fullness of redemption. ↓

OR Jn 6:51-52   [Eternal Life]
I am the living bread from heaven, says the Lord; if anyone eats this bread he will live for ever. ↓

PRAYER AFTER COMMUNION   [One with Christ]

Let us pray.
God of mercy,
by this sacrament you make us one with Christ.
By becoming more like him on earth,
may we come to share his glory in heaven,
where he lives and reigns for ever and ever.
℟. **Amen.**   ➜ No. 32, p. 70

Optional Solemn Blessings, p. 92, and Prayers Over the People, p. 99

"Alleluia. Mary is taken up to heaven."

AUGUST 15

ASSUMPTION OF THE BLESSED VIRGIN MARY

VIGIL MASS

ENTRANCE ANT. [Mary in Glory]
All honor to you, Mary! Today you were raised above the choirs of angels to lasting glory with Christ.

➙ No. 2, p. 10

OPENING PRAYER [Mary's Help]
Let us pray
  [that the Virgin Mary will help us
   with her prayers]
Almighty God,
you gave a humble virgin
the privilege of being the mother of your Son,
and crowned her with the glory of heaven.
May the prayers of the Virgin Mary
bring us to the salvation of Christ
and raise us up to eternal life.
We ask this through our Lord Jesus Christ, your Son,
who lives and reigns with you and the Holy Spirit,
one God, for ever and ever. ℟. **Amen.** ↓

ALTERNATIVE OPENING PRAYER   [Praying with Mary]

Let us pray
  [with Mary to the Father,
  in whose presence she now dwells]
Almighty Father of our Lord Jesus Christ,
you have revealed the beauty of your power
by exalting the lowly virgin of Nazareth
and making her the mother of our Savior.
May the prayers of this woman clothed with the sun
bring Jesus to the waiting world
and fill the void of incompletion
with the presence of her child,
who lives and reigns with you and the Holy Spirit,
one God, for ever and ever. ℟. **Amen.** ↓

FIRST READING 1 Chr 15:3-4, 15-16; 16:1-2

[Procession of Glory]

Under David's direction the Israelites brought the ark of the Lord to the tent prepared for it. They showed great respect for it. They offered holocausts and peace offerings. This becomes a figure of Mary who bore the Son of God.

A reading from the first Book of Chronicles

D AVID assembled all Israel in Jerusalem to bring the ark of the LORD to the place which he had prepared for it. David also called together the sons of Aaron and the Levites.

The Levites bore the ark of God on their shoulders with poles, as Moses had ordained according to the word of the LORD.

David commanded the chiefs of the Levites to appoint their kinsmen as chanters, to play on musical instruments, harps, lyres, and cymbals, to make a loud sound of rejoicing.

They brought in the ark of God and set it within the tent which David had pitched for it. Then they offered up burnt offerings and peace offerings to God. When

David had finished offering up the burnt offerings and peace offerings, he blessed the people in the name of the LORD.—The word of the Lord. ℟. **Thanks be to God.** ↓

RESPONSORIAL PSALM Ps 132   [Mary, Ark of God]

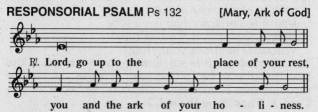

℟. Lord, go up to the place of your rest, you and the ark of your ho - li - ness.

Behold, we heard of it in Ephrathah;
 we found it in the fields of Jaar.
Let us enter into his dwelling,
 let us worship at his footstool.

℟. **Lord, go up to the place of your rest,
 you and the ark of your holiness.**

May your priests be clothed with justice;
 let your faithful ones shout merrily for joy.
For the sake of David your servant,
 reject not the plea of your anointed.

℟. **Lord, go up to the place of your rest,
 you and the ark of your holiness.**

For the LORD has chosen Zion;
 he prefers her for his dwelling.
"Zion is my resting place forever;
 in her will I dwell, for I prefer her."

℟. **Lord, go up to the place of your rest,
 you and the ark of your holiness.** ↓

SECOND READING 1 Cor 15:54b-57   [Victory Over Death]
 Paul reminds the Corinthians that in life after death there is victory. Through his love for us, God has given victory over sin and death in Jesus, his Son.

A reading from the first Letter of Saint Paul
to the Corinthians

BROTHERS and sisters: When that which is mortal
clothes itself with immortality, then the word that
is written shall come about:

Death is swallowed up in victory.
Where, O death, is your victory?
Where, O death, is your sting?

The sting of death is sin, and the power of sin is the
law. But thanks be to God who gives us the victory
through our Lord Jesus Christ.—The word of the
Lord. ℟. **Thanks be to God.** ↓

ALLELUIA Lk 11:28   [Doers of God's Word]

℟. **Alleluia, alleluia.**
Blessed are they who hear the word of God
and observe it.
℟. **Alleluia, alleluia.** ↓

GOSPEL Lk 11:27-28   [Keeping God's Word]

Mary's relationship as the mother of Jesus is unique in all of
history. But Jesus reminds us that those who keep His word
are most pleasing to God. In this Mary has set an example.

℣. The Lord be with you. ℟. **And also with you.**
✠ A reading from the holy Gospel according to Luke.
℟. **Glory to you, Lord.**

WHILE Jesus was speaking, a woman from the
crowd called out and said to him, "Blessed is the
womb that carried you and the breasts at which you
nursed." He replied, "Rather, blessed are those who
hear the word of God and observe it."—The Gospel of
the Lord. ℟. **Praise to you, Lord Jesus Christ.**

➙ No. 14, p. 18

PRAYER OVER THE GIFTS   [Sacrifice of Praise]

Lord,
receive this sacrifice of praise and peace

in honor of the assumption of the Mother of God.
May our offering bring us pardon
and make our lives a thanksgiving to you.
We ask this in the name of Jesus the Lord. ℟. **Amen.** ↓

PREFACE (P 59)   [Assumption—Sign of Hope]
℣. The Lord be with you. ℟. **And also with you.** ℣. Lift
up your hearts. ℟. **We lift them up to the Lord.** ℣. Let
us give thanks to the Lord our God. ℟. **It is right to give
him thanks and praise.**

Father, all-powerful and ever-living God,
we do well always and everywhere to give you thanks
through Jesus Christ our Lord.
Today the virgin Mother of God was taken up into
    heaven
to be the beginning and the pattern of the Church in its
    perfection,
and a sign of hope and comfort for your people on their
    pilgrim way.
You would not allow decay to touch her body,
for she had given birth to your Son, the Lord of all life,
in the glory of the incarnation.
In our joy we sing to your glory
with all the choirs of angels: → No. 23, p. 23

COMMUNION ANT. See Lk 11:27   [Mary Carried Christ]
**Blessed is the womb of the Virgin Mary; she carried
the Son of the eternal Father.** ↓

PRAYER AFTER COMMUNION   [Rejoice]
God of mercy,
we rejoice because Mary, the mother of our Lord,
was taken into the glory of heaven.
May the holy food we receive at this table
free us from evil.
We ask this through Christ our Lord.
℟. **Amen.**   → No. 32, p. 70

Optional Solemn Blessings, p. 92, and Prayers Over the People, p. 99

MASS DURING THE DAY

ENTRANCE ANT. Rv 12:1   [Mary's Glory]

A great sign appeared in heaven: a woman clothed with the sun, the moon beneath her feet, and a crown of twelve stars on her head.

OR   [Joy in Heaven]

Let us rejoice in the Lord and celebrate this feast in honor of the Virgin Mary, at whose assumption the angels rejoice, giving praise to the Son of God.

→ No. 2, p. 10

OPENING PRAYER   [Sharing Mary's Glory]

Let us pray
  [that we will join Mary, the mother of the Lord,
  in the glory of heaven]
All-powerful and ever-living God,
you raised the sinless Virgin Mary,
mother of your Son,
body and soul to the glory of heaven.
May we see heaven as our final goal
and come to share her glory.
We ask this through our Lord Jesus Christ, your Son,
who lives and reigns with you and the Holy Spirit,
one God, for ever and ever. ℟. **Amen.** ↓

ALTERNATIVE OPENING PRAYER   [Following Mary]

Let us pray
  [that with the help of Mary's prayers
  we too may reach our heavenly home]
Father in heaven,
all creation rightly gives you praise,
for all life and all holiness come from you.
In the plan of your wisdom
she who bore the Christ in her womb
was raised body and soul in glory to be with him in
  heaven.

May we follow her example in reflecting your holiness

and join in her hymn of endless life and praise.
We ask this through Christ our Lord. ℟. **Amen.** ↓

FIRST READING Rv 11:19a; 12:1-6a, 10ab

[Ark of the Covenant]

The appearance of the Ark in this time of retribution indicates that God is now accessible—no longer hidden, but present in the midst of his people. Filled with hatred, the devil spares no pains to destroy Christ and his Church. The dragon seeks to destroy the celestial woman and her Son. Its hatred is futile.

A reading from the Book of Revelation

GOD'S temple in heaven was opened, and the ark of his covenant could be seen in the temple.
A great sign appeared in the sky, a woman clothed with the sun, with the moon beneath her feet, and on her head a crown of twelve stars. She was with child and wailed aloud in pain as she labored to give birth. Then another sign appeared in the sky; it was a huge red dragon, with seven heads and ten horns, and on its heads were seven diadems. Its tail swept away a third of the stars in the sky and hurled them down to the earth. Then the dragon stood before the woman about to give birth, to devour her child when she gave birth. She gave birth to a son, a male child, destined to rule all the nations with an iron rod. Her child was caught up to God and his throne. The woman herself fled into the desert where she had a place prepared by God.
    Then I heard a loud voice in heaven say:
        "Now have salvation and power come,
            and the kingdom of our God
            and the authority of his Anointed One."
The word of the Lord. ℟. **Thanks be to God.** ↓

RESPONSORIAL PSALM Ps 45   [Mary the Queen]

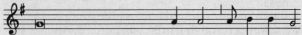

℟. **The queen stands at your   right hand,   ar-rayed in gold.**

The queen takes her place at your right hand in gold
 of Ophir.—℟.

Hear, O daughter, and see; turn your ear,
 forget your people and your father's house.—℟.

So shall the king desire your beauty;
 for he is your lord.—℟.

They are borne in with gladness and joy;
 they enter the palace of the king.—℟. ↓

SECOND READING 1 Cor 15:20-26   [Christ the King]

**The offering of the firstfruits was the symbol of the dedi-
cation of the entire harvest to God. So the Resurrection of
Christ involves the resurrection of all who are in him. Since
his glorious Resurrection, Christ reigns in glory; he is the
Lord.**

A reading from the first Letter of Saint Paul
to the Corinthians

BROTHERS and sisters: Christ has been raised
from the dead, the firstfruits of those who have
fallen asleep. For since death came through man, the
resurrection of the dead came also through man. For
just as in Adam all die, so too in Christ shall all be
brought to life, but each one in proper order: Christ
the firstfruits; then, at his coming, those who belong
to Christ; then comes the end, when he hands over
the kingdom to his God and Father, when he has
destroyed every sovereignty and every authority and
power. For he must reign until he has put all his enemies under his feet. The last enemy to be destroyed is
death, for "he subjected everything under his feet."—
The word of the Lord. ℟. **Thanks be to God.** ↓

ALLELUIA   [Mary in Heaven]

Alleluia, alleluia.
Mary is taken up to heaven;
a chorus of angels exults.
℟. **Alleluia, alleluia.** ↓

GOSPEL Lk 1:39-56   [Blessed among Women]

Mary visits her kinswoman. Mary's song of thanksgiving,
often called the "Magnificat," has been put together from
many Old Testament phrases. The sum of Mary's spirituality is the best and most abundant gift of grace of the
Incarnation of God's Son. Her spirit is filled with goodness
and humility.

℣. The Lord be with you. ℟. **And also with you.**
✤ A reading from the holy Gospel according to Luke.
℟. **Glory to you, Lord.**

MARY set out and traveled to the hill country in
haste to a town of Judah, where she entered the
house of Zechariah and greeted Elizabeth. When
Elizabeth heard Mary's greeting, the infant leaped in
her womb, and Elizabeth, filled with the Holy Spirit,
cried out in a loud voice and said, "Blessed are you
among women, and blessed is the fruit of your womb.
And how does this happen to me, that the mother of
my Lord should come to me? For at the moment the
sound of your greeting reached my ears, the infant in
my womb leaped for joy. Blessed are you who believed
that what was spoken to you by the Lord would be
fulfilled."
And Mary said:
    "My soul proclaims the greatness of the Lord;
        my spirit rejoices in God my Savior
        for he has looked upon his lowly servant.
    From this day all generations will call me blessed:
        the Almighty has done great things for me,
        and holy is his Name.

He has mercy on those who fear him
  in every generation.
He has shown the strength of his arm,
  and has scattered the proud in their conceit.
He has cast down the mighty from their thrones,
  and has lifted up the lowly.
He has filled the hungry with good things,
  and the rich he has sent away empty.
He has come to the help of his servant Israel
  for he has remembered his promise of mercy,
  the promise he made to our fathers,
  to Abraham and his children for ever."

Mary remained with her about three months and then returned to her home.—The Gospel of the Lord.
℟. **Praise to you, Lord Jesus Christ.**   ➔ No. 14, p. 18

PRAYER OVER THE GIFTS   [Living in God's Love]
Lord,
receive this offering of our service.
You raised the Virgin Mary to the glory of heaven.
By her prayers, help us to seek you
and to live in your love.
Grant this through Christ our Lord.
℟. **Amen.**   ➔ Pref. (P 59), p. 474

COMMUNION ANT. Lk 1:48-49   [Mary Aided by Grace]
All generations will call me blessed, for the Almighty has done great things for me. ↓

PRAYER AFTER COMMUNION   [Mary's Intercession]
Lord,
may we who receive this sacrament of salvation
be led to the glory of heaven
by the prayers of the Virgin Mary.
We ask this in the name of Jesus the Lord.
℟. **Amen.**   ➔ No. 32, p. 70

Optional Solemn Blessings, p. 92, and Prayers Over the People, p. 99

"You are Peter, and upon this rock I will build my church."

AUGUST 21

21st SUNDAY IN ORDINARY TIME

ENTRANCE ANT. Ps 86:1-3   [Save Us]

Listen, Lord, and answer me. Save your servant who trusts in you. I call to you all day long; have mercy on me, O Lord.   → No. 2, p. 10

OPENING PRAYER   [One in Mind and Heart]

Let us pray
    [that God will make us one in mind and heart]
Father,
help us to seek the values
that will bring us lasting joy in this changing world.
In our desire for what you promise
make us one in mind and heart.
Grant this through our Lord Jesus Christ, your Son,
who lives and reigns with you and the Holy Spirit,
one God, for ever and ever. ℟. **Amen.** ↓

ALTERNATIVE OPENING PRAYER   [Minds on God]

Let us pray
    [with minds fixed on eternal truth]
Lord our God,
all truth is from you,

and you alone bring oneness of heart.
Give your people the joy
of hearing your word in every sound
and of longing for your presence more than for life
   itself.
May all the attractions of a changing world
serve only to bring us
the peace of your kingdom which this world does not
   give.
Grant this through Christ our Lord. ℟. **Amen.** ↓

FIRST READING Is 22:19-23   [The Gift of Authority]

**Eliakim is given the leadership of the Israelites. He is to
become the father of the Jewish people. He shall have the
key of the House of David. He is to have a place of honor
for his family.**

A reading from the Book of the Prophet Isaiah

T HUS says the LORD, to Shebna, master of the
   palace:
"I will thrust you from your office
   and pull you down from your station.
On that day I will summon my servant
   Eliakim, son of Hilkiah;
I will clothe him with your robe,
   and gird him with your sash,
   and give over to him your authority.
He shall be a father to the inhabitants of Jerusalem,
   and to the house of Judah.
I will place the key of the House of David on Eliakim's shoulder;
   when he opens, no one shall shut,
   when he shuts, no one shall open.
I will fix him like a peg in a sure spot,
   to be a place of honor for his family."
The word of the Lord. ℟. **Thanks be to God.** ↓

RESPONSORIAL PSALM Ps 138   [God's Eternal Love]

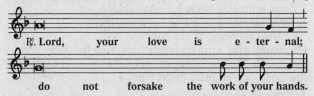

℞. Lord, your love is e-ter-nal; do not forsake the work of your hands.

I will give thanks to you, O LORD, with all my heart,
  for you have heard the words of my mouth;
in the presence of the angels I will sing your praise;
  I will worship at your holy temple.

℞. **Lord, your love is eternal;**
  do not forsake the work of your hands.

I will give thanks to your name,
  because of your kindness and your truth:
when I called, you answered me;
  you built up strength within me.

℞. **Lord, your love is eternal;**
  do not forsake the work of your hands.

The LORD is exalted, yet the lowly he sees,
  and the proud he knows from afar.
Your kindness, O LORD, endures forever;
  forsake not the work of your hands.

℞. **Lord, your love is eternal;**
  do not forsake the work of your hands. ↓

SECOND READING Rom 11:33-36   [Eternal Glory]

Paul offers a description of God, noting his infinite wisdom.
God's ways are unsearchable and no one can really measure
the mind of God. But in him all things have their being.

A reading from the Letter of Saint Paul to the Romans

OH, the depth of the riches and wisdom and knowledge of God! How inscrutable are his judgments and how unsearchable his ways!

For who has known the mind of the Lord
   or who has been his counselor?
Or who has given the Lord anything
   that he may be repaid?

For from him and through him and for him are all things. To him be glory forever. Amen.—The word of the Lord. ℟. **Thanks be to God.** ↓

ALLELUIA Mt 16:18   [Christ's Church]

℟. **Alleluia, alleluia.**

You are Peter and upon this rock I will build my Church
and the gates of the netherworld shall not prevail against it.

℟. **Alleluia, alleluia.** ↓

GOSPEL Mt 16:13-20   [The First Pope]

   Peter acknowledges that Jesus is the Messiah. Jesus in turn declares Peter the rock upon which his Church is to be built. He also gives Peter the power of the keys.

℣. The Lord be with you. ℟. **And also with you.**
✚ A reading from the holy Gospel according to Matthew. ℟. **Glory to you, Lord.**

JESUS went into the region of Caesarea Philippi and he asked his disciples, "Who do people say that the Son of Man is?" They replied, "Some say John the Baptist, others Elijah, still others Jeremiah or one of the prophets." He said to them, "But who do you say that I am?" Simon Peter said in reply, "You are the Christ, the Son of the living God." Jesus said to him in reply, "Blessed are you, Simon son of Jonah. For flesh and blood has not revealed this to you, but my heavenly Father. And so I say to you, you are Peter, and upon this rock I will build my church, and the gates of the netherworld shall not prevail against it. I will give you the keys to the kingdom of heaven. Whatever you bind on earth shall be bound in heaven;

and whatever you loose on earth shall be loosed in heaven." Then he strictly ordered his disciples to tell no one that he was the Christ.—The Gospel of the Lord. ℟. **Praise to you, Lord Jesus Christ.**

➜ No. 14, p. 18

PRAYER OVER THE GIFTS   [Peace and Unity]

Merciful God,
the perfect sacrifice of Jesus Christ
made us your people.
In your love,
grant peace and unity to your Church.
We ask this through Christ our Lord.
℟. **Amen.**   ➜ No. 21, p. 22 (Pref. P 29-36)

COMMUNION ANT. Ps 104:13-15   [Sacred Bread and Wine]

Lord, the earth is filled with your gift from heaven; man grows bread from earth, and wine to cheer his heart. ↓

OR Jn 6:55   [Eternal Life]

The Lord says: The man who eats my flesh and drinks my blood will live for ever; I shall raise him to life on the last day. ↓

PRAYER AFTER COMMUNION   [Pleasing God]

Lord,
may this eucharist increase within us
the healing power of your love.
May it guide and direct our efforts
to please you in all things.
We ask this in the name of Jesus the Lord.
℟. **Amen.**   ➜ No. 32, p. 70

Optional Solemn Blessings, p. 92, and Prayers Over the People, p. 99

"You are thinking not as God does, but as humans do."

AUGUST 28

22nd SUNDAY IN ORDINARY TIME

ENTRANCE ANT. Ps 86:3, 5   [Call Upon God]
**I call to you all day long, have mercy on me, O Lord.
You are good and forgiving, full of love for all who
call to you.**   → No. 2, p. 10

OPENING PRAYER   [Increasing Our Spiritual Gifts]
Let us pray
  [that God will increase our faith
   and bring to perfection the gifts he has given us]
Almighty God,
every good thing comes from you.
Fill our hearts with love for you,
increase our faith,
and by your constant care
protect the good you have given us.
We ask this . . . for ever and ever. ℟. **Amen.**

ALTERNATIVE OPENING PRAYER   [Desire To Please God]
Let us pray
  [to God who forgives all who call upon him]
Lord God of power and might,

nothing is good which is against your will,
and all is of value which comes from your hand.
Place in our hearts a desire to please you
and fill our minds with insight into love,
so that every thought may grow in wisdom
and all our efforts may be filled with your peace.
We ask this through Christ our Lord. ℟. **Amen.** ↓

FIRST READING Jer 20:7-9   [Power of God's Word]

> Jeremiah admits that he has become a mockery for the Lord. He is derided and reproached, but he cannot help speaking out the word of the Lord.

A reading from the Book of the Prophet Jeremiah

YOU duped me, O LORD, and I let myself be duped;
  you were too strong for me, and you triumphed.
All the day I am an object of laughter;
    everyone mocks me.

Whenever I speak, I must cry out,
    violence and outrage is my message;
the word of the LORD has brought me
    derision and reproach all the day.

I say to myself, I will not mention him,
    I will speak in his name no more.
But then it becomes like fire burning in my heart,
    imprisoned in my bones;
I grow weary holding it in, I cannot endure it.
The word of the Lord. ℟. **Thanks be to God.** ↓

RESPONSORIAL PSALM Ps 63   [Longing for God]

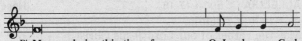

℟. **My soul is thirsting for you,   O Lord my God.**

O God, you are my God whom I seek;
    for you my flesh pines and my soul thirsts
    like the earth, parched, lifeless and without water.

℟. **My soul is thirsting for you, O Lord my God.**

Thus have I gazed toward you in the sanctuary
   to see your power and your glory,
for your kindness is a greater good than life;
   my lips shall glorify you.—℟.

Thus will I bless you while I live;
   lifting up my hands, I will call upon your name.
As with the riches of a banquet shall my soul be sat-
      isfied,
   and with exultant lips my mouth shall praise
      you.—℟.

You are my help,
   and in the shadow of your wings I shout for joy.
My soul clings fast to you;
   your right hand upholds me.—℟. ↓

SECOND READING Rom 12:1-2   [A Living Sacrifice]

**Paul recommends sacrifice, to offer our bodies as a sacri-
fice to the Lord. We must ignore the standards of the world
and become renewed in spirit to be pleasing to God.**

A reading from the Letter of Saint Paul to the Romans

I URGE you, brothers and sisters, by the mercies of
God, to offer your bodies as a living sacrifice, holy
and pleasing to God, your spiritual worship. Do not
conform yourselves to this age but be transformed by
the renewal of your mind, that you may discern what
is the will of God, what is good and pleasing and perfect.—The word of the Lord. ℟. **Thanks be to God.** ↓

ALLELUIA Cf. Eph 1:17-18   [Hope]

℟. **Alleluia, alleluia.**
May the Father of our Lord Jesus Christ
enlighten the eyes of our hearts,
that we may know what is the hope
that belongs to our call.
℟. **Alleluia, alleluia.** ↓

GOSPEL Mt 16:21-27   [Taking Up the Cross]

Jesus foretells his suffering, passion, and death. All those
who wish to follow Jesus must take up their cross.

℣. The Lord be with you. ℟. **And also with you.**
✠   A reading from the holy Gospel according to
Matthew. ℟. **Glory to you, Lord**.

JESUS began to show his disciples that he must go
to Jerusalem and suffer greatly from the elders, the
chief priests, and the scribes, and be killed and on the
third day be raised. Then Peter took Jesus aside and
began to rebuke him, "God forbid, Lord! No such
thing shall ever happen to you." He turned and said to
Peter, "Get behind me, Satan! You are an obstacle to
me. You are thinking not as God does, but as human
beings do."

Then Jesus said to his disciples, "Whoever wishes
to come after me must deny himself, take up his
cross, and follow me. For whoever wishes to save his
life will lose it, but whoever loses his life for my sake
will find it. What profit would there be for one to gain
the whole world and forfeit his life? Or what can one
give in exchange for his life? For the Son of Man will
come with his angels in his Father's glory, and then
he will repay all according to his conduct."—The
Gospel of the Lord. ℟. **Praise to you, Lord Jesus
Christ.**   ➜ No. 14, p. 18

PRAYER OVER THE GIFTS   [Promise of Salvation]

Lord,
may this holy offering
bring us your blessing
and accomplish within us
its promise of salvation.
Grant this through Christ our Lord.
℟. **Amen.**   ➜ No. 21, p. 22 (Pref. P 29-36)

COMMUNION ANT. Ps 31:20   [God's Kindness]
O Lord, how great is the depth of the kindness which you have shown to those who love you. ↓

OR Mt 5:9-10   [Happy the Peacemakers]
Happy are the peacemakers; they shall be called sons of God. Happy are they who suffer persecution for justice' sake; the kingdom of heaven is theirs. ↓

PRAYER AFTER COMMUNION   [Serving God in Others]
Lord,
you renew us at your table with the bread of life.
May this food strengthen us in love
and help us to serve you in each other.
We ask this in the name of Jesus the Lord.
℟. Amen.   ➔ No. 32, p. 70

Optional Solemn Blessings, p. 92, and Prayers Over the People, p. 99

"Where two or three are gathered together in my name, there am I in the midst of them."

SEPTEMBER 4

23rd SUNDAY IN ORDINARY TIME

ENTRANCE ANT. Ps 119:137, 124   [Plea for Mercy]
Lord, you are just, and the judgments you make are right. Show mercy when you judge me, your servant.
                ➔ No. 2, p. 10

OPENING PRAYER   [Christian Freedom]

Let us pray
  [that we may realize the freedom God has given us
  in making us his sons and daughters]
God our Father,
you redeem us
and make us your children in Christ.
Look upon us,
give us true freedom
and bring us to the inheritance you promised.
Grant this through our Lord Jesus Christ, your Son,
who lives and reigns with you and the Holy Spirit,
one God, for ever and ever. R̹. **Amen.** ↓

ALTERNATIVE OPENING PRAYER   [Appreciation of Life]

Let us pray
  [to our just and merciful God]
Lord our God,
in you justice and mercy meet.
With unparalleled love you have saved us from death
and drawn us into the circle of your life.
Open our eyes to the wonders this life sets before us,
that we may serve you free from fear
and address you as God our Father.
We ask this through Christ our Lord. R̹. **Amen.** ↓

FIRST READING Ez 33:7-9   [Warning the Wicked]

**Ezekiel is charged to dissuade evildoers from their faults.
If evildoers do not heed this warning, then they will die for
their guilt.**

A reading from the Book of the Prophet Ezekiel

THUS says the LORD: You, son of man, I have
appointed watchman for the house of Israel; when
you hear me say anything, you shall warn them for
me. If I tell the wicked, "O wicked one, you shall surely die," and you do not speak out to dissuade the
wicked from his way, [the wicked] shall die for his

guilt, but I will hold you responsible for his death. But if you warn the wicked, trying to turn him from his way, and he refuses to turn from his way, he shall die for his guilt, but you shall save yourself.—The word of the Lord. ℟. **Thanks be to God.** ↓

RESPONSORIAL PSALM Ps 95   [Answering the Lord's Call]

℟. If today you hear his voice, harden not your hearts.

Come, let us sing joyfully to the LORD;
  let us acclaim the rock of our salvation.
Let us come into his presence with thanksgiving;
  let us joyfully sing psalms to him.

℟. **If today you hear his voice,
  harden not your hearts.**

Come, let us bow down in worship;
  let us kneel before the LORD who made us.
For he is our God,
  and we are the people he shepherds, the flock he
    guides.

℟. **If today you hear his voice,
  harden not your hearts.**

Oh, that today you would hear his voice:
  "Harden not your hearts as at Meribah,
  as in the day of Massah in the desert,
where your fathers tempted me;
  they tested me though they had seen my works."

℟. **If today you hear his voice,
  harden not your hearts.** ↓

SECOND READING Rom 13:8-10   [Love of Neighbor]

All who love their neighbors truly fulfill the law. The commandments forbidding adultery, stealing, murder, and coveting are all summed up in this law of laws.

A reading from the Letter of Saint Paul to the Romans

BROTHERS and sisters: Owe nothing to anyone, except to love one another; for the one who loves another has fulfilled the law. The commandments, "You shall not commit adultery; you shall not kill; you shall not steal; you shall not covet," and whatever other commandment there may be, are summed up in this saying, namely, "You shall love your neighbor as yourself." Love does no evil to the neighbor; hence, love is the fulfillment of the law.—The word of the Lord. ℟. **Thanks be to God.** ↓

ALLELUIA 2 Cor 5:19   [Reconciliation]

℟. **Alleluia, alleluia.**
God was reconciling the world to himself in Christ
and entrusting to us the message of reconciliation.
℟. **Alleluia, alleluia.** ↓

GOSPEL Mt 18:15-20   [Communal Correction and Prayer]

To correct another person's fault, first speak to him or her. If this fails, invite a witness or two. But if the person continues in this fault, note it before the church assembly. Pray together and make your petitions in the name of Jesus.

℣. The Lord be with you. ℟. **And also with you.**
✠   A reading from the holy Gospel according to Matthew. ℟. **Glory to you, Lord.**

JESUS said to his disciples: "If your brother sins against you, go and tell him his fault between you and him alone. If he listens to you, you have won over your brother. If he does not listen, take one or two others along with you, so that 'every fact may be established on the testimony of two or three witnesses.' If he refuses to listen to them, tell the church. If he refuses to listen even to the church, then treat him as you would a Gentile or a tax collector. Amen, I say to you, whatever you bind on earth shall be bound in heaven, and whatever you loose on earth shall be loosed in heaven. Again, amen, I say to you, if two of you agree on earth about anything for which they are to pray, it shall be granted to them by my heavenly Father. For where two or three are gathered together in my name, there am I in the midst of them."—The Gospel of the Lord. ℟. **Praise to you, Lord Jesus Christ.**   ➜ No. 14, p. 18

PRAYER OVER THE GIFTS   [True Worship]
God of peace and love,
may our offering bring you true worship
and make us one with you.
Grant this through Christ our Lord.
℟. **Amen.**   ➜ No. 21, p. 22 (Pref. P 29-36)

COMMUNION ANT. Ps 42:2-3   [Longing for God]
Like a deer that longs for running streams, my soul longs for you, my God. My soul is thirsting for the living God. ↓

OR Jn 8:12   [The Light of Life]
I am the light of the world, says the Lord; the man who follows me will have the light of life. ↓

PRAYER AFTER COMMUNION   [Word and Sacrament]
Lord,
your word and your sacrament
give us food and life.
May this gift of your Son
lead us to share his life for ever.
We ask this through Christ our Lord.
℟. **Amen.**   ➜ No. 32, p. 70

Optional Solemn Blessings, p. 92, and Prayers Over the People, p. 99

"His master handed him over to the torturers."

SEPTEMBER 11

24th SUNDAY IN ORDINARY TIME

ENTRANCE ANT. See Sir 36:18   [God's Peace]

Give peace, Lord, to those who wait for you and your prophets will proclaim you as you deserve. Hear the prayers of your servant and of your people Israel.

➥ No. 2, p. 10

OPENING PRAYER   [Faithfulness in God's Service]

Let us pray
   [that God will keep us faithful in his service]
Almighty God,
our creator and guide,
may we serve you with all our heart
and know your forgiveness in our lives.
We ask this through our Lord Jesus Christ, your Son,
who lives and reigns with you and the Holy Spirit,
one God, for ever and ever. ℟. **Amen.** ↓

ALTERNATIVE OPENING PRAYER   [Peace of Christ]

Let us pray
   [for the peace which is born of faith and hope]

Father in heaven, Creator of all,
look down upon your people in their moments of
    need,
for you alone are the source of our peace.
Bring us to the dignity which distinguishes the poor
    in spirit
and show us how great is the call to serve,
that we may share in the peace of Christ
who offered his life in the service of all.
We ask this through Christ our Lord. ℟. **Amen.** ↓

FIRST READING Sir 27:30—28:9 [The Need for Forgiveness]

> The sinner abounds in wrath. It is the Lord who punishes
> and we are to forgive injustice and be merciful. We should
> think of our last days.

A reading from the Book of Sirach

WRATH and anger are hateful things,
    yet the sinner hugs them tight.
The vengeful will suffer the LORD's vengeance,
    for he remembers their sins in detail.
Forgive your neighbor's injustice;
    then when you pray, your own sins will be for-
        given.
Could anyone nourish anger against another
    and expect healing from the LORD?
Could anyone refuse mercy to another like himself,
    can he seek pardon for his own sins?
If one who is but flesh cherishes wrath,
    who will forgive his sins?
Remember your last days, set enmity aside;
    remember death and decay, and cease from sin!
Think of the commandments, hate not your neighbor;
    remember the Most High's covenant, and over-
        look faults.
The word of the Lord. ℟. **Thanks be to God.** ↓

RESPONSORIAL PSALM Ps 103   [God's Mercy]

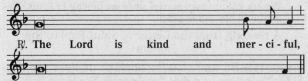

℞. The Lord is kind and mer-ci-ful,

slow to anger, and rich in compassion.

Bless the LORD, O my soul;
  and all my being, bless his holy name.
Bless the LORD, O my soul,
  and forget not all his benefits.

℞. **The Lord is kind and merciful,
  slow to anger, and rich in compassion.**

He pardons all your iniquities,
  heals all your ills,
redeems your life from destruction,
  crowns you with kindness and compassion.

℞. **The Lord is kind and merciful,
  slow to anger, and rich in compassion.**

He will not always chide,
  nor does he keep his wrath forever.
Not according to our sins does he deal with us,
  nor does he requite us according to our crimes.

℞. **The Lord is kind and merciful,
  slow to anger, and rich in compassion.**

For as the heavens are high above the earth,
  so surpassing is his kindness toward those who
    fear him.
As far as the east is from the west,
  so far has he put our transgressions from us.

℞. **The Lord is kind and merciful,
  slow to anger, and rich in compassion.** ↓

SECOND READING Rom 14:7-9   [God's Partners]

We are not our own master since we belong to Jesus. This is true in life and in death.

A reading from the Letter of Saint Paul to the Romans

BROTHERS and sisters: None of us lives for oneself, and no one dies for oneself. For if we live, we live for the Lord, and if we die, we die for the Lord; so then, whether we live or die, we are the Lord's. For this is why Christ died and came to life, that he might be Lord of both the dead and the living. —The word of the Lord. ℟. **Thanks be to God.** ↓

ALLELUIA Jn 13:34   [Love One Another]

℟. **Alleluia, alleluia.**
I give you a new commandment, says the Lord;
love one another as I have loved you.
℟. **Alleluia, alleluia.** ↓

GOSPEL Mt 18:21-35   [Forgiving Our Neighbor]

Jesus answers Peter that we are to forgive our neighbor's faults without any limit. Jesus tells the parable of the unjust steward who was forgiven a large debt by his master but refused to forgive a small debt owed to himself.

℣. The Lord be with you. ℟. **And also with you.**
✝ A reading from the holy Gospel according to Matthew. ℟. **Glory to you, Lord**.

PETER approached Jesus and asked him, "Lord, if my brother sins against me, how often must I forgive? As many as seven times?" Jesus answered, "I say to you, not seven times but seventy-seven times. That is why the kingdom of heaven may be likened to a king who decided to settle accounts with his servants. When he began the accounting, a debtor was brought before him who owed him a huge amount. Since he

had no way of paying it back, his master ordered him
to be sold, along with his wife, his children, and all
his property, in payment of the debt. At that, the servant fell down, did him homage, and said, 'Be patient
with me, and I will pay you back in full.' Moved with
compassion the master of that servant let him go and
forgave him the loan. When that servant had left, he
found one of his fellow servants who owed him a
much smaller amount. He seized him and started to
choke him, demanding, 'Pay back what you owe.'
Falling to his knees, his fellow servant begged him,
'Be patient with me, and I will pay you back.' But he
refused. Instead, he had the fellow servant put in
prison until he paid back the debt. Now when his fellow servants saw what had happened, they were
deeply disturbed, and went to their master and
reported the whole affair. His master summoned him
and said to him, 'You wicked servant! I forgave you
your entire debt because you begged me to. Should
you not have had pity on your fellow servant, as I had
pity on you?' Then in anger his master handed him
over to the torturers until he should pay back the
whole debt. So will my heavenly Father do to you,
unless each of you forgives your brother from your
heart."—The Gospel of the Lord. ℟. **Praise to you,
Lord Jesus Christ.**   ➔ No. 14, p. 18

PRAYER OVER THE GIFTS   [Hear Our Prayer]
Lord,
hear the prayers of your people
and receive our gifts.
May the worship of each one here
bring salvation to all.
Grant this through Christ our Lord.
℟. **Amen.**   ➔ No. 21, p. 22 (Pref. P 29-36)

COMMUNION ANT. Ps 36:8   [God's Mercy]
**O God, how much we value your mercy! All mankind
can gather under your protection. ↓**

OR See 1 Cor 10:16   [Share of Christ]
**The cup that we bless is a communion with the blood
of Christ; and the bread that we break is a communion with the body of the Lord. ↓**

PRAYER AFTER COMMUNION   [Eucharist and the Spirit]
Lord,
may the eucharist you have given us
influence our thoughts and actions.
May your Spirit guide and direct us in your way.
We ask this in the name of Jesus the Lord.
℟. **Amen.**   ➜ No. 32, p. 70

Optional Solemn Blessings, p. 92, and Prayers Over the People, p. 99

"The last will be first, and the first will be last."

SEPTEMBER 18

25th SUNDAY IN ORDINARY TIME

ENTRANCE ANT. [Savior of All]

I am the Savior of all the people, says the Lord. Whatever their troubles, I will answer their cry, and I will always be their Lord. ➔ No. 2, p. 10

OPENING PRAYER [Growth in Love]

Let us pray
   [that we will grow in the love of God
   and of one another]
Father,
guide us, as you guide creation
according to your law of love.
May we love one another
and come to perfection
in the eternal life prepared for us.
Grant this through our Lord Jesus Christ, your Son,
who lives and reigns with you and the Holy Spirit,
one God, for ever and ever. ℟. **Amen.** ↓

ALTERNATIVE OPENING PRAYER [Mutual Love]

Let us pray
   [to the Lord who is a God of love to all peoples]

501

Father in heaven,
the perfection of justice is found in your love
and all mankind is in need of your law.
Help us to find this love in each other
that justice may be attained
through obedience to your law.
We ask this through Christ our Lord. ℟. **Amen.** ↓

FIRST READING Is 55:6-9   [Seek the Lord]

> **Seek the Lord. His ways are far above human ways. The thoughts of God are not the thoughts of human beings. God is rich in forgiving.**

A reading from the Book of the Prophet Isaiah

S EEK the LORD while he may be found,
  call him while he is near.
Let the scoundrel forsake his way,
    and the wicked his thoughts:
let him turn to the LORD for mercy;
    to our God, who is generous in forgiving.
For my thoughts are not your thoughts,
    nor are your ways my ways, says the LORD.
As high as the heavens are above the earth,
    so high are my ways above your ways
    and my thoughts above your thoughts.
The word of the Lord. ℟. **Thanks be to God.** ↓

RESPONSORIAL PSALM Ps 145   [The Nearness of God]

– ℟. **The Lord is   near to   all   who call up - on   him.**
Every day will I bless you,
    and I will praise your name forever and ever.
Great is the LORD and highly to be praised;
    his greatness is unsearchable.

℟. **The Lord is near to all who call upon him.**

The LORD is gracious and merciful,
    slow to anger and of great kindness.

The LORD is good to all
    and compassionate toward all his works.

℟. **The Lord is near to all who call upon him.**

The LORD is just in all his ways
    and holy in all his works.
The LORD is near to all who call upon him,
    to all who call upon him in truth.

℟. **The Lord is near to all who call upon him.** ↓

SECOND READING Phil 1:20c-24, 27a   [Life in Christ]

Paul notes that whether he lives or dies, his life belongs to Christ. It would be more beneficial for the Philippians for Paul to continue living in the flesh to bring them the message of Jesus.

A reading from the Letter of Saint Paul
to the Philippians

BROTHERS and sisters: Christ will be magnified in my body, whether by life or by death. For to me life is Christ, and death is gain. If I go on living in the flesh, that means fruitful labor for me. And I do not know which I shall choose. I am caught between the two. I long to depart this life and be with Christ, for that is far better. Yet that I remain in the flesh is more necessary for your benefit. Only, conduct yourselves in a way worthy of the gospel of Christ. —The word of the Lord. ℟. **Thanks be to God.** ↓

ALLELUIA Cf. Acts 16:14b   [Listen to Jesus]

℟. **Alleluia, alleluia.**
Open our hearts, O Lord,
to listen to the words of your Son.
℟. **Alleluia, alleluia.** ↓

GOSPEL Mt 20:1-16a   [The Workers in the Vineyard]

Jesus teaches that the kingdom of God is like the landowner who hires early in the morning, again at mid-

morning, at noon and midafternoon. At payment time, all the workers receive the same wage. How just and generous God is!

℣. The Lord be with you. ℟. **And also with you.**

✚ A reading from the holy Gospel according to Matthew. ℟. **Glory to you, Lord.**

JESUS told his disciples this parable: "The kingdom of heaven is like a landowner who went out at dawn to hire laborers for his vineyard. After agreeing with them for the usual daily wage, he sent them into his vineyard. Going out about nine o'clock, the landowner saw others standing idle in the marketplace, and he said to them, 'You too go into my vineyard, and I will give you what is just.' So they went off. And he went out again around noon, and around three o'clock, and did likewise. Going out about five o'clock, the landowner found others standing around, and said to them, 'Why do you stand here idle all day?' They answered, 'Because no one has hired us.' He said to them, 'You too go into my vineyard.' When it was evening the owner of the vineyard said to his foreman, 'Summon the laborers and give them their pay, beginning with the last and ending with the first.' When those who had started about five o'clock came, each received the usual daily wage. So when the first came, they thought that they would receive more, but each of them also got the usual wage. And on receiving it they grumbled against the landowner, saying, 'These last ones worked only one hour, and you have made them equal to us, who bore the day's burden and the heat.' He said to one of them in reply, 'My friend, I am not cheating you. Did you not agree with me for the usual daily wage? Take what is yours and go. What if I wish to give this last one the same as you? Or am I not free to do as I wish with my own money? Are you envious because I am generous?' Thus, the last will be first, and the first will be last."—The Gospel of the Lord. ℞. **Praise to you, Lord Jesus Christ.**

→ No. 14, p. 18

PRAYER OVER THE GIFTS   [Gifts Become Eucharist]

Lord,
may these gifts which we now offer
to show our belief and our love
be pleasing to you.
May they become for us
the eucharist of Jesus Christ your Son,
who is Lord for ever and ever.
℞. **Amen.**   → No. 21, p. 22 (Pref. P 29-36)

COMMUNION ANT. Ps 119:4-5 [Keeping God's Commands]
You have laid down your precepts to be faithfully kept. May my footsteps be firm in keeping your commands. ↓

OR Jn 10:14   [The Good Shepherd]
I am the Good Shepherd, says the Lord; I know my sheep, and mine know me. ↓

PRAYER AFTER COMMUNION   [The Eucharist in Action]
Lord,
help us with your kindness.
Make us strong through the eucharist.
May we put into action
the saving mystery we celebrate.
We ask this in the name of Jesus the Lord.
℞. **Amen.**   → No. 32, p. 70

Optional Solemn Blessings, p. 92, and Prayers Over the People, p. 99

"Tax collectors and prostitutes are entering the kingdom of God before you."

SEPTEMBER 25

26th SUNDAY IN ORDINARY TIME

ENTRANCE ANT. Dn 3:31, 29, 30, 43, 42   [God's Kindness]

O Lord, you had just cause to judge men as you did: because we sinned against you and disobeyed your will. But now show us your greatness of heart, and treat us with your unbounded kindness.→No. 2, p. 10

OPENING PRAYER   [God's Forgiveness]

Let us pray
  [for God's forgiveness
  and for the happiness it brings]
Father,
you show your almighty power
in your mercy and forgiveness.
Continue to fill us with your gifts of love.
Help us to hurry toward the eternal life you promise
and come to share in the joys of your kingdom.
Grant this through our Lord Jesus Christ, your Son,
who lives and reigns with you and the Holy Spirit,
one God, for ever and ever. ℟. **Amen.** ↓

ALTERNATIVE OPENING PRAYER   [Radiating Christ]

Let us pray
  [for the peace of the kingdom
  which we have been promised]
Father of our Lord Jesus Christ,
in your unbounded mercy
you have revealed the beauty of your power
through your constant forgiveness of our sins.
May the power of this love be in our hearts
to bring your pardon and your kingdom to all we meet.
We ask this through Christ our Lord. ℟. **Amen.** ↓

FIRST READING Ez 18:25-28 [The Virtuous Man Shall Live]

**The Lord's way is fair and just. It is when sinners repent
from their faults and do what is right that they are to live.
Because of this reform, they deserve to live.**

A reading from the Book of the Prophet Ezekiel

THUS says the LORD: You say, "The LORD's way is
not fair!" Hear now, house of Israel: Is it my way
that is unfair, or rather, are not your ways unfair?
When someone virtuous turns away from virtue to
commit iniquity, and dies, it is because of the iniquity
he committed that he must die. But if he turns from
the wickedness he has committed, and does what is
right and just, he shall preserve his life; since he has
turned away from all the sins that he committed, he
shall surely live, he shall not die.—The word of the
Lord. ℟. **Thanks be to God.** ↓

RESPONSORIAL PSALM Ps 25   [God's Compassion]

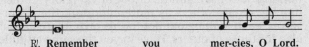

℟. **Remember   you   mer-cies, O Lord.**

Your ways, O LORD, make known to me;
  teach me your paths,

guide me in your truth and teach me,
　for you are God my savior.

℟. **Remember your mercies, O Lord.**

Remember that your compassion, O LORD,
　and your love are from of old.
The sins of my youth and my frailties remember not;
　in your kindness remember me,
　because of your goodness, O LORD.

℟. **Remember your mercies, O Lord.**

Good and upright is the LORD;
　thus he shows sinners the way.
He guides the humble to justice,
　he teaches the humble his way.

℟. **Remember your mercies, O Lord.** ↓

SECOND READING Phil 2:1-11 or 2:1-5   [Jesus Is Lord]

Paul encourages us to unify, to be of one heart and mind, to possess a single love for one another. We should adopt the attitude of Jesus. At his name every knee should bend.

[If the "Shorter Form" is used, the indented text in brackets is omitted.]

A reading from the Letter of Saint Paul
to the Philippians

BROTHERS and sisters: If there is any encouragement in Christ, any solace in love, any participation in the Spirit, any compassion and mercy, complete my joy by being of the same mind, with the same love, united in heart, thinking one thing. Do nothing out of selfishness or out of vainglory; rather, humbly regard others as more important than yourselves, each looking out not for his own interests, but also for those of others. Have in you the same attitude that is also in Christ Jesus,
　[Who, though he was in the form of God,
　　did not regard equality with God

something to be grasped.
Rather, he emptied himself,
taking the form of a slave,
coming in human likeness;
and found human in appearance,
he humbled himself,
becoming obedient to the point of death,
even death on a cross.
Because of this, God greatly exalted him
and bestowed on him the name
which is above every name,
that at the name of Jesus
every knee should bend,
of those in heaven and on earth and under
    the earth,
and every tongue confess that
Jesus Christ is Lord,
to the glory of God the Father.]
The word of the Lord. ℟. **Thanks be to God.** ↓

ALLELUIA Jn 10:27   [Listen]
℟. **Alleluia, alleluia.**
My sheep hear my voice, says the Lord;
I know them, and they follow me.
℟. **Alleluia, alleluia.** ↓

GOSPEL Mt 21:28-32   [Obeying God's Will]
**Jesus cites an example of a son who after having second
thoughts obeyed his father. Even sinners, once they repent
and sincerely search after God, will be saved.**

℣. The Lord be with you. ℟. **And also with you.**
✛ A reading from the holy Gospel according to
Matthew. ℟. **Glory to you, Lord.**

JESUS said to the chief priests and elders of the
people: "What is your opinion? A man had two
sons. He came to the first and said, 'Son, go out and

work in the vineyard today.' He said in reply, 'I will not,' but afterwards changed his mind and went. The man came to the other son and gave the same order. He said in reply, 'Yes, sir,' but did not go. Which of the two did his father's will?" They answered, "The first." Jesus said to them, "Amen, I say to you, tax collectors and prostitutes are entering the kingdom of God before you. When John came to you in the way of righteousness, you did not believe him; but tax collectors and prostitutes did. Yet even when you saw that, you did not later change your minds and believe him."—The Gospel of the Lord. ℟. **Praise to you, Lord Jesus Christ.**   ➔ No. 14, p. 18

PRAYER OVER THE GIFTS   [Offering as a Blessing]

God of mercy,
accept our offering
and make it a source of blessing for us.
We ask this in the name of Jesus the Lord.
℟. **Amen.**   ➔ No. 21, p. 22 (Pref. P 29-36)

COMMUNION ANT. Ps 119:49-50   [Words of Hope]
O Lord, remember the words you spoke to me, your servant, which made me live in hope and consoled me when I was downcast. ↓

OR 1 Jn 3:16   [Offering of Self]
This is how we know what love is: Christ gave up his life for us; and we too must give up our lives for our brothers. ↓

PRAYER AFTER COMMUNION   [Union with Christ]
Lord,
may this eucharist
in which we proclaim the death of Christ
bring us salvation
and make us one with him in glory,

for he is Lord for ever and ever.
℟. **Amen.**   ➔ No. 32, p. 70

Optional Solemn Blessings, p. 92, and Prayers Over the People, p. 99

*"The stone that the builders rejected
has become the cornerstone."*

OCTOBER 2

27th SUNDAY IN ORDINARY TIME

ENTRANCE ANT. Est 13:9, 10-11   [Lord of All]
**O Lord, you have given everything its place in the
world, and no one can make it otherwise. For it is
your creation, the heavens and the earth and the
stars: you are the Lord of all.**   ➔ No. 2, p. 10

OPENING PRAYER   [Peace and Salvation]

Let us pray
   [that God will forgive our failings
   and bring us peace]
Father,
your love for us
surpasses all our hopes and desires.
Forgive our failings,
keep us in your peace

and lead us in the way of salvation.
We ask this through our Lord Jesus Christ, your Son,
who lives and reigns with you and the Holy Spirit,
one God, for ever and ever. ℟. **Amen.** ↓

ALTERNATIVE OPENING PRAYER   [Christian Courage]

Let us pray
  [before the face of God,
  in trusting faith]
Almighty and eternal God,
Father of the world to come,
your goodness is beyond what our spirit can touch
and your strength is more than the mind can bear.
Lead us to seek beyond our reach
and give us the courage to stand before your truth.
We ask this through Christ our Lord. ℟. **Amen.** ↓

FIRST READING Is 5:1-7   [The Lord's Vineyard]

Isaiah uses the story of a vineyard to show how the Lord
respects his people. The vineyard is well cultivated but it
does not produce. The vineyard of the Lord is the house of
Israel and the people of Judah his cherished plants.

A reading from the Book of the Prophet Isaiah

LET me now sing of my friend,
my friend's song concerning his vineyard.
My friend had a vineyard
    on a fertile hillside;
he spaded it, cleared it of stones,
    and planted the choicest vines;
within it he built a watchtower,
    and hewed out a wine press.
Then he looked for the crop of grapes,
    but what it yielded was wild grapes.

Now, inhabitants of Jerusalem and people of Judah,
    judge between me and my vineyard:
What more was there to do for my vineyard
    that I had not done?

Why, when I looked for the crop of grapes,
　　did it bring forth wild grapes?
Now, I will let you know
　　what I mean to do to my vineyard:
take away its hedge, give it to grazing,
　　break through its wall, let it be trampled!
Yes, I will make it a ruin:
　　it shall not be pruned or hoed,
　　but overgrown with thorns and briers;
I will command the clouds
　　not to send rain upon it.
The vineyard of the Lᴏʀᴅ of hosts is the house of
　　Israel,
　　and the people of Judah are his cherished plant;
he looked for judgment, but see, bloodshed!
　　for justice, but hark, the outcry!
The word of the Lord. ℟. **Thanks be to God.** ↓

RESPONSORIAL PSALM Ps 80　　　　[Safety in the Lord]

　　℟. **The vineyard of the　Lord　is　the house of　Is - ra - el.**

A vine from Egypt you transplanted;
　　you drove away the nations and planted it.
It put forth its foliage to the Sea,
　　its shoots as far as the River.

℟. **The vineyard of the Lord is the house of Israel.**

Why have you broken down its walls,
　　so that every passer-by plucks its fruit,
the boar from the forest lays it waste,
　　and the beasts of the field feed upon it?

℟. **The vineyard of the Lord is the house of Israel.**

Once again, O Lᴏʀᴅ of hosts,
　　look down from heaven, and see;

take care of this vine,
   and protect what your right hand has planted
   the son of man whom you yourself made strong.

℞. **The vineyard of the Lord is the house of Israel.**

Then we will no more withdraw from you;
   give us new life, and we will call upon your name.
O LORD of hosts, restore us;
   if your face shine upon us, then we shall be saved.

℞. **The vineyard of the Lord is the house of Israel.** ↓

SECOND READING Phil 4:6-9   [Wholesome Thoughts]

Pray to God for your needs. God will guard over you. Discern what is true, noble, and good and pure, loved and honored, virtuous or worthy of praise. God's peace will be with you.

A reading from the Letter of Saint Paul
to the Philippians

B ROTHERS and sisters: Have no anxiety at all, but in everything, by prayer and petition, with thanksgiving, make your requests known to God. Then the peace of God that surpasses all understanding will guard your hearts and minds in Christ Jesus.

Finally, brothers and sisters, whatever is true, whatever is honorable, whatever is just, whatever is pure, whatever is lovely, whatever is gracious, if there is any excellence and if there is anything worthy of praise, think about these things. Keep on doing what you have learned and received and heard and seen in me. Then the God of peace will be with you.—The word of the Lord. ℞. **Thanks be to God.** ↓

ALLELUIA Cf. Jn 15:16   [Bear Fruit]

℞. **Alleluia, alleluia.**
I have chosen you from the world, says the Lord,
to go and bear fruit that will remain.
℞. **Alleluia, alleluia.** ↓

GOSPEL Mt 21:33-43   [The Tenant Farmers]

Jesus uses the parable of a vineyard owner. Salvation is offered to all. The chosen who reject Christ are really turning him over to the whole world. The vineyard will be leased to others. The kingdom of God will produce fruit.

℣. The Lord be with you. ℟. **And also with you.**
✝ A reading from the holy Gospel according to Matthew. ℟. **Glory to you, Lord.**

JESUS said to the chief priests and the elders of the people:"Hear another parable.There was a landowner who planted a vineyard, put a hedge around it, dug a wine press in it, and built a tower. Then he leased it to tenants and went on a journey.When vintage time drew near, he sent his servants to the tenants to obtain his produce. But the tenants seized the servants and one they beat, another they killed, and a third they stoned. Again he sent other servants, more numerous than the first ones, but they treated them in the same way. Finally, he sent his son to them, thinking, 'They will respect my son.' But when the tenants saw the son, they said to one another, 'This is the heir. Come, let us kill him and acquire his inheritance.' They seized him, threw him out of the vineyard, and killed him. What will the owner of the vineyard do to those tenants when he comes?" They answered him, "He will put those wretched men to a wretched death and lease his vineyard to other tenants who will give him the produce at the proper times." Jesus said to them, "Did you never read in the Scriptures:

The stone that the builders rejected
has become the cornerstone;
by the Lord has this been done,
and it is wonderful in our eyes?

Therefore, I say to you, the kingdom of God will be taken away from you and given to a people that will produce its fruit."—The Gospel of the Lord. ℞. **Praise to you, Lord Jesus Christ.**   ➜ No. 14, p. 18

PRAYER OVER THE GIFTS   [Fullness of Redemption]

Father,
receive these gifts
which our Lord Jesus Christ
has asked us to offer in his memory.
May our obedient service
bring us to the fullness of your redemption.
We ask this in the name of Jesus the Lord.
℞. **Amen.**   ➜ No. 21, p. 22 (Pref. P 29-36)

COMMUNION ANT. Lam 3:25   [Hope in the Lord]

The Lord is good to those who hope in him, to those who are searching for his love. ↓

OR See 1 Cor 10:17   [One Bread, One Body]

Because there is one bread, we, though many, are one body, for we all share in the one loaf and in the one cup. ↓

PRAYER AFTER COMMUNION   [Eucharistic Life]

Almighty God,
let the eucharist we share
fill us with your life.
May the love of Christ
which we celebrate here
touch our lives and lead us to you.
We ask this in the name of Jesus the Lord.
℞. **Amen.**   ➜ No. 32, p. 70

Optional Solemn Blessings, p. 92, and Prayers Over the People, p. 99

"Many are invited, but few are chosen."

OCTOBER 9

28th SUNDAY IN ORDINARY TIME

ENTRANCE ANT. Ps 130:3-4   **[Forgiving God]**
If you, O Lord, laid bare our guilt, who could endure it? But you are forgiving, God of Israel. → No. 2, p. 10

OPENING PRAYER   **[Love in Action]**
Let us pray
  [that God will help us to love one another]
Lord,
our help and guide,
make your love the foundation of our lives.
May our love for you express itself
in our eagerness to do good for others.
Grant this . . . for ever and ever. ℞. **Amen.** ↓

ALTERNATIVE OPENING PRAYER   **[Sincerity]**
Let us pray
  [in quiet for the grace of sincerity]
Father in heaven,
the hand of your loving kindness
powerfully yet gently guides all the moments of our day.
Go before us in our pilgrimage of life,

anticipate our needs and prevent our falling.
Send your Spirit to unite us in faith,
that sharing in your service,
we may rejoice in your presence.
We ask this through Christ our Lord. ℟. **Amen.** ↓

FIRST READING Is 25:6-10a   [God as Savior]

> The Lord will set up a sumptuous feast for his people. He will wipe away their tears. Then the people will recognize him as their Lord and God.

A reading from the Book of the Prophet Isaiah

O N this mountain the LORD of hosts
will provide for all peoples
a feast of rich food and choice wines,
    juicy, rich food and pure, choice wines.
On this mountain he will destroy
    the veil that veils all peoples,
the web that is woven over all nations;
    he will destroy death forever.
The Lord GOD will wipe away
    the tears from every face;
the reproach of his people he will remove
    from the whole earth; for the LORD has spoken.

    On that day it will be said:
"Behold our God, to whom we looked to save us!
    This is the LORD for whom we looked;
    let us rejoice and be glad that he has saved us!"
For the hand of the LORD will rest on this mountain.
The word of the Lord. ℟. **Thanks be to God.** ↓

RESPONSORIAL PSALM Ps 23   [Dwelling with the Lord]

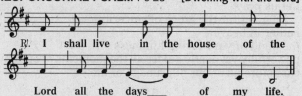

℟. I shall live in the house of the
Lord all the days___ of my life.

The LORD is my shepherd; I shall not want.
  In verdant pastures he gives me repose;
beside restful waters he leads me;
  he refreshes my soul.

℞. **I shall live in the house of the Lord
  all the days of my life.**

He guides me in right paths
  for his name's sake.
Even though I walk in the dark valley
  I fear no evil; for you are at my side
with your rod and your staff
  that give me courage.

℞. **I shall live in the house of the Lord
  all the days of my life.**

You spread the table before me
  in the sight of my foes;
you anoint my head with oil;
  my cup overflows.

℞. **I shall live in the house of the Lord
  all the days of my life.**

Only goodness and kindness follow me
  all the days of my life;
and I shall dwell in the house of the LORD
  for years to come.

℞. **I shall live in the house of the Lord
  all the days of my life.** ↓

SECOND READING Phil 4:12-14, 19-20 [Sharing in Hardships]

**Paul admits that he has learned how to live and accept joy
and sorrows, pleasures and pain. This lesson he has
learned in Jesus.**

A reading from the Letter of Saint Paul
to the Philippians

BROTHERS and sisters: I know how to live in humble circumstances; I know also how to live with

abundance. In every circumstance and in all things I have learned the secret of being well fed and of going hungry, of living in abundance and of being in need. I can do all things in him who strengthens me. Still, it was kind of you to share in my distress. My God will fully supply whatever you need, in accord with his glorious riches in Christ Jesus. To our God and Father, glory forever and ever. Amen.—The word of the Lord. ℟. **Thanks be to God.** ↓

ALLELUIA Cf. Eph 1:17-18   [Hope]

℟. **Alleluia, alleluia.**
May the Father of our Lord Jesus Christ
enlighten the eyes of our hearts,
so that we may know what is the hope
that belongs to our call.
℟. **Alleluia, alleluia.** ↓

GOSPEL Mt 22:1-14 or 22:1-10   [The Wedding Banquet]

Jesus teaches using the parable of a king who gave a wedding banquet. The guests making excuses refused to come to the feast. The king destroyed these and invited the poor and simple. Even one of these did not accept his kindness.

[If the "Shorter Form" is used, the indented text in brackets is omitted.]

℣. The Lord be with you. ℟. **And also with you.**
✛ A reading from the holy Gospel according to Matthew. ℟. **Glory to you, Lord.**

JESUS again in reply spoke to the chief priests and elders of the people in parables, saying, "The kingdom of heaven may be likened to a king who gave a wedding feast for his son. He dispatched his servants to summon the invited guests to the feast, but they refused to come. A second time he sent other servants, saying, 'Tell those invited: "Behold, I have prepared my banquet, my calves and fattened cattle are killed, and everything is ready; come to the feast." ' Some ignored the invitation and went away, one to his farm, another to his business. The rest laid hold of his servants, mistreated them, and killed them. The king was enraged and sent his troops, destroyed those murderers, and burned their city. Then he said to his servants, 'The feast is ready, but those who were invited were not worthy to come. Go out, therefore, into the main roads and invite to the feast whomever you find.' The servants went out into the streets and gathered all they found, bad and good alike, and the hall was filled with guests.

[But when the king came in to meet the guests, he saw a man there not dressed in a wedding garment. The king said to him, 'My friend, how is it that you came in here without a wedding garment?' But he was reduced to silence. Then the king said to his attendants, 'Bind his hands and feet, and cast him into the darkness outside, where there will be wailing and grinding of teeth.' Many are invited, but few are chosen.]"

The Gospel of the Lord. ℟. **Praise to you, Lord Jesus Christ.**   ➜ No. 14, p. 18

PRAYER OVER THE GIFTS   [Faith and Love]

Lord,
accept the prayers and gifts
we offer in faith and love.
May this eucharist bring us to your glory.
We ask this in the name of Jesus the Lord.
℟. **Amen.**   ➜ No. 21, p. 22 (Pref. P 29-36)

COMMUNION ANT. Ps 34:11   [God's Providence]
The rich suffer want and go hungry, but nothing shall be lacking to those who fear the Lord. ↓

OR 1 Jn 3:2   [Vision of God]
When the Lord is revealed we shall be like him, for we shall see him as he is. ↓

PRAYER AFTER COMMUNION　　　[Christ's Life]

Almighty Father,
may the body and blood of your Son
give us a share in his life,
for he is Lord for ever and ever.
℟. **Amen.**　　　　　　　　→ No. 32, p. 70

Optional Solemn Blessings, p. 92, and Prayers Over the People, p. 99

*"Repay to Caesar what belongs to Caesar and to God
what belongs to God."*

OCTOBER 16

29th SUNDAY IN ORDINARY TIME

ENTRANCE ANT. Ps 17:6, 8　　　[Refuge in God]
**I call upon you, God, for you will answer me; bend
your ear and hear my prayer. Guard me as the pupil
of your eye; hide me in the shade of your wings.**

→ No. 2, p. 10

OPENING PRAYER　　　[Faithful Service]

Let us pray
　[for the gift of simplicity and joy
　in our service of God and man]
Almighty and ever-living God,
our source of power and inspiration,

give us strength and joy
in serving you as followers of Christ,
who lives and reigns with you and the Holy Spirit,
one God, for ever and ever. ℟. **Amen.** ↓

ALTERNATIVE OPENING PRAYER   [Spiritual Sight]

Let us pray
  [to the Lord who bends close to hear our prayer]
Lord our God, Father of all,
you guard us under the shadow of your wings
and search into the depths of our hearts.
Remove the blindness that cannot know you
and relieve the fear that would hide us from your sight.
We ask this through Christ our Lord. ℟. **Amen.** ↓

FIRST READING Is 45:1, 4-6   [One God]

**For the sake of the Israelites, the Lord calls Cyrus. He gives
him a title. It is the Lord who arms him, and through him
all people will know that there is only one Lord.**

A reading from the Book of the Prophet Isaiah

THUS says the LORD to his anointed, Cyrus,
  whose right hand I grasp,
subduing nations before him,
    and making kings run in his service,
opening doors before him
    and leaving the gates unbarred:
For the sake of Jacob, my servant,
    of Israel, my chosen one,
I have called you by your name,
    giving you a title, though you knew me not.
I am the LORD and there is no other,
    there is no God besides me.
It is I who arm you, though you know me not,
    so that toward the rising and the setting of the sun
    people may know that there is none besides me.
I am the LORD, there is no other.
The word of the Lord. ℟. **Thanks be to God.** ↓

RESPONSORIAL PSALM Ps 96   [The Lord Is King]

℟. Give   the   Lord   glo - ry and hon - or.

Sing to the LORD a new song;
  sing to the LORD, all you lands.
Tell his glory among the nations;
  among all peoples, his wondrous deeds.

℟. **Give the Lord glory and honor.**

For great is the LORD and highly to be praised;
  awesome is he, beyond all gods.
For all the gods of the nations are things of nought,
  but the LORD made the heavens.

℟. **Give the Lord glory and honor.**

Give to the LORD, you families of nations,
  give to the LORD glory and praise;
  give to the LORD the glory due his name!
Bring gifts, and enter his courts.

℟. **Give the Lord glory and honor.**

Worship the LORD, in holy attire;
  tremble before him, all the earth;
say among the nations: The LORD is king,
  he governs the peoples with equity.

℟. **Give the Lord glory and honor.** ↓

SECOND READING 1 Thes 1:1-5b   [Preaching the Gospel]

**Paul writes to the Thessalonians encouraging them. He
prays for them constantly as they prove their faith through
works of love, for God has chosen them.**

A reading from the first Letter of Saint Paul
to the Thessalonians

PAUL, Silvanus and Timothy to the church of the
Thessalonians in God the Father and the Lord

Jesus Christ: grace to you and peace. We give thanks to God always for all of you, remembering you in our prayers, unceasingly calling to mind your work of faith and labor of love and endurance in hope of our Lord Jesus Christ, before our God and Father, knowing, brothers and sisters loved by God, how you were chosen. For our gospel did not come to you in word alone, but also in power and in the Holy Spirit and with much conviction.—The word of the Lord. ℟. **Thanks be to God.** ↓

ALLELUIA Phil 2:15d, 16a   [Word of Life]

℟. **Alleluia, alleluia.**
Shine like lights in the world
as you hold on to the word of life.
℟. **Alleluia, alleluia.** ↓

GOSPEL Mt 22:15-21   [Lawful Taxes]

The Pharisees try to confound Jesus. They ask about a possible conflict of giving tribute to Caesar and God. Jesus asks for a coin which has Caesar's inscription. Jesus answers by saying: Give to Caesar his due and to God his due.

℣. The Lord be with you. ℟. **And also with you.**
✝ A reading from the holy Gospel according to Matthew. ℟. **Glory to you, Lord**.

THE Pharisees went off and plotted how they might entrap Jesus in speech. They sent their disciples to him, with the Herodians, saying, "Teacher, we know that you are a truthful man and that you teach the way of God in accordance with the truth. And you are not concerned with anyone's opinion, for you do not regard a person's status. Tell us, then, what is your opinion: Is it lawful to pay the census tax to Caesar or not?" Knowing their malice, Jesus said, "Why are you testing me, you hypocrites? Show me the coin that pays the census tax."Then they handed him the Roman coin. He said to them, "Whose image is this and whose inscription?" They replied, "Caesar's." At that he said to them, "Then repay to Caesar what belongs to Caesar and to God what belongs to God."—The Gospel of the Lord. ℟. **Praise to you, Lord Jesus Christ.**   ➜ No. 14, p. 18

PRAYER OVER THE GIFTS   [Lives of Service]

Lord God,
may the gifts we offer
bring us your love and forgiveness
and give us freedom to serve you with our lives.
We ask this in the name of Jesus the Lord.
℟. **Amen.**   ➜ No. 21, p. 22 (Pref. P 29-36)

COMMUNION ANT. Ps 33:18-19   [Divine Protection]

See how the eyes of the Lord are on those who fear him, on those who hope in his love, that he may rescue them from death and feed them in time of famine. ↓

OR Mk 10:45   [Christ Our Ransom]

The Son of Man came to give his life as a ransom for many. ↓

PRAYER AFTER COMMUNION   [Fidelity]

Lord,
may this eucharist help us to remain faithful.
May it teach us the way to eternal life.
Grant this through Christ our Lord.
℟. **Amen.**   ➜ No. 32, p. 70

Optional Solemn Blessings, p. 92, and Prayers Over the People, p. 99

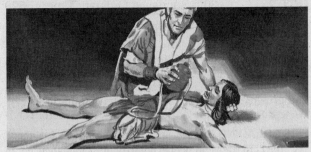

"You shall love your neighbor as yourself."

OCTOBER 23

30th SUNDAY IN ORDINARY TIME

ENTRANCE ANT. Ps 105:3-4   [Seek the Lord]

Let hearts rejoice who search for the Lord. Seek the Lord and his strength, seek always the face of the Lord. ➜ No. 2, p. 10

OPENING PRAYER   [Doing God's Will]

Let us pray
   [for the strength to do God's will]
Almighty and ever-living God,
strengthen our faith, hope, and love.
May we do with loving hearts
what you ask of us
and come to share the life you promise.
We ask this through our Lord Jesus Christ, your Son,
who lives and reigns with you and the Holy Spirit,
one God, for ever and ever. ℞. **Amen.** ↓

ALTERNATIVE OPENING PRAYER   [Faith and Love]

Let us pray
   [in humble hope for salvation]
Praised be you, God and Father of our Lord Jesus
   Christ.

There is no power for good
which does not come from your covenant,
and no promise to hope in
that your love has not offered.
Strengthen our faith to accept your covenant
and give us the love to carry out your command.
We ask this through Christ our Lord. ℟. **Amen.** ↓

FIRST READING Ex 22:20-26   [Kindness to Others]

The Lord warns his people not to oppress foreigners nor to harm widows or orphans. Consideration for the poor and needy should be a prime concern.

A reading from the Book of Exodus

THUS says the Lord: "You shall not molest or oppress an alien, for you were once aliens yourselves in the land of Egypt. You shall not wrong any widow or orphan. If ever you wrong them and they cry out to me, I will surely hear their cry. My wrath will flare up, and I will kill you with the sword; then your own wives will be widows, and your children orphans.

"If you lend money to one of your poor neighbors among my people, you shall not act like an extortioner toward him by demanding interest from him. If you take your neighbor's cloak as a pledge, you shall return it to him before sunset; for this cloak of his is the only covering he has for his body. What else has he to sleep in? If he cries out to me, I will hear him; for I am compassionate."—The word of the Lord. ℟.
Thanks be to God. ↓

RESPONSORIAL PSALM Ps 18   [God Our Rock]

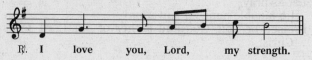

℟. I love you, Lord, my strength.

I love you, O LORD, my strength,
   O LORD, my rock, my fortress, my deliverer.

℟. **I love you, Lord, my strength.**

My God, my rock of refuge,
   my shield, the horn of my salvation, my stronghold!
Praised be the LORD, I exclaim,
   and I am safe from my enemies.

℟. **I love you, Lord, my strength.**

The LORD lives and blessed be my rock!
   Extolled be God my savior,
you who gave great victories to your king
   and showed kindness to your anointed.

℟. **I love you, Lord, my strength.** ↓

SECOND READING 1 Thes 1:5c-10   **[Imitating Christ]**
   You received the word of the Lord in spite of great hardships. You then became model Christians for your neighbors. You turned from idols to worship the true God.

A reading from the first Letter of Saint Paul
to the Thessalonians

BROTHERS and sisters: You know what sort of people we were among you for your sake. And you became imitators of us and of the Lord, receiving the word in great affliction, with joy from the Holy Spirit, so that you became a model for all the believers in Macedonia and in Achaia. For from you the word of the Lord has sounded forth not only in Macedonia and in Achaia, but in every place your faith in God has gone forth, so that we have no need to say anything. For they themselves openly declare about us what sort of reception we had among you, and how you turned to God from idols to serve the living and true God and to await his Son from heaven, whom he raised from the dead, Jesus, who delivers us from the coming wrath.—The word of the Lord. ℟. **Thanks be to God.** ↓

ALLELUIA Jn 14:23   [Keep My Word]

℟. **Alleluia, alleluia.**
Whoever loves me will keep my word,
and my Father will love him and we will come to him.
℟. **Alleluia, alleluia.** ↓

GOSPEL Mt 22:34-40   [The Greatest Commandments]
Jesus tells the scholar of the law that the greatest of all the
commandments is love—to love God above all else and
your neighbor as yourself. This sums up the whole law.

℣. The Lord be with you. ℟. **And also with you.**
✝ A reading from the holy Gospel according to
Matthew. ℟. **Glory to you, Lord.**

WHEN the Pharisees heard that Jesus had
silenced the Sadducees, they gathered together,
and one of them, a scholar of the law tested him by
asking, "Teacher, which commandment in the law is
the greatest?" He said to him,
    "You shall love the Lord, your God,
    with all your heart,
    with all your soul,
    and with all your mind.
This is the greatest and the first commandment. The
second is like it:
    You shall love your neighbor as yourself.
The whole law and the prophets depend on these two
commandments."—The Gospel of the Lord. ℟. **Praise
to you, Lord Jesus Christ.**   → No. 14, p. 18

PRAYER OVER THE GIFTS   [Glorifying God]

Lord God of power and might,
receive the gifts we offer
and let our service give you glory.
Grant this through Christ our Lord.
℟. **Amen.**   → No. 21, p. 22 (Pref. P 29-36)

COMMUNION ANT. Ps 20:6   [Victory of God]
We will rejoice at the victory of God and make our
boast in his great name. ↓

OR Eph 5:2   [Christ's Offering for Us]
Christ loved us and gave himself up for us as a fra-
grant offering to God. ↓

PRAYER AFTER COMMUNION   [Effective Communion]
Lord,
bring to perfection within us
the communion we share in this sacrament.
May our celebration have an effect in our lives.
We ask this in the name of Jesus the Lord.
℟. **Amen.**   → No. 32, p. 70

Optional Solemn Blessings, p. 92, and Prayers Over the People, p. 99

*"Whoever exalts himself will be humbled; but whoever
humbles himself will be exalted."*

OCTOBER 30

31st SUNDAY IN ORDINARY TIME

ENTRANCE ANT. Ps 38:22-23   [Call for God's Help]
Do not abandon me, Lord. My God, do not go away from
me! Hurry to help me, Lord my Savior.   → No. 2, p. 10

OPENING PRAYER [Living the Faith]

Let us pray
  [that our lives will reflect our faith]
God of power and mercy,
only with your help
can we offer you fitting service and praise.
May we live the faith we profess
and trust your promise of eternal life.
Grant this through our Lord Jesus Christ, your Son,
who lives and reigns with you and the Holy Spirit,
one God, for ever and ever. ℟. **Amen.** ↓

ALTERNATIVE OPENING PRAYER
[Eliminating Selfishness]

Let us pray
  [in the presence of God, the source of every good]
Father in heaven, God of power and Lord of mercy,
from whose fullness we have received,
direct our steps in our everyday efforts.
May the changing moods of the human heart
and the limits which our failings impose on hope
never blind us to you, source of every good.
Faith gives us the promise of peace
and makes known the demands of love.
Remove the selfishness that blurs the vision of faith.
Grant this through Christ our Lord. ℟. **Amen.** ↓

FIRST READING Mal 1:14—2:2b, 8-10
[Violating the Covenant]

I have sent a curse upon you, says the Lord, since you have turned from me. You have not kept my ways. Only one God has created us. Why do we break faith with one another?

A reading from the Book of the Prophet Malachi

A GREAT King am I, says the LORD of hosts, and my name will be feared among the nations.

And now, O priests, this commandment is for you:
    If you do not listen,
if you do not lay it to heart,
    to give glory to my name, says the LORD of hosts,
I will send a curse upon you
    and of your blessing I will make a curse.
You have turned aside from the way,
    and have caused many to falter by your instruc-
        tion;
you have made void the covenant of Levi,
    says the LORD of hosts.
I, therefore, have made you contemptible
    and base before all the people,
since you do not keep my ways,
    but show partiality in your decisions.
Have we not all the one father?
    Has not the one God created us?
Why then do we break faith with one another,
    violating the covenant of our fathers?
The word of the Lord. ℟. **Thanks be to God.** ↓

RESPONSORIAL PSALM Ps 131   [Peace in the Lord]

℟. In you, Lord, I have found my   peace.

O LORD, my heart is not proud,
    nor are my eyes haughty;
I busy not myself with great things,
    nor with things too sublime for me.

℟. **In you, Lord, I have found my peace.**

Nay rather, I have stilled and quieted
    my soul like a weaned child.
Like a weaned child on its mother's lap,
    so is my soul within me.

℟. **In you, Lord, I have found my peace.**

O Israel, hope in the LORD,
  both now and forever.

℟. **In you, Lord, I have found my peace.** ↓

SECOND READING 1 Thes 2:7b-9, 13 [God's Good Tidings]

> Paul tells the Thessalonians how he wanted to share the teachings of Jesus with them as well as his own life. He works day and night for them. The word of God works in those who believe.

A reading from the first Letter of Saint Paul
to the Thessalonians

BROTHERS and sisters: We were gentle among you, as a nursing mother cares for her children. With such affection for you, we were determined to share with you not only the gospel of God, but our very selves as well, so dearly beloved had you become to us. You recall, brothers and sisters, our toil and drudgery. Working night and day in order not to burden any of you, we proclaimed to you the gospel of God.

And for this reason we too give thanks to God unceasingly, that, in receiving the word of God from hearing us, you received not a human word but, as it truly is, the word of God, which is now at work in you who believe.—The word of the Lord. ℟. **Thanks be to God.** ↓

ALLELUIA Mt 23:9b, 10b   [One Father]

℟. **Alleluia, alleluia.**
You have but one Father in heaven
and one master, the Christ.

℟. **Alleluia, alleluia.** ↓

GOSPEL Mt 23:1-12   [The Virtue of Humility]
> Jesus warns that the Pharisees speak many words boldy, admonishing others to observe the Law but themselves fail in deeds fulfilling the Law. They act only to be seen. Only the humble will be exalted.

℣. The Lord be with you. ℟. **And also with you.**
✛   A reading from the holy Gospel according to Matthew. ℟. **Glory to you, Lord**.

JESUS spoke to the crowds and to his disciples, saying, "The scribes and the Pharisees have taken their seat on the chair of Moses. Therefore, do and observe all things whatsoever they tell you, but do not follow their example. For they preach but they do not practice. They tie up heavy burdens hard to carry and lay them on people's shoulders, but they will not lift a finger to move them. All their works are performed to be seen. They widen their phylacteries and lengthen their tassels. They love places of honor at banquets, seats of honor in synagogues, greetings in marketplaces, and the salutation 'Rabbi.' As for you, do not be called 'Rabbi.' You have but one teacher, and you are all brothers. Call no one on earth your father; you have but one Father in heaven. Do not be called 'Master'; you have but one master, the Christ. The greatest among you must be your servant. Whoever exalts himself will be humbled; but whoever humbles himself will be exalted."—The Gospel of the Lord. ℟. **Praise to you, Lord Jesus Christ.**   → No. 14, p. 18

PRAYER OVER THE GIFTS   [Forgiveness]
God of mercy,
may we offer a pure sacrifice
for the forgiveness of our sins.
We ask this through Christ our Lord.
℟. **Amen.**   → No. 21, p. 22 (Pref. P 29-36)

COMMUNION ANT. Ps 16:11   [Joy]

Lord, you will show me the path of life and fill me with joy in your presence. ↓

OR Jn 6:58   [Life]

As the living Father sent me, and I live because of the Father, so he who eats my flesh and drinks my blood will live because of me. ↓

PRAYER AFTER COMMUNION   [Hope]

Lord,
you give us new hope in this eucharist.
May the power of your love
continue its saving work among us
and bring us to the joy you promise.
We ask this in the name of Jesus the Lord.
℟. **Amen.**   → No. 32, p. 70

Optional Solemn Blessings, p. 92, and Prayers Over the People, p. 99

"Blessed are the clean of heart, for they will see God."

NOVEMBER 1

ALL SAINTS

ENTRANCE ANT. [Honoring All the Saints]

Let us all rejoice in the Lord and keep a festival in honor of all the saints. Let us join with the angels in joyful praise to the Son of God. → No. 2, p. 10

OPENING PRAYER [Forgiveness and Love]

Let us pray
  [that the prayers of all the saints
  will bring us forgiveness for our sins]
Father, all-powerful and ever-living God,
today we rejoice in the holy men and women
of every time and place.
May their prayers bring us your forgiveness and love.
We ask this through our Lord Jesus Christ, your Son,
who lives and reigns with you and the Holy Spirit,
one God, for ever and ever. ℟. **Amen.** ↓

ALTERNATIVE OPENING PRAYER [Sharing Saints' Peace]

Let us pray
  [as we rejoice and keep festival
  in honor of all the saints]

God our Father,
source of all holiness,
the work of your hands is manifest in your saints,
the beauty of your truth is reflected in their faith.
May we who aspire to have part in their joy
be filled with the Spirit that blessed their lives,
so that having shared their faith on earth
we may also know their peace in your kingdom.
Grant this through Christ our Lord. ℟. **Amen.** ↓

FIRST READING Rv 7:2-4, 9-14   [A Huge Crowd of Saints]
The elect give thanks to God and the Lamb who saved
them. The whole court of heaven joins the acclamation of
the saints.

A reading from the Book of Revelation

I, JOHN, saw another angel come up from the East,
holding the seal of the living God. He cried out in a
loud voice to the four angels who were given power
to damage the land and the sea, "Do not damage the
land or the sea or the trees until we put the seal on the
foreheads of the servants of our God." I heard the
number of those who had been marked with the seal,
one hundred and forty-four thousand marked from
every tribe of the Israelites.

After this I had a vision of a great multitude, which
no one could count, from every nation, race, people,
and tongue. They stood before the throne and before
the Lamb, wearing white robes and holding palm
branches in their hands. They cried out in a loud
voice:

"Salvation comes from our God,
    who is seated on the throne,
and from the Lamb."

All the angels stood around the throne and around
the elders and the four living creatures. They prostrated themselves before the throne, worshiped God, and
exclaimed:

"Amen. Blessing and glory, wisdom and thanksgiving,
honor, power, and might
be to our God forever and ever. Amen."
Then one of the elders spoke up and said to me, "Who
are these wearing white robes, and where did they
come from?" I said to him, "My lord, you are the one
who knows." He said to me, "These are the ones who
have survived the time of great distress; they have
washed their robes and made them white in the blood
of the Lamb."—The word of the Lord. ℟. **Thanks be to
God.** ↓

RESPONSORIAL PSALM Ps 24   [Longing to See God]

℟. Lord, this is the peo - ple that longs to see your face.

The LORD's are the earth and its fullness;
the world and those who dwell in it.
For he founded it upon the seas
and established it upon the rivers.

℟. **Lord, this is the people that longs to see your face.**

Who can ascend the mountain of the LORD?
or who may stand in his holy place?
He whose hands are sinless, whose heart is clean,
who desires not what is vain.

℟. **Lord, this is the people that longs to see your face.**

He shall receive a blessing from the LORD,
a reward from God his Savior.
Such is the race that seeks for him,
that seeks the face of the God of Jacob.

℟. **Lord, this is the people that longs to see your face.** ↓

SECOND READING 1 Jn 3:1-3   [We Shall See God]

God's gift of love has been the gift of His only Son as
Savior of the world. It is this gift that has made it possible
for us to be called the children of God.

A reading from the first Letter of Saint John

BELOVED: See what love the Father has bestowed
on us that we may be called the children of God. Yet
so we are. The reason the world does not know us is
that it did not know him. Beloved, we are God's children now; what we shall be has not yet been revealed.
We do know that when it is revealed we shall be like
him, for we shall see him as he is. Everyone who has
this hope based on him makes himself pure, as he is
pure.—The word of the Lord. ℟. **Thanks be to God.** ↓

ALLELUIA Mt 11:28   [Rest in the Lord]

℟. **Alleluia, alleluia.**
Come to me, all you that labor and are burdened,
and I will give you rest, says the Lord.
℟. **Alleluia, alleluia.** ↓

GOSPEL Mt 5:1-12a   [The Beatitudes]

Jesus is meant to be the new Moses proclaiming the new
revelation on a new Mount Sinai. This is the proclamation of
the reign, or the "Good News." Blessings are pronounced
on those who do not share the values of the world.

℣. The Lord be with you. ℟. **And also with you.**
✝   A reading from the holy Gospel according to
Matthew. ℟. **Glory to you, Lord.**

WHEN Jesus saw the crowds, he went up the
mountain, and after he had sat down, his disciples came to him. He began to teach them, saying:
   "Blessed are the poor in spirit,
      for theirs is the kingdom of heaven.
   Blessed are they who mourn,
      for they will be comforted.

Blessed are the meek,
　　for they will inherit the land.
Blessed are they who hunger and thirst for righ-
　　　teousness,
　　for they will be satisfied.
Blessed are the merciful,
　　for they will be shown mercy.
Blessed are the clean of heart,
　　for they will see God.
Blessed are the peacemakers,
　　for they will be called children of God.
Blessed are they who are persecuted for the sake
　　　of righteousness,
　　for theirs is the kingdom of heaven.
Blessed are you when they insult you and perse-
　　　cute you
　　and utter every kind of evil against you falsely
　　　because of me.
Rejoice and be glad,
　　for your reward will be great in heaven."

The Gospel of the Lord. ℟. **Praise to you, Lord Jesus
Christ.**
➥ No. 14, p. 18

PRAYER OVER THE GIFTS   [The Saints' Concern for Us]

Lord,
receive our gifts in honor of the holy men and women
who live with you in glory.
May we always be aware
of their concern to help and save us.
We ask this in the name of Jesus the Lord. ↓

PREFACE (P 71)   [Saints Give Us Help and Encouragement]

℣. The Lord be with you. ℟. **And also with you.**
℣. Lift up your hearts. ℟. **We lift them up to the Lord.** ℣.
Let us give thanks to the Lord our God. ℟. **It is right to
give him thanks and praise.**

Father, all-powerful and ever-living God,
we do well always and everywhere to give you thanks.
Today we keep the festival of your holy city,
the heavenly Jerusalem, our mother.
Around your throne
the saints, our brothers and sisters,
sing your praise for ever.
Their glory fills us with joy,
and their communion with us in your Church
gives us inspiration and strength,
as we hasten on our pilgrimage of faith,
eager to meet them.
With their great company and all the angels
we praise your glory
as we cry out with one voice:　　　→ No. 23, p. 23

COMMUNION ANT. Mt 5:8-10　[The Saints: Children of God]

**Happy are the pure of heart for they shall see God.
Happy the peacemakers; they shall be called sons of
God. Happy are they who suffer persecution for jus-
tice' sake; the kingdom of heaven is theirs.** ↓

PRAYER AFTER COMMUNION　[Reflectors of God's Glory]

Father, holy one,
we praise your glory reflected in the saints.
May we who share at this table
be filled with your love
and prepared for the joy of your kingdom,
where Jesus is Lord for ever and ever.
℟. **Amen.**　　　　　　　　　　→ No. 32, p. 70

Optional Solemn Blessings, p. 92, and Prayers Over the People, p. 99

"The bridegroom came and [the bridesmaids] who were ready went into the wedding feast with him."

NOVEMBER 6

32nd SUNDAY IN ORDINARY TIME

ENTRANCE ANT. Ps 88:3   [Answer to Prayer]

Let my prayer come before you, Lord; listen, and answer me. ➔ No. 2, p. 10

OPENING PRAYER   [Health of Mind and Body]

Let us pray
  [for health of mind and body]
God of power and mercy,
protect us from all harm.
Give us freedom of spirit
and health in mind and body
to do your work on earth.
We ask this through our Lord Jesus Christ, your Son,
who lives and reigns with you and the Holy Spirit,
one God, for ever and ever. ℟. **Amen.** ↓

ALTERNATIVE OPENING PRAYER   [Aware of God's Plan]

Let us pray
  [that our prayer rise like incense
  in the presence of the Lord]

Almighty Father,
strong is your justice and great is your mercy.
Protect us in the burdens and challenges of life.
Shield our minds from the distortion of pride
and enfold our desire with the beauty of truth.
Help us to become more aware of your loving design
so that we may more willingly give our lives in service to all.
We ask this through Christ our Lord. ℟. **Amen.** ↓

FIRST READING Wis 6:12-16   [Love of Wisdom]

   **Wisdom is found by those who seek after it. Those who
   watch for wisdom shall find it. Wisdom graciously appears.**

   A reading from the Book of Wisdom

R ESPLENDENT and unfading is wisdom,
   and she is readily perceived by those who love her,
   and found by those who seek her.
She hastens to make herself known in anticipation of
      their desire;
   whoever watches for her at dawn shall not be
      disappointed,
   for he shall find her sitting by his gate.
For taking thought of wisdom is the perfection of
      prudence,
   and whoever for her sake keeps vigil shall quickly
      be free from care;
because she makes her own rounds, seeking those
      worthy of her,
   and graciously appears to them in the ways,
   and meets them with all solicitude.
The word of the Lord. ℟. **Thanks be to God.** ↓

RESPONSORIAL PSALM Ps 63   [Seeking the Lord]

℟. My soul is thirsting for you, O Lord my God.

O God, you are my God whom I seek;
　　for you my flesh pines and my soul thirsts
　　like the earth, parched, lifeless and without water.

℟. **My soul is thirsting for you, O Lord my God.**

Thus have I gazed toward you in the sanctuary
　　to see your power and your glory,
for your kindness is a greater good than life;
　　my lips shall glorify you.

℟. **My soul is thirsting for you, O Lord my God.**

Thus will I bless you while I live;
　　lifting up my hands, I will call upon your name.
As with the riches of a banquet shall my soul be sat-
　　isfied,
　　and with exultant lips my mouth shall praise you.

℟. **My soul is thirsting for you, O Lord my God.**

I will remember you upon my couch,
　　and through the night-watches I will meditate on
　　　　you:
you are my help,
　　and in the shadow of your wings I shout for joy.

℟. **My soul is thirsting for you, O Lord my God.** ↓

SECOND READING 1 Thes 4:13-18 or 4:13-14
[Rising from the Dead]

Those who die believing in Jesus will rise with him. They will in the final judgment rise first to enjoy God's life with Jesus.

[If the "Shorter Form" is used, the indented text in brackets is omitted.]

A reading from the first Letter of Saint Paul
to the Thessalonians

W E do not want you to be unaware, brothers and
sisters, about those who have fallen asleep, so

that you may not grieve like the rest, who have no hope. For if we believe that Jesus died and rose, so too will God, through Jesus, bring with him those who have fallen asleep.

[Indeed, we tell you this, on the word of the Lord, that we who are alive, who are left until the coming of the Lord, will surely not precede those who have fallen asleep. For the Lord himself, with a word of command, with the voice of an archangel and with the trumpet of God, will come down from heaven, and the dead in Christ will rise first. Then we who are alive, who are left, will be caught up together with them in the clouds to meet the Lord in the air. Thus we shall always be with the Lord. Therefore, console one another with these words.]

—The word of the Lord. ℟. **Thanks be to God.** ↓

ALLELUIA Mt 24:42a, 44   [Be Ready]

℟. **Alleluia, alleluia.**

Stay awake and be ready!

For you do not know on what day your Lord will come.

℟. **Alleluia, alleluia.** ↓

GOSPEL Mt 25:1-13   [The Need for Watchfulness]

Jesus compares heaven to the five wise and five foolish bridesmaids waiting for the master. Only those who are ever watchful will be ready to meet him.

℣. The Lord be with you. ℟. **And also with you.**

✛ A reading from the holy Gospel according to Matthew. ℟. **Glory to you, Lord.**

JESUS told his disciples this parable: "The kingdom of heaven will be like ten virgins who took their lamps and went out to meet the bridegroom. Five of them were foolish and five were wise. The foolish ones, when taking their lamps, brought no oil with them, but the wise brought flasks of oil with their lamps. Since the bridegroom was long delayed, they all became drowsy and fell asleep. At midnight, there was a cry, 'Behold, the bridegroom! Come out to meet him!' Then all those virgins got up and trimmed their lamps. The foolish ones said to the wise, 'Give us some of your oil, for our lamps are going out.' But the wise ones replied, 'No, for there may not be enough for us and you. Go instead to the merchants and buy some for yourselves.' While they went off to buy it, the bridegroom came and those who were ready went into the wedding feast with him. Then the door was locked. Afterwards the other virgins came and said, 'Lord, Lord, open the door for us!' But he said in reply, 'Amen, I say to you, I do not know you.' Therefore, stay awake, for you know neither the day nor the hour."—The Gospel of the Lord. ℞. **Praise to you, Lord Jesus Christ.**   → No. 14, p. 18

PRAYER OVER THE GIFTS   [Following Christ]

God of mercy,
in this eucharist we proclaim the death of the Lord.
Accept the gifts we present
and help us follow him with love,
for he is Lord for ever and ever.
℞. **Amen.**   → No. 21, p. 22 (Pref. P 29-36)

COMMUNION ANT. Ps 23:1-2   [The Lord Our Shepherd]

The Lord is my shepherd; there is nothing I shall want. In green pastures he gives me rest, he leads me beside the waters of peace. ↓

OR Lk 24:35   [Jesus in the Eucharist]

The disciples recognized the Lord Jesus in the breaking of bread. ↓

PRAYER AFTER COMMUNION   [Serving God]
Lord,
we thank you for the nourishment you give us
through your holy gift.
Pour out your Spirit upon us
and in the strength of this food from heaven
keep us single-minded in your service.
We ask this in the name of Jesus the Lord.
R/. **Amen.**   ➜ No. 32, p. 70

Optional Solemn Blessings, p. 92, and Prayers Over the People, p. 99

"Master, you gave me five talents. See, I have made five more."

NOVEMBER 13
33rd SUNDAY IN ORDINARY TIME

ENTRANCE ANT. Jer 29:11, 12, 14   [God Hears Us]
**The Lord says: my plans for you are peace and not
disaster; when you call on me, I will listen to you, and
I will bring you back to the place from which I exiled
you.**   ➜ No. 2, p. 10

OPENING PRAYER   [Faithful Service]
Let us pray
   [that God will help us to be faithful]

Father of all that is good,
keep us faithful in serving you,
for to serve you is our lasting joy.
We ask this through our Lord Jesus Christ, your Son,
who lives and reigns with you and the Holy Spirit,
one God, for ever and ever. ℟. **Amen.** ↓

ALTERNATIVE OPENING PRAYER   [God's Truth]

Let us pray
   [with hearts that long for peace]
Father in heaven,
ever-living source of all that is good,
from the beginning of time you promised man salvation
through the future coming of your Son, our Lord
   Jesus Christ.
Help us to drink of his truth
and expand our hearts with the joy of his promises,
so that we may serve you in faith and in love
and know for ever the joy of your presence.
We ask this through Christ our Lord. ℟. **Amen.** ↓

FIRST READING Prv 31:10-13, 19-20, 30-31   [A Worthy Wife]

**A true wife is valued beyond all pearls. She brings good to
her husband. She works for the household. She helps the
poor. She fears the Lord. She deserves her reward.**

A reading from the Book of Proverbs

W HEN one finds a worthy wife,
      her value is far beyond pearls.
Her husband, entrusting his heart to her,
      has an unfailing prize.
She brings him good, and not evil,
      all the days of her life.
She obtains wool and flax
      and works with loving hands.
She puts her hands to the distaff,
      and her fingers ply the spindle.

She reaches out her hands to the poor,
  and extends her arms to the needy.
Charm is deceptive and beauty fleeting;
  the woman who fears the LORD is to be praised.
Give her a reward for her labors,
  and let her works praise her at the city gates.
The word of the Lord. ℟. **Thanks be to God.** ↓

RESPONSORIAL PSALM Ps 128   [Fear of the Lord]

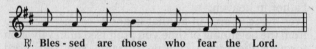

℟. Bles - sed are those who fear the Lord.

Blessed are you who fear the LORD,
  who walk in his ways!
For you shall eat the fruit of your handiwork;
  blessed shall you be, and favored.

℟. **Blessed are those who fear the Lord.**

Your wife shall be like a fruitful vine
  in the recesses of your home;
your children like olive plants
  around your table.

℟. **Blessed are those who fear the Lord.**

Behold, thus is the man blessed
  who fears the LORD.
The LORD bless you from Zion:
  may you see the prosperity of Jerusalem
  all the days of your life.

℟. **Blessed are those who fear the Lord.** ↓

SECOND READING 1 Thes 5:1-6   [The Day of the Lord]
  The day of the Lord will come like a thief in the night. It
  will be sudden. There will be no escape.

A reading from the first Letter of Saint Paul
to the Thessalonians

CONCERNING times and seasons, brothers and sisters, you have no need for anything to be written to you. For you yourselves know very well that the day of the Lord will come like a thief at night. When people are saying, "Peace and security," then sudden disaster comes upon them, like labor pains upon a pregnant woman, and they will not escape.

But you, brothers and sisters, are not in darkness, for that day to overtake you like a thief. For all of you are children of the light and children of the day. We are not of the night or of darkness. Therefore, let us not sleep as the rest do, but let us stay alert and sober.—The word of the Lord. ℟. **Thanks be to God.** ↓

ALLELUIA Jn 15:4a, 5b   [Live in Christ]

℟. **Alleluia, alleluia.**
Remain in me as I remain in you, says the Lord.
Whoever remains in me bears much fruit.
℟. **Alleluia, alleluia.** ↓

GOSPEL Mt 25:14-30 or 25:14-15, 19-21   [The Faithful Servant]

Jesus speaks of the master who is going on a journey. He entrusts his property to three servants. Upon his return the first two are rewarded for their work. But the third who did not increase his wealth is chastised and punished.

[If the "Shorter Form" is used, the indented text in brackets is omitted.]

℣. The Lord be with you. ℟. **And also with you.**
✣ A reading from the holy Gospel according to Matthew. ℟. **Glory to you, Lord.**

JESUS told his disciples this parable: "A man going on a journey called in his servants and entrusted his possessions to them. To one he gave five talents; to another, two; to a third, one—to each according to his ability. Then he went away.

[Immediately the one who received five talents went and traded with them, and made another five. Likewise, the one who received two made another two. But the man who received one went off and dug a hole in the ground and buried his master's money.]

After a long time the master of those servants came back and settled accounts with them. The one who had received five talents came forward bringing the additional five. He said, 'Master, you gave me five talents. See, I have made five more.' His master said to him, 'Well done, my good and faithful servant. Since you were faithful in small matters, I will give you great responsibilities. Come, share your master's joy.'

[Then the one who had received two talents also came forward and said, 'Master, you gave me two talents. See, I have made two more.' His master said to him, 'Well done, my good and faithful servant. Since you were faithful in small matters, I will give you great responsibilities. Come, share your master's joy.' Then the one who had received the one talent came forward and said, 'Master, I knew you were a demanding person, harvesting where you did not plant and gathering where you did not scatter; so out of fear I went off and buried your talent in the ground. Here it is back.' His master said to him in reply, 'You wicked, lazy servant! So you knew that I harvest where I did not plant and gather where I did not scatter? Should you not then have put my money in the bank so that I could have got it back with interest on my return? Now then! Take the talent from him and give it to the one with ten. For to every-

one who has, more will be given and he will grow
rich; but from the one who has not, even what he
has will be taken away. And throw this useless
servant into the darkness outside, where there
will be wailing and grinding of teeth.'] "

The Gospel of the Lord. ℟. **Praise to you, Lord Jesus
Christ.** → No. 14, p. 18

PRAYER OVER THE GIFTS [Eternal Life]

Lord God,
may the gifts we offer
increase our love for you
and bring us to eternal life.
We ask this in the name of Jesus the Lord.
℟. **Amen.** → No. 21, p. 22 (Pref. P 29-36)

COMMUNION ANT. Ps 73:28 [Hope in God]

**It is good for me to be with the Lord and to put my
hope in him.** ↓

OR Mk 11:23, 24 [Believing Prayer]

**I tell you solemnly, whatever you ask for in prayer,
believe that you have received it, and it will be yours,
says the Lord.** ↓

PRAYER AFTER COMMUNION [Growth in Love]

Father,
may we grow in love
by the eucharist we have celebrated
in memory of the Lord Jesus,
who is Lord for ever and ever.
℟. **Amen.** → No. 32, p. 70

Optional Solemn Blessings, p. 92, and Prayers Over the People, p. 99

"The Son of Man . . . will sit upon his glorious throne. . . ."

NOVEMBER 20

CHRIST THE KING

ENTRANCE ANT. Rv 5:12; 1:6   [Christ's Glory]
**The Lamb who was slain is worthy to receive
strength and divinity, wisdom and power and honor:
to him be glory and power for ever.**   ➡ No. 2, p. 10

OPENING PRAYER   [King of the Universe]
Let us pray
  [that all men will acclaim Jesus as Lord]
Almighty and merciful God,
you break the power of evil
and make all things new
in your Son Jesus Christ, the King of the universe.
May all in heaven and earth acclaim your glory
and never cease to praise you.
We ask this . . . for ever and ever. ℟. **Amen.** ↓

ALTERNATIVE OPENING PRAYER   [Spiritual Kingdom]
Let us pray
  [that the kingdom of Christ
  may live in our hearts and come to our world]

Father all-powerful, God of love,
you have raised our Lord Jesus Christ from death to life,
resplendent in glory as King of creation.
Open our hearts,
free all the world to rejoice in his peace,
to glory in his justice, to live in his love.
Bring all mankind together in Jesus Christ, your Son,
whose kingdom is with you and the Holy Spirit,
one God, for ever and ever. ℟. **Amen.** ↓

FIRST READING Ez 34:11-12, 15-17   [The Lord's Care]

The Lord looks after his own flock. He takes them to pasture and rescues them. He goes after those who are lost. He will also judge them.

A reading from the Book of the Prophet Ezekiel

THUS says the Lord GOD: I myself will look after and tend my sheep. As a shepherd tends his flock when he finds himself among his scattered sheep, so will I tend my sheep. I will rescue them from every place where they were scattered when it was cloudy and dark. I myself will pasture my sheep; I myself will give them rest, says the Lord GOD. The lost I will seek out, the strayed I will bring back, the injured I will bind up, the sick I will heal, but the sleek and the strong I will destroy, shepherding them rightly.

As for you, my sheep, says the Lord GOD, I will judge between one sheep and another, between rams and goats.—The word of the Lord. ℟. **Thanks be to God.** ↓

RESPONSORIAL PSALM Ps 23   [The Good Shepherd]

℟.   The Lord is my shep-herd; there is noth-ing I shall want.

The LORD is my shepherd; I shall not want.
  In verdant pastures he gives me repose.

℟. **The Lord is my shepherd;**
    there is nothing I shall want.

Beside restful waters he leads me;
  he refreshes my soul.
He guides me in right paths
  for his name's sake.

℟. **The Lord is my shepherd;**
    there is nothing I shall want.

You spread the table before me
  in the sight of my foes;
you anoint my head with oil;
  my cup overflows.

℟. **The Lord is my shepherd;**
    there is nothing I shall want.

Only goodness and kindness follow me
  all the days of my life;
and I shall dwell in the house of the LORD
  for years to come.

℟. **The Lord is my shepherd;**
    there is nothing I shall want. ↓

SECOND READING 1 Cor 15:20-26, 28 [Christ the Firstfruits]

  Christ has risen, and he is the firstfruits of the dead. All
  have life in him. He will reign and all will be subjected to
  him.

A reading from the first Letter of Saint Paul
to the Corinthians

BROTHERS and sisters: Christ has been raised
from the dead, the firstfruits of those who have
fallen asleep. For since death came through man, the
resurrection of the dead came also through man. For
just as in Adam all die, so too in Christ shall all be
brought to life, but each one in proper order: Christ

the firstfruits; then, at his coming, those who belong
to Christ; then comes the end, when he hands over
the kingdom to his God and Father, when he has
destroyed every sovereignty and every authority and
power. For he must reign until he has put all his enemies under his feet. The last enemy to be destroyed is
death. When everything is subjected to him, then the
Son himself will also be subjected to the one who
subjected everything to him, so that God may be all in
all.—The word of the Lord. ℟. **Thanks be to God.** ↓

ALLELUIA Mt 11:9, 10   [Son of David]

℟. **Alleluia, alleluia.**
Blessed is he who comes in the name of the Lord!
Blessed is the kingdom of our father David that is to
   come!
℟. **Alleluia, alleluia.** ↓

GOSPEL Mt 25:31-46   [The Last Judgment]

All people will come to be judged by the Son of Man seated
on his royal throne. The sheep will be on his right, the goats
on his left. He will reward all good and punish all evil.

℣. The Lord be with you. ℟. **And also with you.**
✠ A reading from the holy Gospel according to
Matthew. ℟. **Glory to you, Lord.**

JESUS said to his disciples: "When the Son of Man
comes in his glory, and all the angels with him, he
will sit upon his glorious throne, and all the nations
will be assembled before him. And he will separate
them one from another, as a shepherd separates the
sheep from the goats. He will place the sheep on his
right and the goats on his left. Then the king will say
to those on his right, 'Come, you who are blessed by
my Father. Inherit the kingdom prepared for you from
the foundation of the world. For I was hungry and you
gave me food, I was thirsty and you gave me drink, a

stranger and you welcomed me, naked and you clothed me, ill and you cared for me, in prison and you visited me.' Then the righteous will answer him and say, 'Lord, when did we see you hungry and feed you, or thirsty and give you drink? When did we see you a stranger and welcome you, or naked and clothe you? When did we see you ill or in prison, and visit you?' And the king will say to them in reply, 'Amen, I say to you, whatever you did for one of the least brothers of mine, you did for me.' Then he will say to those on his left, 'Depart from me, you accursed, into the eternal fire prepared for the devil and his angels. For I was hungry and you gave me no food, I was thirsty and you gave me no drink, a stranger and you gave me no welcome, naked and you gave me no clothing, ill and in prison, and you did not care for me.' Then they will answer and say, 'Lord, when did we see you hungry or thirsty or a stranger or naked or ill or in prison, and not minister to your needs?' He will answer them, 'Amen, I say to you, what you did not do for one of these least ones, you did not do for me.' And these will go off to eternal punishment, but the righteous to eternal life."—The Gospel of the Lord. ℟. **Praise to you, Lord Jesus Christ.**   ➙ No. 14, p. 18

PRAYER OVER THE GIFTS   [Unity and Peace]
Lord,
we offer you the sacrifice
by which your Son reconciles mankind.
May it bring unity and peace to the world.
We ask this through Christ our Lord. ℟. **Amen.** ↓

PREFACE (P 51)   [Marks of Christ's Kingdom]
℣. The Lord be with you. ℟. **And also with you.**
℣. Lift up your hearts. ℟. **We lift them up to the Lord.**
℣. Let us give thanks to the Lord our God. ℟. **It is right to give him thanks and praise.**

Father, all-powerful and ever-living God,
we do well always and everywhere to give you thanks.
You anointed Jesus Christ, your only Son, with the
    oil of gladness,
as the eternal priest and universal king.
As priest he offered his life on the altar of the cross
and redeemed the human race
by this one perfect sacrifice of peace.
As king he claims dominion over all creation,
that he may present to you, his almighty Father,
an eternal and universal kingdom:
a kingdom of truth and life,
a kingdom of holiness and grace,
a kingdom of justice, love, and peace.
And so, with all the choirs of angels in heaven
we proclaim your glory
and join in their unending hymn of praise:

➜ No. 23, p. 23

COMMUNION ANT. Ps 29:10-11   [Gift of Peace]

**The Lord will reign for ever and will give his people
the gift of peace.** ↓

PRAYER AFTER COMMUNION   [Joy of Christ's Kingdom]

Lord,
you gave us Christ, the King of all creation,
as food for everlasting life.
Help us to live by his gospel
and bring us to the joy of his kingdom,
where he lives and reigns for ever and ever.
℟. **Amen.**   ➜ No. 32, p. 70

Optional Solemn Blessings, p. 92, and Prayers Over the People, p. 99

PASTORAL HELPS

- **The New Luminous Mysteries of the Rosary**

- **Christ's Presence in Liturgical Celebrations**

- **The Liturgical Year and the History of Salvation**

THE NEW LUMINOUS MYSTERIES
OF THE ROSARY

O N October 16, 2002, Pope John Paul II issued an Apostolic Letter entitled *The Rosary of the Blessed Virgin Mary,* encouraging all Catholics to recite the Rosary. In it the Pope said:

"There are some who think that the centrality of the Liturgy, rightly stressed by the Second Vatican Ecumenical Council, necessarily entails giving lesser importance to the Rosary. Yet, as Pope Paul VI made clear, not only does this prayer not conflict with the Liturgy, *[the Rosary] sustains [the Liturgy],* since it serves as an excellent introduction and a faithful echo of the Liturgy, enabling people to participate fully and interiorly in it and to reap its fruits in their daily lives. . . .

"But the most important reason for strongly encouraging the practice of the Rosary is that it represents a most effective means of fostering among the faithful that *commitment to the contemplation of the Christian Mystery* which I have proposed in the Apostolic Letter *On the Threshold of the New Millennium* as a genuine 'training in holiness': 'What is needed is a Christian life distinguished above all in the *art of prayer.'*

"Inasmuch as contemporary culture, even amid so many indications to the contrary, has witnessed the flowering of a new call for spirituality, due also to the influence of other religions, it is more urgent than ever that our Christian communities should become 'genuine schools of prayer.' "

At the same time, the Pope also suggested five new Mysteries that might supplement the meditation on the traditional Joyful, Sorrowful, and Glorious Mysteries of the Rosary. The new Mysteries, called the Luminous Mysteries (or Mysteries of Light), are intended to offer contemplation on important parts of Christ's Public Life in addition to the contemplation on his Childhood, his Sufferings, and his Risen Life offered by the traditional Mysteries:

"Of the many Mysteries of Christ's life, only a few are indicated by the Rosary in the form that has become generally established with the seal of the Church's approval. . . .

"I believe, however, that to bring out fully the Christological depth of the Rosary it would be suitable to make an addition to the traditional pattern which, while left to the freedom of individuals and communities, could broaden it to include *the Mysteries of Christ's Public Ministry between his Baptism and his Passion.*

"In the course of those Mysteries we contemplate important aspects of the person of Christ as the definitive revelation of God. Declared the beloved Son of the Father at the Baptism in the Jordan, Christ is the One who announces the coming of the Kingdom, bears witness to it in his works, and proclaims its demands. It is during the years of his Public Ministry that *the Mystery of Christ is most evidently a Mystery of Light:* 'While I am in the world, I am the light of the world' (Jn 9:5).

"Consequently . . . it is fitting to add, following reflection on the Incarnation and the Hidden Life of Christ *(the Joyful Mysteries)* and before focusing on the sufferings of his Passion *(the Sorrowful Mysteries)* and the triumph of his Resurrection *(the Glorious Mysteries),* a meditation on *certain particularly significant moments in his Public Ministry (the Luminous Mysteries).*"

The Pope assigned these new Mysteries to Thursday while transferring the Joyful Mysteries—normally said on that day—to Saturday (the traditional day for honoring Mary) because of the special Marian presence in them.

1. The Baptism of Jesus in the Jordan

Meditation

Think of Christ's Baptism at the hands of John the Baptist when the Father called him his beloved Son and the Holy Spirit descended on him to invest him with the mission he was to carry out.

Scripture Text (Mt 3:13-17 and Is 42:1-2, 4-5)

1. Jesus arrived from Galilee and came to John at the Jordan to be baptized by him.

2. John tried to dissuade him, saying, "Why do you come to me? I am the one who needs to be baptized by you."

3. But Jesus said to him in reply, "For the present, let it be thus. It is proper for us to do this to fulfill all that righteousness demands."

4. Then John acquiesced.

5. After Jesus had been baptized, as he came up from the water, the heavens were opened.

6. And he beheld the Spirit of God descending like a dove and alighting on him.

7. And a voice came from heaven, saying, "This is my beloved Son, in whom I am well pleased."

8. [These words recall the words of the Lord spoken by the Prophet Isaiah about the Suffering Servant:] "This is my Servant whom I uphold, my chosen one in whom I delight."

9. "I will put my Spirit in him, and he will bring justice to the nations."

10. "In his law the coastlands will place their hope. This is what the Lord says."

Grace Desired

To live my Baptismal Promises.

———————

2. Christ's Self-Manifestation at the Wedding in Cana

Meditation

Think of Christ's self-manifestation at the wedding in Cana when he changed water into wine and opened the hearts of the disciples to faith, thanks to the intervention of Mary, the first among believers.

Scripture Text (Jn 2:1-11)

1. On the third day, there was a wedding feast at Cana in Galilee. The Mother of Jesus was there, and Jesus and his disciples had also been invited.

2. When the supply of wine was exhausted, the Mother of Jesus said to him, "They have no wine."

3. Jesus responded, "Woman, why should this be of any concern to me? My hour has not yet come."

4. His Mother said to the servants, "Do whatever he tells you."

5. Standing nearby there were six stone water jars, of the type used for Jewish rites of purification, each holding twenty to thirty gallons.

6. Jesus instructed the servants, "Fill the jars with water."

7. When they had filled them to the brim, he ordered them, "Now draw some out and take it to the chief steward," and they did so.

8. When the chief steward tasted the water that had become wine, he did not know where it came from, although the servants who had drawn the water knew.

9. He called over the bridegroom and said, "Everyone serves the choice wine first, and then an inferior vintage when the guests have had too much to drink. However, you have saved the best wine until now."

10. Jesus performed this, the first of his signs, at Cana in Galilee, thereby revealing his glory, and his disciples believed in him.

Grace Desired

To do whatever Jesus says.

---

3. Christ's Proclamation of the Kingdom of God

Meditation

Think of Christ's preaching of the Kingdom of God (by means of its Magna Carta, the Sermon on the Mount, and especially the Beatitudes), and its call to forgiveness as he inaugurated the ministry of mercy ("The time of fulfillment has arrived, and the Kingdom of God is close at hand. Repent, and believe in the Gospel"—Mk 1:15), which he continues to exercise until the end of the world, particularly through the Sacrament of Reconciliation.

Scripture Text (Mk 1:15 and Mt 5:1-11)

1. The time of fulfillment has arrived, and the Kingdom of God is close at hand. Repent, and believe the Gospel.

2. Blessed are the poor in spirit, for theirs is the Kingdom of heaven.

3. Blessed are those who mourn, for they will be comforted.

4. Blessed are the meek, for they will inherit the earth.

5. Blessed are those who hunger and thirst for justice, for they will have their fill.

6. Blessed are the merciful, for they will obtain mercy.

7. Blessed are the pure of heart, for they will see God.

8. Blessed are the peacemakers, for they will be called children of God.

9. Blessed are those who are persecuted in the cause of justice, for theirs is the Kingdom of heaven.

10. Blessed are you when you are forced to endure insults and cruel treatment and all kinds of calumnies for my sake. Rejoice and be glad, for your reward will be great in heaven.

Grace Desired

God's forgiveness for my sins.

4. The Transfiguration of Our Lord

Meditation

Think of Christ's Transfiguration when the glory of the Godhead shone forth from his face as the Father commanded the Apostles to listen to him and experience his Passion and Resurrection and be transfigured by the Holy Spirit.

Scripture Text (Mt 17:1-8)

1. Six days later, Jesus took Peter and James and his brother John with him and led them up a high mountain by themselves.

2. And in their presence he was transfigured; his face shone like the sun, and his clothes became dazzling white.

3. Suddenly there appeared to them Moses and Elijah, conversing with him.

4. Then Peter said to Jesus, "Lord, it is good for us to be here."

5. "If you wish, I will make three shelters here—one for you, one for Moses, and one for Elijah."

6. While he was still speaking, suddenly a bright cloud cast a shadow over them.

7. Then a voice from the cloud said, "This is my beloved Son, with whom I am well pleased. Listen to him."

8. When the disciples heard this, they fell on their faces and were greatly frightened.

9. But Jesus came and touched them, saying, "Stand up, and do not be frightened."

10. And when they raised their eyes, they saw no one, but only Jesus.

Grace Desired

To be a new person in Christ.

---

5. Christ's Institution of the Eucharist

Meditation

Think of Christ's Institution of the Eucharist, in which he offered his Body and Blood as food under the signs of bread and wine and testified to his love for humanity, for whose sake he would offer himself in sacrifice.

Scripture Text (Lk 22:7-8, 14-20)

1. The day of the feast of Unleavened Bread arrived, on which the Passover lamb had to be sacrificed.

2. Jesus sent Peter and John, saying, "Go and make preparations for us to eat the Passover."

3. When the hour came, Jesus took his place at table along with the Apostles.

4. He said to them, "I have eagerly desired to eat this Passover with you before I suffer."

5. "For I tell you that from this moment on I shall never eat it again until it is fulfilled in the Kingdom of God."

6. Then he took a cup, and after giving thanks he said, "Take this and divide it among yourselves."

7. "For I tell you that from this moment I will not drink of the fruit of the vine until the Kingdom of God comes."

8. Then he took bread, and after giving thanks he broke it and gave it to them, saying, "This is my body, which will be given for you."

9. "Do this in memory of me."

10. And he did the same with the cup after supper, saying, "This cup is the new covenant in my blood, which will be poured out for you."

Grace Desired

To attain active participation at Mass.

PRAYER AFTER THE ROSARY

O GOD, whose, only-begotten Son, by his Life, Death, and Resurrection, has purchased for us the rewards of eternal life; grant, we beseech you, that, meditating upon these Mysteries of the Most Holy Rosary of the Blessed Virgin Mary, we may imitate what they contain and obtain what they promise, through the same Christ our Lord. Amen.

℣. May the divine assistance remain always with us. ℟. Amen.

℣. And may the souls of the faithful departed, through the mercy of God, rest in peace. ℟. Amen.

CHRIST'S PRESENCE IN LITURGICAL CELEBRATIONS

Christ Is Personally Present to Us

WE know of two types of presence—local and personal. The first is a simple accident of space and involves no interrelation between the things that are close to one another or even touch. The second is a substantial presence of heart, mind, and will. This is the only true presence for conscious beings in our experience. It is the only way in which the union of hearts and minds takes place.

The Liturgy makes Christ personally present to us. Furthermore, Christ's Presence in the Liturgy is not a static thing, an object of adoration. It is a living achievement in which we cooperate and in which we actively share. To attain the salvation wrought by God in Christ we must enter into the event of Jesus' sacrificial Death and Glorification, which breaks the bonds of time and is accessible to all ages. We do this by participating fully, consciously, and actively in liturgical celebrations of the Church.

Generally speaking, there are four liturgical presences of Christ and each is a different mode of his presence for a specific purpose in regard to us. A brief look at them may make it possible for us to share more fully in the benefits of this astonishing gift of Christ's presence among us.

Christ's Presence in the Assembly

On any given Sunday (or weekday for that matter), a group of persons come together to perform the sacred actions of Christian worship in a particular place. At first they are barely aware of one another; then they begin to act in unison: they rise, sing, perform actions, pray, and utter responses. They welcome the presiding member of the gathering (the priest who acts in the person of Christ) as indispensable for what they are doing, they listen to him, and they give their assent to the prayer that he makes in the name of all.

This is the Christian Assembly. It is rooted in the profoundly human reality of "togetherness" and in the words of Christ: "Where two or three are gathered together in my name, I am in their midst" (Mt 18:20).

572

The Assembly is the overwhelming manifestation and realization-in-action of the unity of the Body of Christ, the oneness of the baptized. It is the covenant-celebration of the mission entrusted by God to his people to Christianize the world. The Liturgy that flows from the Assembly is a series of prayerful and self-sustaining actions of a faith-community. Members of the Assembly are more than simply consumers, clients, or patients. They are the Church, which is the fundamental doer, actor, and minister of the Liturgy.

Out of the Assembly come the priest who presides, the deacon who ministers to him, the acolytes who assist him, the lectors who proclaim God's Word, the extraordinary ministers who administer Christ's Body and Blood (to those physically present as well as to those who make up its extension because o their inability to be present), the choristers who create the mood of the celebration, and various others.

In the celebrant's greeting, we discern the Presence of the Risen Lord among us. As we accomplish the Eucharistic Sacrifice, which is a prayer (and indeed the Greatest Prayer), Jesus prays with us. In the words of St. Augustine, "He prays for us and in us, and is prayed to by us: he prays for us as our Priest and in us as our Head. As our God, he is prayed to by us." Thus, Jesus is among us as our Friend and Intercessor with the Father.

Christ's Presence in His Priest or Minister

Christ is present in liturgical services in the Priest or Minister who celebrates. At Mass he is present in the Priest who offers the Holy Sacrifice "in the person of Christ," that is, "in specific sacramental identification with the eternal High Priest, who is the Author and principal Subject of this Sacrifice of his, a sacrifice in which, in truth, nobody can take his place" (John Paul II).

Christ is the sole Priest. He alone accomplishes the full communion of human beings with God. He is not only a possible way—he is the Way. He brings not only a truth—he is the Truth. He is not only a living being—he is the Life. All this is summed up in the phrase one Mediator.

"Whoever hears you hears me" (Lk 10:16). In mysterious fashion, the presence of the Lord is manifested also by the one who is called to preside at our Eucharist. Even though he is one of us, he has been chosen to become the sign of the Other. The priest is not the one who presides at our Eucharist; he is the sign of Christ who presides. The priest is a sign of Christ, Head of the Church, and at the same time a sign of the union of the Body with its Head.

In every Sacrament, Christ is also present in his Minister. Through actions and words that "signify" his Presence and his actions, he communicates to us the intention of salvation that he pursues in the world, and that he is in the process of achieving it in us here and now.

The priest consecrates and offers the sacrifice in the name of Christ; he (or a minister) baptizes, confirms, absolves, anoints the sick in the name of Christ. But through him it is Christ who is re-presented, made present anew.

Thus, Jesus is among us as our Representative and Companion who pleads our cause before the Father.

Christ's Presence in His Word

The Word of God acts in many ways—e.g., through private Bible reading and through people. However, it is especially in the Liturgy that the Word is present and active.

In the Liturgy of the Word, the speaker is the Crucified and Risen Christ, who is both the content and the key to the understanding of the Old and New Testament. In him the Father has said everything to us and given everything to us.

The reading from the Old Testament (usually the Prophets) looks forward to Christ the Messiah—bringing Christ before us. The reading from the New Testament (usually from the apostles) looks back to Christ the Lord—bringing Christ in our midst.

No doubt it is "Christ himself who speaks while the Scriptures are read in the Church" (Vatican II: *Constitution on the Sacred Liturgy*, no. 7). But in the Gospel he speaks to us in a way that is clearer, more personal, more decisive, and more enriching that in the other texts.

The Gospel is the high point of the Liturgy of the Word, because in it the Good News of Christ is preached by the

Risen Lord. It is Christ living and present among us who continues to speak to us as he calls us to faith and conversion. He is as present to us as he was to the people who gathered to hear him along the roads of the Holy Land. He comes to us as our Teacher who leads us to all truth.

It is our task to discern the saving event of Christ's Presence among us and God's intervention in our lives that flow out of the reading. More important, we must embrace Christ's Word with an open heart and mind and respond in positive fashion to it. In this task our faith is paramount. It will help us to respond to Christ who leads us to the One who is all Truth.

Christ's Presence in the Eucharist

The last way in which Christ is present in liturgical celebrations is in the Eucharist under the signs of Bread and Wine. This is known as the Presence of Christ par excellence, his Real Presence. One of the reasons for this is that it is the only one that remains. The Bread and Wine remain the Body and Blood, Soul and Divinity of Christ as long as they last after they are consecrated.

In the Eucharistic celebration, Christ is present in a way that is absolutely special: as Priest and Victim, offering himself in a sacrifice of covenant and thanksgiving, recapitulating and appropriating his whole People to make this People in turn priest and victim of the unique Sacrifice. He comes as our God who unites us to himself and to one another.

This presence is active, dynamic, substantial, and permanent. When Communion is over, the Hosts that remain continue to realize Christ's presence among us!

This is the most important presence of Christ and is intended to be the means for our close union with our brothers and sisters who share that Presence with us. It provides our entrance into the Sacred Banquet in which the living Memory of Christ's Passion is recalled, our souls are filled with grace, and we receive a pledge of future glory.

The Eucharist is the vehicle by which Christ comes to us daily in the Spirit. It is the vehicle that effects a transformation in Christians and in the world that is wrought by the Risen Christ.

THE LITURGICAL YEAR AND THE HISTORY OF SALVATION

1. THE LITURGICAL YEAR

Every Sunday the Church keeps the memory of our Lord's Paschal Mystery. She sanctifies time, consecrates it to God, and as it were inserts us into the History of Salvation. Within the cycle of a year she unfolds the whole mystery of Christ—from his foreshadowings in the Old Testament to his majestic Life and Work in the New Testament.

Thus, the feasts of the Liturgical Year are first of all celebrations of the History of Salvation. The mysteries of our Salvation are to be honored not as something past but as something present, for while the act itself (e.g., Christ's birth, death, resurrection, ascension, and the descent of the Holy Spirit) is past, its effects are present. Each feast puts before our mind the sign of some hidden sacred reality, which must be applied to us. We should celebrate the mysteries of our Salvation as happening now to us and we should undergo their mystical effect with an open heart. The best way to do so is by an active participation in Public Worship, aided by the Missal.

We can also be aided by the following summary of the major events of the History of Salvation.

2. ABRAHAM

a) The time around 1850 B.C. was a turning point in the long history of human beings. Almighty God interfered in the course of things and spoke to a man called Abraham. This man lived in what we call now the Fertile Crescent, i.e., the fertile countries along the Tigris and Euphrates rivers, the Jordan river and the Nile river, that surround the Syrian desert as a crescent. God gave the gift of faith to a simple Bedouin, Abraham, who surrendered himself and his family entirely to God. Note that God blessed Abraham, promised to give the land of Canaan to his descendants, made a covenant (alliance) with him and wanted Abraham's faith to be sealed with a sign—circumcision (see Rom 4:11). This is the first establishment of the Kingdom of God on this earth. Read: Gen 11:27—12:9; Gen 17:1-14.

b) It is St. Paul who explains this simple beginning of God's dealings with humanity. Read: Gal 3:16, 26-29, 7-9; Rom 4:18-25. The Church considers Abraham the Father of all the faithful.

c) During the time that the Kingdom of God was restricted to Abraham's carnal offspring, initiation into it was achieved by the sign of circumcision. Now that it is open to all, through Christ's Death and Resurrection, Baptism and Confirmation are the signs (sacraments) of initiation into God's people on earth. Read: Acts 15:1-12; Col 2:11-14.

3. PASSOVER AND EXODUS

a) "Abraham was the father of Isaac, and Isaac the father of Jacob, and Jacob the father of Judah and his brothers" (Mt 1:2). The clan of Jacob emigrated to Egypt where it later fell into slavery. However, God did not forget his chosen people. He bestowed a leader upon the people of Israel (Moses) who led them out of slavery in Egypt. This is called the Exodus. Read: Gen 37; 41:37-46; 46:1-7, 28-34; Ex 1:1-14; 2:1-21; 3:1-14; 11; 12; 14:10-31.

b) God's people were saved from bondage and evil by the Passover sacrifice and its Sacrificial Repast—which foreshadowed the perfect Sacrifice of Jesus

Christ on the Cross. Because Jesus was man, he could offer a sacrifice. Because he was also God, his Sacrifice symbolized an infinitely perfect obedience and self-surrender and was worthy of God the Father. We are saved from evil because of the blood of our Passover Lamb, Jesus Christ. We partake in this Sacrifice, made present to us under the signs of bread and wine, and eat the Sacrificial Repast. Read: Heb 10:4-10; Mk 14:12-16, 22-24; 1 Cor 5:6-8.

4. GOD'S PROTECTION

a) Israel, God's people, went through the Red Sea and obtained their freedom from slavery in Egypt. Under the leadership of Moses they wandered in the desert for forty years and hoped to enter the Promised Land. Whatever they needed in the desert—water, meat, and bread—they received through the prayer of Moses. Read: Ex 16:4-15, 31-35; 17:1-7.

b) We, who are the new people of God, obtained our freedom from the bondage of Satan by going through the water of Baptism (best symbolized in the ancient Church by immersion!). Under the leadership of Christ the Church passes through the desert of life, hoping to enter the Promised Land: heaven. All that the people need in order to reach their supreme goal is given through Christ, our Lord. Read: 1 Cor 10:1-11; 2 Cor 5:1-10; Jn 6:48-71.

5. THE COVENANT

a) Moses ascended Mount Sinai as the mediator between God and the people. It was on this mountain that God proclaimed the Ten Commandments. The Covenant of God with Abraham was then four hundred years old (see Gen 17:1-8). It is a perpetual Covenant, unfolded gradually and consummated with the blood of sacrifice, which reaches its final perfection in its renewed form on Calvary. Read: Ex 19:1-8, 16-25; 20:1-17; 24:4-8.

b) The Mediator of the New Covenant is Jesus Christ. It is established on Calvary with all peoples of the world. The New Covenant is consummated with the Sacrifice of Christ's Precious Blood. Read: Heb 3:1-6; 8:6-13; Lk 22:14-20.

6. FIRST FULFILLMENT OF GOD'S PROMISE

God promised Abraham to give the land of Canaan to his descendants (Gen 12:7). God began to fulfill his promise when the Jews crossed the river Jordan at Jericho under the leadership of Joshua. He realized it under the kingship of David and of Solomon. This great kingdom, ever more idealized in Jewish history, was actually the Kingdom of God. The king was merely his representative and servant (2 Sam 7:5). Since the kings were anointed to be king (2 Sam 5:3) they were called: "The anointed of Yahweh," which means in Hebrew: "Mashiah." Hence the Bible speaks of the "Messiah" or "Christ" (from the Greek), being the king of the great Kingdom of God to come. But this first fulfillment of God's promise contained a further promise, namely, of the Universal Kingdom of God, the Church. God gradually revealed that David's kingdom merely prefigured this great Kingdom to come. Read: 2 Sam 5:1-5; 7:1-17 (esp. 12-16); Ps 71:1-17; Lk 1:31-33; Mk 1:14-15; Mt 9:35-38; Lk 22:24-30; Jn 18:33-38.

7. THE EXILE (BABYLONIAN CAPTIVITY)

a) Israel knew that all the blessings and promises of God depended on faithfulness to the Covenant. But Israel was not faithful. God sent prophets to remind his people of the Covenant. He threatened them and finally had to punish them. Israel was carried away into exile. Read: 1 Kings 19:1-4; 21; Am 3; Isa 1:1-4; 5:1-7; Jer 2:4-7; 6:16-19; 15:5-6; Bar 6:1-6.

b) It was in the exile of Babylon that God's people started praying again. We should pray the psalms of God's chosen people and make them our prayer. Exile and punishment may be seen as separation from God, when we have sinned. We are now: Israel, House of Jacob, House of Judah, Zion or Jerusalem. Read: Ps 136:1-6; 78; 41; 125; 135:1-9, 26.

8. GOD'S PLAN OF SALVATION

a) The wise men of Israel, moved by the Holy Spirit (Gen 1:1—2:7) tell us that God created everything. To make "everything" more understandable for the people of their time, they divided it up in six portions, calling them "days," in order to suggest that the Jews had six days to work and were supposed to rest on the Sabbath. Compare this story about creation with the lesson about it by St. Paul to the Athenians. Read: Gen 1:1—2:7; Acts 17:22-34.

b) They give us God's plan: Human beings would share in God's own life. They would be only a little less than the angels (Ps 8:6). They would live in happiness without pain, frustration, hard labor, or sickness and without dying would be admitted to see God in heaven. But this plan could not be realized, because Adam ate from the tree of knowledge of good and evil (committed sin). The Bible speaks of: "sin of the world" or simply: "sin." This is called "original sin"—the sinful condition in which all of us are born because of the sins of our first parents and everybody's sin. Read: Gen 1:26-30; 2:8-25.

c) God chose a people for himself. He began with Abraham. Patiently, he revealed his plans more clearly and finally established the Kingdom of God through Christ. God did not give up his original plan. He restored all things in Jesus. Read: Eph 1:3-10.

9. PREPARATION

a) The punishment of the exile was the punishment of a loving Father. The prophet Ezekiel, who was with the exiled Jews in Babylon, taught them these things. This punishment was to cleanse the people from evil and to prepare them gradually for the coming of the Universal Kingdom of God with the true "Anointed," Jesus Christ. Read: Ezek 36:24-28, 33-38.

b) In the past centuries before the coming of Christ, the pious Jews, called "The Holy Remnant" or sometimes "The Poor of Yahweh," fostered that waiting and desire for the Kingdom of God. They knew their Bible and prayed. Their prayer should be our prayer during our celebration of Advent. Read: Gen 3:14-15; Isa 7:14; 9:1-7; 11:1-9; 40:1-11; 53:1-7; Ps 21; Isa 45:8.

c) John the Baptist is the last of the prophets in the time of preparation. He introduced the Promised Messiah to his contemporaries. Read: Mt 3.

10. THE KINGDOM OF GOD IS AT HAND

a) When Jesus of Nazareth began preaching and establishing the Kingdom of God, he taught plainly: "I have come, not to abolish [the law and the prophets], but to fulfill them" (Mt 5:17). The kingdom of David was only a first fulfillment of God's promise to Abraham. It contained a further promise, which has been fulfilled in the Kingdom of the Anointed of Yahweh par excellence: Christ Jesus. Read: Mk 1:14-22; Mt 5:17-20; 4:23-25; Jn 1:35-51.

b) Christ Jesus explained that it was he of whom the prophets had spoken (see Jn 1:45) and he worked many miracles to manifest the glory and power of God in him. Read: Lk 4:14-22; Mt 11:16 and Isa 35:5 and 61:1; Lk 18:31-34; 24:13-35 (esp. 25-27); Jn 2:1-12 (esp. 11); 11:1-44 (esp. 42); 12:37-43.

c) With both plain words and parables Jesus explained the nature of the Kingdom and what it means to us. It is a universal Kingdom for all people of faith, who are henceforth the real children of Abraham (see Gal 3:7). It is a people cleansed from iniquity (see Eph 5:25-27) and sharing God's life as originally planned by him (see No. 8b). Read: Mt 22:1-4; 21:33-43; Jn 10:11-16; 15:1-11; 3:1-6; Mt 13.

d) Jesus established a hierarchy of bishops to rule the Kingdom, to teach and to distribute God's blessings in his name, while he resides in heaven, sitting at God's right hand, i.e., as Man sharing power with God, being King and High Priest, interceding for us at God's throne (see Heb 7:25). Read: Mt 28:16-20; Lk 10:1-16 (esp. 16); Jn 20:19-23; Mt 16:13-20; Jn 21:15-17; 1 Cor 11:23-26 (esp. 24).

e) The gradually more perfect realization of the Kingdom in every person follows the universal law of birth and growth: Through pain and death to life everlasting! But it is worthwhile to give up everything to gain it. Read: Jn 12:20-26; Mt 10:16-20; Lk 22:15-30; 12:22-34; 18:18-30; 24:25-27.

11. THE UNIVERSAL CHURCH

The History of our Salvation began with Abraham, reached a peak in the Death and Resurrection of our Lord and became complete with the descent of the Holy Spirit. But it goes on. Christ leads the Church through the Holy Spirit (see Jn 14:16 and Mt 10:20). He continues to teach us and to bless us through holy Signs, the Sacraments. And our grateful answer to God by good behavior is possible only with the help of Christ. Read: Acts 8:26-40; 8:14-17; 2:42-47; 2 Tim 1:6-9; Eph 5:22-33; Rom 8:26.

12. THE FINAL FULFILLMENT

When Christ Jesus established the Kingdom of God, the promise to Abraham was fulfilled. God's original plan was restored in human beings. Sin and evil were defeated. Human beings shared in God's life. But like David's kingdom (see No. 6) this first fulfillment contains a promise, namely, the glorious Kingdom of God in the future world. This will be realized when Jesus will surrender the Kingdom to the Father and God will be all in all. Read: Mt 25:33-46; 1 Cor 15:22-28; Rev 21:1-4; Titus 2:11-15; Mt 6:10.

Saint Joseph

HYMNAL

Praise My Soul, The King of Heaven **1**

F. Lyte

John Goss

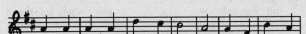

1. Praise my soul, the King of hea - ven; To his feet thy
2. Praise him for his grace and fa - vor; To his children
3.   Fa-ther-like he tends and spares us; Well our feeble
4. An-gels help us to a - dore him; You be-hold him

1.   tri-bute bring; Ran-somed, healed, re-stored, for-giv-en
2.   in dis - tress; Praise him still the same as ev - er
3. frame he knows; In his hand he gen - tly bears us,
4. face to face; Sun and moon, bow down be-fore him,

1.   Ev - er more his prais - es sing: Al - le - lu - ia!
2. Slow to chide, and swift to bless: Al - le - lu - ia!
3. Re-cues us from all our foes: Al - le - lu - ia!
4. Dwell-ers all in time and space. Al - le - lu - ia!

1. Al - le - lu - ia! Praise the ev - er - last - ing King.
2. Al - le - lu - ia! Glo - rious in his faith - ful - ness.
3. Al - le - lu - ia! Wide - ly yet his mer - cy flows.
4. Al - le - lu - ia! Praise with us the God of grace.

All Are Welcome

Tune: TWO OAKS 9 6 8 6 8 7 10
with refrain; Marty Haugen, b. 1950

Text: Marty Haugen, b. 1950

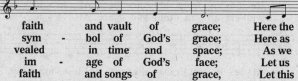

1. Let us build a house where love can dwell And
2. Let us build a house where proph-ets speak, And
3. Let us build a house where love is found In
4. Let us build a house where hands will reach Be -
5. Let us build a house where all are named, Their

all can safe - ly live, A place where saints and
words are strong and true, Where all God's chil-dren
wa - ter, wine and wheat: A ban - quet hall on
yond the wood and stone To heal and strength-en,
songs and vi - sions heard And loved and treas-ured,

chil - dren tell How hearts learn to for -
dare to seek To dream God's reign a -
ho - ly ground, Where peace and jus - tice
serve and teach, And live the Word they've
taught and claimed As words with - in the

give. Built of hopes and dreams and vi - sions, Rock of
new. Here the cross shall stand as wit-ness And as
meet. Here the love of God, through Je - sus, Is re-
known. Here the out - cast and the stran-ger Bear the
Word. Built of tears and cries and laugh-ter, Prayers of

faith and vault of grace; Here the
sym - bol of God's grace; Here as
vealed in time and space; As we
im - age of God's face; Let us
faith and songs of grace, Let this

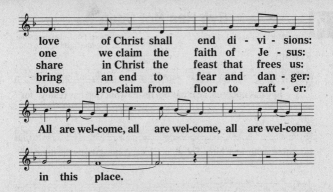

love   of Christ shall   end di - vi - sions:
one   we claim the   faith of   Je - sus:
share   in Christ the   feast that frees us:
bring   an end to   fear and dan - ger:
house   pro-claim from floor to raft - er:

All are wel-come, all are wel-come, all are wel-come

in this place.

Praise to the Lord

3

1. Praise to the Lord,
   The almighty, the King of creation;
   O my soul, praise him,
   For he is our health and salvation;
   Hear the great throng,
   Joyous with praises and song,
   Sounding in glad adoration.

2. Praise to the Lord,
   Who doth prosper thy way and defend thee;
   Surely his goodness
   And mercy shall ever attend thee;
   Ponder anew
   What the almighty can do,
   Who with his love doth befriend thee.

3. Praise to the Lord,
   O let all that is in me adore him!
   All that hath breath join
   In our praises now to adore him!
   Let the "Amen"
   Sung by all people again
   Sound as we worship before him. Amen.

4 Eye Has Not Seen

Tune: Marty Haugen, b. 1950

Text: 1 Corinthians 2:9-10;
Marty Haugen, b. 1950

Refrain

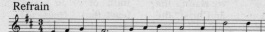

Eye has not seen, ear has not heard what God has read-y for

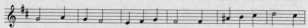

those who love him; Spir-it of love, come, give us the mind of

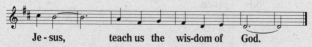

Je - sus, teach us the wis-dom of God.

Verses 1-3

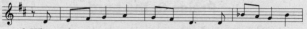

1. When pain and sor-row weigh us down, be near to us, O
2. Our lives are but a sin-gle breath, we flow-er and we
3. To those who see with eyes of faith, the Lord is ev - er

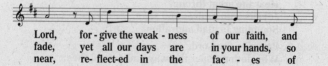

Lord, for - give the weak - ness of our faith, and
fade, yet all our days are in your hands, so
near, re - flect-ed in the fac - es of

D.C.

bear us up with-in your peace-ful word.
we re-turn in love what love has made.
all the poor and low-ly of the world.

Verse 4

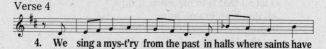

4. We sing a mys-t'ry from the past in halls where saints have

trod,   yet ev-er new the   mu-sic rings   to

D.C.

Je-sus, Liv-ing Song of God.

Praise God from Whom All Blessings Flow 5

1. Praise God, from whom all blessings flow;
   Praise him, all creatures here below;
   Praise him above, ye heav'nly host:
   Praise Father, Son, and Holy Ghost.

2. All people that on earth do dwell.
   Sing to the Lord with cheerful voice;
   Him serve with mirth, his praise forth tell,
   Come ye before him and rejoice.

3. Know that the Lord is God indeed;
   Without our aid he did us make;
   We are his flock, he doth us feed.
   And for his sheep he doth us take.

4. O enter then his gates with praise,
   Approach with joy his courts unto;
   Praise, laud, and bless his name always,
   For it is seemly so to do. Amen.

Faith of Our Fathers 6

1. Faith of our fathers! living still,
   In spite of dungeon, fire, and sword;
   O how our hearts beat high with joy,
   Whene'er we hear that glorious word!

   Refrain: Faith of our fathers holy faith,
             We will be true to thee till death.

2. Faith of our fathers! We will love
   Both friend and foe in all our strife,
   And preach thee too, as love knows how,
   By kindly words and virtuous life.

3. Faith of our fathers! Mary's prayers
   Shall keep our country close to thee;
   And through the truth that comes from God,
   O we shall prosper and be free.

589

7 God Father, Praise and Glory

1. God Father, praise and glory
   Thy children bring to thee.
   Good will and peace to mankind
   Shall now forever be.

Refrain: O most Holy Trinity,
                Undivided Unity; Holy God,
                Mighty God, God immortal be adored.

2. And thou, Lord Coeternal.
   God's sole begotten Son;
   O Jesus, King anointed,
   Who hast redemption won.—*Refrain*

3. O Holy Ghost, Creator.
   Thou gift of God most high;
   Life, love and sacred Unction
   Our weakness thou supply.—*Refrain*

8 Praise the Lord of Heaven

Praise the Lord of Heaven,
Praise Him in the height.
Praise Him all ye angels,
Praise Him stars and light;
Praise Him skies and waters
   which above the skies
When His word commanded,
Mighty did arise,

Praise Him man and maiden,
Princes and all kings,
Praise Him hills and mountains,
All created things;
Heav'n and earth He fashioned
   mighty oceans raised;
This day and forever
His name shall be praised.

9 Holy, Holy, Holy

1. Holy, holy, holy! Lord God almighty.
   Early in the morning our song shall rise to thee:
   Holy, holy, holy! Merciful and mighty,
   God in three persons, blessed Trinity.

2. Holy, holy, holy! Lord God almighty.
   All thy works shall praise thy name in earth and sky
      and sea;
   Holy, holy, holy! Merciful and mighty,
   God in three persons, blessed Trinity.

3. Holy, holy, holy! All thy saints adore thee,
   Praising thee in glory, with thee to ever be;
   Cherubim and Seraphim, falling down before thee,
   Which wert and art and evermore shall be.

Now Thank We All Our God

1. Now thank we all our God,
   With heart and hands and voices,
   Who wondrous things hath done,
   In whom the world rejoices;
   Who from our mother's arms
   Hath blessed us on our way
   With countless gifts of love,
   And still is ours today.

2. All praise and thanks to God,
   The Father now be given,
   The Son, and him who reigns
   With them in highest heaven,
   The one eternal God
   Whom earth and heav'n adore;
   For thus it was, is now,
   And shall be ever more.

The Church's One Foundation

1
The Church's one foundation
Is Jesus Christ her Lord.
She is his new creation,
By water and the Word;
From heav'n he came and sought her,
To be his holy bride;
With his own blood he bought her,
And for her life he died.

2
Elect from ev'ry nation,
Yet one o'er all the earth.
Her charter of salvation,
One Lord, one faith, one birth;
One holy Name she blesses,
Partakes one holy food;
And to one hope she presses,
With ev'ry grace endued.

3
Mid toil and tribulation,
And tumult of her war.
She waits the consummation
Of peace for evermore;
Till with the vision glorious
Her loving eyes are blest,
And the great Church victorious
Shall be the Church at rest.

12 Awake, Awake and Greet the New Morn

Tune: REJOICE, REJOICE, 9 8 9 8 8 7 8 9;
Marty Haugen, b. 1950

Text: Marty Haugen, b. 1950

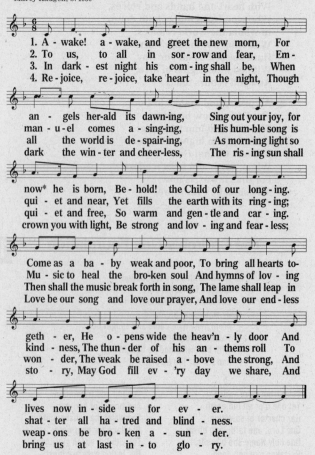

1. A-wake! a-wake, and greet the new morn, For an-gels her-ald its dawn-ing, Sing out your joy, for now* he is born, Be-hold! the Child of our long-ing. Come as a ba-by weak and poor, To bring all hearts to-geth-er, He o-pens wide the heav'n-ly door And lives now in-side us for ev-er.

2. To us, to all in sor-row and fear, Em-man-u-el comes a-sing-ing, His hum-ble song is qui-et and near, Yet fills the earth with its ring-ing; Mu-sic to heal the bro-ken soul And hymns of lov-ing kind-ness, The thun-der of his an-thems roll To shat-ter all ha-tred and blind-ness.

3. In dark-est night his com-ing shall be, When all the world is de-spair-ing, As morn-ing light so qui-et and free, So warm and gen-tle and car-ing. Then shall the music break forth in song, The lame shall leap in won-der, The weak be raised a-bove the strong, And weap-ons be bro-ken a-sun-der.

4. Re-joice, re-joice, take heart in the night, Though dark the win-ter and cheer-less, The ris-ing sun shall crown you with light, Be strong and lov-ing and fear-less; Love be our song and love our prayer, And love our end-less sto-ry, May God fill ev-'ry day we share, And bring us at last in-to glo-ry.

* During Advent: "soon"

Canticle of the Sun

Tune: Marty Haugen, b. 1950   Text: Marty Haugen, b. 1950

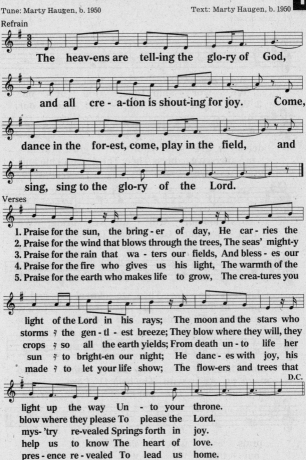

Refrain

The heav-ens are tell-ing the glo-ry of God, and all cre - a-tion is shout-ing for joy. Come, dance in the for-est, come, play in the field, and sing, sing to the glo-ry of the Lord.

Verses

1. Praise for the sun, the bring - er of day, He car - ries the light of the Lord in his rays; The moon and the stars who light up the way Un - to your throne.

2. Praise for the wind that blows through the trees, The seas' might-y storms ℣ the gen - tl - est breeze; They blow where they will, they blow where they please To please the Lord.

3. Praise for the rain that wa - ters our fields, And bless - es our crops ℣ so all the earth yields; From death un - to life her mys - 'try re-vealed Springs forth in joy.

4. Praise for the fire who gives us his light, The warmth of the sun ℣ to bright-en our night; He danc - es with joy, his help us to know The heart of love.

5. Praise for the earth who makes life to grow, The crea-tures you made ℣ to let your life show; The flow-ers and trees that pres - ence re - vealed To lead us home.

D.C.

14 We Praise Thee, O God, Our Redeemer

Ps 26:12
Tr. Julia B. Cady

E. Kremser

1. We praise Thee, O God, our Re-deem-er, Cre-a-tor, In grate-ful de-vo-tion our trib-ute we bring; We lay it be-fore Thee, we kneel and a-dore Thee, We bless Thy ho-ly name, glad prais-es we sing.

2. We wor-ship Thee, God of our fa-thers, we bless Thee; Thro' trou-ble and tem-pest our Guide hast Thou been; When per-ils o'er-take us, es-cape Thou wilt make us, And with Thy help, O Lord, our bat-tles we win.

3. With voic-es u-nit-ed our prais-es we of-fer, To Thee, great Je-ho-vah, glad an-thems we raise. Thy strong arm will guide us, our God is be-side us, To Thee, our great Re-deem-er for-ev-er be praise. A-men.

Rejoice, the Lord Is King

15

C. Wesley, alt.   J. Darwall, 1770

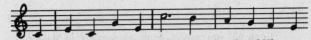

1. Re - joice, the Lord is King! Your Lord and King a-
2. The Lord, the Sav - ior reigns, The God of truth and
3. His king-dom can - not fail; He rules o'er earth and

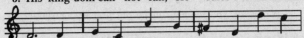

1. dore! Let all give thanks and sing, And tri-umph
2. love, When he had purged our stains, He took his
3. heav'n; The King of vic - t'ry hail, all praise to

Refrain

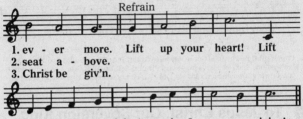

1. ev - er more. Lift up your heart! Lift
2. seat a - bove.
3. Christ be giv'n.

up your voice! Re - joice! a-gain I say re - joice!

We Gather Together

16

(Same Melody as Hymn No. 14)

1. We gather together to ask the Lord's blessing;
   He chastens and hastens his will to make known;
   The wicked oppressing now cease from distressing;
   Sing praises to his name; he forgets not his own.

2. Beside us to guide us, our God with us joining,
   Ordaining, maintaining his kingdom divine;
   So from the beginning the fight we were winning;
   Thou Lord, wast at our side: all glory be thine.

3. We all do extol thee, thou leader triumphant,
   And pray that thou still our defender wilt be.
   Let thy congregation escape tribulation:
   Thy name be ever praised! O Lord, make us free!

17 Come All You People

Tune: Alexander Gondo;
arr. by John L. Bell, b. 1949

Text: Alexander Gondo

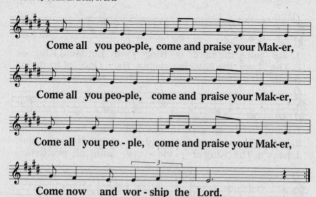

Come all you peo-ple, come and praise your Mak-er,

Come all you peo-ple, come and praise your Mak-er,

Come all you peo - ple, come and praise your Mak-er,

Come now and wor - ship the Lord.

18 To Jesus Christ, Our Sovereign King

1. To Jesus Christ, our sov'reign King,
   Who is the world's Salvation,
   All praise and homage do we bring
   And thanks and adoration.

2. Your reign extend, O King benign,
   To ev'ry land and nation;
   For in your kingdom, Lord divine,
   Alone we find salvation.

3. To you and to your Church, great King,
   We pledge our heart's oblation;
   Until before your throne we sing
   In endless jubilation.

   Refrain:
   Christ Jesus, Victor! Christ Jesus, Ruler!
   Christ Jesus, Lord and Redeemer!

Crown Him with Many Crowns

1. Crown him with many crowns,
   The Lamb upon his throne;
   Hark how the heav'nly anthem drowns
   All music but its own;

   Awake my soul, and sing
   Of him who died for thee,
   And hail him as thy matchless King
   Through all eternity.

2. Crown him of lords the Lord,
   Who over all doth reign,
   Who once on earth, the incarnate Word,
   For ransomed sinners slain.

   Now lives in realms of light,
   Where saints with angels sing
   Their songs before him day and night,
   Their God, Redeemer, King.

O Perfect Love

1. O perfect Love, all human thought transcending.
   Lowly we kneel in prayer before thy throne,
   That theirs may be the love that knows no ending,
   Whom thou for evermore dost join in one.

2. O perfect Life, be thou their full assurance
   Of tender charity and steadfast faith,
   Of patient hope, and quiet, brave endurance,
   With child-like trust that fears not pain nor death.

On Jordan's Bank

1. On Jordan's bank the Baptist's cry
   Announces that the Lord is nigh,
   Awake and hearken, for he brings
   Glad tidings of the King of Kings.

2. Then cleansed be ev'ry breast from sin;
   Make straight the way of God within,
   Oh, let us all our hearts prepare
   For Christ to come and enter there.

Gather Us In

Tune: GATHER US IN, Irreg.,
Marty Haugen, b. 1950

Text: Marty Haugen, b. 1950

1. Here in this place   new light is stream-ing,
2. We are the young—our lives are a mys-t'ry,
3. Here we will take the wine and the wa - ter,
4. Not in the dark of build-ings con - fin - ing,

Now is the dark - ness van-ished a - way,
We are the old— who yearn for your face,
Here we will take the bread of new birth,
Not in some heav - en, light-years a -way, But

See in this space our fears and our dream-ings,
We have been sung through-out all of his - t'ry,
Here you shall call your sons and your daugh-ters,
here in this place the new light is shin-ing,

Brought here to you in the light of this day.
Called to be light to the whole hu-man race.
Call us a - new to be salt for the earth.
Now is the King-dom, now is the day.

Gath - er us in— the lost and for - sak - en,
Gath - er us in— the rich and the haugh-ty,
Give us to drink the wine of com - pas-sion,
Gath - er us in and hold us for ev - er,

Gath-er us in— the blind and the lame;
Gath-er us in— the proud and the strong;
Give us to eat the bread that is you;
Gath-er us in and make us your own;

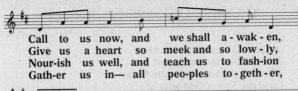

Call to us now, and we shall a-wak-en,
Give us a heart so meek and so low-ly,
Nour-ish us well, and teach us to fash-ion
Gath-er us in— all peo-ples to-geth-er,

We shall a-rise at the sound of our name.
Give us the cour-age to en-ter the song.
Lives that are ho-ly and hearts that are true.
Fire of love in our flesh and our bone.

Confitemini Domino / Come and Fill

23

Tune: Jacques Berthier, 1923–1994

Text: Psalm 137,
Give thanks to the Lord for he is good;
Taizé Community, 1982

Ostinato Refrain

Con-fi-te-mi-ni Do-mi-no
Come and fill our hearts with your peace.

quo-ni-am bo-nus. Con-fi-te-mi-ni
You a-lone, O Lord, are ho-ly. Come and fill our hearts

Do-mi-no, Al-le-lu - ia!
with your peace, Al-le-lu - ia!

24

O Come, O Come, Emmanuel

John M. Neal, Tr.   Melody adapted by T. Helmore

O come, O come, Emmanuel,
And ransom captive Israel,
That mourns in lowly exile here,
Until the Son of God appear.

Refrain: Rejoice! Rejoice! O Israel,
To thee shall come Emmanuel.

25

Come, Thou Long Expected Jesus

1. Come, thou long expected Jesus,
Born to set thy people free;
From our sins and fears release us,
Let us find our rest in thee.

2. Israel's strength and consolation,
Hope of all the earth thou art;
Dear desire of every nation,
Joy of every longing heart.

3. Born thy people to deliver,
Born a child and yet a king.
Born to reign in us for ever,
Now thy gracious kingdom bring.

26

O Come Little Children

O come little children, O come one and all
Draw near to the crib here in Bethlehem's stall
And see what a bright ray of heaven's delight,
Our Father has sent on this thrice holy night.

He lies there, O children, on hay and straw,
Dear Mary and Joseph regard HIm with awe,
The shepherds, adoring, how humbly in pray'r
Angelical choirs with song rend the air.

O children bend low and adore Him today,
O lift up your hands like the shepherds, and pray
Sing joyfully children, with hearts full of love
In jubilant song join the angels above.

O Come, All Ye Faithful

1. O come, all ye faithful, joyful and triumphant,
   O come ye, O come ye to Bethlehem;
   Come and behold Him born, the King of angels.

   Refrain:
   O come, let us adore Him,
   O come, let us adore Him,
   O come, let us adore Him, Christ the Lord.

2. Sing choirs of angels, Sing in exultation.
   Sing all ye citizens of Heav'n above;
   Glory to God, Glory to the highest.—*Refrain*

3. Yea, Lord, we greet thee, born this happy morning,
   Jesus to thee be all glory giv'n;
   Word of the Father, now in flesh appearing.—*Refrain*

The First Noel

1. The first Noel the angel did say,
   Was to certain poor shepherds in fields as they lay;
   In fields where they lay keeping their sheep
   On a cold winter's night that was so deep.

   Refrain:
   Noel, Noel, Noel, Noel,
   Born is the King of Israel.

2. They looked up and saw a star,
   Shining in the east, beyond them far,
   And to the earth it gave great light,
   And so it continued both day and night.—*Refrain*

3. This star drew nigh to the northwest,
   O'er Bethlehem it took its rest,
   And there it did stop and stay,
   Right over the place where Jesus lay.—*Refrain*

4. Then entered in those wise men three,
   Full reverently upon their knee,
   And offered there, in his presence,
   Their gold and myrrh and frankincense.—*Refrain*

29 A Child Is Born in Bethlehem
Three Magi Kings

Carlton

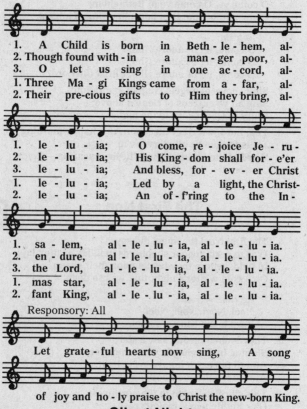

1. A Child is born in Beth-le-hem, al-
2. Though found with-in a man-ger poor, al-
3. O let us sing in one ac-cord, al-
1. Three Ma-gi Kings came from a-far, al-
2. Their pre-cious gifts to Him they bring, al-

1. le-lu-ia; O come, re-joice Je-ru-
2. le-lu-ia; His King-dom shall for-e'er
3. le-lu-ia; And bless, for-ev-er Christ
1. le-lu-ia; Led by a light, the Christ-
2. le-lu-ia; An of-f'ring to the In-

1. sa-lem, al-le-lu-ia, al-le-lu-ia.
2. en-dure, al-le-lu-ia, al-le-lu-ia.
3. the Lord, al-le-lu-ia, al-le-lu-ia.
1. mas star, al-le-lu-ia, al-le-lu-ia.
2. fant King, al-le-lu-ia, al-le-lu-ia.

Responsory: All

Let grate-ful hearts now sing, A song

of joy and ho-ly praise to Christ the new-born King.

Silent Night

30

Silent night, holy night!
All is calm, all is bright.
'Round yon Virgin Mother and Child,
Holy Infant so tender and mild:
Sleep in heavenly peace,
Sleep in heavenly peace.

Silent night, holy night!
Shepherds quake at the sight!
Glories stream from heaven afar,
Heav'nly hosts sing Alleluia:
Christ, the Savior is born,
Christ, the Savior is born!

3. Silent night, holy night!
   Son of God, love's pure light.
   Radiant beams from thy holy face,
   With the dawn of redeeming grace,
   Jesus, Lord, at thy birth,
   Jesus, Lord, at thy birth.

Hark! The Herald Angels Sing

31

1. Hark! The herald angels sing.
   "Glory to the new-born King.
   Peace on earth, and mercy mild
   God and sinners reconciled."
   Joyful all ye nations rise,
   Join the triumph of the skies.
   With th' angelic host proclaim,
   "Christ is born in Bethlehem."

   Refrain:
   Hark! The herald angels sing,
   "Glory to the new-born King."

2. Christ, by highest heaven adored,
   Christ, the everlasting Lord.
   Late in time behold Him come,
   Off-spring of a virgin's womb.
   Veiled in flesh, the God-head see;
   Hail th' incarnate Deity!
   Pleased as Man with men to appear,
   Jesus, our Immanuel here!—*Refrain*

O Sing a Joyous Carol

32

1. O sing a joyous carol
Unto the Holy Child,
And praise with gladsome
       voices
His mother undefiled.
Our gladsome voices greeting
Shall hail our Infant King;
And our sweet Lady listens
When joyful voices sing.

2. Who is there meekly lying
In yonder stable poor?
Dear children, it is Jesus;
He bids you now adore.
Who is there kneeling by him
In virgin beauty fair?
It is our Mother Mary,
She bids you all draw near.

Good Christian Men Rejoice

Tr. John Mason Neale

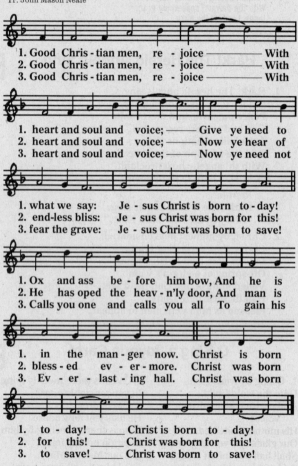

1. Good Chris-tian men, re - joice ——————— With
2. Good Chris-tian men, re - joice ——————— With
3. Good Chris-tian men, re - joice ——————— With

1. heart and soul and voice; —— Give ye heed to
2. heart and soul and voice; —— Now ye hear of
3. heart and soul and voice; —— Now ye need not

1. what we say: Je - sus Christ is born to - day!
2. end-less bliss: Je - sus Christ was born for this!
3. fear the grave: Je - sus Christ was born to save!

1. Ox and ass be - fore him bow, And he is
2. He has oped the heav - n'ly door, And man is
3. Calls you one and calls you all To gain his

1. in the man - ger now. Christ is born
2. bless - ed ev - er - more. Christ was born
3. Ev - er - last - ing hall. Christ was born

1. to - day! _____ Christ is born to - day!
2. for this! _____ Christ was born for this!
3. to save! _____ Christ was born to save!

Angels We Have Heard on High

1. Angels we have heard on high,
   Sweetly singing o'er the plains,
   And the mountains in reply
   Echoing their joyous strains.

   Refrain: Gloria in excelsis Deo. (Repeat)

2. Shepherds, why this jubilee,
   Why your rapturous song prolong?
   What the gladsome tidings be
   Which inspire your heav'nly song?—*Refrain*

3. Come to Bethlehem and see
   Him whose birth the angels sing;
   Come, adore on bended knee
   Christ the Lord, the new-born King.—*Refrain*

Away in a Manger

1. Away in a manger, no crib for his bed,
   The little Lord Jesus laid down his sweet head.
   The stars in the bright sky looked down where he lay,
   The little Lord Jesus asleep on the hay.

2. The cattle are lowing, the baby awakes,
   But little Lord Jesus no crying he makes.
   I love thee, Lord Jesus! Look down from the sky,
   And stay by my side until morning is nigh.

3. Be near me Lord Jesus, I ask thee to stay
   Close by me forever, and love me I pray.
   Bless all the dear children in thy tender care,
   And fit us for heaven to live with thee there.

O Little Town of Bethlehem

O little town of Bethlehem,
How still we see thee lie!
Above the deep and dreamless sleep
The silent stars go by;
Yet in the dark streets shineth
The everlasting Light;
The hopes and fears of all the years
Are met in thee tonight.

For Christ is born of Mary,
And gathered all above,
While mortals sleep, the angels keep
Their watch of wondering love.
O morning stars, together
Proclaim the holy birth!
And praising sing to God the King
And peace to men on earth.

O holy Child of Bethlehem!
Descend on us we pray;
Cast out our sin, and enter in,
Be born in us today.
We hear the Christmas angels,
The great glad tidings tell;
O come to us, abide with us,
Our Lord Emmanuel.

37

What Child Is This?

What child is this, who laid to rest,
On Mary's lap is sleeping?
Whom angels greet with anthems sweet,
While shepherds watch are keeping?

> *Refrain:*
> This, this is Christ the King,
> Whom shepherds guard and angels sing;
> Haste, haste to bring him laud,
> The Babe, the Son of Mary.

Why lies he in such mean estate
Where ox and ass are feeding?
Good Christian fear, for sinners here
The silent Word is pleading.—*Refrain*

So bring him incense, gold, and myrrh,
Come peasant, king to own him,
The King of kings salvation brings,
Let loving hearts enthrone him.—*Refrain*

We Three Kings

1. We three kings of Orient are
   Bearing gifts we traverse afar,
   Field and fountain, moor and mountain,
   Following yonder star.

   Refrain:
   O Star of wonder, Star of night,
   Star with royal beauty bright,
   Westward leading, still proceeding,
   Guide us to thy perfect light.

2. Born a king on Bethlehem's plain,
   Gold I bring to crown Him again,
   King forever, ceasing never,
   Over us all to reign.—*Refrain*

3. Frankincense to offer have I
   Incense owns a Deity high,
   Prayer and praising, all men raising,
   Worship Him, God most High.—*Refrain*

4. Myrrh is mine, its bitter perfume
   Breathes a life of gathering gloom:
   Sorrowing, sighing, bleeding, dying,
   Sealed in the stone-cold tomb.—*Refrain*

5. Glorious now behold Him arise,
   King and God and Sacrifice,
   Alleluia, Alleluia,
   Earth to the heavens replies.—*Refrain*

Holy God, We Praise Thy Name

1. Holy God, we praise Thy Name!
   Lord of all, we bow before Thee!
   All on earth Thy sceptre claim,
   All in heaven above adore Thee.
   Infinite Thy vast domain,
   Everlasting is Thy reign. *Repeat last two lines*

2. Hark! the loud celestial hymn,
   Angel choirs above are raising;
   Cherubim and seraphim,
   In unceasing chorus praising,
   Fill the heavens with sweet accord;
   Holy, holy, holy Lord! *Repeat last two lines*

40 Lord, Who throughout These 40 Days

1. Lord, who throughout these forty days
   For us did fast and pray,
   Teach us with you to mourn our sins,
   And close by you to stay.

2. And through these days of penitence,
   And through your Passiontide,
   Yea, evermore, in life and death,
   Jesus! with us abide.

3. Abide with us, that so, this life
   Of suff'ring over past,
   An Easter of unending joy
   We may attain at last. Amen.

41 When I Behold the Wondrous Cross

1. When I   be - hold the won-drous cross
2. For - bid   it, Lord, that I should boast,
3. See   from his head, his hands, his feet,
4. Were   all   the realms of na - ture mine,

1. On which the prince of glo - ry died,_
2. Save in the death of Christ, my God;_
3. What grief and love flow min - gled down;_
4. It would be off - 'ring far too small;_

1. My rich - est gain I count_ but loss,
2. The vain things that at - tract_ me most,
3. Did e'er such love that sor - row meet,
4. Love so a - maz - ing, so_ di - vine,

1. And pour con - tempt on all_ my pride.
2. I sac - ri - fice them to_ his blood.
3. Or thorns com - pose so rich_ a crown?
4. De - mands my soul, my life,_ my all.

608

Jesus, Remember Me

Tune: Jacques Berthier, 1923-1994

Text: Luke 23:42
Taizé Community, 1981

Ostinato Refrain

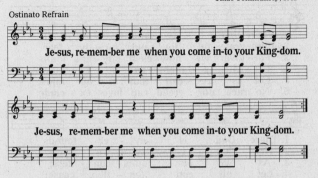

Je-sus, re-mem-ber me when you come in-to your King-dom.

Je-sus, re-mem-ber me when you come in-to your King-dom.

O Sacred Head Surrounded

1. O sacred Head surrounded
   By crown of piercing thorn!
   O bleeding Head, so wounded,
   Reviled, and put to scorn!
   Death's pallid hue comes ov'r you,
   The glow of life decays,
   Yet angel hosts adore you,
   And tremble as they gaze.

2. I see your strength and vigor
   All fading in the strife,
   And death with cruel rigor,
   Bereaving you of life.
   O agony and dying!
   O love to sinners free!
   Jesus, all grace supplying,
   O turn your face on me.

Where Charity and Love Prevail

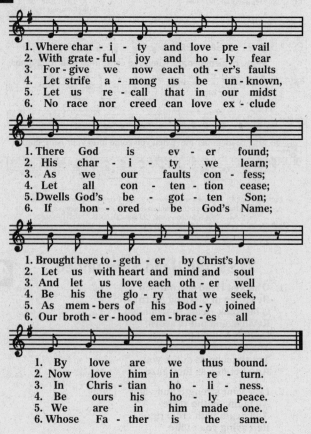

1. Where char - i - ty and love pre - vail
2. With grate - ful joy and ho - ly fear
3. For - give we now each oth - er's faults
4. Let strife a - mong us be un - known,
5. Let us re - call that in our midst
6. No race nor creed can love ex - clude

1. There God is ev - er found;
2. His char - i - ty we learn;
3. As we our faults con - fess;
4. Let all con - ten - tion cease;
5. Dwells God's be - got - ten Son;
6. If hon - ored be God's Name;

1. Brought here to - geth - er by Christ's love
2. Let us with heart and mind and soul
3. And let us love each oth - er well
4. Be his the glo - ry that we seek,
5. As mem - bers of his Bod - y joined
6. Our broth - er - hood em - brac - es all

1. By love are we thus bound.
2. Now love him in re - turn.
3. In Chris - tian ho - li - ness.
4. Be ours his ho - ly peace.
5. We are in him made one.
6. Whose Fa - ther is the same.

O Faithful Cross

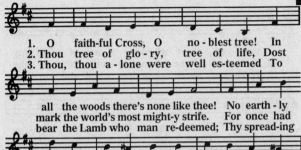

1. O faith-ful Cross, O no - blest tree! In
2. Thou tree of glo - ry, tree of life, Dost
3. Thou, thou a - lone were well es-teemed To

all the woods there's none like thee! No earth - ly
mark the world's most might-y strife. For once had
bear the Lamb who man re-deemed; Thy spread-ing

grooves, no shad - y bowers. Pro-duce such leaves, such
been the sigh of shame, For Je - sus now the
arms, like bal-ance true; Weighed out the price for

fruit, such flowers. Sweet are the nails and sweet the
world doth claim. Lo, from the cross, his al - tar
sin-ners due. And on thy al - tar, meek - ly

wood That bears a load so sweet, so good!
throne, He gent - ly draws and rules his own.
laid, The Lamb of God a - tone-ment made.

O God, Our Help in Ages Past

I. Watts

1.
O God, our help in ages past,
Our hope for years to come,
Our shelter from the stormy blast,
And our eternal home.

2.
Under the shadow of Thy throne,
Thy saints have dwelt secure.
Sufficient is Thine arm alone,
And our defense is sure.

3.
A thousand ages in Thy sight,
Are like an evening gone;
Short as the watch that ends the night,
Before the rising sun.

4.
O God, our help in ages past,
Our hope for years to come,
Be Thou our guide while troubles last,
And our eternal home.

Were You There

1. Were you there when they cru-ci-fied my
2. Were you there when they nailed him to the
3. Were you there when they laid him in the

1. Lord? Were you there when they
2. tree? Were you there when they
3. tomb? Were you there when they

1. cru-ci-fied my Lord?
2. nailed him to the tree? } Oh_____
3. laid him in the tomb? }

Some-times it caus-es me to

trem-ble, trem-ble trem-ble. {
1. Were you
2. Were you
3. Were you

1. there when they cru-ci-fied my Lord?
2. there when they nailed him to the tree?
3. there when they laid him in the tomb?

At the Cross Her Station Keeping

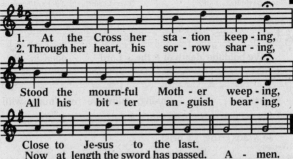

1. At the Cross her sta-tion keep-ing,
2. Through her heart, his sor-row shar-ing,

Stood the mourn-ful Moth-er weep-ing,
All his bit-ter an-guish bear-ing,

Close to Je-sus to the last.
Now at length the sword has passed. A - men.

3. Oh, how sad and sore distressed
Was that Mother highly blessed
Of the sole begotten One!

4. Christ above in torment hangs,
She beneath beholds the pangs
Of her dying, glorious Son.

5. Is there one who would not weep
'Whelmed in miseries so deep
Christ's dear Mother to behold?

6. Can the human heart refrain
From partaking in her pain,
In that mother's pain untold?

7. Bruised, derided, cursed, defiled,
She beheld her tender Child,
All with bloody scourges rent.

8. For the sins of His own nation
Saw Him hang in desolation
Till His spirit forth He sent.

9. O sweet Mother! fount of love,
Touch my spirit from above,
Make my heart with yours accord.

10. Make me feel as you have felt.
Make my soul to glow and melt
With the love of Christ, my Lord.

11. Holy Mother, pierce me through,
In my heart each wound renew
Of my Savior crucified.

12. Let me share with you His pain,
Who for all our sins was slain,
Who for me in torments died.

13. Let me mingle tears with you
Mourning Him Who mourned for me,
All the days that I may live.

14. By the Cross with you to stay,
There with you to weep and pray,
Is all I ask of you to give.

15. Virgin of all virgins blest!
Listen to my fond request.
Let me share your grief divine.

16. Let me, to my latest breath
In my body bear the death
Of that dying Son of yours.

17. Wounded with His every wound,
Steep my soul till it has swooned
In His very blood away.

18. Be to me, O Virgin, nigh,
Lest in flames I burn and die,
In His awful judgment day.

19. Christ, when You shall call me hence
Be Your Mother my defense.
Be Your Cross my victory.

20. While my body here decays,
May my soul Your goodness praise
Safe in heaven eternally.
Amen. Alleluia.

Now We Remain

Tune: David Haas, b. 1957

Text: Corinthians, 1 John, 2 Timothy;
David Haas, b. 1957

Refrain

We hold the death of the Lord deep in our hearts. Liv-ing; now we re-main with Je-sus the Christ.

Verses

1. Once we were peo-ple a-fraid, lost in the night. Then by our cross we were saved; Dead be-came liv-ing, Life from your giv-ing.

2. Some-thing which we have known, some-thing we've touched, What we have seen with our eyes: This we have heard; Life giv-ing word.

3. He chose to give of him-self, be-came our bread. Bro-ken, that we might live. Love be-yond love, Pain for our pain.

1.–3. ... *D.C.* *4.* ... for to live with the Lord, we must die with the Lord.

O Lord, Hear My Prayer

50

Tune: Jaques Berthier, 1923-1994

Text: Psalm 102
Taizé Community, 1982

Ostinato Chorale

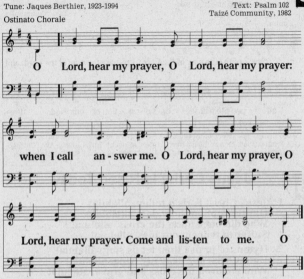

O Lord, hear my prayer, O Lord, hear my prayer:

when I call an-swer me. O Lord, hear my prayer, O

Lord, hear my prayer. Come and lis-ten to me. O

Stay Here and Keep Watch

51

Tune: Jaques Berthier, 1923-1994

Text: from Matthew 26;
Taizé Community

Stay here and keep watch with me. The hour has come.

Stay here and keep watch with me. Watch and pray.

52 Prepare the Way of the Lord

Tune: Jaques Berthier, 1923-1994

Text: Luke 3:4, 6;
Taizé Community

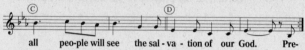

Pre - pare the way of the Lord. Pre-pare the way of the Lord, and

all peo-ple will see the sal - va - tion of our God. Pre-

53 Jesus Christ Is Risen Today

1. Jesus Christ is ris'n today, alleluia!
   Our triumphant holy day, alleluia!
   Who did once upon the cross, alleluia!
   Suffer to redeem our loss, alleluia!

2. Hymns of praise then let us sing, alleluia!
   Unto Christ our heav'nly King, alleluia!
   Who endured the cross and grave, alleluia!
   Sinners to redeem and save, alleluia!

3. Sing we to our God above, alleluia!
   Praise eternal as his love, alleluia!
   Praise him, all ye heav'nly host, alleluia!
   Father, Son and Holy Ghost, alleluia!

54 At the Lamb's High Feast We Sing

1. At the Lamb's high feast we sing
   Praise to our victor'ous King,
   Who has washed us in the tide
   Flowing from his pierced side;
   Praise we him whose love divine
   Gives the guests his Blood for wine,
   Gives his Body for the feast,
   Love the Victim, Love the Priest.

2. When the Paschal blood is poured,
   Death's dark Angel sheathes his sword;
   Israel's hosts triumphant go
   Through the wave that drowns the foe.

Christ, the Lamb whose Blood was shed,
Paschal victim, Paschal bread;
With sincerity and love
Eat we Manna from above.

Christ the Lord Is Risen Today

Tr. Jane E. Leeson, 1807-1882   Traditional

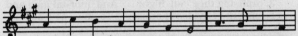

1. Christ, the Lord is risn' to-day,
2. Christ, the Vic-tim un-de-filed,
3. Christ, Who once for sin-ners bled,

Chris-tians, haste your vows to pay; Of-fer ye your
Man to God hath re-con-ciled; When in strange and
Now the first born of the dead, Thron'd in end-less

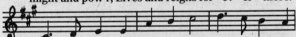

prais-es meet   At the Pas-chal Vic-tim's feet.
aw-ful strife   Met to-geth-er death and life;
might and pow'r, Lives and reigns for-ev-er more.

For the sheep the Lamb hath bled; Sin-less in the
Chris-tians on this hap-py day Haste with joy your
Hail, e-ter-nal Hope on high! Hail, Thou King of

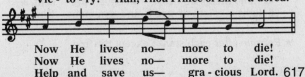

sin-ner's stead; Christ, the Lord, is ris'n on high,
vows to pay. Christ, the Lord, is ris'n on high,
Vic-to-ry!   Hail, Thou Prince of Life a-dored!

Now He lives no— more to die!
Now He lives no— more to die!
Help and save us— gra-cious Lord. 617

All Glory, Laud, and Honor

Tr. John Mason Neale, 1851

Melchior Teschner, pub. 1615

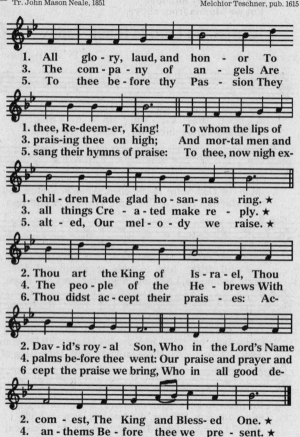

1. All glo - ry, laud, and hon - or To
3. The com - pa - ny of an - gels Are
5. To thee be - fore thy Pas - sion They

1. thee, Re - deem - er, King! To whom the lips of
3. prais - ing thee on high; And mor - tal men and
5. sang their hymns of praise: To thee, now nigh ex -

1. chil - dren Made glad ho - san - nas ring. ★
3. all things Cre - a - ted make re - ply. ★
5. alt - ed, Our mel - o - dy we raise. ★

2. Thou art the King of Is - ra - el, Thou
4. The peo - ple of the He - brews With
6. Thou didst ac - cept their prais - es: Ac -

2. Dav - id's roy - al Son, Who in the Lord's Name
4. palms be - fore thee went: Our praise and prayer and
6 cept the praise we bring, Who in all good de -

2. com - est, The King and Bless - ed One. ★
4. an - thems Be - fore thee we pre - sent. ★
6 light - est, thou good and gra - cious King. ★

★ *Refrain:* after each stanza except the first.

The Strife Is O'er

Alleluia! Alleluia! Alleluia!

1. The strife is o'er, the battle done!
   The victory of life is won!
   The song of triumph has begun! Alleluia!

2. The powers of death have done their worst,
   But Christ their legions has dispersed;
   Let shouts of holy joy outburst! Alleluia!

3. The three sad days are quickly sped,
   He rises glor'ous from the dead;
   All glory to our risen Head! Alleluia!

4. He closed the yawning gates of hell;
   The bars from heaven's high portals fell;
   Let hymns of praise His triumph tell! Alleluia!

O Sons and Daughters, Let Us Sing!

Alleluia! Alleluia! Alleluia!

1. O sons and daughters, let us sing!
   The King of heav'n, the glorious King,
   Today is ris'n and triumphing. Alleluia!

2. On Easter morn, at break of day,
   The faithful women went their way
   To seek the tomb where Jesus lay. Alleluia!

3. An angel clad in white they see,
   Who sat and spoke unto the three,
   "Your Lord doth go to Galilee." Alleluia!

4. On this most holy day of days,
   To you our hearts and voice we raise,
   In laud and jubilee and praise. Alleluia!

5. Glory to Father and to Son,
   Who has for us the vict'ry won
   And Holy Ghost; blest Three in One. Alleluia!

59. Christ the Lord Is Risen Again

1. Christ the Lord is ris'n a-gain!
2. He who gave for us his life,
3. He who bore all pain and loss

Christ has bro-ken ev-'ry chain!
Who for us en-dured the strife,
Com-fort-less up-on the Cross,

Hark, the an-gels shout for joy,
Is our Pas-chal Lamb to-day!
Lives in glo-ry now on high,

Sing-ing ev-er more on high,_
We too sing for joy and say,_
Pleads for us and hears our cry,_

Al-le-lu-ia. Al-le-lu-

ia. Al-le-lu-ia.

60. Creator Spirit, Lord of Grace

Creator Spirit, Lord of Grace,
Make thou our hearts thy dwelling place;
And, with thy might celestial, aid
The souls of those whom thou hast made.

O to our souls thy light impart,
And give thy love to every heart;
Turn all our weakness into might,
O thou the source of life and light.

Send Us Your Spirit

Tune: David Haas, b. 1957
acc. by Jeanne Cotter, b. 1964

Text: David Haas, b. 1957

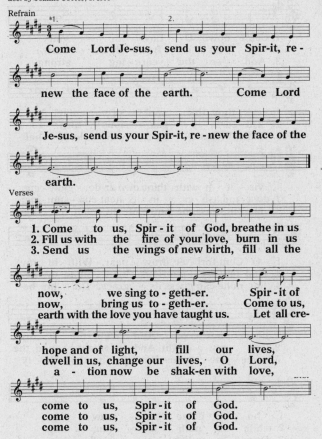

Refrain

Come Lord Je-sus, send us your Spir-it, re-new the face of the earth. Come Lord Je-sus, send us your Spir-it, re-new the face of the earth.

Verses

1. Come to us, Spir-it of God, breathe in us now, we sing to-geth-er. Spir-it of hope and of light, fill our lives, come to us, Spir-it of God.

2. Fill us with the fire of your love, burn in us now, bring us to-geth-er. Come to us, dwell in us, change our lives, O Lord, come to us, Spir-it of God.

3. Send us the wings of new birth, fill all the earth with the love you have taught us. Let all cre-a-tion now be shak-en with love, come to us, Spir-it of God.

* May be sung in canon.

Come Down, O Love Divine

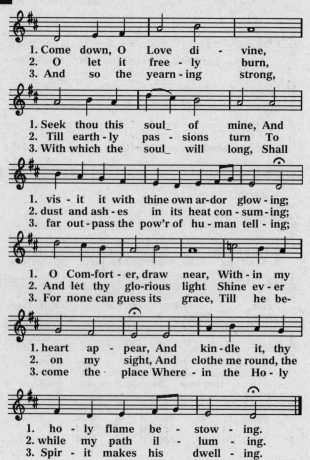

1. Come down, O Love di - vine,
2. O let it free - ly burn,
3. And so the yearn - ing strong,

1. Seek thou this soul_ of mine, And
2. Till earth - ly pas - sions turn To
3. With which the soul_ will long, Shall

1. vis - it it with thine own ar-dor glow - ing;
2. dust and ash - es in its heat con - sum - ing;
3. far out - pass the pow'r of hu - man tell - ing;

1. O Com-fort - er, draw near, With - in my
2. And let thy glo-rious light Shine ev - er
3. For none can guess its grace, Till he be-

1. heart ap - pear, And kin - dle it, thy
2. on my sight, And clothe me round, the
3. come the place Where - in the Ho - ly

1. ho - ly flame be - stow - ing.
2. while my path il - lum - ing.
3. Spir - it makes his dwell - ing.

Come, Holy Ghost, Creator Blest

1. Come, Holy Ghost, Creator blest,
   And in our hearts take up thy rest;
   Come with thy grace and heav'nly aid
   To fill the hearts which thou hast made,
   To fill the hearts which thou hast made.

2. O Comforter, to thee we cry,
   Thou heav'nly gift of God most high;
   Thou fount of life and fire of love
   And sweet anointing from above,
   And sweet anointing from above.

3. Praise we the Father, and the Son,
   And the blest Spirit with them one;
   And may the Son on us bestow
   The gifts that from the Spirit flow,
   The gifts that from the Spirit flow.

O God of Loveliness

1. O God of loveliness, O Lord of Heav'n above,
   How worthy to possess my heart's devoted love!
   So sweet Thy Countenance, so gracious to behold,
   That one, and only glance to me were bliss untold.

2. Thou are blest Three in One, yet undivided still;
   Thou art that One alone whose love my heart can fill,
   The heav'ns and earth below, were fashioned by Thy
        Word;
   How amiable art Thou, my ever dearest Lord!

3. O loveliness supreme, and beauty infinite
   O everflowing Stream, and Ocean of delight;
   O life by which I live, my truest life above,
   To You alone I give my undivided love.

65 Psalm 23: Shepherd Me, O God

Music: Marty Haugen

Text: Psalm 23; Marty Haugen

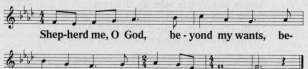

Refrain

Shep-herd me, O God, be - yond my wants, be-yond my fears, from death in-to life.

Verses

1. God is my shepherd, so nothing shall I want,
   I rest in the meadows of faithfulness and love,
   I walk by the quiet waters of peace.

2. Gently you raise me and heal my weary soul,
   you lead me by pathways of righteousness and truth,
   my spirit shall sing the music of your name.

3. Though I should wander the valley of death,
   I fear no evil, for you are at my side, your rod and your
       staff,
   my comfort and my hope.

4. Surely your kindness and mercy follow me all the days
       of my life;
   I will dwell in the house of my God for evermore.

66 Eat This Bread

Tune: Jacques Berthier, 1923-1994   Text: John 6; adapt. by Robert J. Batastini, b. 1942
and the Taizé Community

Refrain

Eat this bread, drink this cup, come to him and nev-er be hun-gry.

Eat this bread, drink this cup, trust in him and you will not thirst.

When Morning Gilds the Skies

E. Caswall, Tr.   Traditional

1. When morn - ing gilds the skies   My
2. Be   this, while life   is   mine,   My
3. To   God, the Word, on   high   The
4. Let   earth's wide cir - cle   round   In

1. heart a - wak-ing cries; May Je - sus Christ be
2. cant - i - cle   di - vine; May Je - sus Christ be
3. hosts of an - gels cry; May Je - sus Christ be
4. joy - ful song re - sound; May Je - sus Christ be

1. praised!   A - like at work and   prayer To
2. praised!   Be   our e - ter - nal   song, Through
3. praised!   Let   na - tions too up - raise Their
4. praised!   Let   air, and sea, and   sky, Through

1. Je - sus I re - pair: May Je-sus Christ be
2. all   the   a - ges   long. May Je-sus Christ be
3. voice in hymns of   praise: May Je-sus Christ be
4. depth and height re - ply   May Je-sus Christ be

1. praised!   May Je - sus Christ be   praised!
2. praised!   May Je - sus Christ be   praised!
3. praised!   May Je - sus Christ be   praised!
4. praised!   May Je - sus Christ be   praised!

68 Take and Eat

Tune: Michael Joncas, b. 1951

Text: Verse text, James Quinn, SJ, b. 1919, © 1989.
Used by permission of Selah Publishing Co., Inc.
refrain text, Michael Joncas, b. 1951

Refrain

Take and eat;   take and eat: this is my bod-y giv-en up for you.   Take and drink;   take and drink: this is my blood   giv-en up for   you.

Verses

1. I am the Word that spoke and light was made;
2. I am the way that leads the   ex - ile home;
3. I am the Lamb that takes a - way your sin;
4. I am the cor - ner - stone that God has laid;
5. I am the light that came in - to the world;

   I am the seed that died   to   be re - born;
   I am the truth that sets the   cap - tive free;
   I am the gate that guards you   night and day;
   A cho-sen stone and pre - cious   in his eyes;
   I am the light   that dark - ness can - not hide;

   I am   the bread that comes from heav'n a - bove;
   I am   the life that rais - es   up the dead;
   You are   my flock: you know the shep-herd's voice;
   You are God's dwell-ing place, on   me you rest;
   I am   the morn-ing star that nev - er sets;

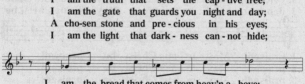

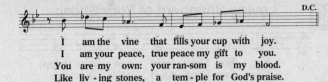

I am the vine that fills your cup with joy.
I am your peace, true peace my gift to you.
You are my own: your ran-som is my blood.
Like liv-ing stones, a tem-ple for God's praise.
Lift up your face, in you my light will shine.

Holy Is Your Name / Luke 1:46-55

69

Music: WILD MOUNTAIN THYME, Irreg.
Irish traditional; arr. by David Haas

Text: Luke 1:46-55, David Haas

Refrain

And ho-ly is your name through all gen-er-

a-tions! Ev-er-last-ing is your mer-cy to the

peo-ple you have cho-sen, and ho-ly is your name.

Verses

1. My soul is filled with joy as I sing to God my savior:
   you have looked upon your servant, you have visited your
   people.

2. I am lowly as a child, but I know from this day forward
   that my name will be remembered, for all will call me
   blessed.

3. I proclaim the pow'r of God, you do marvels for your
   servants;
   though you scatter the proud hearted, and destroy the might
   of princes.

4. To the hungry you give food, send the rich away empty.
   In your mercy you are mindful of the people you have
   chosen.

5. In your love you now fulfill what you have promised to your
   people.
   I will praise you, Lord, my savior, everlasting is your mercy.

70. Loving Shepherd of Your Sheep

1. Lov - ing Shep - herd of your sheep,
2. Lov - ing Shep - herd you did give,
3. Lov - ing Shep - herd ev - er near,

Keep us Lord in safe - ty keep;
Your own life that we might live;
Teach us still your voice to hear;

Noth - ing can your pow'r with - stand,
May we love you day by day,
Suf - fer not our steps to stray

None can pluck us from your hand.
Glad - ly your sweet Will o - bey.
From the straight and nar - row way.

Good Shep - herd, shield us.
Good Shep - herd, shield us.
Good Shep - herd, shield us.

71. In the Lord's Atoning Grief

1. In the Lord's atoning grief
   Be our rest and sweet relief;
   Deep within our hearts we'll store
   Those dear pains and wrongs he bore.

2. Thorns and cross and nail and spear,
   Wounds that faithful hearts revere,
   Vinegar and gall and reed
   And the pang his soul that freed.

3. Crucified we thee adore,
   Thee with all our hearts implore;
   With the saints our soul unite,
   In the realms of heav'nly light.

Taste and See

72

Tune: James E. Moore, Jr., b. 1951

Text: Psalm 34;
James E. Moore, Jr., b. 1951

Refrain

Taste and see, taste and see the good-ness of the
Lord. O taste and see, taste and see the
good - ness of the Lord, of the Lord.

Verses

1. I will bless the Lord at all times.
2. Glo - ri - fy the Lord with me,
3. Wor-ship the Lord, all you peo-ple.

Praise shall al-ways be on my lips;
To-geth-er let us all praise God's name.
You'll want for noth-ing if you ask.

my soul shall glo-ry in the Lord
I called the Lord who an - swered me;
Taste and see that the Lord is good;

D.C.

for God has been so good to me.
from all my tou-bles I was set free.
in God we need put all our trust.

73 Song of the Body of Christ / Canción del Cuerpo de Cristo

Tune: NO KE ANO' AHI, Irreg.,
Hawaiian traditional,
arr. by David Haas, b. 1957

Text: David Haas, b. 1957,
Spanish translation by Donna Peña, b. 1955,
and Ronald F. Krisman, b. 1946

Refrain

We come to share our sto-ry we
Hoy ve-ni-mos a con-tar nues-tra_his-to-ria, com-par-

come to break the bread, We come to
tien-do_el pan ce-les-tial. Hoy ve-ni-mos jun-tos

know our ris-ing from the dead.
a ce-le-brar tu mis-te-rio pas-cual.

Verses

1. We come as your peo-ple, we
2. We are called to heal the bro-ken, to be
3. Bread of life and cup of prom-ise, in this
4. You will lead and we shall fol-low, you will
5. We will live and sing: your prais-es, "Al-le-

1. come as your own, u-nit-ed with each
2. hope for the poor, we are called to feed the
3. meal we all are one. In our dy-ing and our
4. be the breath of life; liv-ing wa-ter, we are
5. lu-ia" is our song. May we live in love and

D.C.

1. oth-er, love finds a home.
2. hun-gry at our door.
3. ris-ing, may your king-dom come.
4. thirst-ing for your light.
5. peace our whole life long.

1. Hoy ve-ni-mos por-que so-mos tu pue-blo, re-na-
2. A sa-nar al en-fer-mo nos lla-mas, al an-
3. Pan de vi-da y san-gre de la a-lian-za, haz-nos
4. Nos guia-rás y te se-gui-re-mos. Nues-tro a-
5. Vi-vi-re-mos can-tan-do "A-lo-ja." "A-le-

ci - dos por tu per-dón, re-u-ni-dos
sio-so, tu_es-pe-ran-za tra-er, y al ham-brien-to,
u-no_en es-ta co-mu-nión. Que tu rei-no
lien-to vi-tal tú se-rás. Nuse-tra luz en el
lu-ya" es nues-tra can-ción. Que vi-va-mos por

D.C.

en tu a-mor, y de un co-ra-zón.
nues-tro a-li-men-to o-fre-cer.
ven-ga en nues-tra trans-for-ma-ción.
dí-a y en la no-che bri-lla-rás.
siem-pre en paz y fra-ter-na u-nión.

Ubi Caritas

74

Tune: Jacques Berthier 1923-1994   Text: 1 Corinthians 13:2-8

Refrain

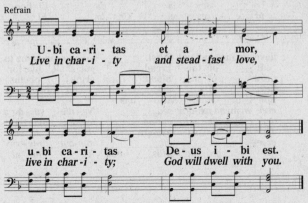

U-bi ca-ri-tas et a-mor,
Live in char-i-ty and stead-fast love,

u-bi ca-ri-tas De-us i-bi est.
live in char-i-ty; God will dwell with you.

I Am the Bread of Life

Tune: BREAD OF LIFE, Irreg with refrain;
Suzanne Toolan, SM, b. 1927.

Text: John 6;
Suzanne Toolan, SM, b. 1927

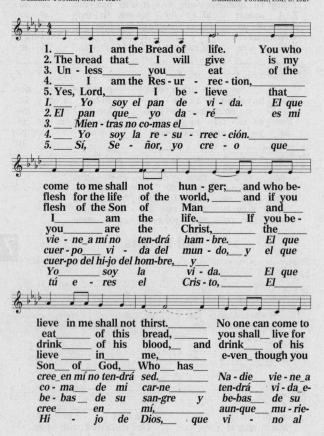

1. ___ I am the Bread of life. You who
2. The bread that___ I will give is my
3. Un-less___ you eat of the
4. ___ I am the Res-ur-rec-tion,___
5. Yes, Lord,___ I be-lieve that___

1. Yo soy el pan de vi-da. El que
2. El pan que___ yo da-ré es mi
3. ___ Mien-tras no co-mas el___
4. ___ Yo soy la re-su-rrec-ción.___
5. ___ Sí, Se-ñor, yo cre-o que___

come to me shall not hun-ger;___ and who be-
flesh for the life of the world,___ and if you
flesh of the Son of Man___ and___
I___ am the life. If you be-
you___ are the Christ,___ the___

vie-ne_a mí no ten-drá ham-bre.___ El que
cuer-po___ vi-da del mun-do,___ y el que
cuer-po del hi-jo del hom-bre,___ y___
Yo___ soy la vi-da.___ El que
tú e-res el Cris-to,___ El___

lieve in me shall not thirst.___ No one can come to
eat___ of this bread,___ you shall__ live for
drink___ of his blood,__ and drink___ of his
lieve in___ me,___ e-ven__ though you
Son___ of God,___ Who___ has___

cree_en mí no ten-drá sed.___ Na-die___ vie-ne_a
co-ma___ de mi car-ne___ ten-drá___ vi-da_e-
be-bas__ de su san-gre y be-bas___ de su
cree en mí,___ aun-que___ mu-rie-
Hi-jo de Dios,___ que vi-no al

me   un - less the___ Fa - ther   beck-ons.
ev - er,_____ you shall__ live   for   ev - er.
blood,   you shall not have life with - in   you.
die,_____   you shall__ live for   ev - er.
come   in - to_____the_____   world.___
mí_____ mien-tras el Pa - dre   lla - me.
ter - na,_____ ten - drá___ vi - da_e - ter - na.
san - gre,   no ten - drá___ vi - da   en ti.
ra,_____ ten - drá vi - da   e - ter - na.
mun-do_____ pa-ra sal-var-nos.

And I will raise you up,   and I will
Yo   le re - su - ci - ta - ré,   Yo lo re-

raise   you up,   and I will raise   you
su - ci - ta - ré,   Yo lo re - su - ci - ta-

up   on the last   day.
ré   el   di - a   de_El.

O Lord, I Am Not Worthy

76

1. O Lord, I am not worthy,
   That thou should come to me,
   But speak the word of comfort
   My spirit healed shall be.

2. And humbly I'll receive thee,
   The bridegroom of my soul,
   No more by sin to grieve thee
   Or fly thy sweet control.

3. O Sacrament most holy,
   O Sacrament divine,
   All praise and all thanksgiving
   Be every moment thine.

The Summons

Tune: KELVINGROVE, 7 6 7 6 777 6;
Scottish traditional; arr. by John L. Bell, b. 1949

Text: John L. Bell, b. 1949;

1. Will you come and fol-low me If I but call your name? Will you go where you don't know And nev-er be the same? Will you let my love be shown, Will you let my name be known, Will you let my life be grown In you and you in me?

2. Will you leave your-self be-hind If I but call your name? Will you care for cruel and kind And nev-er be the same? Will you risk the hos-tile stare Should your life at-tract or scare? Will you let me an-swer prayer In you and you in me?

3. Will you let the blind-ed see If I but call your name? Will you set the pris-'ners free And nev-er be the same? Will you kiss the lep-er clean, And do such as this un-seen, And ad-mit to what I mean In you and you in me?

4. Will you love the 'you' you hide If I but call your name? Will you quell the fear in-side And nev-er be the same? Will you use the faith you've found To re-shape the world a-round, Through my sight and touch and sound In you and you in me?

You Are Mine

78

Tune: David Haas, b. 1957

Text: David Haas, b. 1957

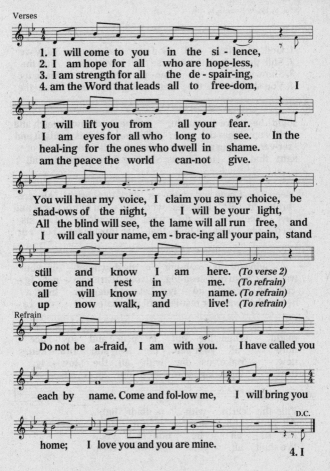

Verses

1. I will come to you in the si - lence,
2. I am hope for all who are hope-less,
3. I am strength for all the de - spair-ing,
4. am the Word that leads all to free-dom, I

I will lift you from all your fear.
I am eyes for all who long to see. In the
heal-ing for the ones who dwell in shame.
am the peace the world can-not give.

You will hear my voice, I claim you as my choice, be
shad-ows of the night, I will be your light,
All the blind will see, the lame will all run free, and
I will call your name, em - brac-ing all your pain, stand

still and know I am here. *(To verse 2)*
come and rest in me. *(To refrain)*
all will know my name. *(To refrain)*
up now walk, and live! *(To refrain)*

Refrain

Do not be a-fraid, I am with you. I have called you

each by name. Come and fol-low me, I will bring you

D.C.

home; I love you and you are mine.

4. I

79 God of Day and God of Darkness

Tune: BEACH SPRING, 8 7 8 7 D;
The Sacred Harp, 1844;
harm. by Marty Haugen, b. 1950

Text: Marty Haugen, b. 1950

1. God of day and God of dark - ness, Now we
2. Still the na - tions curse the dark - ness, Still the
3. Show us Christ in one an - oth - er, Make us
4. You shall be the path that guides us, You the

stand be - fore the night; As the shad - ows stretch and
rich op - press the poor; Still the earth is bruised and
ser - vants strong and true; Give us all your love of
light that in us burns; Shin-ing deep with - in all

deep - en, Come and make our dark-ness bright. All cre-
brok - en By the ones who still want more. Come and
jus - tice So we do what you would do. Let us
peo - ple, Yours the love that we must learn, For our

a - tion still is groan-ing For the dawn-ing of your
wake us from our sleep-ing, So our hearts can - not ig -
call all peo-ple ho - ly, Let us pledge our lives a -
hearts shall wan-der rest-less 'Til they safe to you re -

might, When the Sun of peace and jus - tice
nore all your peo - ple lost and bro - ken,
new, Make us one with all the low - ly,
turn; Find - ing you in one an - oth - er,

Fills the earth with ra - diant light.
All your chil - dren at our door.
Let us all be one in you.
We shall all your face dis - cern.

We Walk by Faith

Tune: SHANTI, CM;
Marty Haugen, b. 1950

Text: Henry Alford, 1810-1871, alt.

1. , 5. We walk by faith and not by sight: No
2. We may not touch his hands and side, Nor
3. Help then, O Lord, our un - be - lief, And
4. That when our life of faith is done In

gra-cious words we hear Of him who spoke as
fol - low where he trod; Yet in his prom - ise
may our faith a - bound; To call on you when
realms of clear - er light We may be-hold you

none e'er spoke, But we be-lieve him near.
we re-joice, And cry "My Lord and God!"
you are near, And seek where you are found:
as you are In full and end - less sight.

Amazing Grace

81

1. Amazing grace! how sweet the sound
   That saved a wretch like me!
   I once was lost, but now am found,
   Was blind, but now I see.

2. 'Twas grace that taught my heart to fear,
   And grace my fears relieved;
   How precious did that grace appear
   The hour I first believed!

3. Through many dangers, toils, and snares,
   I have already come;
   'Tis grace hath brought me safe thus far,
   And grace will lead me home.

4. The Lord has promised good to me,
   His word my hope secures;
   He will my shield and portion be,
   As long as life endures.

Whatsoever You Do

Refrain:
Whatsoever you do to the least of my brothers
That you do unto me.

1. When I was hungry you gave me to eat.
   When I was thirsty you gave me to drink.
   Now enter into the home of my Father.

2. When I was homeless you opened your door.
   When I was naked you gave me your coat.
   Now enter into the home of my Father.

3. When I was weary you helped me find rest.
   When I was anxious you calmed all my fears.
   Now enter into the home of my Father.

4. When in prison you came to my cell.
   When on a sick bed you cared for my needs.
   Now enter into the home of my Father.

5. In a strange country you made me at home.
   Seeking employment you found me a job.
   Now enter into the home of my Father.

6. Hurt in a battle you bound up my wounds.
   Searching for kindness you held out your hands.
   Now enter into the home of my Father.

7. When I was aged you bothered to smile.
   When I was restless you listened and cared.
   Now enter into the home of my Father.

8. When I was laughed at you stood by my side.
   When I was happy you shared in my joy.
   Now enter into the home of my Father.

Hear, O Lord

Refrain:
Hear, O Lord, the sound of my call;
Hear, O Lord, and have mercy.
My soul is longing for the glory of you.
O hear, O Lord, and answer me.

1. Ev'ry night before I sleep I pray my soul to take,
   Or else I pray that loneliness is gone when I awake.

2. Why do I no longer feel like I've a place to stay?
   O take me where someone will care, so fear will go
   away.

Sing My Tongue the Savior's Glory

1. Sing my tongue, the Savior's glory,
   Of his flesh the mystr'y sing;
   Of the Blood all price exceeding,
   Shed by our immortal King,
   Destined for the world's redemption,
   From a noble womb to spring.

2. Of a pure and spotless Virgin
   Born for us on earth below,
   He, as Man, with man conversing,
   Stayed, the seeds of truth to sow;
   Then he closed in solemn order
   Wondrously his life of woe.

3. On the night of that Last Supper,
   Seated with his chosen band,
   He the Paschal victim eating,
   First fulfills the Law's command;
   Then as food to his Apostles
   Gives himself with his own hand.

4. Word made flesh the bread of nature
   By his word to Flesh he turns;
   Wine into his blood he changes
   What though sense no change discerns?
   Only be the heart in earnest,
   Faith her lesson quickly learns.

(Tantum ergo)

5. Down in adoration falling
   Lo! the sacred Host we hail,
   Lo! o'er ancient forms departing,
   Newer rites of grace prevail;
   Faith for all defects supplying,
   Where the feeble senses fail.

6. To the Everlasting Father,
   And the Son who reigns on high,
   With the Holy Ghost proceeding
   Forth from each eternally
   Be salvation, honor, blessing,
   Might, and endless majesty. Amen.

Sing of Mary, Pure and Lowly

Trier, 1695

1. Sing of Ma-ry, pure and low-ly,
2. Sing of Je-sus, son of Ma-ry,
3. Glo-ry be to God the Fa-ther,

Vir-gin moth-er un-de-filed,
In the home at Na-za-reth.
Glo-ry be to God the Son;

Sing of God's own Son most ho-ly,
Toil and la-bor can-not wea-ry
Glo-ry be to God the Spir-it;

Who be-came her lit-tle child.
Love en-dur-ing un-to death.
Glo-ry to the Three in One.

Fair-rest child of fair-est moth-er,
Con-stant was the love he gave her,
From the heart of bless-ed Ma-ry,

God the Lord who came to earth,
Though he went forth from her side,
From all saints the song as-cends,

Word made flesh, our ve-ry broth-er,
Forth to preach, and heal, and suf-fer,
And the Church the strain re-ec-hoes

Takes our na - ture by his birth.
Till on Cal - va - ry he died.
Un - to earth's re - mo - test ends.

Immaculate Mary

86

1. Immaculate Mary, thy praises we sing,
   Who reignest in splendor with Jesus, our King.

   Refrain:
   Ave, ave, ave, Maria! Ave, ave, Maria!

2. In heaven, the blessed thy glory proclaim,
   On earth, we thy children invoke thy fair name.
   —*Refrain*

3. Thy name is our power, thy virtues our light,
   Thy love is our comfort, thy pleading our might.
   —*Refrain*

4. We pray for our mother, the Church upon earth,
   And bless, dearest Lady, the land of our birth.
   —*Refrain*

Hail, Holy Queen Enthroned Above

87

1. Hall, holy Queen enthroned above, O Maria!
   Hail, Mother of mercy and of love, O Maria!

   Refrain:
   Triumph, ail ye cherubim,
   Sing with us, ye seraphim,
   Heav'n and earth resound the hymn.
   Salve; salve, salve Regina.

2. Our life, our sweetness here below, O Maria!
   Our hope in sorrow and in woe, O Maria!
   —*Refrain*

3. To thee we cry, poor sons of Eve, O Maria!
   To thee we sigh, we mourn, we grieve, O Maria!
   —*Refrain*

4. Turn, then, most gracious Advocate, O Maria!
   Toward us thine eyes compassionate, O Maria!
   —*Refrain*

5. When this our exile's time is o'er, O Maria!
   Show us thy Son for evermore, O Maria!
   —*Refrain*

88
For All the Saints

William W. How
Moderately, in unison

R. Vaughan Williams, 1872-1958

1. For all the saints,
   who from their labors
       rest,
   Who Thee by faith
   before the world con-
       fessed,
   Thy Name, O Jesus, be
       for ever blest.
   Alleluia, alleluia!

2. O blest communion!
   fellowship divine!
   We feebly struggle,
   they in glory shine;
   Yet all are one in Thee,
       for all are Thine.
   Alleluia, alleluia!

3. From earth's wide
       bounds,
   from ocean's farthest
       coast,
   Through gates of pearl
       streams
   in the countless host,
   Singing to Father, Son
       and Holy Ghost.
   Alleluia, alleluia!

89
America

1.
My country, 'tis of thee,
Sweet land of liberty,
Of thee I sing;
Land where my fathers died,
Land of the pilgrim's pride
From ev'ry mountainside
Let freedom ring.

2.
My native country, thee,
Land of the noble free,
Thy name I love;
I love thy rocks and rills,
Thy woods and templed hills;
My heart with rapture thrills
Like that above.

90
America the Beautiful

1. O beautiful for spacious skies,
   For amber wave of grain,
   For purple mountain majesties
   Above the fruited plain.
   America! America! God shed his grace on thee.
   And crown thy good with brotherhood
   From sea to shining sea.

2. O beautiful for pilgrim feet
   Whose stern impassioned stress
   A thoroughfare for freedom beat
   Across the wilderness.
   America! America! God mend thy ev'ry flaw,
   Confirm thy soul in self control,
   Thy liberty in law.

91

Ye Watchers and Ye Holy Ones

Athelstan Riley, 1858-1945

Cologne, 1623

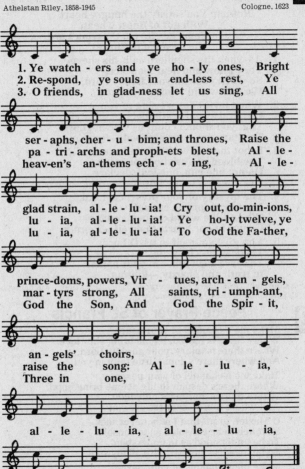

1. Ye watch - ers and ye ho - ly ones, Bright
2. Re-spond, ye souls in end-less rest, Ye
3. O friends, in glad-ness let us sing, All

ser - aphs, cher - u - bim; and thrones, Raise the
pa - tri - archs and proph-ets blest, Al - le -
heav-en's an-thems ech - o - ing, Al - le -

glad strain, al - le - lu - ia! Cry out, do-min-ions,
lu - ia, al - le - lu - ia! Ye ho-ly twelve, ye
lu - ia, al - le - lu - ia! To God the Fa-ther,

prince-doms, powers, Vir - tues, arch - an - gels,
mar - tyrs strong, All saints, tri - umph-ant,
God the Son, And God the Spir - it,

an - gels' choirs,
raise the song: Al - le - lu - ia,
Three in one,

al - le - lu - ia, al - le - lu - ia,

al - le - lu - ia, al - le - lu - ia!

92 Gift of Finest Wheat

Omer Westendorf   Robert E. Kreutz

Refrain: **You satisfy the hungry heart**
With gift of finest wheat;
Come give to us, O saving Lord,
The bread of life to eat.

1. As when the shepherd calls his sheep,
   They know and hear his voice;
   So when you call your fam'ly Lord,
   We follow and rejoice.—*Refrain*

2. When joyful lips we sing to you
   Our praise and gratitude,
   That you should count us worthy, Lord,
   To share this heav'nly food.—*Refrain*

3. Is not the cup we bless and share
   The blood of Christ out-poured?
   Do not one cup, one loaf, declare
   Our oneness in the Lord?—*Refrain*

4. The myst'ry of your presence, Lord,
   No mortal tongue can tell;
   Who all the world cannot contain
   Comes in our hearts to dwell.—*Refrain*

5. You give yourself to us, O Lord;
   Then selfless let us be,
   To serve each other in your name,
   In truth and charity.—*Refrain*

93 Peace Prayer of St. Francis

Make me a channel of your peace.
Where there is hatred, let me bring your love.
Where there is injury, your pardon, Lord.
And where there's doubt, true faith in you.

Make me a channel of your peace.
Where there's despair in life, let me bring hope.
Where there is darkness only light.
And where there's sadness ever joy.

O Master, grant that I may never seek,
So much to be consoled as to console.
To be understood as to understand.
To be loved, as to love, with all my soul.

Make me a channel of your peace.
It is in pardoning that we are pardoned.
In giving of ourselves that we receive.
And in dying that we're born to eternal life.

TREASURY OF PRAYERS

MORNING PRAYERS

Most holy and adorable Trinity, one God in three Persons, I praise you and give you thanks for all the favors you have bestowed upon me. Your goodness has preserved me until now. I offer you my whole being and in particular all my thoughts, words and deeds, together with all the trials I may undergo this day. Give them your blessing. May your Divine Love animate them and may they serve your greater glory.

I make this morning offering in union with the Divine intentions of Jesus Christ who offers himself daily in the holy Sacrifice of the Mass, and in union with Mary, his Virgin Mother and our Mother, who was always the faithful handmaid of the Lord.

Glory be to the Father, and to the Son, and to the Holy Spirit. Amen.

Prayer for Divine Guidance through the Day

*Partial indulgence (No. 21) ***

Lord, God Almighty, you have brought us safely to the beginning of this day. Defend us today by your mighty power, that we may not fall into any sin, but that all our words may so proceed and all our thoughts and actions be so directed, as to be always just in your sight. Through Christ our Lord. Amen.

* The indulgences quoted in this Missal are taken from the 1968 Vatican edition of the "Enchiridion Indulgentiarum" (published by Catholic Book Publishing Corp.).

Partial indulgence (No. 1)

Direct, we beg you, O Lord, our actions by your holy inspirations, and carry them on by your gracious assistance, that every prayer and work of ours may begin always with you, and through you be happily ended. Amen.

NIGHT PRAYERS

I adore you, my God, and thank you for having created me, for having made me a Christian and preserved me this day. I love you with all my heart and I am sorry for having sinned against you, because you are infinite Love and infinite Goodness. Protect me during my rest and may your love be always with me. Amen.

Eternal Father, I offer you the Precious Blood of Jesus Christ in atonement for my sins and for all the intentions of our Holy Church.

Holy Spirit, Love of the Father and the Son, purify my heart and fill it with the fire of your Love, so that I may be a chaste Temple of the Holy Trinity and be always pleasing to you in all things. Amen.

Plea for Divine Help

Partial indulgence (No. 24)

Hear us, Lord, holy Father, almighty and eternal God; and graciously send your holy angel from heaven to watch over, to cherish, to protect, to abide with, and to defend all who dwell in this house. Through Christ our Lord. Amen.

PRAYERS BEFORE HOLY COMMUNION

Act of Faith

Lord Jesus Christ, I firmly believe that you are present in this Blessed Sacrament as true God and true Man, with your Body and Blood, Soul and Divinity. My Redeemer and my Judge, I adore your Divine Majesty together with the angels and saints. I believe, O Lord; increase my faith.

Act of Hope

Good Jesus, in you alone I place all my hope. You are my salvation and my strength, the Source of all good. Through your mercy, through your Passion and Death, I hope to obtain the pardon of my sins, the grace of final perseverance and a happy eternity.

Act of Love

Jesus, my God, I love you with my whole heart and above all things, because you are the one supreme Good and an infinitely perfect Being. You have given your life for me, a poor sinner, and in your mercy you have even offered yourself as food for my soul. My God, I love you. Inflame my heart so that I may love you more.

Act of Contrition

O my Savior, I am truly sorry for having offended you because you are infinitely good and sin displeases you. I detest all the sins of my life and I desire to atone for them. Through the merits of your Precious Blood, wash from my soul all stain of sin, so that, cleansed in body and soul, I may worthily approach the Most Holy Sacrament of the Altar.

PRAYERS AFTER HOLY COMMUNION

Act of Faith

Jesus, I firmly believe that you are present within me as God and Man, to enrich my soul with graces and to fill my heart with the happiness of the blessed. I believe that you are Christ, the Son of the living God!

Act of Adoration

With deepest humility, I adore you, my Lord and God; you have made my soul your dwelling place. I adore you as my Creator from whose hands I came and with whom I am to be happy forever.

Act of Love

Dear Jesus, I love you with my whole heart, my whole soul, and with all my strength. May the love of your own Sacred Heart fill my soul and purify it so that I may die to the world for love of you, as you died on the Cross for love of me. My God, you are all mine; grant that I may be all yours in time and in eternity.

Act of Thanksgiving

From the depths of my heart I thank you, dear Lord, for your infinite kindness in coming to me. How good you are to me! With your most holy Mother and all the angels, I praise your mercy and generosity toward me, a poor sinner. I thank you for nourishing my soul with your Sacred Body and Precious Blood. I will try to show my gratitude to you in the Sacrament of your love, by obedience to your holy commandments, by fidelity to my duties, by kindness to my neighbor and by an earnest endeavor to become more like you in my daily conduct.

Act of Offering

Jesus, you have given yourself to me, now let me give myself to you; I give you my body, that it may be chaste and pure. I give you my soul, that it may be free from sin. I give you my heart, that it may always love you. I give you every thought, word, and deed of my life, and I offer all for your honor and glory.

Prayer to Christ the King

O Christ Jesus, I acknowledge you King of the universe. All that has been created has been made for you. Exercise upon me all your rights. I renew my baptismal promises, renouncing Satan and all his works and pomps. I promise to live a good Christian life and to do all in my power to procure the triumph of the rights of God and your Church.

Divine Heart of Jesus, I offer you my poor actions in order to obtain that all hearts may acknowledge your sacred Royalty, and that thus the reign of your peace may be established throughout the universe. Amen.

Indulgenced Prayer before a Crucifix

Look down upon me, good and gentle Jesus, while before your face I humbly kneel, and with a burning soul pray and beseech you to fix deep in my heart lively sentiments of faith, hope and charity, true contrition for my sins, and a firm purpose of amendment, while I contemplate with great love and tender pity your five wounds, pondering over them within me, calling to mind the words which David, your prophet, said of you, my good Jesus: "They have pierced my hands and my feet; they have numbered all my bones" (Ps 22:17-18).

A *plenary indulgence* is granted on each Friday of Lent and Passiontide to the faithful, who after Communion piously recite the above prayer before an image of Christ crucified; on other days of the year the indulgence is partial. *(No. 22)*

Prayer to Mary

O Jesus living in Mary, come and live in your servants, in the spirit of your holiness, in the fullness of your power, in the perfection of your ways, in the truth of your mysteries. Reign in us over all adverse powers by your Holy Spirit, and for the glory of the Father. Amen.

Anima Christi

Partial indulgence (No. 10)

Soul of Christ, sanctify me.
Body of Christ, save me.
Blood of Christ, inebriate me.
Water from the side of Christ, wash me.
Passion of Christ, strengthen me.
O good Jesus, hear me.
Within your wounds hide me.
Separated from you let me never be.
From the malignant enemy, defend me.
At the hour of death, call me.
And close to you bid me.
That with your saints I may be
Praising you, for all eternity. Amen.

THE SCRIPTURAL WAY OF THE CROSS

The Way of the Cross is a devotion in which we accompany, in spirit, our Blessed Lord in his sorrowful journey to Calvary, and devoutly meditate on his suffering and death.

A plenary indulgence is granted to those who make the Way of the Cross. (No. 63)

1. Jesus Is Condemned to Death — God so loved the world that he gave his only-begotten Son to save it (John 3:16).

2. Jesus Bears His Cross— If anyone wishes to come after me, let him deny himself, and take up his cross daily (Luke 9:23).

3. Jesus Falls the First Time—The Lord laid upon him the guilt of us all (Isaiah 53:6).

4. Jesus Meets His Mother—Come, all you who pass by the way, look and see whether there is any suffering like my suffering (Lam 1:13).

5. Jesus Is Helped by Simon—As long as you did it for one of these, the least of my brethren, you did it for me (Mt 25:40).

6. Veronica Wipes the Face of Jesus—He who sees me, sees also the Father (John 14:9).

7. Jesus Falls a Second Time—Come to me, all you who labor, and are burdened, and I will give you rest (Mt 11:28).

8. Jesus Speaks to the Women—Daughters of Je-rusalem, do not weep for me, but weep for yourselves and for your children (Luke 23:2).

9. Jesus Falls a Third Time—Everyone who exalts himself shall be humbled, and he who humbles himself shall be exalted (Luke 14:11).

10. Jesus Is Stripped of His Garments—Every one of you who does not renounce all that he possesses cannot be my disciple (Luke 14:33).

11. Jesus Is Nailed to the Cross—I have come down from heaven, not to do my own will, but the will of him who sent me (John 6:38).

12. Jesus Dies on the Cross — He humbled himself, becoming obedient to death, even to death on a cross. Therefore God has exalted him (Phil 2:8-9).

13. Jesus Is Taken Down from the Cross—Did not the Christ have to suffer those things before entering into his glory? (Luke 24:26).

14. Jesus Is Placed in the Tomb—Unless the grain of wheat falls into the ground and dies, it remains alone. But if it dies, it brings forth much fruit (John 12:24-25).

STATIONS
of the
CROSS

1. Jesus Is Condemned to Death

O Jesus, help me to appreciate Your sanctifying grace more and more.

2. Jesus Bears His Cross

O Jesus, You chose to die for me. Help me to love You always with all my heart.

3. Jesus Falls the First Time

O Jesus, make me strong to conquer my wicked passions, and to rise quickly from sin.

4. Jesus Meets His Mother

O Jesus, grant me a tender love for Your Mother, who offered You for love of me.

STATIONS
of the
CROSS

5. Jesus is Helped by Simon

O Jesus, like Simon lead me ever closer to You through my daily crosses and trials.

6. Jesus and Veronica

O Jesus, imprint Your image on my heart that I may be faithful to You all my life.

7. Jesus Falls a Second Time

O Jesus, I repent for having offended You. Grant me forgiveness of all my sins.

8. Jesus Speaks to the Women

O Jesus, grant me tears of compassion for Your sufferings and of sorrow for my sins.

9. Jesus Falls a Third Time

O Jesus, let me never yield to despair. Let me come to You in hardship and spiritual distress.

10. He is Stripped of His Garments

O Jesus, let me sacrifice all my attachments rather than imperil the divine life of my soul.

11. Jesus is Nailed to the Cross

O Jesus, strengthen my faith and increase my love for You. Help me to accept my crosses.

12. Jesus Dies on the Cross

O Jesus, I thank You for making me a child of God. Help me to forgive others.

STATIONS
of the
CROSS

13. Jesus is Taken down from the Cross

O Jesus, through the intercession of Your holy Mother, let me be pleasing to You.

14. Jesus is Laid in the Tomb

O Jesus, strengthen my will to live for You on earth and bring me to eternal bliss in heaven.

Prayer after the Stations

JESUS, You became an example of humility, obedience and patience, and preceded me on the way of life bearing Your Cross. Grant that, inflamed with Your love, I may cheerfully take upon myself the sweet yoke of Your Gospel together with the mortification of the Cross and follow You as a true disciple so that I may be united with You in heaven. Amen.

The Five
Joyful
Mysteries

Said on Mondays and Saturdays [except during Lent], and the Sundays from Advent to Lent.

3. The Nativity
For the spirit of poverty.

1. The Annunciation
For the love of humility.

4. The Presentation
For the virtue of obedience.

2. The Visitation
For charity toward my neighbor.

5. Finding in the Temple
For the virtue of piety.

The Five Luminous Mysteries*

Said on Thursdays [except during Lent].

*Added to the Mysteries of the Rosary by Pope John Paul II in his Apostolic Letter of October 16, 2002, entitled *The Rosary of the Virgin Mary*.

1. The Baptism of Jesus
For living my Baptismal Promises.

3. Proclamation of the Kingdom
For seeking God's forgiveness.

4. The Transfiguration
Becoming a New Person in Christ.

5. Institution of the Eucharist
For active participation at Mass.

2. The Wedding at Cana
For doing whatever Jesus says.

The Five Sorrowful Mysteries

Said on Tuesdays and Fridays throughout the year, and every day from Ash Wednesday until Easter.

3. Crowning with Thorns
For moral courage.

1. Agony in the Garden
For true contrition.

4. Carrying of the Cross
For the virtue of patience.

2. Scourging at the Pillar
For the virtue of purity.

5. The Crucifixion
For final perseverance.

The Five Glorious Mysteries

Said on Wednesdays [except during Lent], and the Sundays from Easter to Advent.

1. The Resurrection
For the virtue of faith.

2. The Ascension
For the virtue of hope.

4. Assumption of the B.V.M.
For devotion to Mary.

3. Descent of the Holy Spirit
For love of God.

5. Crowning of the B.V.M.
For eternal happiness.

PRAYER TO ST. JOSEPH

O Blessed St. Joseph, loving father and faithful guardian of Jesus, and devoted spouse of the Mother of God, I beg you to offer God the Father his divine Son, bathed in blood on the Cross. Through the holy Name of Jesus obtain for us from the Father the favor we implore.

FOR THE SICK

Father, your Son accepted our sufferings to teach us the virtue of patience in human illness. Hear the prayers we offer for our sick brothers and sisters. May all who suffer pain, illness or disease realize that they are chosen to be saints, and know that they are joined to Christ in his suffering for the salvation of the world, who lives and reigns with you and the Holy Spirit, one God, for ever and ever.

FOR RELIGIOUS VOCATIONS

Father, you call all who believe in you to grow perfect in love by following in the footsteps of Christ your Son. May those whom you have chosen to serve you as religious provide by their way of life a convincing sign of your kingdom for the Church and the whole world.

FOR THE ASSEMBLY OF NATIONAL LEADERS

Father, you guide and govern everything with order and love. Look upon the assembly of our national leaders and fill them with the spirit of your wisdom. May they always act in accordance with your will and their decisions be for the peace and well-being of all.

PRAYER FOR HEALTH

O Sacred Heart of Jesus, I come to ask of Your infinite mercy the gift of health and strength that I may serve You more faithfully and love You more sincerely than in the past. I wish to be well and strong if this be Your good pleasure and for Your greater glory. Filled with high resolves and determined to perform my tasks most perfectly for love of You, I wish to be enabled to go back to my duties.

PRAYER FOR PEACE AND JOY

Jesus, I want to rejoice in You always. You are near. Let me have no anxiety, but in every concern by prayer and supplication with thanksgiving I wish to let my petitions be made known in my communing with God.

May the peace of God, which surpasses all understanding, guard my heart and my thoughts in You.

PRAYER TO KNOW GOD'S WILL

God the Father of our Lord Jesus Christ, the Author of glory, grant me spiritual wisdom and revelation. Enlighten the eyes of my mind with a deep knowledge of You and Your holy will. May I understand of what nature is the hope to which You call me, what is the wealth of the splendor of Your inheritance among the Saints, and what is the surpassing greatness of Your power toward me.

PRAYER FOR CIVIL AUTHORITIES

Almighty and everlasting God, You direct the powers and laws of all nations; mercifully regard those who rule over us, that, by Your protecting right hand, the integrity of religion and the security of each country might prevail everywhere on earth. Through Christ our Lord. Amen.

GUIDELINES FOR THE RECEPTION
OF COMMUNION

For Catholics

As Catholics, we fully participate in the celebration of the Eucharist when we receive Holy Communion. We are encouraged to receive Communion devoutly and frequently. In order to be properly disposed to receive Communion, participants should not be conscious of grave sin and normally should have fasted for one hour. A person who is conscious of grave sin is not to receive the Body and Blood of the Lord without prior sacramental confession except for a grave reason where there is no opportunity for confession. In this case, the person is to be mindful of the obligation to make an act of perfect contrition, including the intention of confessing as soon as possible (*Code of Canon Law*, *canon 916*). A frequent reception of the Sacrament of Penance is encouraged for all.

For Fellow Christians

We welcome our fellow Christians to this celebration of the Eucharist as our brothers and sisters. We pray that our common baptism and the action of the Holy Spirit in this Eucharist will draw us closer to one another and begin to dispel the sad divisions that separate us. We pray that these will lessen and finally disappear, in keeping with Christ's prayer for us "that they may all be one" (John 17:21).

Because Catholics believe that the celebration of the Eucharist is a sign of the reality of the oneness of faith, life, and worship, members of those churches with whom we are not yet fully united are ordinarily not admitted to Holy Communion. Eucharistic sharing in exceptional circumstances by other Christians requires permission according to the directives of the diocesan bishop and the provisions of canon law (*canon 844 § 4*). Members of the Orthodox Churches, the Assyrian Church of the East, and the Polish National Catholic Church are urged to respect the discipline of their own Churches. According to Roman Catholic discipline, the Code of Canon Law does not object to the reception of Communion by Christians of these Churches (*canon 844 § 3*).

For Those Not Receiving Holy Communion

All who are not receiving Holy Communion are encouraged to express in their hearts a prayerful desire for unity with the Lord Jesus and with one another.

For Non-Christians

We also welcome to this celebration those who do not share our faith in Jesus Christ. While we cannot admit them to Holy Communion, we ask them to offer their prayers for the peace and the unity of the human family.

NEW RITE OF PENANCE
(Extracted from the Rite of Penance)

Texts for the Penitent

The penitent should prepare for the celebration of the sacrament by prayer, reading of Scripture, and silent reflection. The penitent should think over and should regret all sins since the last celebration of the sacrament.

RECEPTION OF THE PENITENT

The penitent enters the confessional or other place set aside for the celebration of the sacrament of penance. After the welcoming of the priest, the penitent makes the sign of the cross saying:

In the name of the Father, and of the Son, and of the Holy Spirit. Amen.

The penitent is invited to have trust in God and replies:

Amen.

READING OF THE WORD OF GOD

The penitent then listens to a text of Scripture which tells about God's mercy and calls man to conversion.

CONFESSION OF SINS AND ACCEPTANCE OF SATISFACTION

The penitent speaks to the priest in a normal, conversational fashion. The penitent tells when he or she last celebrated the sacrament and then confesses his or her sins. The penitent then listens to any advice the priest may give and accepts the satisfaction from the priest. The penitent should ask any appropriate questions.

PRAYER OF THE PENITENT AND ABSOLUTION

Prayer

Before the absolution is given, the penitent expresses sorrow for sins in these or similar words:

**My God,
I am sorry for my sins with all my heart.
In choosing to do wrong
and failing to do good,
I have sinned against you
whom I should love above all things.
I firmly intend, with your help,
to do penance,
to sin no more,
and to avoid whatever leads me to sin.
Our Savior Jesus Christ
suffered and died for us.
In his name, my God, have mercy.**

OR:

> Remember, Lord, your compassion and mercy
> which you showed long ago.
> Do not recall the sins and failings of my youth.
> In your mercy remember me, Lord, because of your good-
> ness.

OR:

> Wash me from my guilt
> and cleanse me of my sin.
> I acknowledge my offense;
> my sin is before me always.

OR:

> Father, I have sinned against you
> and am not worthy to be called your son.
> Be merciful to me, a sinner.

OR:

> Father of mercy,
> like the prodigal son
> I return to you and say:
> "I have sinned against you
> and am no longer worthy to be called your son."
> Christ Jesus, Savior of the world,
> I pray with the repentant thief
> to whom you promised Paradise:
> "Lord, remember me in your kingdom."
> Holy Spirit, fountain of love,
> I call on you with trust:
> "Purify my heart,
> and help me to walk as a child of light."

OR:

> Lord Jesus,
> you opened the eyes of the blind,
> healed the sick,
> forgave the sinful woman,
> and after Peter's denial confirmed him in your love.
> Listen to my prayer,
> forgive all my sins,
> renew your love in my heart,
> help me to live in perfect unity with my fellow Chris-
> tians
> that I may proclaim your saving power to all the world.

OR:

> Lord Jesus,
> you chose to be called the friend of sinners.
> By your saving death and resurrection
> free me from my sins.

May your peace take root in my heart
and bring forth a harvest
of love, holiness, and truth.

OR:

Lord Jesus Christ,
you are the Lamb of God;
you take away the sins of the world.
Through the grace of the Holy Spirit
restore me to friendship with your Father,
cleanse me from every stain of sin
and raise me to new life
for the glory of your name.

OR:

Lord God,
in your goodness have mercy on me:
do not look on my sins,
but take away all my guilt.
Create in me a clean heart
and renew within me an upright spirit.

OR:

Lord Jesus, Son of God,
have mercy on me, a sinner.

ABSOLUTION

*If the penitent is not kneeling, he or she bows his or her head
as the priest extends his hands (or at least extends his right
hand).*

God, the Father of mercies,
through the death and resurrection of his Son
has reconciled the world to himself
and sent the Holy Spirit among us
for the forgiveness of sins;
through the ministry of the Church
may God give you pardon and peace,
and I absolve you from your sins
in the name of the Father, and of the Son,
and of the Holy Spirit. Amen.

PROCLAMATION OF PRAISE OF GOD AND DISMISSAL

Penitent and priest give praise to God.

Priest: Give thanks to the Lord, for he is good.
Penitent: His mercy endures for ever.

Then the penitent is dismissed by the priest.

Form of Examination of Conscience

This suggested form for an examination of conscience should be completed and adapted to meet the needs of different individuals and to follow local usages.

In an examination of conscience, before the sacrament of penance, each individual should ask himself these questions in particular:

1. What is my attitude to the sacrament of penance? Do I sincerely want to be set free from sin, to turn again to God, to begin a new life, and to enter into a deeper friendship with God? Or do I look on it as a burden, to be undertaken as seldom as possible?

2. Did I forget to mention, or deliberately conceal, any grave sins in past confessions?

3. Did I perform the penance I was given? Did I make reparation for any injury to others? Have I tried to put into practice any resolution to lead a better life in keeping with the Gospel?

Each individual should examine his life in the light of God's word.

I. The Lord says: "You shall love the Lord your God
with your whole heart."

1. Is my heart set on God, so that I really love him above all things and am faithful to his commandments, as a son loves his father? Or am I more concerned about the things of this world? Have I a right intention in what I do?

2. God spoke to us in his Son. Is my faith in God firm and secure? Am I wholehearted in accepting the Church's teaching? Have I been careful to grow in my understanding of the faith, to hear God's word, to listen to instructions on the faith, to avoid dangers to faith? Have I been always strong and fearless in professing my faith in God and the Church? Have I been willing to be known as a Christian in private and public life?

3. Have I prayed morning and evening? When I pray, do I really raise my mind and heart to God or is it a matter of words only? Do I offer God my difficulties, my joys, and my sorrows? Do I turn to God in time of temptation?

4. Have I love and reverence for God's name? Have I offended him in blasphemy, swearing falsely, or taking his name in vain? Have I shown disrespect for the Blessed Virgin Mary and the saints?

5. Do I keep Sundays and feast days holy by taking a full part, with attention and devotion, in the liturgy, and especially in the Mass? Have I fulfilled the precept of annual confession and of communion during the Easter season?

6. Are there false gods that I worship by giving them greater attention and deeper trust than I give to God: money, superstition, spiritism, or other occult practices?

II. The Lord says: "Love one another as I have loved you."

1. Have I a genuine love for my neighbors? Or do I use them for my own ends, or do to them what I would not want done to myself? Have I given grave scandal by my words or actions?

2. In my family life, have I contributed to the well-being and happiness of the rest of the family by patience and genuine love? Have I been obedient to parents, showing them proper respect and giving them help in their spiritual and material needs? Have I been careful to give a Christian upbringing to my children, and to help them by good example and by exercising authority as a parent? Have I been faithful to my husband/wife in my heart and in my relations with others?

3. Do I share my possessions with the less fortunate? Do I do my best to help the victims of oppression, misfortune, and poverty? Or do I look down on my neighbor, especially the poor, the sick, the elderly, strangers, and people of other races?

4. Does my life reflect the mission I received in confirmation? Do I share in the apostolic and charitable works of the Church and in the life of my parish? Have I helped to meet the needs of the Church and of the world and prayed for them: for unity in the Church, for the spread of the Gospel among the nations, for peace and justice, etc.?

5. Am I concerned for the good and prosperity of the human community in which I live, or do I spend my life caring only for myself? Do I share to the best of my ability in the work of promoting justice, morality, harmony, and love in human relations? Have I done my duty as a citizen? Have I paid my taxes?

6. In my work or profession am I just, hard-working, honest, serving society out of love for others? Have I paid a fair wage to my employees? Have I been faithful to my promises and contracts?

7. Have I obeyed legitimate authority and given it due respect?

8. If I am in a position of responsibility or authority, do I use this for my own advantage or for the good of others, in a spirit of service?

9. Have I been truthful and fair, or have I injured others by deceit, calumny, detraction, rash judgment, or violation of a secret?

10. Have I done violence to others by damage to life or limb, reputation, honor, or material possessions? Have I involved them in loss? Have I been responsible for advising an abortion or procuring one?

Have I kept up hatred for others? Am I estranged from others through quarrels, enmity, insults, anger? Have I been guilty of refusing to testify to the innocence of another because of selfishness?

11. Have I stolen the property of others? Have I desired it unjustly and inordinately? Have I damaged it? Have I made restitution of other people's property and made good their loss?

12. If I have been injured, have I been ready to make peace for the love of Christ and to forgive, or do I harbor hatred and the desire for revenge?

III. Christ our Lord says: "Be perfect as your Father is perfect."

1. Where is my life really leading me? Is the hope of eternal life my inspiration? Have I tried to grow in the life of the Spirit through prayer, reading the word of God and meditating on it, receiving the sacraments, self-denial? Have I been anxious to control my vices, my bad inclinations and passions, e.g., envy, love of food and drink? Have I been proud and boastful, thinking myself better in the sight of God and despising others as less important than myself? Have I imposed my own will on others, without respecting their freedom and rights?

2. What use have I made of time, of health and strength, of the gifts God has given to me to be used like the talents in the Gospel? Do I use them to become more perfect every day? Or have I been lazy and too much given to leisure?

3. Have I been patient in accepting the sorrows and disappointments of life? How have I performed mortification so as to "fill up what is wanting to the sufferings of Christ"? Have I kept the precept of fasting and abstinence?

4. Have I kept my senses and my whole body pure and chaste as a temple of the Holy Spirit consecrated for resurrection and glory, and as a sign of God's faithful love for men and women, a sign that is seen most perfectly in the sacrament of matrimony? Have I dishonored my body by fornication, impurity, unworthy conversation or thoughts, evil desires or actions? Have I given in to sensuality? Have I indulged in reading, conversation, shows, and entertainments that offend against Christian and human decency? Have I encouraged others to sin by my own failure to maintain these standards? Have I been faithful to the moral law in my married life?

5. Have I gone against my conscience out of fear or hypocrisy?

6. Have I always tried to act in the true freedom of the sons of God according to the law of the Spirit, or am I the slave of forces within me?

HYMN INDEX

WHY . . . You should have a
MISSAL . . . of Your OWN!

AT MASS . . . for complete participation and understanding

- ✔ TO RECITE or SING . . . your parts with understanding and devotion.
- ✔ TO LISTEN . . . attentively to the Word of God.
- ✔ TO UNITE . . . with the prayers of the Priest.
- ✔ TO HOLD . . . attention and increase your devotion.
- ✔ TO HELP . . . during short periods recommended for personal prayer.

AT HOME . . . to guide your Christian Life and personal spiritual reading

- ✔ TO PREPARE . . . yourself for Mass by reading over the texts and helpful commentary.
- ✔ TO SEE . . . the liturgical year as a whole.
- ✔ TO GUIDE . . . your life in the spirit of the liturgy.
- ✔ TO MODEL . . . your prayers on liturgical sources.
- ✔ TO MEDITATE . . . often on the Word of God.